Beginning Fedora

From Novice to Professional

*The complete guide to Fedora—includes
everything you need to know to master this
popular Linux-based operating system.*

Shashank Sharma and Keir Thomas

Beginning Fedora: From Novice to Professional

Copyright © 2007 by Shashank Sharma and Keir Thomas

ISBN-13 (pbk): 978-1-59059-855-9

ISBN-10 (pbk): 1-59059-855-5

Printed and bound in the United States of America 9 8 7 6 5 4 3 2 1

Lead Editor: Jason Gilmore
Technical Reviewer: Paul Frields
Editorial Board: Steve Anglin, Ewan Buckingham, Gary Cornell, Jonathan Gennick, Jason Gilmore,
    Jonathan Hassell, Chris Mills, Matthew Moodie, Jeffrey Pepper, Ben Renow-Clarke,
    Dominic Shakeshaft, Matt Wade, Tom Welsh
Project Manager: Tracy Brown Collins
Copy Edit Manager: Nicole Flores
Copy Editor: Damon Larson
Assistant Production Director: Kari Brooks-Copony
Production Editor and Artist: Katie Stence
Compositor: Linda Weidemann, Wolf Creek Press
Proofreader: Lori Bring
Indexer: John Collin
Cover Designer: Kurt Krames
Manufacturing Director: Tom Debolski

Distributed to the book trade worldwide by Springer-Verlag New York, Inc., 233 Spring Street, 6th Floor, New York, NY 10013. Phone 1-800-SPRINGER, fax 201-348-4505, e-mail orders-ny@springer-sbm.com, or visit http://www.springeronline.com.

For information on translations, please contact Apress directly at 2855 Telegraph Avenue, Suite 600, Berkeley, CA 94705. Phone 510-549-5930, fax 510-549-5939, e-mail info@apress.com, or visit http://www.apress.com.

Contents at a Glance

PART 1 ■■■ Introducing the World of Linux

PART 2 ■■■ Installing Fedora

PART 3 ■■■ The No-Nonsense Getting Started Guide

PART 4 ■■■ The Shell and Beyond

PART 5 ■■■ Multimedia

PART 6 ■■■ Office Tasks

PART 7 ■■■ Keeping Your System Running

Contents

PART 1 ■■■ Introducing the World of Linux

PART 2 ∎∎∎ Installing Fedora

PART 3 ■ ■ ■ The No-Nonsense Getting Started Guide

PART 4 ■ ■ ■ The Shell and Beyond

PART 5 ■■■ Multimedia

PART 6 ■ ■ ■ Office Tasks

PART 7 ■ ■ ■ Keeping Your System Running

About the Authors

SHASHANK SHARMA has contributed articles extensively to Linux.com and NewsForge. He conducts classes on various aspects of Linux at the Indian Institute of Technology (IIT), Delhi.

Using Linux since 1997, Shashank has helped several newbies with his 1000-plus posts at the popular LinuxQuestions.org forum board. Interested in the workings of free/open source software licenses, he actively participates in the discussions on the Creative Commons mailing list. His blog on licensing (www.linuxlala.net/) is regularly linked to by major web sites such as IPcentral and LXer.

KEIR THOMAS is an award-winning author who has written several best-selling beginning-level Linux titles for Apress. A former computer magazine editor, he has been writing about computers, operating systems, and software for a decade. He has also edited many computing titles.

Keir currently works as a full-time author and has written four books for Apress. He lives on the side of a mountain in England, and his hobbies include hiking and playing musical instruments.

About the Technical Reviewer

PAUL W. FRIELDS is an engineer with a background in digital forensics and investigation who has taught Linux to hundreds of technical and law enforcement professionals. He has been a Linux user and advocate since 1997, and spends some of his spare time working on various parts of the Fedora Project, which he joined before the release of Fedora Core 1 in 2003. He serves as one of the senior managers of the Fedora Documentation Project, packages software for inclusion in the distribution, and evangelizes Fedora and Linux to entities in both the private and public sectors. He also served as one of the inaugural members of the Fedora Project Board from 2006 to 2007, joining a select few community members in managing the overall program direction for Fedora.

The remainder of his time is devoted to his wife and children, and his part-time work as a professional musician.

Acknowledgments

Books like the one you're holding now take an enormous amount of work by a lot of people to come to fruition. To this end, I'd like to acknowledge the help of the following individuals in the production of this book: Tracy Brown Collins, Jason Gilmore, Paul W. Frields, Damon Larson, Katie Stence, and the many other people at Apress whose work behind the scenes made *Beginning Fedora* possible.

In addition, I'd like to thank the Fedora community at large, which often helped me figure out some aspects of Fedora, particularly when it came to hardware configuration. Thanks must also go to Red Hat for continuing to support the Fedora Project and the Fedora developers for creating one of the most exciting and innovative Linux distributions I've had the pleasure of using.

Shashank Sharma

Introduction

Linux has come a long way in a short time. Computing itself is still relatively young by any standard; if the era of modern computing started with the invention of the microchip, it's still less than 50 years old. But Linux is a youngster compared even to this; it has been around for only 16 of those years.

In that brief time span, a student's personal project has grown to where it now runs many computers throughout the world. It has rampaged through the computing industry, offering an alternative to commercial solutions such as those offered by Microsoft, and toppling long-held beliefs about the way things should be done. This is all by virtue of the fact that Linux is simply better than every other choice out there. Many argue that it's more secure and faster than other operating systems. But here's the kicker—Linux is free of charge. Yes, that's right. It doesn't have to cost a penny.

I was bitten by the Linux bug in the mid-1990s. I learned of its existence when my dad read a version of the Halloween documents in a local daily. In those days, the Internet as we now know it was still in its infancy and there was very little documentation. But the euphoria of discovering something new urged us on and we quickly became hooked.

Still, getting your monitor to work or configuring the sound card was a major concern. Now, it's much easier to get started with Linux; you don't even have to install it! The arrival of LiveCD has definitely aided Linux adoption.

With an ever-increasing Linux user base, this book answers the need for a fundamental, authoritative, and down-to-earth guide to Linux. This book purely and simply focuses on what you need to know to use Linux, done in the context of one of the most popular flavors of Linux.

Beginning Fedora is concise and to the point, aiming to re-create under Linux all the stuff you are used to doing under Windows. This doesn't mean that *Beginning Fedora* cuts corners. Wherever justified, this book spends time examining the topics you need to know in order to gain a complete and comprehensive understanding. For example, you'll find a hefty chapter dedicated to the command line—arguably the heart of Linux and all the elements that gives Linux most of its power. There's also an entire chapter discussing (and illustrating) how to initially install Fedora on your computer. *Beginning Fedora* really is a complete guide.

About Fedora

Linux applies an alternative philosophy to computing that revolves around the sharing of not only software, but also knowledge. To use Linux is to become part of a huge global community of people who have caught on to a phenomenon that is changing the world.

Fedora (http://fedoraproject.org) is the natural continuation of these goals. The first version of Fedora, Fedora Core 1, was released in November 2003, and the next, Fedora Core 2, was released in May 2004. Roughly six moths separate each Fedora release, the latest being Fedora 7.

Fedora has its roots in Red Hat Linux, a popular Linux distribution from Red Hat (a company dedicated to open source software). When Red Hat Linux was discontinued in 2003, Red Hat urged its commercial users to shift to Red Hat Enterprise Linux and its home users to Fedora Core. Fedora (previously known as Fedora Core) aims to promote the rapid progress of free and open source software and content.

The release of Fedora 7 (included with this book on DVD) marks a major milestone for Fedora, with the merger of the Core and Extras repositories. Fedora traditionally had two main software repositories: Core and Extras. While Core was maintained by Red Hat employees, the Extras repository was maintained by the community. There no longer is any distinction between these two software repositories.

Fedora is available for use by anyone in the world, no matter who or where they are. As such, many different languages are supported, and the operating system can also be accessed by those with disabilities, such as partial sight or hearing. Fedora might just as easily be found on a Wall Street banker's laptop as on a battered, old computer in a Brazilian favela.

Fedora focuses largely on the desktop. It provides a powerful office suite by default, for example, as well as some excellent pieces of Internet software. It's also very easy to use. Fedora works "straight out of the box." As soon as it's installed, you should be ready to start using it without any further work. In addition, tasks such as updating your software are as easy under Fedora as they are under Windows.

Above all, however, Fedora is designed to be shared. You can take the DVD-ROM included with this book and install Fedora on as many machines as you want. You can also copy it as many times as you want and give those copies to your friends. This isn't some kind of trick—Fedora isn't a trial version that will shut up shop in a month. You will never find yourself having to pay a fee further down the line, even if you want to install additional software. Fedora will always be free of charge.

What You'll Find in This Book

Beginning Fedora is split into seven parts, each of which contains chapters about a certain aspect of Fedora use. You can read these parts in sequence, or you can dip in and out of them at will. Whenever a technical term is mentioned, a reference is made to the chapter where that term is explained.

Part 1 examines the history and philosophy behind the Linux operating system. We aim to answer many of the common questions about Linux. Such knowledge is considered to be as important as understanding the technical details on how Linux works. But while these chapters should be read sooner rather than later, they don't contain any technical information that's absolutely required to get started with Fedora.

Part 2 covers installing Fedora on your computer. An illustrated guide is provided, and all installation choices are explained in depth. Additionally, you'll find a problem-solving chapter to help in case anything goes wrong.

Part 3 focuses on getting started with Fedora. It covers setting up the Linux system so that it's ready to use. One chapter is dedicated to setting up common hardware devices, such as printers and modems, and another explains how you can secure your system. Other chapters in this part explore the desktop, explaining what you need to know to begin using Fedora on a daily basis.

In Part 4, we take a look at how the underlying technology behind Linux functions. You'll be introduced to the command-line prompt and learn how the file system works. It's in these chapters that you'll really master controlling Linux!

Part 5 covers multimedia functions built into Fedora, which among other things let you watch movies and play back music. We also take a look at the image-editing software built into Fedora.

Part 6 moves on to explain how typical office tasks can be accomplished under Fedora. We investigate OpenOffice.org, the complete office suite built into Fedora. After an introduction to OpenOffice.org, separate chapters explore its word processor, spreadsheet, database, and presentation packages. You'll also learn how to use Evolution, Fedora's e-mail program.

Part 7 carries on from Part 4, taking an even more in-depth look at the underlying technology behind Fedora. This time, the emphasis is on giving you the skills you need to keep your system running smoothly. You'll learn how to install software, manage users, optimize your system, back up essential data, schedule tasks, and access computers remotely.

Finally, at the back of the book, you'll find three appendixes. The first is a glossary of Linux terms used not only in this book, but also in the Linux and UNIX world. The second appendix is a quick reference to commands typically used at the command-line prompt under Linux. The third appendix explains how to get further help when using Fedora.

Conventions Used in This Book

The goal when writing *Beginning Fedora* was to make it as readable as possible while providing the facility for readers to learn at their own pace.

Throughout the book, you'll find various types of notes and sidebars complementing the regular text. These are designed to provide handy information to help further your knowledge. They also make reading the book a bit easier.

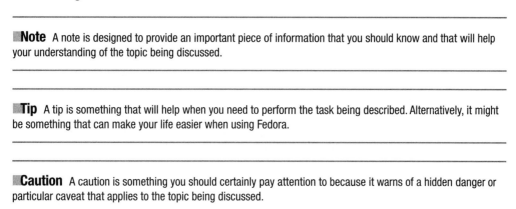

Note A note is designed to provide an important piece of information that you should know and that will help your understanding of the topic being discussed.

Tip A tip is something that will help when you need to perform the task being described. Alternatively, it might be something that can make your life easier when using Fedora.

Caution A caution is something you should certainly pay attention to because it warns of a hidden danger or particular caveat that applies to the topic being discussed.

In the sidebars, we take a moment to explain something that you should know but isn't vital to an understanding of the main topic being discussed. You don't need to read the sidebars there and then; you can return to them later if you wish.

Support from Apress

Finally, we'd like to mention the online help offered by Apress, the publisher of this book. When you visit www.apress.com, you can click a link at the top of the page to visit the forums. Here, you'll be able to make comments about this book and find help with any issues it raises.

PART 1

■ ■ ■

Introducing the World of Linux

■■■

## CHAPTER 1

Welcome!

If you're an avid computer user, there's a good chance that you've heard of Linux. You might have read about it, or perhaps you've seen TV ads that refer to it.

One of the odd things about Linux is that the more you learn about it, the more questions you have. For instance, it's generally thought that Linux is free of charge, but this then raises the question of how, in our modern world, something like an entire computer operating system can cost nothing. After all, who pays the programmers?

In the following introductory chapters, we're going to try to answer some of these questions. In this chapter, we'll explain what Linux is and its benefits compared to Windows.

What Is Linux?

There are two ways of looking at a PC. The first is to see it as a magical box that lets you do cool stuff like browse the Internet or play games. Seen in this way, it's like a VCR—put in a tape, press a button, and a picture appears on your TV. On your PC, you click the Internet Explorer icon, type a web address, and a web site somehow appears. The astonishing technical complexity behind these simple procedures isn't important to most people.

The other way of looking at a PC is as a collection of components that are made by various manufacturers. You might be familiar with this way of thinking if you've ever tried to upgrade your PC's hardware. In that case, you'll know that your PC consists of a CPU, a hard disk, a graphics card, and so on. You can swap any of these out to put in newer and better components that upgrade your PC's performance or allow more data storage.

What almost no one realizes is that operating systems such as Linux and Windows are just components of your PCs. The operating system, too, can be swapped out for a better replacement. Windows doesn't come free of charge, and Microsoft isn't performing a public service by providing it. Around $50 to $100 of the price you pay for a PC goes straight into Microsoft's pocket. Bearing in mind that hundreds of millions of PCs are built each year, it's not hard to see why Microsoft is one of the world's richest corporations.

It would be difficult to question this state of affairs if Microsoft gave us our money's worth. But it often falls far short. Its products are full of serious security holes, which at best inconvenience us and at worst make us lose data. And that's before we consider the instability of Microsoft products—hardly a day goes by without something unexpected happening. One of the first things people are taught when attending Windows training is how to use the Ctrl+Alt+Delete keyboard combination, which helps you recover after a crash!

Microsoft became rich, and maintains its wealth, by a virtual monopoly over PC manufacturers. While the intelligent computer buyer can choose between components to put together a better PC—deciding between an AMD or Intel processor, for example—you usually have little choice but to buy Windows with a new PC. Try it now. Phone your favorite big-name computer retailer. Say that you want a PC but you *don't* want Windows installed. Then listen as the salesperson on the other end of the phone struggles to understand.

■**Note** Some PC manufacturers actually will sell you a PC without Windows installed on it. All you have to do is ask, although you might need to speak to a senior salesperson to get through to someone who understands your request. Smaller local companies, in particular, will be more than willing to sell you a PC without Windows. Some larger multinational companies, such as Hewlett-Packard, sell workstations with Linux preinstalled instead of Windows. However, these computers are usually aimed at businesses rather than home users.

Wouldn't it be terrific if you could get rid of Windows? Would you like to finally say goodbye to all those security holes and not have to worry about virus infections anymore, yet not lose out on any features or need to make sacrifices or compromises?

There is an alternative. Welcome to the world of Linux.

Linux is an operating system, which is to say that it's a bit like Windows. It's the core software that runs your computer and lets you do stuff on it. By the strictest definition of the term, an *operating system* is the fundamental software that's needed to make your PC work. Without an operating system installed on your PC, it would merely be an expensive doorstop. When you turned it on, it would beep in annoyance—its way of telling you that it can't do much without a whole set of programs to tell it what to do next.

An operating system allows your PC's hardware to communicate with the software you run on it. It's hundreds of programs, system libraries, drivers, and more, all tightly integrated into a whole. In addition, an operating system lets programs talk to other programs and, of course, communicate with you, the user. In other words, the operating system runs everything and allows everything to work.

■**Note** Some companies and individuals, including Microsoft, define an operating system as much more than this fundamental software. They add in the basic tools you run on an operating system, such as web browsers and file management programs.

Linux consists of a central set of programs that run the PC on a low level, referred to as the *kernel*, and hundreds (if not thousands) of additional programs provided by other people and various companies. Technically speaking, the word *Linux* refers explicitly just to the core kernel program. However, most people generally refer to the entire bundle of programs that make up the operating system as *Linux*.

GNU/LINUX

Although most of us refer to Linux as a complete operating system, the title "Linux" hides a lot of confusing but rather important details. Technically speaking, the word *Linux* refers merely to the kernel file: the central set of programs that lie at the heart of the operating system. Everything else that comes with a typical version of Linux, such as programs to display graphics on the screen or let the user input data, is supplied by other people, organizations, or companies. The Linux operating system is the combination of many disparate projects (we'll explain how this works in the next chapter).

The GNU organization, in particular, supplies a lot of vital programs and also system library files, without which Linux wouldn't run. These programs and files were vital to the acceptance of Linux as an operating system in its early days. Because of this, and the fact that Linux completed a long-running goal of the GNU project to create a UNIX-like operating system, some people choose to refer to Linux as GNU/Linux.

A fierce debate rages over the correct way to refer to the Linux operating system and whether the GNU prefix should be used. For what it's worth, an equally fierce debate rages over how we should define an operating system. It can all get very confusing. It's also very easy to accidentally offend someone by not using the correct terminology!

It's not the purpose of this book to get involved in this debate. Suffice it to say that we acknowledge the vital input of the GNU project into the operating system many people refer to simply as Linux, as well as that of other vital projects. However, readers should note that when we refer to Linux throughout this book, we mean the entire operating system. If we intend to refer simply to the kernel program, we will make that clear.

The Age of Linux

At the time of writing this book, Linux is a little over 16 years old. It has gone from a hobbyist project maintained by just one man to a professional and corporate-sponsored solution for virtually every level of computer user.

Linux has also gone from being a server operating system, designed for central computers that hand out files and other computer resources to other computers, to becoming a full-fledged graphical desktop operating system like Windows. In fact, it's gone even further. Today, it's very likely that you'll find Linux running your digital video recorder and other computerized household gadgets.

Getting technical for a moment, Linux is a 32-bit and 64-bit multitasking, multiuser operating system. This is a complicated way of saying that it's pretty darn powerful. Linux is as capable of running supercomputers as it is of running a desktop PC. Linux builds on the foundation laid by UNIX, which itself was based on Multics, which was one of the first modern computer operating systems. It's not an exaggeration to say that Linux can trace its family tree all the way back to the pioneering days of computing.

CORRECT PRONUNCIATION

What most people refer to as the Linux operating system takes its name from the kernel program, one of its most important system components. This, in turn, was named after its creator, Linus Torvalds.

The name Linus is commonly pronounced *LIE-nus* in many English-speaking countries, but Torvalds speaks Swedish. He pronounces his name *LEEN-us* (imagine this spoken with a gentle Scandinavian lilt, and you've got it about right).

Because of this, he pronounces Linux as *LIN-ux*, and most people copy this pronunciation. You can hear this spoken by Torvalds himself by visiting www.paul.sladen.org/pronunciation/.

Some people refer to the Linux operating system by its full title of GNU/Linux. In this case, GNU is pronounced with a hard *G: guh-NOO*. The full pronunciation is therefore *guh-NOO LIN-ux*.

Finally, the DVD that comes with this book contains a version of Linux called Fedora. The Fedora Project, sponsored by Red Hat, is responsible for producing the Fedora distribution.

The Problems with Windows

The world's most popular operating system is Windows, which is made by the Microsoft Corporation. Linux has no links with Windows at all. Microsoft doesn't contribute anything to Linux and, in fact, is rather hostile toward it because it threatens Microsoft's market dominance. This means that installing Linux can give you an entirely Microsoft-free PC. How enticing does *that* sound?

Windows is used on 91 percent of the world's desktop computers. In other words, it must be doing a good job for it to be so popular, right?

Let's face facts. Windows is not without problems, and that's putting it mildly. It's stunningly insecure, and virtually every day a new security hole is uncovered. This leads to the creation of worms by malevolent programmers. *Worms* are small programs that exploit security holes within operating systems, leaping from computer to computer and spreading like wildfire via the Internet. Examples include Sasser (as well as its variations), which causes your computer to crash and shut down as soon as you go online.

Then there are the viruses—hundreds and hundreds of them. This has led to an entire industry that creates antivirus programs, which are additional pieces of software. Antivirus software is vital if you want to use Windows without losing data or running the risk of your files being stolen!

Some argue that Windows is hit by so many viruses merely because it's so popular. But consider that many of these viruses are simple programs that merely take advantage of security holes in Windows. For example, one particular virus took advantage of a bug in such a way that just viewing an e-mail message caused the virus to infect your computer! And we're *paying* for this quality of software?

■**Note** Although we're being disparaging about Windows here, unlike many books, *Beginning Fedora Linux: From Novice to Professional* doesn't ignore Windows. Throughout its pages, you'll find frequent references to Windows and the software that runs under it. You'll find direct comparisons with actual Windows programs. The intention is that anyone with prior experience will be able to get started with Fedora much more quickly.

And how about the speed at which Windows runs? It's just dandy when your PC is brand new. But after just a few months, it seems like someone has opened up the case and poured molasses inside. It takes quite a few seconds for My Computer to open, and there's time for a coffee break while Internet Explorer starts up.

So is Linux the solution to these problems? Most would agree that it's a step in the right direction, at the very least. Linux doesn't need antivirus programs, because there are virtually no Linux-specific viruses. As with all software, security holes are occasionally discovered in Linux, but the way it is built means exploiting those holes is much more difficult.

■**Note** There have been a couple of viruses for Linux, but they're no longer "in the wild" (that is, they're no longer infecting PCs). This is because the security holes they exploited were quickly patched, causing the viruses to die out. This happened because the majority of Linux users update their systems regularly, so any security holes that viruses might exploit are patched promptly. Compare that to Windows, where most users aren't even aware they can update their systems, even when Microsoft gets around to issuing a patch (which has been known to take months).

There's also the fact that Linux encourages you to take control of your computer, as opposed to treating it like a magical box. As soon as you install Linux, you become a power user. Every aspect of your PC is under your control, unlike with Windows. This means fixing problems is a lot easier, and optimizing your system becomes part and parcel of the user experience. You no longer have to take poor performance lying down. You can do something about it!

WINDOWS COMPATIBLE?

One of the biggest questions asked by most newcomers to Linux is whether it can run Windows software. The answer is yes . . . and no.

Linux is completely different from Windows on a fundamental technical level. Its creators based it on UNIX, an industrial-strength operating system, and deliberately steered clear of emulating Windows. This means that Linux isn't a swap-in replacement for Windows. You cannot take the installation CD of a Windows program and use it to install that program on Linux, just as you cannot install an Apple Mac program on Windows.

However, several current projects let you run Windows programs on Linux. Wine (www.winehq.com/) is an example of such a project, and you can download a commercial, easy-to-use variation of it from www.codeweavers.com/. You can also use programs like VMware (www.vmware.com/) to create a "virtual PC" running on Linux. Then you can install the Windows operating system and, therefore, any Windows software you like.

In most cases, however, you'll find that there's a Linux equivalent of your favorite Windows software. Frequently, you'll find that this Linux version is actually superior to the Windows program you've been using. We'll discuss many of these in Chapter 11.

The Benefits of Linux

People have been known to exaggerate about Linux when singing its praises, and there's certainly some hyperbole around. But there are a couple of cast-iron facts about its benefits.

Crash-Free

A primary benefit of Linux is that it doesn't crash. In years and years of using Linux, you will never experience your mouse cursor freezing on the screen. A strange error box won't appear and not go away until you reboot. It's possible to leave a Linux system running for years without ever needing to reboot (although most desktop Fedora users shut down their PCs when they won't be using it for a while, just like the rest of us).

Of course, programs that run on top of Linux sometimes crash, but they don't take the rest of the system down with them, as can happen under Windows. Instead, you can clean up after a crash and just carry on.

■Note Actually, very few programs under Linux crash. Because Linux programmers use a different method of bug testing than Microsoft developers, there are arguably fewer bugs, and those that are discovered are fixed very quickly.

Security

The next benefit is that Linux is far, far more secure than Windows. Linux is based on years of proven computer science research. It works on the principle of users who have permissions to undertake various tasks on the system. If you don't have the correct permission, then you cannot, for example, access a particular piece of hardware. Additionally, privacy can be ensured because the files on the PC are "owned" by individual users, who can permit or deny others access to those files.

Free and Shareable

Another big benefit is that Linux can be obtained free of charge. Once it's installed, the latest updates for all your programs are also free of charge. Not only that, but if you want any new software, it will also usually be free of charge (and normally just a download away). Is this starting to sound attractive yet?

Because the software is free, you can share it with friends. Suppose that you find a really great image editor. You mention it to a friend, and he asks for a copy. Under Windows, copying the program is strictly illegal—to do so turns you into a software pirate! Unless that image editor is freeware, your friend will need to buy the software himself. Under Linux, sharing software is normally entirely legal. In fact, it's encouraged! We'll explain why in Chapter 2.

Compatible with Older Hardware

Another benefit of Linux is that it works very well on older hardware and doesn't require a cutting-edge PC system. The latest OS offering from Microsoft, Windows Vista, requires high-powered hardware, to the extent that upgrading to that operating system usually means buying a new PC, even if your old one still works fine!

In contrast, Linux works on computers dating back as far as the early 1990s. One of our test systems, a five-year-old Pentium II 450 MHz notebook can still run several distributions of Linux, including Fedora. Although it would be an exaggeration to claim that the computer is lightning-fast, there's little waiting around for programs to start. On the same machine, Windows 2000 (which came installed on the computer) grinds and churns, and using it can be a frustrating experience.

Linux encourages an attitude of both recycling and making the most of what you have, rather than constantly upgrading and buying new hardware. You can pull out that "old" PC and bring it back to life by installing Linux. You might even be able to give it away to a family member or friend who does not have a PC. Perhaps it's time for grandma to get online, or perhaps you can give the kids their own PC so they'll stop using yours.

Alternatively, you might consider turning old hardware into a server. Linux is capable of just about any task. As well as running desktop computers, it also runs around 60 percent of the computers that make the Internet work. Linux is extremely flexible. You could turn an old PC into a web server, e-mail server, or firewall that you can attach to a broadband Internet connection. If you were to do this with Microsoft software, it would cost hundreds of dollars, not to mention requiring an advanced computer. It's free with Linux.

The Linux Community

So we've established that Linux is powerful, secure, and flexible. But we've saved the best for last. Linux is more than a computer operating system. It's an entire community of users spread across the globe. When you start to use Linux, you become part of this community (whether you like it or not).

One of the benefits of membership is that you're never far from finding a solution to a problem. The community likes to congregate online around forums and newsgroups, which you can join in order to find help.

Your placement in the ranks of the community is "newbie." This is a popular way of describing someone who is new to Linux. Although this sounds derisory, it will actually help when you talk to others. Advertising your newbie status will encourage people to take the time to help you. After all, they were newbies once upon a time!

There's another reason not to be disheartened by your newbie tag: you'll outgrow it very quickly. By the time you reach the end of this book, you'll have advanced to the other end of the spectrum: "guru." You'll be one of those giving out the advice to those poor, clueless newbies, and you'll be 100 percent confident in your skills.

Note One of the best ways to learn about Linux is under the auspices of a knowledgeable friend. It's very beneficial to have your own guru to help you along when you get stuck—someone who is just an e-mail message or phone call away. If you have a friend who uses Linux, consider taking him or her out for a drink and getting friendlier!

But being part of a community is not just about getting free technical support. It's about sharing knowledge. Linux is as much about a political ideal as it is about software. It was created to be shared among those who want to use it. There are no restrictions, apart from one: any changes you make must also be made available to others.

The spirit of sharing and collaboration has been there since day one. One of the first things Linus Torvalds did when he produced an early version of Linux was to ask for help from others. And he got it. Complete strangers e-mailed him and said they would contribute their time, skills, and effort to help his project. This has been the way Linux has been developed ever since. Hundreds of people around the world contribute their own small pieces, rather than there being one overall company in charge. And the same concept applies to knowledge of Linux. When you learn something, don't be afraid to share this knowledge with others. "Giving something back" is a very important part of the way Linux works.

To understand why Linux is shared, you need to understand its history, as well as the history of what came before it. This is the topic of Chapter 2.

Summary

This chapter has provided an introduction to Linux. It explained what Linux can be used for and also its many advantages when compared to Microsoft Windows. It also introduced the community surrounding Linux, which adds to its benefits. You should be starting to realize what makes millions of people around the world use Linux as their operating system of choice.

The next chapter covers the history of Linux. It also discusses another curious aspect: the political scene that drives the operating system forward.

CHAPTER 2

■■■

A History and Politics Lesson

Linux is more than just software. It's an entire community of users, and as such, there's a detailed social history behind it. In this chapter, we'll look at the origins of Linux, both in terms of where it came from and the people who make it.

You might be tempted to skip this chapter and move on to the information about installing Fedora. To be fair, nothing of vital technical importance is mentioned here. But it's important that you read this chapter at some stage, because Linux is more than simply the sum of its parts. It's far more than simply a set of computer programs.

If nothing else, this chapter explains the fundamental philosophies behind Linux and attempts to answer some of the often-baffling questions that arise when Linux is considered as a whole.

In the Beginning

Linux was created in 1991, 16 years ago (at the time of writing). Such a span is considered a lifetime in the world of computing, but Linux actually harks back even further, into the early days of modern computing in the mid-1970s.

Linux was created by a Finnish student named Linus Torvalds. At the time, he was studying in Helsinki and had bought a desktop PC. His new computer needed an operating system. Torvalds's operating system choices were limited: there were various versions of DOS and something called MINIX. It was the latter that Torvalds decided to use.

MINIX was a clone of the popular UNIX operating system. UNIX was used on huge computers in businesses and universities, including those at Torvalds's university. UNIX was created in the early 1970s and has evolved since then to become what many considered the cutting edge of computing. UNIX brought to fruition a large number of computing concepts in use today and, many agree, got almost everything just right in terms of features and usability.

Versions of UNIX were available for smaller computers like Torvalds's PC, but they were considered professional tools and were very expensive. This was in the early days of the home computer craze, and the only people who used IBM PCs were businesspeople and hobbyists.

Note Linux is a pretty faithful clone of UNIX. If you were to travel back in time 20 or 30 years, you would find that using UNIX on those old mainframe computers, complete with their teletype interfaces, would be similar to using Linux on your home PC. Many of the fundamental concepts of Linux, such as the file system hierarchy and user permissions, are taken directly from UNIX.

Torvalds liked UNIX because of its power, and he liked MINIX because it ran on his computer. MINIX was created by Andrew Tanenbaum, a professor of computing, to demonstrate the principles of operating system design to his students. Because MINIX was also a learning tool, people

11

could also view the *source code* of the program—the original listings that Tanenbaum had entered to create the software.

MINIX was lacking in some significant areas. Many people, including Torvalds, found using it very frustrating. Torvalds decided to create from scratch his own version of MINIX, but to make it better, avoiding what many considered the pitfalls of MINIX. He managed to produce version 0.01 of Linux in just over half a year.

■Note Most clones or implementations of UNIX are named so that they end in an *x*. One story has it that Torvalds wanted to call his creation Freax, but a containing directory was accidentally renamed Linux on an Internet server. The name stuck.

From day one, Torvalds intended his creation to be shared among everyone who wanted to use it. He encouraged people to copy it and give it to friends. He didn't charge any money for it, and he also made the source code freely available. The idea was that people could take the code and improve it.

This was a master stroke. Many people contacted Torvalds, offering to help out. Because they could see the program code, they realized he was onto a good thing. Soon, Torvalds wasn't the only person developing Linux. He became the leader of a team that used the fledgling Internet to communicate and share improvements.

■Note The popular conception of Linux is that it is created by a few hobbyists who work on it in their spare time. This might have been true in the very early days. Nowadays, in addition to these "bedroom programmers," Linux is programmed by hundreds of professionals around the world, many of whom are employed specifically for the task. Torvalds adds to the effort himself and also coordinates the work.

It's important to note that when we talk here about Linux, we're actually talking about the kernel—the central program that runs the PC hardware and keeps the computer ticking. This is all that Torvalds initially produced back in 1991. It was an impressive achievement, but needed a lot of extra add-on programs to take care of even the most basic tasks. Torvalds's kernel needed additional software so that users could enter data, for example. It needed a way for users to be able to enter commands so that they could manipulate files, such as deleting or copying them. And that's before you even consider more complicated stuff like displaying graphics on the screen or printing documents.

Linux itself didn't offer these functions. It simply ran the computer's hardware. Once it booted up, it expected to find other programs. If they weren't present, then all you saw was a blank screen.

LINUS TORVALDS

Linus Benedict Torvalds was born in Helsinki, Finland, in 1969. A member of the minority Swedish-speaking population, he attended the University of Helsinki from 1988 to 1996, graduating with a masters degree in computer science.

He started Linux not through a desire to give the world a first-class operating system but with other goals in mind. Its inspiration is in part due to Helsinki winters being so cold. Rather than leave his warm flat and trudge through the snow to the university's campus in order to use its powerful minicomputer, he wanted to be able to connect to it from home. He also wanted to have a platform to use to experiment with the properties of the Intel 386, but that's another story. Torvalds needed an operating system capable of such tasks. Linux was born.

It took Torvalds the better part of a year to come up with the very first version of Linux, during which he worked alone in a darkened room. In 1991, he announced his creation to the world, describing Linux as "just a hobby," and saying it would never be big. It wouldn't be until 1994 that it reached version 1.0.

In the early days, Torvalds's creation was fairly primitive. He was passionate that it should be free for everyone to use, and so he released it under a software license that said that no one could ever sell it. However, he quickly changed his mind, adopting the GNU Public License.

Torvalds was made wealthy by his creation, courtesy of the dot-com boom of the late 1990s, even though this was never his intention; he was driven by altruism. Nowadays, he lives in Portland, Oregon, with his wife and children, having moved to the United States from Finland in the late 1990s.

Initially, Torvalds worked for Transmeta, developing CPU architectures as well as overseeing kernel development, although this wasn't part of his official work. He still programs the kernel, but currently he oversees the Open Source Development Lab, an organization created to encourage open-source adoption in industry (and also referred to as the home of Linux).

The GNU Project

Around the time Linus created Linux, another project, called GNU, also existed. This project team also hoped to create an operating system that used UNIX as its inspiration, although avoiding some of the pitfalls that had blighted that operating system, both technically and in terms of its licensing. GNU is a so-called recursive acronym that stands for "GNU's Not UNIX," a play on words favored by computer programmers.

GNU's parent organization, the Free Software Foundation (FSF), had been formed eight years prior to Torvalds's effort, and in that time had produced the majority of the core software that Linux desperately needed. However, as luck would have it, FSF lacked the essential functionality of the kernel. The developers were in the process of creating their own kernel, but it had not come to fruition.

The GNU software was distributed for free to anyone who wanted it. The source code was also made available so users could adapt and change the programs to meet their own needs (in fact, Torvalds had used the GNU model when deciding how to distribute Linux).

Richard Stallman is the man behind GNU and, along with Linus Torvalds, is the second accidental hero in our story. Stallman had been around since the dark ages of computing, back when wardrobe-sized computers were "time-shared" among users who used small desktop terminals to access them. Like Torvalds, Stallman started GNU as a personal project, but then found others who were more than willing to join his cause.

■**Note** Stallman created the Emacs text editor and the GNU C Compiler (GCC). Together, they allow the creation of yet more software, so it's no surprise that one of the very first programs Torvalds used in the early days to create Linux was Stallman's GCC.

Back in Stallman's day at the legendary Massachusetts Institute of Technology (MIT), computer software was shared. If you came up with a program to perform a particular task, you offered it to practically anyone who wanted it. Alternatively, if you found an existing program wasn't adequate or had a bug, you improved it yourself, and then made the resulting program available to others. People might use your improved version, or they might not; it was up to them.

This way of sharing software was disorganized and done on an ad hoc basis, but came about of its own accord. Nobody questioned it, and it seemed the best way of doing things. There certainly wasn't any money involved, any more than there would be money involved in one friend explaining an idea to another.

RICHARD STALLMAN

Richard Matthew Stallman, usually referred to as RMS, was born in 1953 in Manhattan. He comes from the old school of computing forged during the 1970s and was a member of MIT's legendary Artificial Intelligence Lab.

Seemingly destined for a life in academia, Stallman left MIT in 1984 to found the GNU Project. This was a reaction to the increasing commercialization of computer software. Whereas once all hackers—that is, programmers—had shared ideas and program code, the trend in the 1980s was toward proprietary, nonshared code, as well as legal contracts, which forced programmers to keep secrets from one another.

Stallman is a very talented programmer and is considered a genius by many observers. He single-handedly created many essential programming tools in his initial efforts to get GNU off the ground. Many of these find a home in Linux.

Stallman is also widely applauded for the creation of the GNU Public License. This is a legal document that lets people share software. It introduces the concept of *copyleft* and is opposed to the legal concept of copyright, which attempts to limit the freedom of individuals when using a piece of software (or any other creative work). Nowadays, the concept of copyleft has been applied to literature, music, and other arts in an attempt to avoid restricting who can and cannot access various items, as well as to encourage a collaborative working environment.

Proprietary Software and the GPL

In the 1980s, everything changed. The world became more corporate, and with the rise of the desktop PC, the concept of proprietary software became prevalent. More and more companies started to sell software. They reasoned that this was impossible to do if they shared it with everybody else, so they kept it secret. Microsoft led this charge and did very well with its proprietary software.

To Stallman, this "trade secrets" approach to software was anathema. He had nothing against software being sold for a profit, but he hated the fundamental ideas behind software being kept secret. He felt passionately that sharing software and being able to understand how it worked was akin to free speech—necessary and vital for the furthering of technology, and therefore society itself. How could the new generation of programmers improve on the previous generation's work if they were unable to see how it worked? It was absurd to need to create software from scratch each time, rather than taking something that already existed and making it better.

Because of his beliefs, Stallman resigned from his job in the MIT Artificial Intelligence Lab and founded GNU. His aim initially was to produce a complete clone of UNIX that would be shared in the ways he knew from the early days of computing. This software would be available for everyone to use, to study, and to adapt. It would be free, in the same sense as free speech—shared and unrestricted. This gave rise to the vital concept of "free software," and soon GNU, and the FSF, became not just a programming venture, but also a political movement.

■**Note** A very common misconception of "free software" is that it is always free of charge. This isn't correct. The word *free* is used here in its political sense, as in "free speech." Many companies and individuals make a healthy profit from selling free software and, in fact, selling free software is encouraged by the GNU Project.

To protect the rights of people to share and adapt the GNU software, Stallman came up with the GNU Public License (GPL). Various drafts of this license were produced over time, until it became a completely watertight legal contract, which furthered the concept of free software.

Most software you buy comes with a license agreement—that big chunk of text you must agree to when installing software (in the case of Windows desktop software, it's frequently referred to as the End-User License Agreement, or EULA). The license agreement usually says that you cannot copy the software or share it with friends. If others want to use the software, they must buy their own version.

The GPL turns this on its head. Rather than restricting what people can do with the software, it gives them permission to share the software with whomever they wish. However, if they modify the program in any way and then distribute it to others, the program they come up with must also be licensed under the GPL. In other words, people cannot make changes to a program that has a GPL, and then sell the modified program, keeping their improvements secret.

■**Note** An interesting side note is that the actual wording of the GPL says that any changes you make should be shared with others *only if the software is redistributed*. This means that if you modify some GPL software and don't give it to anyone else, there's no need for you to publish your changes or make others aware of those changes.

GNU and Linux Together

The Linux kernel, developed by Torvalds, and the GNU software, developed by Stallman, were a perfect match. It's important to note that this doesn't mean the two projects joined forces. It simply means that the Linux project took some of the GNU software and gave it a good home. This was done with Stallman's blessing, but there wasn't any official union between the two groups. Remember that Stallman had intended everyone to freely share and use the GNU tools. Linux represented a set of people doing just that. GNU is still working on its own kernel, called Hurd, which may provide an alternative to using Torvalds's Linux kernel.

■**Note** Hurd was first planned back in the 1980s and, at the time of writing, still has yet to see the light of day (although testing versions are available). Hurd is a hugely ambitious project and will set a gold standard when it is released.

GNU and Linux together formed a complete operating system, which mimicked the way UNIX operated. Other projects and individuals spotted the success of Linux and came on board, and it wasn't long before Linux realized the potential for a graphical user interface (GUI), the fundamentals of which were provided by the XFree86 Project. A lot of additional software was also provided by individuals and organizations, all using the same "share and share alike" example set by Stallman, with the GNU tools, and Torvalds, with his kernel.

Many people refer to Linux as GNU/Linux. This gives credit to the GNU Project that provided the majority of tools vital to making Linux into a usable operating system. However, like the majority of people in the computing world, we use the term *Linux* throughout this book to avoid confusion.

Different Flavors of Linux

All the pieces of GNU software were available for free download and were therefore free of charge. But this brought its own problems. Not everyone had the know-how to put all the bits and pieces together into a complete operating system. Those who could do this didn't necessarily have the time for it.

Because of this, a number of companies stepped in to do the hard work. They put together versions of Linux, complete with all the software from the GNU Project, which they then sold for a fee on floppy disks, CDs, or DVDs. They also added in bits of their own software, which made it possible to install Linux easily onto a computer's hard disk, for example. They produced their own manuals and documentation, too, and did other things such as bug testing to ensure that it all worked well.

What they came up with became known as *distributions* of Linux, or *distros* for short. Examples of these companies include Red Hat, SUSE, and Mandrake. Additionally, a number of enthusiasts got together and formed organizations to create their own distros, such as Debian and Slackware.

Modern distros are very advanced. They make it easy to install Linux on your PC, and they usually come with everything you need, so you can get started immediately. Additionally, they have their own look and feel, as well as unique ways of working and operating. This means that Fedora is not the same as SUSE Linux, for example, although they share a lot of common features and, of course, they all share the core GNU software.

Linux Today

Nowadays, Linux is a thoroughly modern, capable operating system, considered cutting edge by many. It also runs on many different types of computer hardware, including Apple Macintosh computers, Sun SPARC machines, and the ubiquitous desktop PCs equipped with Intel or AMD processors. One of the ironies is that although Linux was based on UNIX, it has slowly come to dominate the computer operating system market. According to industry sources, Linux is on its way to making commercial varieties of UNIX redundant. Companies that sell their own versions of UNIX, such as Hewlett-Packard and IBM, have added Linux to their traditional product range.

Recent innovations in the latest versions of the kernel mean that it finds uses on the smallest computers in the world, as well as on the biggest. Linux is run on several of the top supercomputers in the world; at the same time it can be used on handheld PDAs or even digital watches! You'll even find it running things like digital video recorders and other household devices, where it sits invisibly in the background and makes everything work. Remember that one of the fundamental principles of Linux is that you can use it for whatever you want. You don't need to ask for permission first or tell anyone what you're doing.

Linux initially found mainstream use by software developers, and on server computers, such as those that run the Internet. However, in recent years, it has become increasingly popular on desktop computers. This is the area where experts suggest it will see massive growth over the coming years.

Modern Linux Development

Nowadays, Linux is developed not only by Torvalds, who manages the huge project, but also by hundreds of volunteers and corporations who contribute resources. Most recently, IBM and Novell have gotten involved and contribute hundreds of people to the effort of creating Linux. Sun contributes the OpenOffice.org office suite and sells its own version of Linux. Corporations like Computer Associates contribute their own software, too.

These companies have realized that the best way of producing software is to share and share alike, rather than develop their own proprietary software and keep it secret. The proprietary ways of the 1980s are starting to seem like an ill-conceived flash in the pan.

Most recently, Novell found that by embracing Linux, it could massively enhance the functions of its aging NetWare product without needing to return to the drawing board and start from scratch. It could just take what it wanted from the pile of Linux software. This shows the philosophy of Linux in action.

Linux has software for just about every need, ranging from simply receiving e-mail to running a huge e-mail server. There are databases, office suites, web browsers, video games, movie players, audio tools, and more, as well as thousands of pieces of specialized software used in various niches of industry (and too boring to mention here). Most of this software is available to anyone who wants it, free of charge. What more could you want?

Summary

This chapter has detailed the history of Linux and explained its origins. It also explained *why* Linux came into being. We looked at how Linux formed one of the building blocks of a political movement geared toward producing software that can be shared.

We discussed the creator of Linux, Linus Torvalds. We also looked at the massive input the GNU Project has made and, in particular, that of its philosopher king, Richard Stallman.

In the next chapter, we'll move on to look at what you can expect from day-to-day use of Linux.

CHAPTER 3

■ ■ ■

The Realities of Running Linux

Now that you've learned about the politics, history, and personalities behind Linux, the questions remain: what's Linux actually like when used day to day? What should the average user expect from the experience?

These are the questions we hope to answer in this brief chapter.

Learning to Use Linux

What should you expect from Linux once you've installed it? Well, it's a little like running Windows, except there are no viruses, fewer crashes, and no inexplicable slowdowns.

In addition, you have complete control over the system. This doesn't mean Linux is necessarily complicated. It's just that you have the control if you wish to make use of it. We'll look into this in the later chapters of this book.

Most software you use under Windows has at least one equivalent under Fedora, installed by default. It's unlikely that you'll need to download or install any additional software, and even if you do, you'll probably find it's available for free.

In most cases, the Linux swap-ins are at least as powerful and easy to use as their Windows alternatives. Tabbed browsing in the Mozilla Firefox web browser lets you visit more than one site at once, for example, without needing to have a lot of browser instances running, as you do with Microsoft Internet Explorer. The Beagle program lets you look through your e-mail messages, chat conversations, web browsing history, and other data files quickly for a variety of criteria, and it puts the features in a similar Microsoft product to shame.

Does this sound too good to be true? There is just one caveat. Linux isn't a clone of Windows and doesn't aim to be. It has its own way of doing certain things, and sometimes works differently from Windows. This means that many people experience a learning curve when they first begin using Linux.

Note Several Linux distributions aim to mimic Windows pretty faithfully. For example, Xandros and Linspire copy the look and feel of Windows to the extent that (allegedly) some people are unable to tell the difference.

But in just a few weeks after your move to Linux, everything will start to seem entirely normal. Most of the time, you won't even be aware you're running Linux. Of course, some patience is required during those initial few weeks. Linux can be illogical and frustrating; on the other hand, so can Windows. We simply got used to it.

Who Uses Linux?

Who uses Linux? The myth from the old days is that it's only for techies and power users. When you needed to put everything together by hand, this was clearly true. But modern distributions make Linux accessible to all. It's no exaggeration to say that you could install Linux on a computer Luddite's PC and have that person use it in preference to Windows.

Up until quite recently, Linux was largely seen as a developer's tool and a server operating system. It was geared toward programmers or was destined for a life running backroom computers, serving data, and making other computer resources available to users.

To this end, Linux continues to run a sizable proportion of the computers that make the Internet work, largely because it provides an ideal platform for the Apache web server, as well as various databases and web-based programming languages. This has lead to the LAMP acronym, which stands for Linux, Apache (a web server), MySQL (a database), and PHP, Python, or Perl (three programming languages that can be used in an online environment).

Despite its technical origins, recent years have seen a strong push for Linux on desktop computers. Linux has stepped out of the dark backrooms, with the goal of pushing aside Microsoft Windows and Mac OS in order to dominate the corporate workstation and home user market.

Running Linux on the desktop has always been possible, but the level of knowledge required was often prohibitively high, putting Linux out of the reach of most ordinary users. It's only comparatively recently that the companies behind the distributions of Linux have taken a long, hard look at Windows and attempted to mirror its user-friendly approach. In addition, the configuration software in distributions like Fedora has progressed in leaps and bounds. Now, it's no longer necessary to know arcane commands in order to do something as simple as switch the screen resolution. The situation has also been helped by the development of extremely powerful office software, such as OpenOffice.org and KOffice.

Is Linux for you? There's only one way of finding out, and that's to give it a go. Linux doesn't require much of you except an open mind and the will to learn new ways of doing things. You shouldn't see learning to use Linux as a chore. Instead, you should see it as an adventure—a way of finally getting the most from your PC and not having to worry about things going wrong for reasons outside your control.

Linux puts you in charge. You're the mechanic of the car as well as its driver, and you'll be expected to get your hands dirty every now and then. Unlike Windows, Linux doesn't hide any of its settings or stop you from doing things for your own protection; everything is available to tweak. Using Linux requires commitment and the realization that there are probably going to be problems, and they're going to need to be overcome.

However, using Linux should be enjoyable. In his initial newsgroup posting announcing Linux back in 1992, Linus Torvalds said that he was creating Linux "just for fun." This is what it should be for you.

Getting Ahold of Linux

Getting ahold of Linux is easy. You'll already have spotted the version of Fedora packaged with this book. Fedora is the main focus of this book, and we consider it to be one of the very best versions of Linux out there. It's ideal for both beginners and power users, and it really does match the functionality offered in Windows. It includes several easy-to-use configuration tools, which makes changing your system settings a breeze. For example, the Pirut Package Manager software can automate the download and installation of new software with just a few clicks.

Fedora is also a very good-looking distribution. You'll find your friends and colleagues "wowing" when they happen to pass by and glance at your PC.

Quite a number of Linux distributions are available. If you want to explore other Linux distributions as well as Fedora, by far the most fuss-free method of getting ahold of Linux is to pop over to your local computer store (or online retailer) and buy a boxed copy. You can choose from Ubuntu, SUSE, Mandriva, Turbolinux (if you want foreign language support, although nearly all commercial distributions do a good job of supporting mainstream languages), and many others. Many distributions come on more than a single CD—typically up to five CDs at the moment. Some versions of Linux, Fedora included, come on DVD.

Caution Bearing in mind what we've said about the sharing nature of Linux, you might think it possible to buy a boxed copy of Linux and run off copies for friends, or even sell them for a profit. However, you shouldn't assume this is the case. A minority of distribution companies, such as Xandros and Linspire, incorporate copyrighted corporate logos into their distributions that place restrictions on redistribution. Sometimes they include proprietary software along with the Linux tools, which you cannot copy without prior permission. However, in many cases, reproducing the CDs in small volumes for friends or for use on workstations in a company environment is permitted.

Many of the Linux distributions are also available to download free of charge. In fact, many community-run distributions—such as Slackware, Debian, Gentoo, and even Fedora—are *only* available this way (although you can often buy "homemade" CDs from smaller retailers, who effectively burn the CDs for you and produce makeshift packaging). If your PC has a CD-R/RW drive and you have some CD-burning software under Windows (such as Nero), you can download an ISO image and make your own installation CD from it.

Note An *ISO image* is a very large file (typically 700 MB) that you can burn to CD. This CD is then used to install Linux.

Using Fedora

Fedora is a relatively young Linux distribution. It is based on the original Red Hat Linux distribution. Red Hat Linux was suspended in 2003, branching into two products: Fedora for regular users and Red Hat Enterprise Linux for commercial users. Red Hat has been in existence for almost as long as the Linux kernel, and it embraces the spirit and philosophy of Linux, which says software should be shared and made available to anyone who wants it.

Fedora takes this one step further. Its goal is to promote the rapid progress of free and open-source software and content. Using public forums, rapid innovation and meritocracy, the intention is to create the best operating system that free software can offer. Fedora supports a large number of languages, so it can be used in most countries around the world. In addition, it includes accessibility tools, so it can be used by partially sighted, deaf, or disabled people.

From the very start, Fedora's creators decided it would always be free of charge, freely available, and freely redistributable. Unlike many versions of Linux, no commercial version of Fedora exists (discounting Red Hat Enterprise Linux, which just like Fedora branched from Red Hat Linux).

But perhaps Fedora's greatest strength is its community, which extends across the world. If you have a question about Fedora, you'll find hundreds of people willing to help. Just as the software is designed to be shared, a strong belief within the Fedora community is that knowledge should be shared, too.

Fedora Linux was the name of a volunteer project that provided additional software for the Red Hat Linux distribution. In late 2003, Red Hat Linux merged with the Fedora Linux Project to form the Fedora Project, a group sponsored by Red Hat to produce the Fedora distribution.

Fedora is primarily geared toward desktop users, although with a little adapting, it can also be used to run server computers.

Fedora is designed to be easy to use. Anyone who has used Windows or Mac OS will feel right at home. It features every piece of software you could wish for or would find within a well-equipped modern operating system. It includes a web browser, an e-mail client, instant messaging software, an office suite, a graphics editor, and much more. And don't think that these are cut-down versions designed to lure you into purchasing the full version later on. In every case, they're full-featured pieces of software that give proprietary programs a run for their money.

Perhaps more importantly, Fedora is very user-friendly. Updating the system can be done with just a few clicks of the mouse, as can downloading and installing new software.

Summary

This chapter has explained what you can realistically expect when using Linux every day, and also discussed the kind of company you'll be keeping in terms of fellow users.

You learned how people usually get ahold of Linux. Of course, with this book, you already have a version of Linux—Fedora—which was introduced in this chapter.

This completes the general overview of the world of Linux. In the next part of the book, you'll move on to actually installing Linux on your hard disk. This sounds more daunting than it actually is. The next chapter gets you started by explaining a few basic preinstallation steps.

PART 2

■ ■ ■

Installing Fedora

CHAPTER 4

■ ■ ■

Preinstallation Steps

The first part of this book discussed the pros and cons of using Linux as part of your day-to-day life. It was intended to help you evaluate Linux and understand what you're buying into should you decide to make it your operating system of choice. Now, we move on to actually installing Linux and, specifically, Fedora, which is included with this book on a DVD.

Installing any kind of operating system is a big move and can come as something of a shock to your PC. However, Fedora makes this complicated maneuver as easy as possible. Its installation routines are very advanced compared to previous versions of Linux, and even compared to other current distributions.

What does saying that you're going to install Fedora actually mean? This effectively implies three things:

- Somehow all the files necessary to run Fedora are going to be put onto your hard disk.
- The PC will be configured so that it knows where to find these files when it first boots up.
- The Fedora operating system will be set up so that you can use it.

However, in order to do all this and get Fedora onto your PC, you must undertake some preparatory work, which is the focus of this chapter.

Understanding Partitioning

Chances are, if you're reading this book, your PC already has Windows installed on it. This won't present a problem. In most cases, Fedora can live happily alongside Windows in what's called a *dual-boot setup*, where you can choose at startup which operating system to run. However, installing Fedora means that Windows must make certain compromises. It needs to cohabit your hard disk with another operating system—something it isn't designed to do.

The main issue with such a situation is that Windows needs to shrink and make some space available for Fedora (unless you install a second hard disk, which is discussed later in this chapter). Fedora isn't able to use the same file system as Windows, and it needs its own separately defined part of the disk. Actually, it requires more than one part of the disk. Each of these parts is known as a *partition*. All of this can be handled automatically by the Fedora installation routine, but it's important that you know what happens.

All hard disks are split into partitions, which are large chunks of the disk created to hold operating systems (just like a large farm is partitioned into separate fields). A partition is usually multiple gigabytes in size, although it can be smaller. You can view your disk's partitions using the Disk Management tool in Windows XP and Windows 2000, as shown in Figure 4-1. You can access this tool by opening Control Panel, clicking the Administrative Tools icon, selecting Computer Management, and then choosing Disk Management.

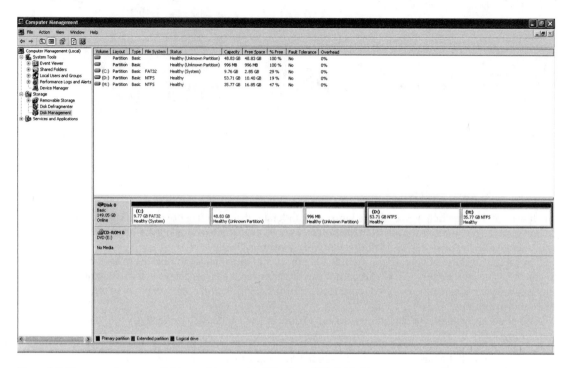

Figure 4-1. *You can view your disk's partitions using Windows XP's Disk Management tool.*

Most desktop PC systems have just one partition, unless the user has specifically created new partitions. As mentioned, Fedora needs two partitions of its own. During installation, Fedora creates fresh partitions alongside the Windows partition. It creates two partitions: the /boot and a Logical Volume Management (LVM) partition that contains root (/) and the swap partitions.

In addition, the Fedora installation routine writes a new *boot sector* (also known as a *boot loader*). The boot sector is located at the very beginning of the disk and contains a small program that then runs another program that lets you choose between operating systems (and therefore partitions) when you first boot up.

■**Note** Not all Linux distributions have the ability to repartition the hard disk. In fact, at the time of writing, it's pretty rare. Most expect to simply take over the entire hard disk, wiping Windows in the process (although they'll always ask the user to confirm this beforehand). We suggest that you use the KNOPPIX Live CD to resize NTFS partitions.

Of course, Fedora cannot shrink a Windows partition that is packed full of data, because no space is available for it to reclaim; and perhaps more importantly, Fedora does not completely support NTFS yet.

FEDORA AND WINDOWS FILE SYSTEMS

One of the benefits of dual-booting Linux and Windows is that Fedora lets you access the files on the Windows partition. This is quite handy and facilitates the easy exchange of data.

If the Windows partition is FAT32—used on Windows 95, 98, Me, and (sometimes) XP—then Fedora can both read and write files to the partition. However, if the file system is NTFS—used with Windows NT, 2000, and (sometimes) XP—then Fedora will make the file system available as read-only. We discuss in Chapter 14 software that enables you to write to an NTFS partition.

Freeing Up Space

The first step before installing Fedora alongside Windows is to check how much free space you have in your Windows partition. To see the amount of free space you have, double-click My Computer, right-click your boot drive, and select Properties. The free space is usually indicated in purple on a pie-chart diagram, as shown in Figure 4-2.

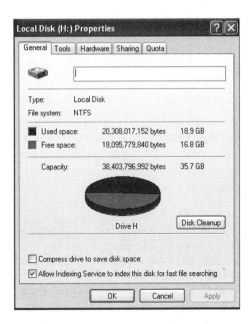

Figure 4-2. *Fedora needs free disk space in which to install, so you might need to clean up your Windows partition.*

You need to have at least 2 GB of free space in your Windows partition for Fedora to use. You'll need more space if you wish to install a lot of programs. If you don't have enough free space, you have several options: reclaim space, remove Windows, or use a second hard disk.

Reclaiming Space

On Windows XP, you can run the Disk Cleanup tool to free some space on your hard disk. Click the Disk Cleanup button beneath the pie-chart diagram showing the free disk space (see Figure 4-2). Disk Cleanup is also accessible by choosing Start ➤ All Programs ➤ Accessories ➤ System Tools ➤ Disk Cleanup.

You might also consider turning off System Restore. This consumes a lot of disk space, which you can therefore reclaim. However, deactivating System Restore will mean that you lose the possibility of returning your system to a previous state should anything go wrong. To access the System Restore control, right-click My Computer, click Properties, and then click the System Restore tab.

If you still cannot free up enough disk space, consider uninstalling unused software via the Add/Remove Programs applet within Control Panel. If you have any large games installed, consider removing them first, because they usually take up substantial amounts of hard disk space. You might also consider deleting movie and MP3 music files, which are renowned for eating up hard disk space. The average MP3 is around 4 MB, for example, and one minute of video at 240 × 180 resolution typically takes up 10 MB of disk space!

Removing Windows

Some users might prefer a second, more radical option: getting rid of Windows completely and letting Fedora take over the entire hard disk. If you feel confident that Fedora will fulfill your needs, this is undoubtedly the most straightforward solution. You'll be able to do this during installation. However, this will also mean that any personal data you have will be lost, so you should first back up your data (as described shortly).

■**Caution** You should be aware that installing Windows back onto a hard disk that has Fedora on it is troublesome. Windows has a Darwinian desire to wipe out the competition. If you attempt to install Windows on a Fedora hard disk, it will overwrite Linux.

Using Another Hard Disk

A third option for making room for Fedora is attractive and somewhat safer in terms of avoiding the potential for data loss, but also potentially expensive: fitting a second hard disk to your PC. You can then install Fedora on this other hard disk, letting it take up the entire disk. Unlike Windows, Fedora doesn't need to be installed on the primary hard disk and is happy on a secondary drive.

A second hard disk is perhaps the best solution if you're low on disk space and want to retain Windows on your system. However, you'll need to know how to install the new drive or find someone to do it for you (although step-by-step guides can be found on the Web—just search using Google or another search engine). In addition, if your PC is less than 12 months old, there is a possibility that you'll invalidate your guarantee by opening up your PC.

If you have an old PC lying around, you might also consider installing Fedora on it, at least until you're sure that you want to run it on your main PC. As noted in Chapter 1, one of the best features of Fedora is that it runs relatively well on older hardware. For example, a Pentium II with 256 MB of memory should allow for a decent performance.

NO-INSTALL LINUX

If you want to use the Linux operating system but leave your hard disk untouched, you might consider a number of additional options. Perhaps the most popular is to use a "live" version of Linux. A live version of Linux is one that boots and runs entirely from a CD (or DVD); it doesn't touch the user's hard disk. The most popular is KNOPPIX (www.knoppix.org/). The distribution we discuss throughout this book, Fedora, also offers two live CD versions, albeit ones that can be installed as well.

Using Linux in this way involves downloading an ISO image (a single large file of around 650 MB), which then must be burned to CD using a Windows program like Nero. Once the CD has been created, you simply boot from it in order to run Linux (after you ensure that your PC's BIOS is set to boot from CD, as explained in Chapter 5).

Alternatively, you might consider using virtual PC software. This type of software runs under Windows and re-creates an entire PC hardware system within software—effectively a PC within a PC. The hard disk is contained within one or two Windows files. Linux can then be installed on these virtual PC systems. When the program is switched to full-screen mode, it's impossible to tell you're running inside a computer system created in software. Two commercially available examples are considered worthwhile by many: VMware (www.vmware.com/) and Microsoft's Virtual PC (www.microsoft.com/windowsxp/virtualpc/). You should be aware that both are designed to be professional-level tools, so they are quite expensive. You can also obtain open source renditions of virtual PC software, such as QEMU (http://fabrice.bellard.free.fr/qemu/).

Another option in its infancy at the time of writing is Cooperative Linux, or coLinux for short (www.colinux.org/). This is a set of Windows programs that aims to let Linux run under Windows using emulation. Unfortunately, setting up and using coLinux requires some expert knowledge, so you might want to wait until you have more experience with Linux.

Backing Up Your Data

Whichever route you decide to take when installing Fedora, you should back up the data currently on your computer beforehand. Possibly the easiest way of doing this is to burn the data to CD-R/RW discs using a program like Nero and a CD-R/RW drive.

If you take the coexistence route, installing Fedora alongside Windows, backing up your data should be done for insurance purposes. Although the Fedora Project tests all its software thoroughly and relies on community reporting of bugs, there's always the chance that something will go wrong. Repartitioning a hard disk is a major operation and carries with it the potential for data loss.

If you intend to erase the hard disk when installing Fedora (thereby removing Windows), you can back up your data, and then import it into Fedora.

Table 4-1 shows a list of common personal data file types, their file extensions, where they can be typically found on a Windows XP system, and notes on importing the data into Fedora. Note that earlier versions of Windows (95, 98, and Me) may differ when it comes to data storage locations.

Table 4-1. *Data That Should Be Backed Up*

Type of File	File Extensions	Typical Location	Notes
Office files	.doc, .xls, .ppt, .pdf, etc.	My Documents	Microsoft Office files can be opened, edited, and saved under Fedora using the OpenOffice.org suite. PDF documents can be viewed with the Evince program.
E-mail files	N/A	N/A	The Evolution mail client used by Fedora cannot import data directly from Microsoft Outlook or Outlook Express. However, there is a convoluted but effective workaround, which is described in the next section.
Digital images	.jpg, .bmp, .tif, .png, .gif, etc.	My Pictures (within My Documents)	Fedora includes a variety of programs to both view and edit image files.
Multimedia files	.mp3, .mpg, .avi, etc.	Various	With some additional downloads (discussed in Chapter 18), programs under Fedora can play MP3 music files and most movie file formats.
Internet Explorer Favorites	None	\Documents and Settings\ <username>\ Favorites	Your Favorites list cannot be imported into Fedora, but the individual files can be opened in a text editor in order to view their URLs, which can then be opened in the Fedora web browser.
Miscellaneous Internet files	Various	Various	You might also want to back up web site archives or instant messenger chat logs, although hidden data such as cookies cannot be imported.

Backing Up E-mail Files

Microsoft e-mail cannot be easily imported into Fedora because Microsoft prefers to create its own proprietary file formats, rather than use open standards recognized by the rest of industry. Most e-mail programs use the MBOX format, and this is true of Fedora as well as programs created by the Mozilla Foundation (the organization behind the Firefox web browser). However, Microsoft uses its own DBX file format for Outlook Express and PST format for Outlook.

As a workaround, you can download and install the free Mozilla Thunderbird e-mail client (available from www.mozilla.com) on your Windows system. In Thunderbird, select Tools ➤ Import to import your messages from Outlook, Outlook Express, or even the popular Eudora mail client. You will then be able to back up Thunderbird's mail files and import them into Evolution under Fedora.

To find where the mail files are stored, in Thunderbird, select Tools ➤ Account Settings, and then look in the Local Directory box. Back up each file that corresponds to a folder within your mail program—for example, Inbox, Sent, and so on. Note that you only need to back up the files *without* file extensions. You can ignore the .sbd folders as well as the .msf files.

Making Notes

When you're backing up data, a pencil and paper come in handy, too. You should write down any important usernames and passwords, such as those for your e-mail account and other online services. You might want to write down the phone number of your dial-up connection, for example, or your DSL/cable modem technical settings.

■**Caution** Don't forget to back up "hidden" data, such as Internet passwords.

In addition, remember to jot down essential technical details, such as your IP address if you are part of a network of computers using static addresses (this will usually be relevant only if you work in an office environment).

■Tip If you've forgotten any passwords, several freeware/shareware applications are able to "decode" the asterisks that obscure Windows passwords and show what's beneath them. A good example is Asterisk Password Reveal, which you can download from `www.paqtool.com/product/pass/pass_001.htm`. Sites like Download.com (`www.download.com/`) offer similar applications.

Note that you don't need to write down information such as hardware interrupt (IRQ) or memory addresses, because hardware is configured automatically by Fedora. However, it might be worth making a note of the make and model of some items of internal hardware, such as your graphics card, modem (dial-up, DSL, or cable), and sound card. This will help if Fedora is unable to automatically detect your hardware, although such a situation is fairly unlikely to arise. You can garner this information by right-clicking My Computer on your desktop, selecting Properties, and then clicking the Hardware tab. Then click the Device Manager button. Instead of writing everything down, you might consider taking a screenshot by pressing the Print Scr button and then using your favorite image editor to print it.

■Tip Fedora works with a wide variety of hardware, and in most cases, it will automatically detect your system components. If you're in any doubt, you can consult the forums at `www.fedoraforum.org` (in particular, the Hardware Help forums). You might also consider subscribing to one or more of the Fedora mailing lists at `www.redhat.com/mailman/listinfo`. Remember that an important element of Fedora is its community of users, many of whom will be very willing to answer any questions you might have!

Once you're certain that all your data is backed up, you can move on to the next chapter, which provides a step-by-step guide to installing the operating system.

Summary

The aim of this chapter has been to prepare both you and your computer for the installation of Fedora. We've looked at how your hard disk will be partitioned prior to installation and the preparations you should make to ensure your hard disk has sufficient free space. You also learned about the types of files you might choose to back up, in addition to vital details you should record, such as usernames and passwords for your online accounts.

In the next chapter, we move on to a full description of the Fedora installation procedure, which will guide you through getting Fedora onto your computer.

CHAPTER 5

■ ■ ■

Installing Fedora

It's now time to install Linux. This chapter details how to install Fedora, the version of Linux supplied with this book. Fedora offers a special installation program for this purpose.

Installing Linux is a surprisingly quick task and shouldn't take more than 45 minutes on a modern PC. It's also relatively simple, with very few decisions to make throughout. Fedora's installation program automates the task to a high degree. However, you should examine all the options you're offered to make sure they're correct.

Installing an operating system involves a couple of serious maneuvers that, via an incorrect click of the mouse or accidental keystroke, bring with them the possibility of data loss. Read and consider every warning message you see, and be sure to keep your wits about you. Above all, make a backup of your data, as described in Chapter 4.

An Overview of the Installation Process

Installing Fedora requires little more of you than the ability to use the keyboard. The initial stage of the installation program is a little old-fashioned in that you can't use a mouse. Instead, you choose options by highlighting them using various keys and then pressing Enter. Don't worry—it's really easy. Besides, the rest of the installer is graphical, so you will be able to use the mouse. You'll notice during the installation that in most cases, the default choices are best, but we advise you to be attentive when installing Linux.

The installation works through a few stages to get Linux on your computer's hard disk. After a few preliminary setup options, you'll need to partition your hard disk in order to create space for Fedora. After this, Fedora is installed onto your hard disk. Occasionally during the installation, you'll have to answer a few questions. For example, you'll need to set a username and password.

At the end of the procedure, your PC will boot straight into the Fedora login screen, and you're set to go. There's no need to mess around configuring hardware because that's done automatically. Neat, eh?

In most cases, the installation of Fedora will run smoothly without a hitch. But if you do run into problems, head over to Chapter 6, which addresses many of the most common issues and provides solutions.

Step-by-Step Guide

As outlined in Chapter 4, you shouldn't start the installation process until you've made sure that there's enough space for Fedora on your hard disk and you've backed up all your data. With those preparations complete, you're ready to install Fedora. The remainder of this chapter guides you through the process.

Step 1: Booting from the DVD-ROM

With your computer booted up, insert the Fedora disc into the CD/DVD-ROM drive. Close the tray, and then reboot your computer.

Fedora is installed by booting the installation program from DVD-ROM. Therefore, the first step is to ensure that your computer's BIOS is set to boot from the CD/DVD-ROM drive. How this is achieved depends on your particular computer, but it's always done via the BIOS setup program. Most PCs let you enter BIOS setup by pressing the Delete key just after the computer is first booted, although some use another key or key combination. Review the information displayed on your particular screen at boot time for more information.

When the BIOS menu appears, look for an option such as Boot and select it (you can usually navigate the BIOS menu by using the cursor keys and select options by pressing Enter). On the new menu, look for a separate entry such as Boot Device Priority or perhaps Boot Sequence. Ensure that the entry for the CD-ROM is at the top of the list, as shown in Figure 5-1. Arrange the list so that it's followed by the floppy drive and then your main hard disk (which will probably be identified as IDE-0 or First Hard Disk). You can usually press the F1 key for help on how the menu selection system works.

Once you've made the changes, be sure to select the Exit Saving Changes option on the main BIOS setup menu. Your PC will then restart and boot from the Fedora DVD-ROM, and you'll be greeted by the Fedora welcome screen, as shown in Figure 5-2. Press Enter to start the installation program.

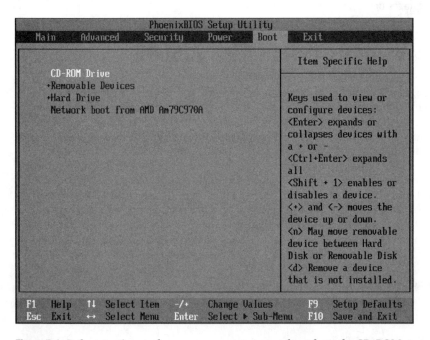

Figure 5-1. *Before starting, make sure your computer can boot from the CD-ROM.*

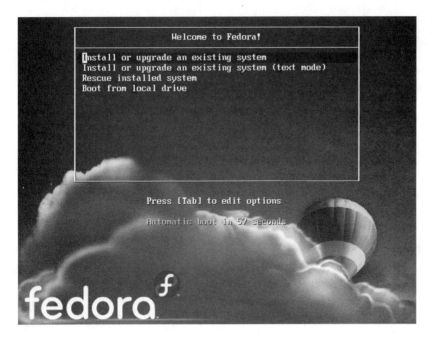

Figure 5-2. *Press Enter to start the installation program.*

The next screen gives you the option to test the installation disk. The test is to make sure the disk is not corrupt. You can choose to skip this test. Press the Tab key once such that the skip option is highlighted, and then press Enter.

From here on you get a graphical installation. Press the Next button to start the installation.

Step 2: Selecting Your Language

One of the design goals of Fedora is to be usable by just about anyone in the world. Fedora supports a massive list of languages, and the first step in the installation routine is to select one, as shown in Figure 5-3. It offers many eastern and western European languages, as well as Asian languages. The default is English.

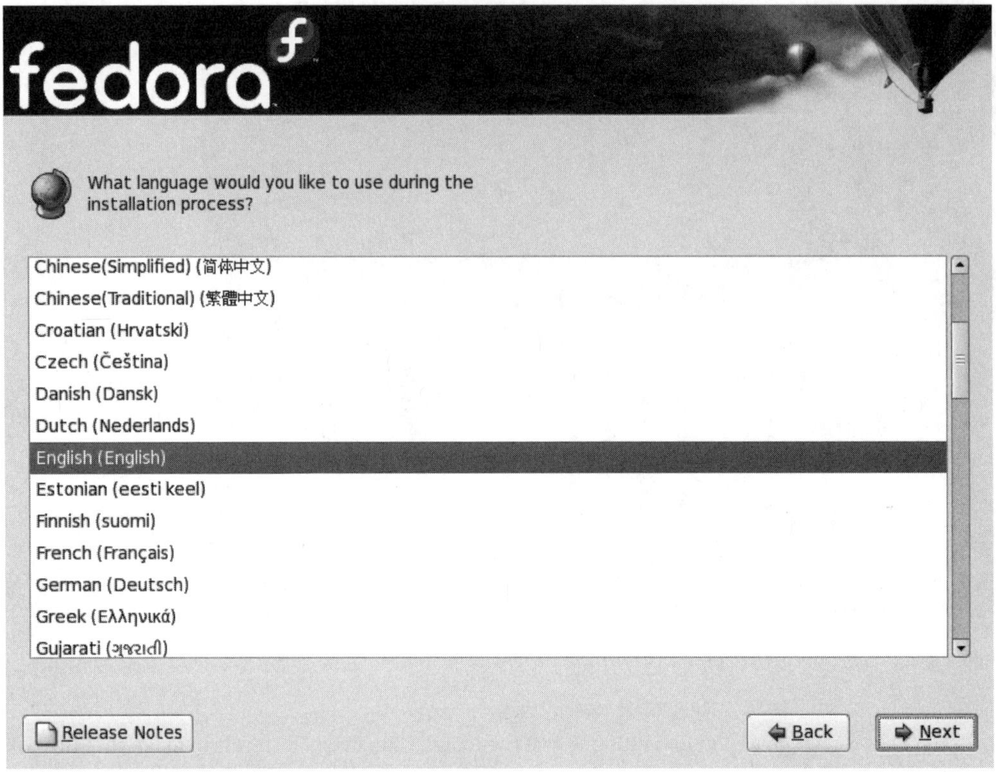

Figure 5-3. *Choose your language.*

This will be your first experience with Fedora's graphical installation program, Anaconda. It's pretty straightforward to navigate. You can scroll through the list and select the language you want, and then click the Next button at the bottom right of the screen.

Step 3: Confirming Your Keyboard Layout

Next, you'll be asked to confirm the keyboard layout you'll be using. This should correspond to your setting, and will be automatically selected, so you can just click Next.

Step 4: Installing or Upgrading Fedora

Fedora looks through your hard disk to determine if there is an existing version of Fedora installed. Depending on the outcome of this search, you will be presented with the option of installing or upgrading Fedora (see Figure 5-4). Choosing Install Fedora brings up the partitioning screen, shown in Figure 5-5.

Alternately, if you're installing Fedora for the first time, you'll be dropped directly to the partitioning screen.

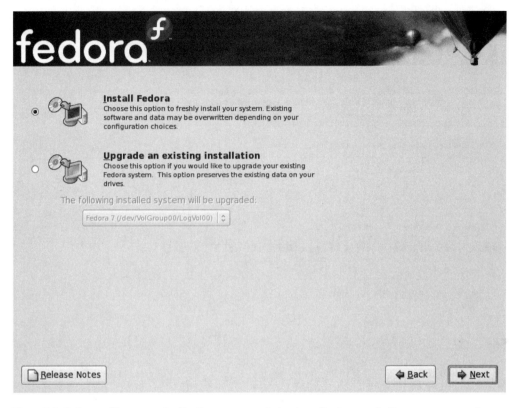

Figure 5-4. *Fedora will automatically discover any existing installations and allow you to upgrade or do a fresh install.*

Step 5: Partitioning the Disk

Partitioning the disk is one of the most important steps during installation, but it's unfortunately couched in some difficult terminology. Fedora does its best to make partitioning easy, though.

You have three main options when it comes to disk partitioning: installing on a hard disk that also contains Windows using existing free space, installing on a second hard disk, or deleting an existing Windows partition.

All available drives are listed under the "Select the drive(s) to use for installation" heading. Choose the one on which you wish to install Fedora by clicking the associated check box.

■**Caution** Ensure that only the drive you wish to install Fedora on has the check box marked.

From the drop-down list, select "Use free space on selected drives and create default layout" (see Figure 5-5), and then click Next.

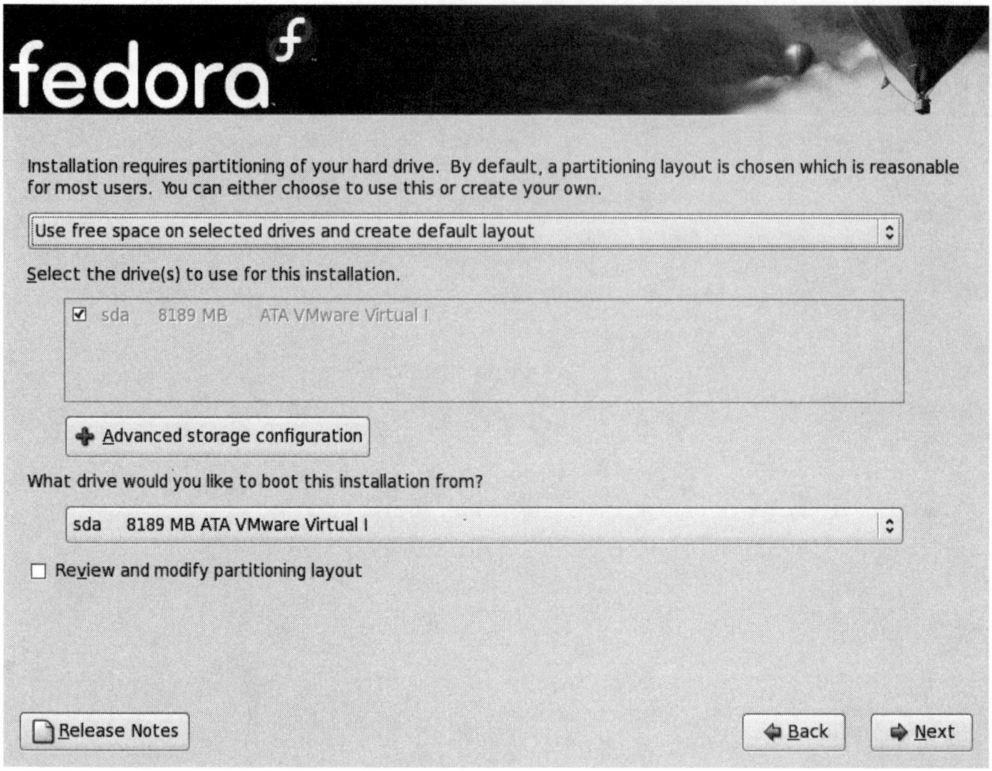

Figure 5-5. *Creating a default layout for installing Fedora*

With this option, you don't have to worry about creating different partitions for Fedora. For details of the partitions Fedora created for you, click the "Review and modify partitioning layout" check box before clicking Next.

You will be presented with a graphical representation of the partitions Fedora created. Figure 5-6 shows the partitions on our test machine.

Apart from the size of each partition, you can also see each partition's file system type. Windows partitions are either of type NTFS or FAT32.

Fedora, on the other hand, uses the ext3 file system. Before proceeding to the next step, read the "Default Partitions" sidebar, which details the purpose of each of these partitions.

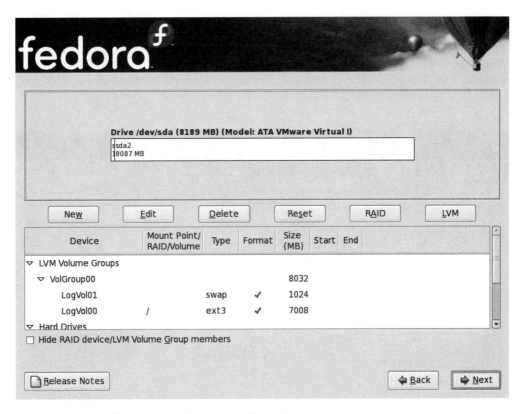

Figure 5-6. *Fedora will automatically create partitions for you.*

DEFAULT PARTITIONS

You might have noticed a partition of type *swap*. As a rule of thumb, the size of the swap partition is twice that of your physical RAM. All Linux distributions use the swap space to extend their memory pool. You can think of swap space as scratch paper you might use when performing mathematical calculations.

Next is the */boot* partition. This contains all the files that are required to initialize the system.

Finally, there is the *root* partition (/). This is formatted as ext3 and is the topmost directory on Linux systems.

The most intriguing aspect of the default partition layout is the use of Logical Volume Management (LVM). LVM partitions comprise *physical volumes*. A *volume group* consists of one or more physical volumes. The volume group is then divided into *logical volumes*. A logical volume is like any regular partition.

In Figure 5-6, the partition formatted as ext3—the root partition (/)—is a logical volume. The biggest advantage of using LVM partitions is that you can increase or shrink logical volumes without losing data. Standard partitions don't allow you to modify the size.

The default partitioning scheme allocates all free space to the root partition. Typically, you only need about 6 GB to install Fedora (this depends on the packages you choose to install), so you can reduce this partition size. To reduce its size, select LogVol00 and click the Edit button. The Edit LVM Volume Group: VolGroup00 window will come up, as shown in Figure 5-7. Select LogVol00 and again click Edit. You can now specify the new size for this partition. Click OK, and then click OK again in the main window.

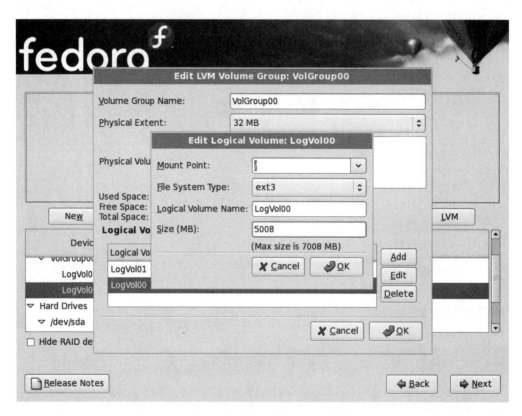

Figure 5-7. *You can specify a custom size for the logical volume.*

Once you are satisfied with the partitions, click the Next button at the bottom right of the screen.

Deleting the Windows Partition

You can choose the "Remove all partitions on selected drive and create default layout" option if you no longer wish to use Windows. Remember that this will erase all your partitions and data, so please back everything up before proceeding with this step.

Installing Fedora on a Separate Disk

If you have installed an additional hard disk for installing Fedora, choose the "Remove all partitions on selected drive and create default layout" option. Depending on whether the hard disk is formatted or not, Fedora will ask you if it should initialize the hard disk for you. Click Yes.

Fedora will then take up the entire hard disk. As discussed, you can shrink the space allocated to the root partition. Refer to Figure 5-7.

Step 6: Installing the GRUB Boot Loader

If Windows is installed on the same hard disk as Fedora, you'll be asked if you want to install the GRUB boot loader onto the PC's master boot record (MBR), as shown in Figure 5-8. The GRUB boot loader is the menu that will appear when you first boot, from which you'll be able to choose either Fedora or Windows. It's pretty essential, so you should select the first option. Then click Next.

■**Caution** On older hardware, you can easily dual-boot Windows and Fedora by installing the GRUB boot loader to the MBR. But certain newer systems with Windows Vista come with TPM (Trusted Platform Module), a chip in the motherboard that stops the computer from booting if the MBR does not have the Vista files. If you have a newer machine with Windows Vista, you should inquire whether it has the TPM chip before you install GRUB to the boot loader. You can use Vista's boot manager to dual-boot Fedora if you follow the instructions at http://209.34.241.68/voy/archive/2006/10/13/building-a-dual-boot-system-with-windows-vista-bitlocker-protection-with-tpm-support.aspx—but this is recommended for expert users only. Another option is using EasyBCD (http://neosmart.net/dl.php?id=1), but once again, this requires an expert understanding of the system. However, keep in mind that only the Enterprise and Ultimate editions of Vista have the Bitlocker Drive Encryption feature that, in conjunction with the TPM, raises this issue.

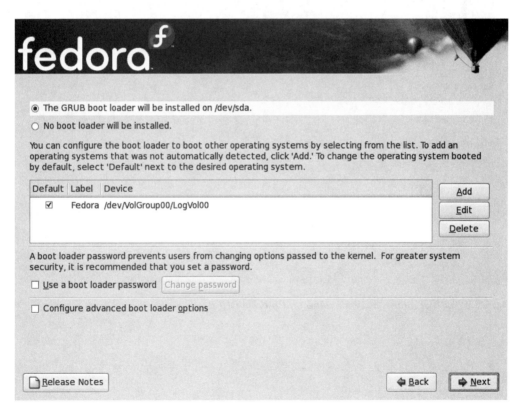

Figure 5-8. *The GRUB boot loader is the menu that appears when you boot, allowing you to choose between Fedora and Windows.*

Step 7: Configuring Network Devices

Fedora will automatically configure your network devices. You can choose to use DHCP (Dynamic Host Configuration Protocol) to determine the hostname, as shown in Figure 5-9, or explicitly mention it and other settings like your DNS.

■**Note** You should use the DHCP option to automatically obtain an IP address in case your service provider didn't give you a static IP address. You should talk to your system administrator or service provider regarding the IP address and DNS settings.

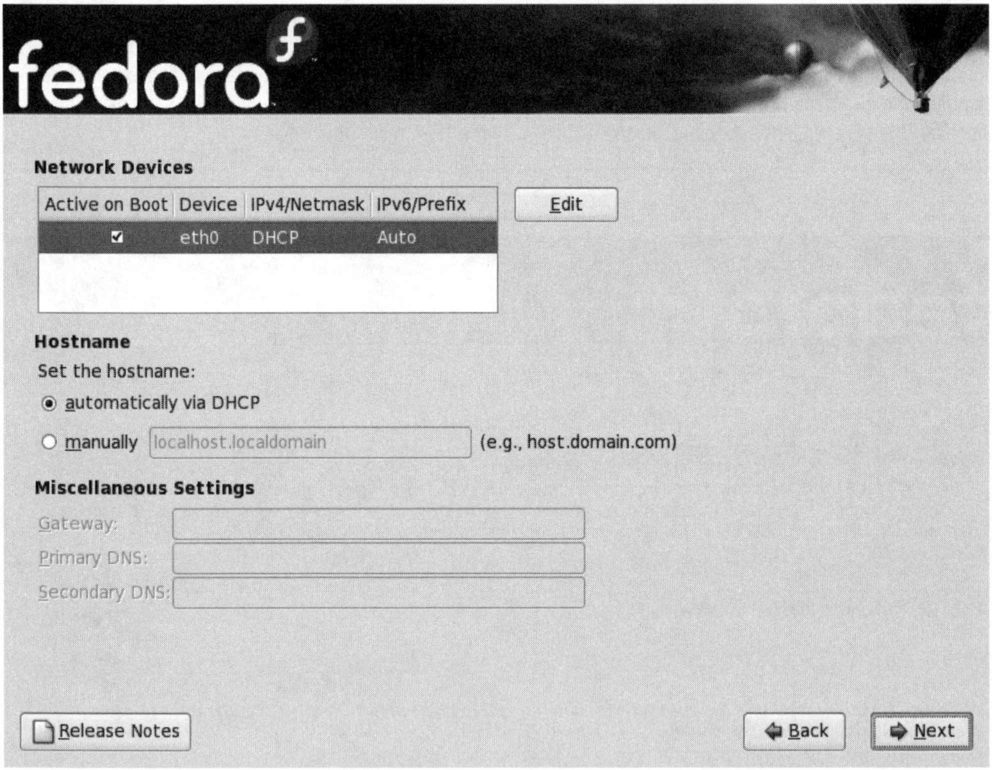

Figure 5-9. *The hostname is picked up automatically via DHCP.*

Step 8: Setting the Time Zone

The next step is to set the time zone for your region, as shown in Figure 5-10. You need to pick up your region either from the drop-down list or using the map. For example, users in New York should pick America/New York while those in London should pick Europe/London.

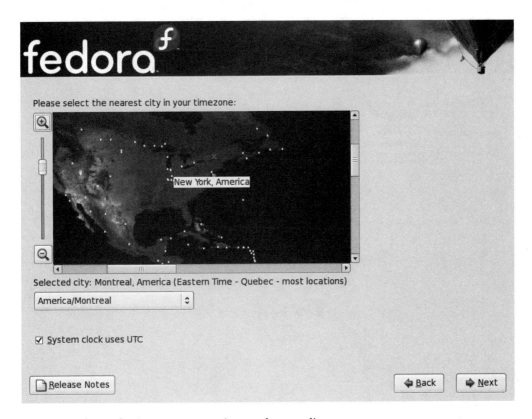

Figure 5-10. *Choose the time zone appropriate to where you live.*

Depending on your location, you may choose to use Coordinated Universal Time (UTC). If you're dual-booting with Windows, you should remove the check from the "System clock uses UTC" check box.

Step 9: Setting the Root Account Password

Next, you need to provide the password for the root account, as shown in Figure 5-11. The root account is the administrator account, meaning that you can use the root account to configure your system.

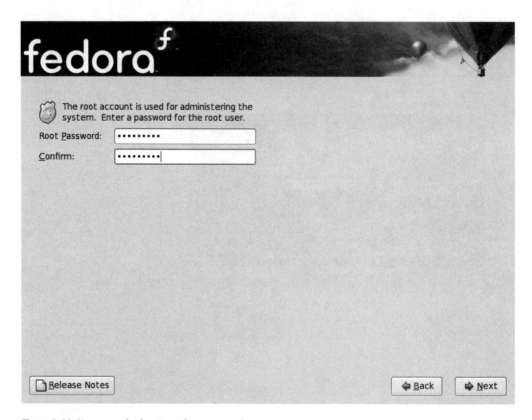

Figure 5-11. *You are asked to type the password twice.*

Step 10: Selecting Software to Install

Fedora allows you to custom select the software that it installs to your hard disk. The three broad categories, as shown in Figure 5-12, are Office and Productivity, Software Development, and Web server. You can choose the Customize now option at the bottom of the screen to further scrutinize the packages within each of these categories.

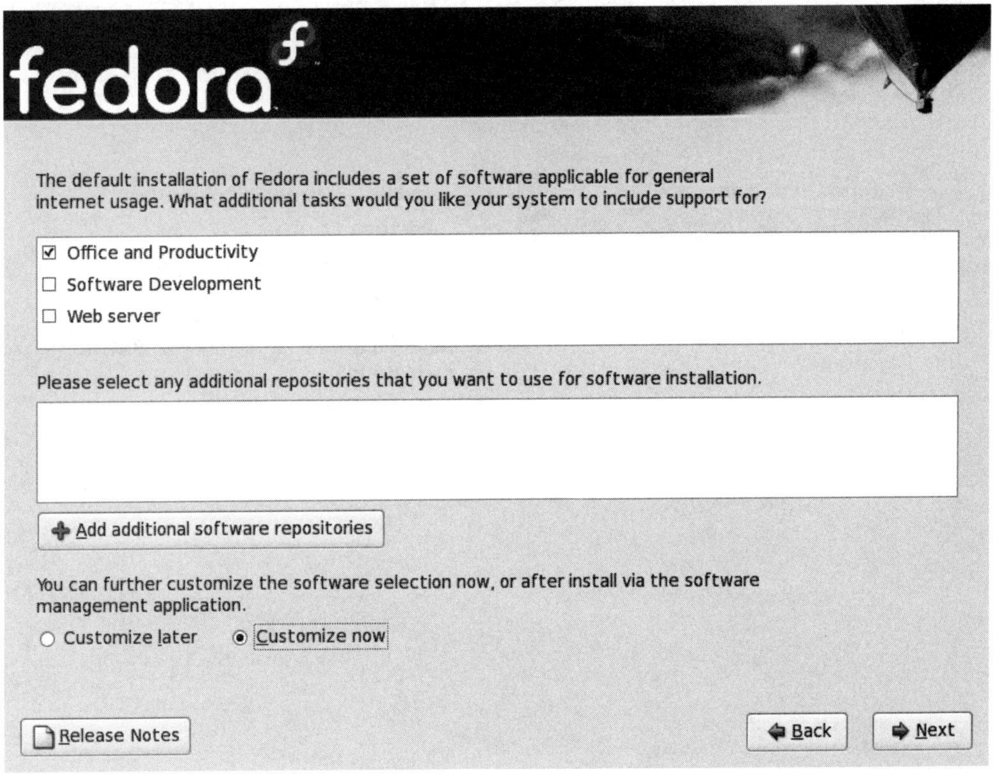

Figure 5-12. *Choose the Customize now option to select the software you wish to install.*

Caution It is recommended that you choose the Customize now option as it allows complete control over the packages that get installed.

Using Other Software Repositories

If you configured your network as described in step 7, you can click the "Add additional software repositories" button to install packages that are not on the installation disk.

Custom Software Selection

When you click Next after choosing the Customize now option, you're presented with the software selection screen, as shown in Figure 5-13. This screen is divided into three frames.

Various software categories are listed on the left of the screen. When you click a category, the frame on the right will display further software sections within that category.

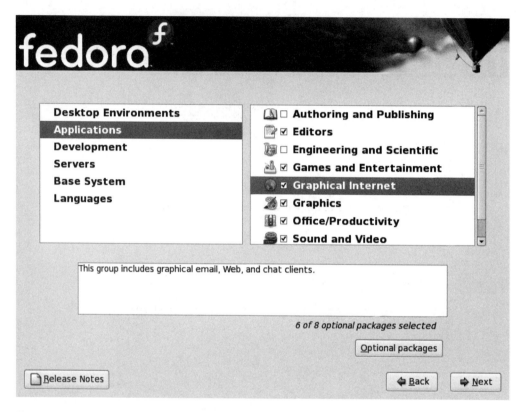

Figure 5-13. *Software packages are divided into several different categories and sections.*

You can custom select packages from a section by selecting it and then clicking the Optional packages button (see Figure 5-14).

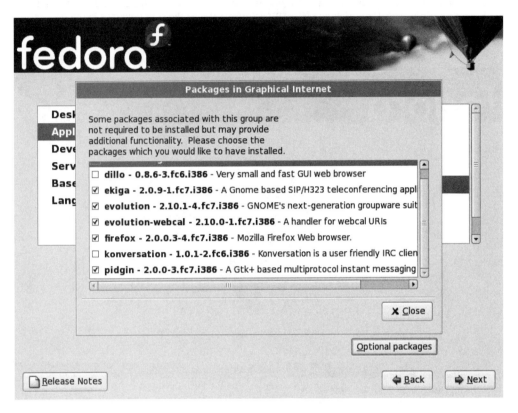

Figure 5-14. *Selecting packages from a software section.*

All the packages whose boxes you check will be installed on your system.

Click the Next button when you are finished selecting the packages you wish to install. At this time, Fedora will compute the dependencies for the packages you selected. It does so to determine if there is enough space on your hard disk to install all the packages. Click Next on the screen that appears to begin package installation.

Don't worry if you forget to add certain packages. You can add and remove packages easily once Fedora is up and running. Refer to Chapter 28 to learn more about managing software on Fedora.

Step 11: Waiting During Package Installation

Package installation now begins. It is difficult to estimate how long it will take to install Fedora on your system, since it depends on a lot of factors such as package selection and method of installation (e.g., via the Internet, a network, or the DVD). During the package installation you'll see a progress bar on the screen, as shown in Figure 5-15.

Figure 5-15. *You are informed about each package that Fedora installs.*

Below the progress bar you'll see the package Fedora is installing and its size and description. Don't worry about the names of the packages as they flash by on the screen. Some of them might seem strange, complicated, or irrelevant. The way Linux works is that certain software packages rely on other software packages, so sometimes software that might never be used directly is also installed.

When Fedora is done installing packages, you'll be told to remove the installation disk from the CD/DVD-ROM drive and reboot your computer, as shown in Figure 5-16.

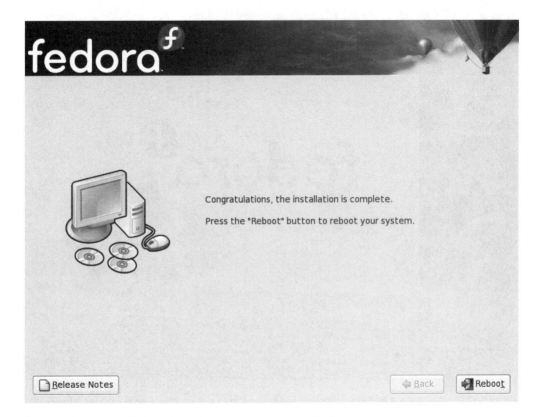

Figure 5-16. *You are asked to reboot the computer once installation is complete.*

Step 12: Postinstallation Configuration

When installation has finished, the system will spit the disc out and ask you to reboot the machine. The system will then boot straight into the postinstall configuration screen shown in Figure 5-17.

Click Forward to begin the configuration. You will then be informed about Fedora's license. Click Forward to continue with the configuration.

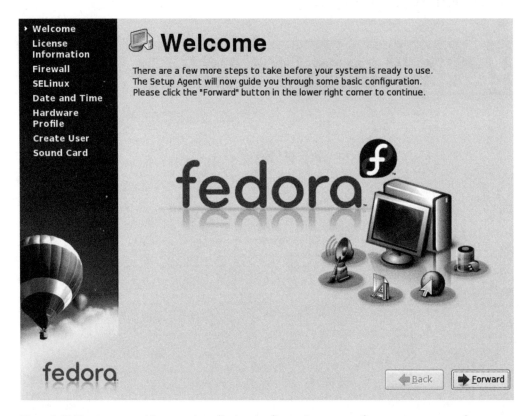

Figure 5-17. *You are greeted by a postinstallation configuration screen after your computer reboots.*

Configuring the Firewall

Next on the agenda is the firewall. Depending on your needs, you can enable other services, such as FTP (Figure 5-18).

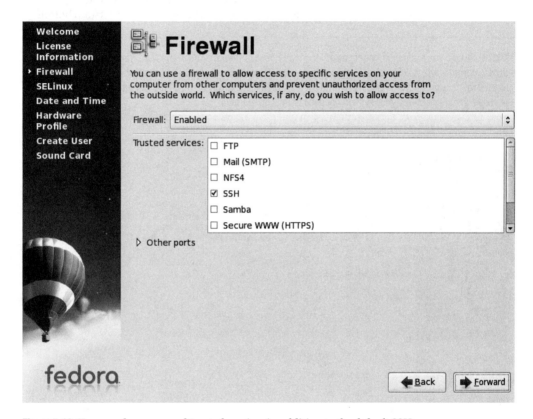

Figure 5-18. *You can choose several trusted services in addition to the default SSH.*

We discuss configuring the firewall in Chapter 9, and urge you to not make any changes to the default settings at this time. Click Forward to continue with the setup.

Configuring SELinux

Security Enhanced Linux (SELinux) provides excellent security control over your system as compared to traditional Linux systems. There are three SELinux states that you can select from the drop-down list, as shown in Figure 5-19. These are Enforcing, Permissive, and Disabled.

Unless you know what you are doing, keep the default settings and click the Forward button.

■Note SELinux works on the principles of Mandatory Access Control (MAC). The MAC framework governs how a program interacts with other parts of the system (files, other programs, devices, etc.). With SELinux, you can prevent an attacker from causing harm from exploiting a vulnerability in some program, and even eliminate the possibility of corrupting your system because of misconfiguration.

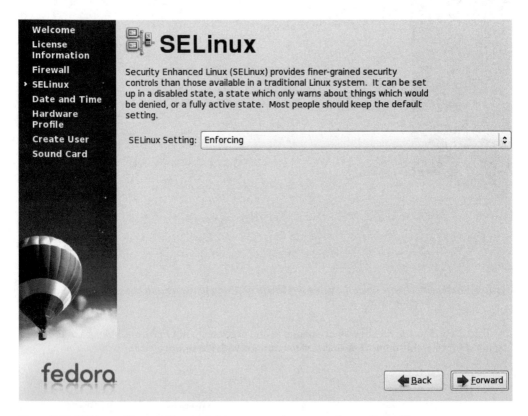

Figure 5-19. *SELinux offers excellent security measures, but cannot be configured by new users.*

Fedora will again prompt you to confirm your selection. Click the Yes button to continue.

Setting the Date and Time

This screen allows you to specify the date and time for your system. If you set your time zone correctly in step 8, this screen will show the correct time. Click Forward to move on.

Creating a User

Enter your real name and your username, as shown in Figure 5-20. The *real name* is how you'll be formally identified on the system. The standard practice is to use your full name (first and last, separated by a space).

The *username* is how the computer itself will identify you. It's what you'll use to log into the system. This needs to be unique, as two users on the same computer cannot have the same username.

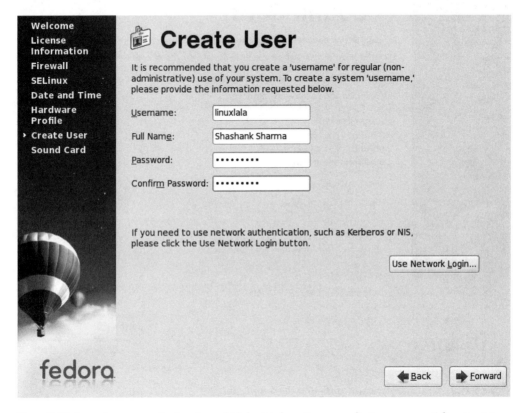

Figure 5-20. *A good username is simple, and it's best to base it on your first name or a nickname you are comfortable with.*

Try to keep your username uncomplicated. Do not use symbols as part of your username, and keep it entirely in one case—preferably lowercase. After this, you fill in your password.

The rules for passwords are inverse of those for your username. A good password contains numbers, uppercase and lowercase letters, and other symbols, like # and $. This makes your password almost impossible for someone else to guess, and thus makes your system more secure. Your password must be at least six characters long. You'll need to enter the password twice; the second time confirms that you didn't mistype it the first time.

Configuring the Sound Card

Figure 5-21 shows the sound card configuration screen. This is the last step in the configuration. To test your sound card, click the play button under Sound test. You will be asked if you were able to hear the test music. Click Finish once you are satisfied with the sound settings. Click Finish once you are satisfied with the sound settings.

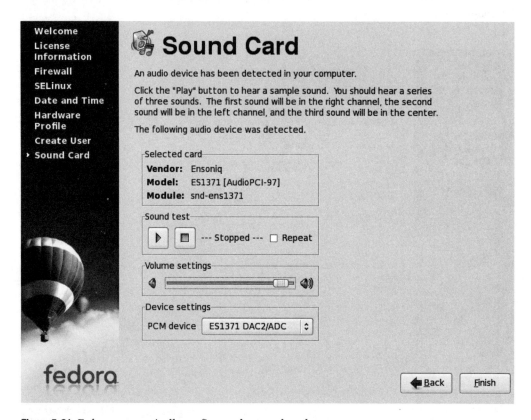

Figure 5-21. *Fedora automatically configures the sound card.*

Your Fedora system is now ready to use! You will be delivered to the standard Fedora login screen, as shown in Figure 5-22.

From here, you can progress to Chapter 7 to learn how to get started with Fedora. Alternatively, if you've run into any problems, see Chapter 6.

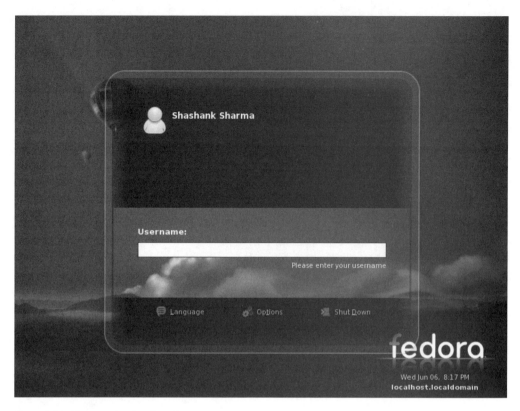

Figure 5-22. *The standard Fedora login screen.*

Summary

By following the steps outlined in this chapter, you should now have Fedora installed on your computer. We've tried to provide you with enough information to get around any problems, as well as explain exactly what's happening every step of the way.

Alas, it's still possible that you've encountered hurdles that weren't addressed here. In the next chapter, you'll find solutions to many common problems associated with Fedora installation.

CHAPTER 6

■ ■ ■

Solving Installation Problems

Chances are that your installation of Fedora will complete without a hitch, and you'll find yourself with a first-rate operating system up and running within just a few minutes. However, if a problem rears its ugly head, you should be able to find the solution in this chapter, which addresses the most common installation problems. These problems are organized by when they occur: before you begin the installation, during the installation, and after the installation. The final section of the chapter describes how to configure the graphical subsystem with the X.org configuration utility, which can be useful if graphical glitches arise.

Preinstallation Problems

Some problems might arise before you even begin the installation process, or very early in the process, before the main installer program starts to run. This section addresses such issues.

Problem

The PC is unable to boot from the CD-ROM.

Solution

All modern computers are able to boot from a CD-ROM. Check your BIOS settings, as described in Chapter 5, to ensure that your BIOS is set correctly. In particular, check onscreen messages at boot time to see if any special key combination needs to be pressed to ensure your computer boots from the CD-ROM. On certain computers, you may need to press a key combination even if the BIOS is set to boot from the CD-ROM.

Some very old computers might not be able to boot from a CD-ROM. In this case you are stuck. Many Linux distributions allow you to make a bootable floppy disk that you can use to install the distribution. Unfortunately, Fedora's kernel is too big to fit onto a floppy disk.

You might want to contact the manufacturer for a BIOS upgrade, but it's unlikely that there will be one for very old systems.

Problem

The computer boots from the CD-ROM, but when the initial boot screen appears, pressing Enter doesn't start the installation. In fact, nothing happens at all!

Solution

If your PC uses a USB keyboard, it might be that it's not being recognized by the Fedora boot loader. It's possible to make most computers pretend that USB keyboards are older PS/2 keyboards. This is done on a fundamental hardware level and is invisible to the operating system. Here are the steps:

1. Enter the BIOS setup program by pressing Delete during the initial stages of your computer boot routine (while memory testing and drive identification are still taking place). Some computers might use a different key combination to enter BIOS setup, such as Ctrl+Insert or F2, but this information will be displayed on the screen.

2. Use the cursor keys to navigate to the Integrated Peripherals section, and then look for an entry along the lines of "USB Legacy Support." Set it to Enabled.

3. Press Escape to return to the main menu and opt to save the changes.

4. Reboot the computer.

Note that you should repeat this procedure and deactivate USB Legacy Support once Fedora has been installed. At that stage, Fedora should be able to recognize the USB keyboard properly.

In case your BIOS does not have the USB Legacy Support, contact your vendor and ask him to upgrade your BIOS. You can alternatively use a PS/2 keyboard during the installation and hook up the USB keyboard later.

Problem

After I've pressed Enter to clear the initial loading screen, the screen fills with text, and then the computer hangs with a message along the lines of "Kernel Panic."

Solution

Kernel panic errors occur when the operating system cannot continue to load for various reasons. In this context, it's likely that either the CD is faulty (or dirty) or that your PC has a defective item of hardware.

First, check to make sure the CD is both clean and not scratched. If possible, try it on a different computer. If it works, then it's clearly not at fault, and your computer most likely has a hardware issue. In particular, bad memory can cause problems. Does the computer already have an operating system installed? Does this run without problems? If not, consider replacing your memory modules.

Also, certain power management configurations can also cause this problem. Try to boot with the `acpi=off` option. At the initial graphical prompt, press Esc twice, and then at the boot: prompt type `linux acpi=off` and press Enter.

Problem

After I press Enter on the loading screen, the screen fills with text. A message about configuring the framebuffer appears, and then the screen is corrupted and/or the text looks odd.

Solution

Your graphics card may be incompatible with the framebuffer mode used by Fedora's installation routine. You can overcome this problem by rebooting and, when you normally press Enter to start the installation routine, press Esc twice and type `linux nofb` and then press Enter.

Problem

The installation program freezes or reboots almost as soon as it begins.

Solution

The power-saving feature in your computer is causing problems. Boot from the CD-ROM and, instead of pressing Enter at the boot prompt, press Esc twice and type `linux acpi=off` and then press Enter.

Installation Problems

During installation, you may get error messages or experience other difficulties. This section offers some solutions to common installation problems.

Problem

During the installation, I see an error message about an unhandled exception regarding the network configuration. Then the installer shuts down.

Solution

The Fedora installer automatically activates all network devices on your computer. The problem occurs when you choose to install software from an online repository without properly configuring your network interface. Ensure that you specified the correct configuration details illustrated in step 7 of Chapter 5.

Problem

When the installation reaches the stage where it's installing packages, it freezes on a particular package. It then returns a message along the lines of "Cannot read from disk."

Solution

The problem might be that the installation DVD-ROM is faulty. It could be dirty, in which case you should consider wiping it with a tissue. Alternatively, it might be scratched, in which case you should seek a replacement. You might consider downloading an ISO file from `http://fedoraproject.org/` and burning your own replacement copy of the DVD-ROM. This will require a CD-burning program such as Nero (`www.nero.com/`).

You can also try installing through the Internet. Depending on the packages you wish to install and your connection, this might be a more suitable option.

Problem

I'm using the same keyboard, mouse, and monitor across several computers courtesy of a keyboard, video, and monitor (KVM) switch. During installation, it appears that the autoprobing of my video hardware produces the wrong results.

Solution

It's impossible to correctly probe a monitor if a KVM switch is attached to the computer. Consider attaching the monitor directly to the computer for the duration of the installation.

Postinstallation Problems

Problems might also occur after you install Fedora. This section addresses several possible postinstallation problems. This section covers only problems that appear immediately after installation—those that prevent Fedora from working correctly immediately after its first boot. Issues surrounding the configuration of hardware or software are dealt with in the next part of this book.

Problem

After installation has finished, I find myself with a blank screen (or a screen that's full of corrupted graphics). If I reboot, the computer appears to boot Fedora correctly, but again, it ends with a blank screen.

Solution

For some reason, your graphical configuration isn't working. See the "Graphical Problems" section later in this chapter for the steps to fix this problem.

Problem

During bootup, the Fedora logo and/or onscreen status messages are corrupted. However, the computer will eventually boot to the desktop just fine.

Solution

The Fedora graphical boot process is probably causing problems for your particular hardware configuration. Follow these steps to correct the problem:

1. At the Fedora desktop, select Applications ➤ System Tools ➤ Terminal.

2. At the command prompt, type the following:

    ```
    su -c "gedit /boot/grub/grub.conf"
    ```

3. Type the root password when requested.

4. Your boot menu configuration file will open in a simple text editor. Navigate to the line that reads as follows:

```
kernel vmlinuz. . .
```

This will be toward the end of the file and, unlike many of the lines above it, won't be preceded by a hash symbol.

5. At the end of the line, you will see the word `rhgb`. Move the cursor to that word and delete it.

6. Save the file and press Ctrl+Q to quit the Gedit program.

Following this, the system's boot will be text only, although the system will boot into a graphical desktop as usual.

Problem

When I boot for the first time, the resolution is too low/high.

Solution

As soon as you're logged in, select System ➤ Preferences ➤ Hardware ➤ Screen Resolutions from the main menu (at the top of the screen). In the dialog box, choose a resolution more appropriate to your screen and a refresh rate to match. For most CRT screens, a refresh rate of 70 or 75 Hz should be fine; for LCD panels or notebooks, a refresh rate of 60 Hz is appropriate.

In case Fedora doesn't detect your monitor correctly, try to use a generic device. Open the display settings tool (System ➤ Administration ➤ Display) and click the Hardware tab. Click Configure to choose a generic monitor. In the case of LCD, click the Generic LCD Display drop-down list and select a suitable screen resolution. Use the Generic CRT Display list to select a CRT monitor.

Problem

After booting up, my USB mouse and/or USB keyboard are not recognized.

Solution

Try unplugging the keyboard and/or mouse, and then reattaching them. If you find they now work, log into Fedora, and then perform an online system upgrade. See Chapter 9 for more information.

If this fails to solve the problem, you can configure your BIOS to pretend your mouse and keyboard are traditional PS/2-style devices, as follows:

1. Enter the BIOS setup program by pressing Delete during the initial stages of your computer boot routine (while memory testing and drive identification are still taking place). Some computers might use a different key combination to enter BIOS setup, such as Ctrl+Insert or F2, but this information will be displayed on the screen.

2. Use the cursor keys to navigate to the Integrated Peripherals section, and then look for an entry along the lines of "USB Legacy Support." Set it to Enabled.

3. Press Escape to return to the main menu and opt to save the changes.

4. Reboot the computer.

Problem

When I boot for the first time, all I see shortly after the PC is switched on is a command prompt that reads grub>.

Solution

For some reason, your installation of the GRUB boot menu went wrong. Try this solution, which involves reinstalling it:

1. Insert the Fedora installation DVD-ROM and boot from it. At the splash screen press Esc twice and type linux rescue and then press Enter.

2. The installer will start, and you'll need to answer the initial questions again, such as which language you wish to use. You won't get graphical screens under the rescue environment. Pressing the spacebar or Enter key selects an option. You can move between options by pressing the Tab key.

3. Eventually, Fedora will inform you that the root partition has been detected and ask you if it should mount it. Choose continue. Fedora will then mount the root partition under /mnt/sysimage. Run the command chroot /mnt/sysimage. Next, type the command grub-install /dev/hda.

4. If you receive an error message, start over from step 1.

5. Press Ctrl+D to exit from the chroot environment and then again to restart the computer.

6. Remove the CD-ROM from the drive. You should now see the boot menu.

Graphical Problems

Although Fedora is extremely good at automatically detecting and configuring your PC's graphics hardware, it sometimes configures your GUI incorrectly. This is characterized by one of the following:

- Fedora freezes when the desktop would normally appear.
- You see onscreen graphical corruption, either of text or graphics.
- You see a message that the X server isn't working.
- You see a black screen with only a text login prompt.

If you experience any of these problems, you will need to reconfigure Fedora's graphical subsystem, called X.org (often referred to simply as X). To begin, press Alt+Ctrl+F2. This will drop you to one of the virtual text consoles. Log into your account and then run the following command:

```
su -c "gedit /etc/X11/xorg.conf"
```

After you enter the root account's password, you'll see a configuration file that has details about your monitor, the graphics card, and so on.

```
Section "Monitor"
      Identifier   "Monitor0"
      ModelName    "LCD Panel 1440x900"
EndSection

Section "Device"
      Identifier   "Videocard0"
      Driver       "i810"
EndSection

Section "Screen"
      Identifier "Screen0"
      Device     "Videocard0"
      Monitor    "Monitor0"
      DefaultDepth    24
      SubSection "Display"
              Viewport   0 0
              Depth      24
              Modes    "1152x864" "1024x768" "800x600" "640x480"
      EndSubSection
EndSection
```

Check if all the details are correct. You may find, for instance, that the monitor resolutions are wrong. Press Ctrl+A, scroll down to the Modes line under the Screen section and type the correct value.

When you are done, press Esc and then type :wq. This will save the file and quit the vi text editor. Refer to Chapter 15 for more details about the vi text editor.

Installing a Graphics Card

If you find that Fedora did not correctly install the NVIDIA or ATI card, you can easily install the driver using the livna repository. From a virtual text console (Alt+Ctrl+F1), set up the livna repository with the command su -c 'rpm -Uvh http://rpm.livna.org/livna-release-6.rpm'.

Once livna is set up, run the command su -c 'yum install kmod-nvidia' to install the NVIDIA drivers. At the time of writing, there were some issues with the ATI drivers on Fedora 7. Hopefully, the situation will be resolved by the time you read this, so you should check the Livna repository for available ATI drivers.

You now need to restart the X server. Log in as root (use the su - command) and then run the command init 3. Now run the command init 5. After login, click System ➤ Administration ➤ Display. Click the Hardware tab and see if your card is properly configured.

Monitor Configuration

If you find that the screen flickers or the text seems stretched, you might need to configure your display settings. You can do so as follows:

1. Click System ➤ Administration ➤ Display. Enter the root password.

2. Check if the Resolution and Color Depth settings under the Settings tab are fine.

3. Click the Hardware tab. If the monitor or graphics card are incorrectly detected, click the Configure button. If you find that your monitor is not listed, you can select a more generic option. Choose the Generic CRT Display option and pick a relevant resolution if you have a CRT monitor, or choose one from the Generic LCD Display list if it's LCD. You should refer to your monitor guide for guidance on which resolutions you should choose. Most notebooks run at 1024×768, regardless of screen size, although some higher-end models might run at higher resolutions, particularly if they are wide-screen models (refer to your notebook documentation).

For a complete list of all supported monitors, click the "Show all available monitors" check box, as shown in Figure 6-1.

Figure 6-1. *You can choose your monitor from a list of supported models.*

■**Note** TFT screens are designed to run at a single optimal resolution, rather than at a range of resolutions. Therefore, you should select only one resolution from the list if you have this type of monitor.

Refer to your monitor's manual to determine its ideal resolution. If you don't have the manual, you can search online for the specifications of your model, as shown in Figure 6-2.

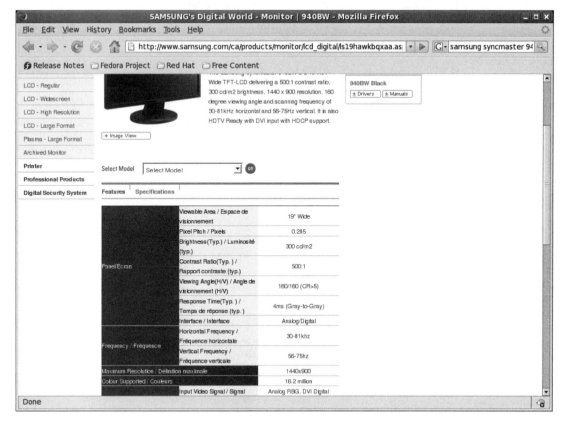

Figure 6-2. *A quick search on the Web will reveal the specifications of most monitors.*

Summary

This chapter's goal was to address problems that might occur during the installation of Fedora. It discussed preinstallation, installation, and postinstallation issues. It also covered how to use the X.org reconfiguration utility to configure the graphics subsystem, which may be necessary if the installation program fails to properly recognize your graphics card or monitor.

You should now have Fedora installed. The next part of this book focuses on helping you get everything up and running. You'll learn essential skills and become a confident Linux user.

## PART 3

The No-Nonsense Getting Started Guide

CHAPTER 7

■■■

Booting Fedora for the First Time

Now that Fedora is installed, you'll no doubt want to get started immediately, and that's what Part 3 of this book is all about. In later chapters, we'll examine specific details of using Fedora and getting essential hardware up and running. We'll also look at personalizing Fedora so that it works in a way that's best for you on a day-to-day basis. But right now, the goal of this chapter is to get you doing the same things you did under Windows as quickly as possible.

This chapter explains how to start up Fedora for the first time and work with the desktop. It also looks at how some familiar aspects of your computer, such as using the mouse, are slightly enhanced under Fedora.

Starting Up

If you've chosen to dual-boot with Windows, the first Fedora screen you'll see is the boot loader menu, which appears shortly after you switch on your PC. If Fedora is the only operating system on your hard disk, you'll see a brief one-line message pointing out that if you press a key, you can access this boot menu. In fact, if Fedora is the only operating system on your computer, you can skip to the next section.

■**Note** The boot loader is actually a separate program called GRUB. This program kicks everything off and starts Fedora.

The boot loader menu you see when your PC is set to dual-boot has two choices, as shown in Figure 7-1.

■**Note** This is actually a hidden menu. You will have to press a key to see this menu. Fedora will automatically boot if you do nothing.

The top entry is what you need to boot Fedora. The Fedora option will be selected automatically within 5 seconds, but you can press Enter to start immediately.

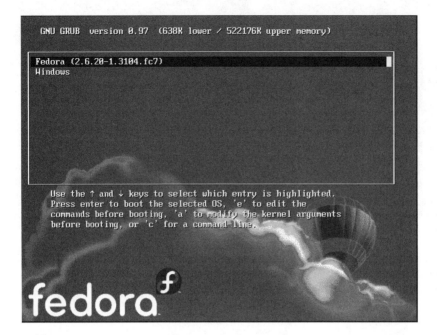

Figure 7-1. *The default choice is fine on the boot menu, so press Enter to start Fedora.*

You should find that you also have an entry for Windows, located at the bottom of the list. To boot into Windows, simply use the cursor keys to move the selection to the appropriate option, and then press Enter.

When you update your system software, you might find new entries are added to the boot menu list. Almost always, the topmost entry is the one you'll want each time Fedora boots. This will ensure that you start the system with the newest version of the system software. The entries beneath this will start the system with older versions of the system software and are provided in the unlikely situation that the latest software causes problems.

■**Note** All operating systems need a boot loader—even Windows. However, the Windows boot loader is hidden and simply starts the operating system. Under Fedora, the boot loader usually has a menu, so you can select Linux or perhaps an option that lets you access your PC for troubleshooting problems. When you gain some experience with Fedora, you might choose to install two or more versions of Linux on the same hard disk, and you'll be able to select among them using the boot menu.

Logging In

After Fedora has booted, you should see the login screen, as shown in Figure 7-2. Here, you enter the username and the password you created during the installation process. By clicking one of the buttons on the bottom-left side of the screen, you can also opt to reboot the system or shut it down.

Figure 7-2. *Type your username, then enter your password, and then press Enter to log in.*

The user account you created during the post-installation configuration is not the administrator account. (You should already have the administrator or root account set up, as described in the "Step 9" section of Chapter 5.)

It is important to understand the difference between a user account and the root account. While the account you use on a day-to-day basis can change important system settings and reconfigure the system, as is the case with Windows, the main difference with Fedora is that you'll need to enter the root account's password to make any serious system-level changes. Don't worry about damaging anything accidentally; trying to reconfigure the system or access a serious system setting will invariably bring up a password prompt. You can simply click the Cancel button if you don't want to continue.

■**Note** Using the actual root (or administrator) account for everyday tasks such as browsing the Internet, instant messaging, and so on, is not a good idea. The root account should only be used when you wish to modify system settings. A regular user account will prompt you for the root account's password if you try to change any system settings; you don't have to log out of your user account and log in again as the root user.

Exploring the Desktop

After you've logged in, you'll see the welcoming black and blue DNA theme of the Fedora desktop, as shown in Figure 7-3. Feel free to click around and see what you can discover. There's little chance of you doing serious damage, so let yourself go wild and play around with your new operating system!

■Tip Although you can't damage the system by messing around, you might find that you somehow cause programs to work incorrectly. Don't worry if this happens. You can always create a new account for yourself following the instructions in Chapter 30. When using this new account, you should find that all the settings are returned to normal, and you'll be back to square one!

Figure 7-3. *Feel free to experiment with the Fedora desktop and see what you can discover.*

First Impressions

The first thing you'll notice is that the desktop is clean compared to older variants of Windows. You don't have a lot of icons littering the screen.

Of course, you can fill the desktop with stuff if you want to do that. As with Windows, you can save files to the desktop for easy access. In addition, you can click and drag icons from any of the menus onto the desktop in order to create shortcuts.

Along the top of the desktop, there are three menus:

- *The Applications menu*: This is the equivalent of the Windows Start menu. Here, you'll find access to all the software available under Fedora.

- *The Places menu*: This is somewhat like My Computer in Windows, in that it gives quick access to locations within the file system.

- *The System menu*: This is a little like the Windows Control Panel, in that it allows you to change various system settings.

The counterpart of the Windows Recycle Bin lives at the bottom right of the screen as a small icon and is called the Trash. Although diminished in stature compared to the Windows representation, it works in a similar way: you can drag icons and files onto the icon in order to delete them, and you can click the icon to open it and salvage files.

The mouse works largely as it does in Windows, in that you can move it around and click things. You can also right-click virtually everything and everywhere to bring up context menus, which usually let you alter settings. And you should find that the scroll wheel in between the mouse buttons lets you scroll windows.

Whenever Fedora is busy, an animated icon will appear that is similar in principle to the hourglass icon used in Windows. It also appears when programs are being launched.

You can shut down or reboot your PC by selecting the System ➤ Shut Down menu option.

■**Caution** Bear in mind that Fedora isn't a clone of Windows and doesn't try to be. Although it works in a similar way—by providing menus and icons, and containing programs within windows—there are various potholes in the road that can trip up the unwary.

WRONG RESOLUTION!

You might find when you boot up that Fedora has defaulted to the wrong resolution. In other words, everything might be a little too large or too small. You might have trouble reading text, for example, or you might find that program windows fill the screen to the extent that their contents partially disappear off the edges.

Changing the resolution is simple. Select System ➤ Preferences ➤ Screen Resolution from the menu (at the top of the screen). In the Resolution drop-down list, select the appropriate resolution for your monitor. For a 17-inch CRT monitor, the standard resolution is 1024×768 (although some people prefer 800×600). Most 17-inch TFT screens run at 1280×1024 resolution. If you have a 15-inch CRT monitor (common on PCs made before 2000), you'll probably find 800×600 a maximum setting; others prefer 640×480. A 15-inch TFT screen will usually run at 1024 × 768 resolution. If in doubt as to your monitor's resolution, consult your monitor's manual for more information. You can also use the Administration ➤ Display tool to configure your monitor in case Fedora didn't pick it up.

Desktop Elements

The Fedora desktop is similar to that of Windows. It has the following elements:

- *Menus*: The three menus at the top left of the screen provide access to all of Fedora's functionality. As noted earlier, the Applications menu provides access to programs, the Places menu provides access to the file system, and the System menu provides access to configuration settings (as well as the Shutdown option). You can click and drag practically every menu entry onto the desktop in order to create a quick-and-easy shortcut.

- *Icons*: Although the Fedora desktop is clean, some icons are tucked away at the top and bottom of the screen. Those at the top are located to the right of the menus and allow you to start the browser, e-mail client, and various office applications (and are arranged in that order). At the top right is a speaker icon that lets you alter the sound volume, while at the bottom left is the Hide Windows button that instantly minimizes all open windows to give access to the desktop underneath. At the bottom right are the four virtual desktop buttons, which we'll discuss in the "Working with Virtual Desktops" section later in this chapter, and also the Trash icon. Apart from these, the desktop itself has three icons: Computer, which allows quick access to removable drives; Home, which is similar to My Documents; and Trash, which was just discussed.

- *Panel*: The bar at the bottom of the screen, called the Panel, shows which programs are currently running (if any). As with Windows, you can simply click the button for any program to bring that window "to the top." Alternatively, you can right-click each entry to instantly minimize or maximize that particular window.

- *User Switcher*: To the left of the clock you will find the complete name you provided when creating your user account. This lets you quickly switch to a different user account on your system, without logging out of the current account. Refer to Chapter 29 to learn how the User Switcher works.

- *Clock*: The clock is located in the top right of the screen. Clicking it brings up a handy monthly calendar. Right-clicking it brings up a context menu. On this menu, the Preferences option lets you alter the way the date and time are displayed. The Adjust Date & Time option lets you change the time and/or date if they're incorrect.

- *Notification area*: The speaker icon and clock are located in the notification area, which is similar to the Windows system tray. Programs that like to hang around in memory, such as Pup Software Updater or Rhythmbox media player, will add an icon in this top-right area to allow quick access to their functions. Usually, you simply need to click (or right-click) their icons to access the program features.

Note The small bar marks the leftmost boundary of the notification area. The notification area expands when needed to fit all the icons.

BEHIND THE DESKTOP: GNOME

Although we refer to the Fedora desktop, the fundamental software behind it is created by GNOME: The Free Software Desktop Project. This is one of the most well-established organizations currently producing desktop interfaces for Linux, as well as for other versions of UNIX. Its home page is at www.gnome.org/.

Although it's based on GNOME, Fedora's desktop has its own set of individual features and programs, as well as a unique look and feel. That said, it works in an almost identical way to versions of GNOME that are used in other Linux distributions, such as Ubuntu.

The nature of open source software—whereby anyone can take the source code and create their own version of a program—makes Fedora's remodeling of the GNOME desktop possible. Unlike with Windows software, more than one current version of a particular program or software suite can exist, and each is usually tailored to the particular needs of one of the various Linux distributions.

Quick Desktop Guides

Refer to Figure 7-4 for an annotated diagram of the desktop. The figure includes an open menu, a browser window, and a program window so that you can get an idea of working from the desktop.

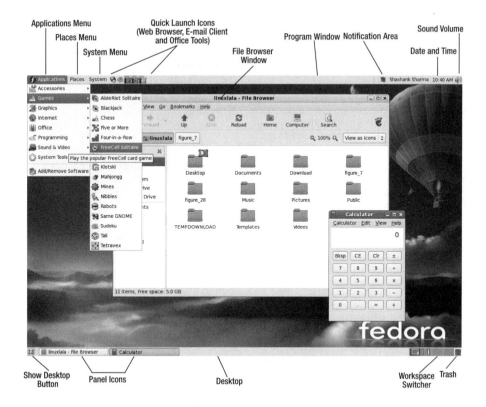

Figure 7-4. *The Fedora desktop is similar to the Windows desktop, with a few minor differences.*

As another handy reference, Table 7-1 lists standard Windows desktop features and where similar functionality can be found on the Fedora desktop.

Table 7-1. *Windows Desktop Feature Equivalents Under Fedora*

Windows Function	Description	Fedora Equivalent
My Computer	Double-clicking the My Computer icon gives you access to the PC system. In particular, it lets you browse the file system.	Click the Computer icon on the desktop or click Places ➤ Computer to see all the drives attached to the computer in the file browser window. If you wish to browse the file system, double-click the File System icon.
Recycle Bin	The Recycle Bin is the repository of deleted files.	Click the small Trash icon located at the bottom-right corner of the Fedora desktop or the larger icon on the desktop.
Start menu	The Start menu provides access to many computer functions, as well as a list of the programs installed on the system.	This function is split between the Applications and System menus. The Applications menu provides access to every piece of software installed under Fedora. The System menu lets you configure and administer the system, rather like the Windows Control Panel.
Quick Launch toolbar	Located just to the right of the Start button, these small icons let you launch popular programs with a single click.	Similar icons are located to the right of the main menus at the top of the Fedora desktop. You can add you own entries here by clicking and dragging program icons from the Applications menu.
My Network Places/ Network Neighborhood	This icon is used to access network services, usually within a business environment (on newer versions of Windows, this icon is often hidden by default).	To browse the local network, click Places ➤ Network.
My Documents	The My Documents folder, accessed via its icon on the Windows desktop, is a storage space set aside for a user's documents.	The Documents folder under the user's Home serves this purpose and can be accessed by clicking Places ➤ Documents. You will also find folders for your music and movies.
Control Panel	The Windows Control Panel, available via the Start menu, allows the user to change system settings and preferences.	Similar functionality can be found under the System ➤ Administration and System ➤ Preferences menu options.
Find Files	Located on the Start menu, the Find Files function lets a user search the file system for missing items.	To find files, click Places ➤ Search.
Shut Down	At the bottom of the Start menu within Windows is the Shut Down button.	Clicking System ➤ Shutdown brings up a dialog box that is almost identical to the one displayed in Windows. It gives you the option of rebooting, shutting down, or hibernating the system (suspending the RAM to disk and then shutting down the computer). You can also click System ➤ Log Out to return to the initial username/password prompt.

It will take some time to get used to the look and feel of Fedora; everything will initially seem odd. You'll find that the onscreen fonts look a little different from those in Windows, for example. The icons also won't be the same as you're used to in Windows. This can be a little disconcerting, but that feeling will quickly pass, and everything will become second nature. We'll look at how you can personalize the desktop in Chapter 10.

Running Programs

Starting a new program is easy. Just click the Applications menu and then choose a program from the list, as you would in Windows using the Start menu. The menu, shown in Figure 7-5, is split into various subcategories of programs, such as office tools, graphics programs, and even games.

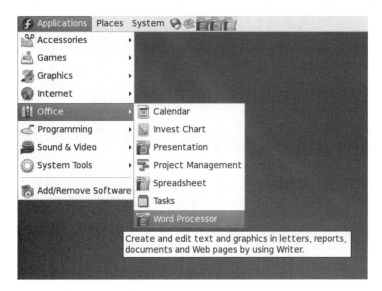

Figure 7-5. *The programs on the Applications menu are split into various categories.*

If you want to start the web browser or e-mail client (arguably two of the most popular programs offered by Fedora), you can click their icons on the desktop, just to the right of the menus at the top of the screen (see Figure 7-4).

At the top right of every program window under Fedora, you'll see the familiar close, minimize, and maximize buttons, albeit with a slightly different look and feel than you're used to. Clicking Close will end each program, as in Windows.

Working with Virtual Desktops

Windows works on the premise of everything taking place on top of a "desktop." When you start a new program, it runs on top of the desktop, effectively covering up the desktop. In fact, all programs are run on this desktop, so it can get a bit confusing when you have more than a couple of programs running at the same time. Which Microsoft Word window contains the document you're working on, and which contains the one you've opened to take notes from? Where is that My Computer window you were using to copy files?

Fedora overcomes this problem by having more than one desktop area. By using the Workspace Switcher tool, located at the bottom right of the desktop, you can switch between four virtual desktops. This is best explained by a demonstration:

1. Make sure that you're currently on the first virtual desktop (click the leftmost square on the Workspace Switcher) and start up the web browser by clicking its icon at the top of the screen (the globe icon located to the right of the menus).

2. Click the second square on the Workspace Switcher. This will switch you to a clean desktop, where no programs are running—desktop number two.

3. Start up the file browser by selecting the Places ➤ Home menu option. A file browser window appears.

4. Click the *first square* in the Workspace Switcher again. You should switch back to the desktop that is running the web browser.

5. Click the *second square*, and you'll switch back to the other desktop, which is running the file browser.

■**Tip** Right-clicking any of the program entries in the Panel will bring up a menu where you can move a program from one virtual desktop to another. Just select Move to Another Workspace.

See how it works? You can create more than a couple virtual desktops—as many as 36! To set the number of workspaces, right-click the Workspace Switcher and select Preferences. In the window that appears, click the up arrow next to the Number of Workspaces entry, as shown in Figure 7-6. You might choose to have fewer than four virtual desktops. For example, some people use only two: one main desktop and one "spare," to take the excess when the main desktop gets full.

Figure 7-6. *Fedora makes 4 virtual desktops available by default, but you can have as many as 36.*

You can also rename each virtual desktop by double-clicking its entry in the list in the Preferences window. This allows you to be even more organized. For example, you might reserve desktop 1 for running Internet programs and give it a name that indicates this, such as Net Programs. You might then use desktop 2 to run office programs, giving it an appropriate title; use desktop 3 for file browsing; and so on. This name will then appear whenever you right-click a program's entry on the Panel and attempt to move it to a different desktop. Additionally, these titles will appear whenever you right-click and choose to send each program window to a different desktop.

■Tip Putting your mouse over the Workspace Switcher and scrolling the mouse wheel switches between the various virtual desktops instantly.

The Workspace Switcher provides a way of organizing your programs and also reducing the clutter. You can experiment with virtual desktops to see if you want to organize your work this way. Some people swear by them. Other users think multiple desktops are a waste of time. In fact, on many Linux forum boards, this is one of the most discussed topics! They're certainly worth trying out to see if they suit the way you work.

Using the Mouse

As noted earlier, the mouse works mostly the same under Fedora as it does under Windows: a left-click selects things, and a right-click usually brings up a context menu. Try right-clicking various items, such as icons on the desktop or even the desktop itself.

■Tip Right-clicking a blank spot on the desktop and selecting Create Launcher lets you create shortcuts to applications. Clicking Create Folder lets you create new empty folders.

You can use the mouse to drag icons on top of other icons. For example, you can drag a file onto a program icon in order to run it. You can also click and drag in certain areas to create an elastic band and, as in Windows, this lets you select more than one icon at once.

You can resize windows using the mouse in much the same way as in Windows. Just click and drag the edges and corner of the windows. In addition, you can double-click the title bar to maximize and subsequently restore windows.

Fedora also makes use of the third mouse button for middle-clicking. You might not think your mouse has one of these, but actually, if it's relatively modern, it probably does. Such mice have a scroll wheel between the buttons, and this can act as a third button when pressed.

In Fedora, the main use of the middle mouse button is in copying and pasting, as described in the next section. Middle-clicking also has a handful of other functions; for example, middle-clicking the title bar of any open window will switch to the window underneath.

■Tip If your mouse doesn't have a scroll wheel, or if it has one that doesn't click, you can still middle-click. Simply press the left and right mouse buttons at the same time. This emulates a middle-click, although it takes a little skill to get it right. Generally speaking, you need to press one button a fraction of a second before you press the other button.

Copying and Pasting Text

Fedora offers two separate methods of copying and pasting text. The first method is identical to that under Windows. In a word processor or another application that deals with text, you can click and drag the mouse to highlight text, right-click anywhere on it, and then select to copy or cut the text. In many programs, you can also use the keyboard shortcuts of Ctrl+X to cut, Ctrl+C to copy, and Ctrl+V to paste.

However, there's a quicker method of copying and pasting. Simply click and drag to highlight some text, and then immediately click the middle mouse button where you want the text to appear. This will copy and paste the highlighted text automatically, as shown in Figure 7-7.

This special method of copying and pasting bypasses the usual clipboard, so you should find that any text you've copied or cut previously should still be there. The downside is that it doesn't work across all applications within Fedora, although it does work with the majority of them.

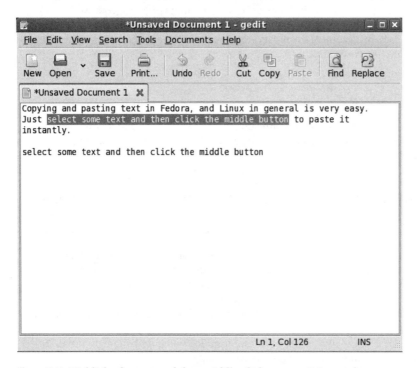

Figure 7-7. *Highlight the text, and then middle-click to paste it instantly.*

Summary

This chapter has covered booting into Fedora for the first time and discovering the desktop. We looked at starting programs, working with virtual desktops, using the mouse on the Fedora desktop, and much more. You should have become confident in some basic Fedora skills and now be ready to learn more!

In the next chapter, we'll look at getting your system up and running, focusing in particular on items of hardware that experience day-to-day use.

■ ■ ■

## CHAPTER 8

Getting Everything Up and Running

This chapter guides you through setting up all the essential components of your Fedora installation. This includes hardware configuration, as well as setting up e-mail and online software repositories. It covers the postinstallation steps necessary for getting your system up and running efficiently.

Like all modern Linux distributions, Fedora is practically automated when it comes to setting up key hardware and software components. Key software will work from the start, and hardware will be automatically configured. However, you might need to tweak a few settings to make everything work correctly. Read on to learn more.

Fedora Hardware Support

The age-old criticism that the Linux operating system lags behind Windows in terms of hardware support is long dead. The majority of add-ins, such as digital cameras and printers, will all work with Fedora immediately, with little, if any, configuration.

In fact, most underlying PC hardware is preconfigured during installation without your knowledge and without further work required. Both your graphics card and sound card should work without a hitch, for example. In addition, nearly all USB and FireWire devices you plug in after installation will be supported.

Fedora doesn't support a few hardware items. Generally, it's a black-and-white situation; Fedora either works with a piece of hardware or it doesn't.

The types of hardware that Fedora doesn't support tend to be esoteric devices that rely on custom software provided by the hardware manufacturer. It's also sometimes the case that brand new models of hardware won't work with Fedora because support has yet to be added. However, as soon as a new piece of hardware comes out, work is usually undertaken to ensure that Linux is made compatible with it. This work is carried out by the people who produce the Linux kernel, although sometimes the companies behind the hardware will supply their own code. This means that you can get the latest hardware drivers by grabbing the latest kernel files. This is one more reason why you should regularly update your system online, as explained in Chapter 9.

■**Tip** Before you buy a new piece of hardware, ask the salesperson if it runs under Linux. You can only hope that the salesperson knows or can find out for you. Also, compatibility with Linux is often listed on the hardware box or at the manufacturer's web site (even if you sometimes need to search through the FAQ section to find out about it!). You can also try running a LiveCD distribution to test if the device works under Linux.

Unfortunately, unlike with Windows, it's rare to find Linux drivers on the CD that comes with the hardware. Even if you do find a Linux driver supplied, chances are that it will work with only certain distributions of Linux, such as Red Hat or SUSE Linux.

Proprietary vs. Open Source Drivers

As discussed earlier in this book, Linux is an open source operating system. This means that the source code underlying Linux programs is available for inspection. This is a good thing when it comes to hardware drivers, because bugs in the code can be spotted and repaired by anyone with an interest in doing so. If you consider that a bug in a graphics driver could mean your PC crashes every 5 minutes, the value of such an approach is abundantly clear.

Unfortunately, some hardware manufacturers don't like to disclose how their hardware works, because they want to protect their trade secrets. This makes it impossible for them to release open source drivers, because such drivers would expose exactly how the hardware operates. Such companies are not blind to the fact that growing numbers of people use Linux, so they release proprietary drivers whose source code is not made publicly available.

■**Note** Sometimes, it's actually possible to use Windows drivers under Linux, such as with the NDISwrapper project (`http://ndiswrapper.sourceforge.net/`).

Proprietary drivers bring with them a number of problems. The first relates to bugs. To use a proprietary driver is to be at the mercy of the hardware manufacturer's own development and release schedule. If the driver has a serious bug, you'll either have to work around it or put up with troubling issues until the manufacturer offers an update. Additionally, proprietary drivers are usually tied into particular versions of Linux. Sometimes, they can be hacked to work with other versions of Linux, but this isn't something that beginners can take on themselves.

Although the folks behind Fedora strongly support open source software, even they realize that proprietary drivers need to be used in certain situations. For example, it's impossible to use the 3D graphics elements of most modern graphics cards unless you have a proprietary driver. Because of this, it's often possible to grab proprietary drivers from one of the unofficial Fedora online software repositories. We'll look at connecting to these software repositories later in this chapter, in the "Setting Up Online Software Repositories" section, and we'll also show you how to download 3D graphics card drivers, in the "Installing 3D Graphics Card Drivers" section.

■**Note** Linux sees hardware in a technical way, rather than in the way humans do. If you attach something like a USB CD-R/RW drive, Linux will recognize the drive hardware and attempt to make it work. It won't try to find a driver for that specific make and model of CD-R/RW drive. Thus, Linux is able to work with a wide range of hardware because a lot of hardware is actually very similar on a technical level, despite the differences in case design, model names, and even prices!

WHAT HARDWARE WORKS?

The question of what hardware works under Fedora is one that's not easily answered. There are several incomplete hardware compatibility lists that you can look at, such as `http://fedora-linux.nl/wiki/index.php/HCL`. There is no single complete and accurate HCL for Fedora, so it's generally a good idea to look at popular Linux compatibility lists, such as the LinuxQuestions.org Hardware Compatibility List (`http://www.linuxquestions.org/hcl/`). Another very popular hardware list is hosted at `http://www.linuxcompatible.org/`.

The Fedora Smolt Project, although still in the early testing stage, attempts to profile what hardware works with Fedora. Visit `http://smolt.fedoraproject.org/` for more details about Smolt and supported hardware. Since the Fedora Smolt Project is still growing, you can contribute to it by sending a report of your hardware installation. Open a Terminal window (Applications ➤ Accessories ➤ Terminal) and run the command `smoltSendProfile`. This will anonymously submit a list of your computer's hardware.

A search engine like Google is your best friend if the Fedora hardware lists don't help. Simply search for the brand and model of your hardware and add "Fedora" to the search string. This should return results, usually from the Fedora forums (`www.fedoraforum.org/`), which has an exclusive forum dedicated to discussing hardware, or an individual's blog, written by someone who has found a way to make that type of hardware work.

Viewing Your Hardware

When using Windows, you might have come across Device Manager, the handy tool that lists your PC's hardware (see Figure 8-1). You can install similar software for Fedora using the online software repositories. Start Pirut Package Manager (Applications ➤ Add/Remove Software) and click the Search tab. Type **device manager**. In the search results, select `hal-gnome` by clicking the check box next to it. Now click Apply. Once Pirut has installed Device Manager, you will find it under System ➤ Administration ➤ Hardware.

You should be aware of a few important differences between the Windows and Fedora versions of Device Manager. Under Fedora, the list is for information only. You can't tweak any settings and must instead rely on separate pieces of configuration software. On the other hand, Fedora's list is far more comprehensive than that in Windows. Fedora's Device Manager thoroughly probes the hardware to discover its capabilities.

Perhaps the biggest difference, however, is that just because a piece of hardware is listed within Fedora's Device Manager doesn't mean that the hardware is configured to work with Fedora. In fact, it doesn't even imply that the hardware will *ever* work under Fedora. Device Manager's list is simply the result of probing devices attached to the various system buses (PCI, AGP, USB, etc.) and reporting back the data.

Nonetheless, Device Manager is the best starting place if you find that a certain piece of hardware isn't working. If a piece of hardware is listed, then it proves, if nothing else, that the system recognizes that the hardware is attached.

That said, it's very unlikely that you'll need to use Fedora's Device Manager, because most hardware will work after you install Fedora. At the very most, all you'll need to do is configure a few settings for the hardware.

■**Note** To configure most hardware devices, you'll be asked for the root password, because configuring hardware requires superuser privileges.

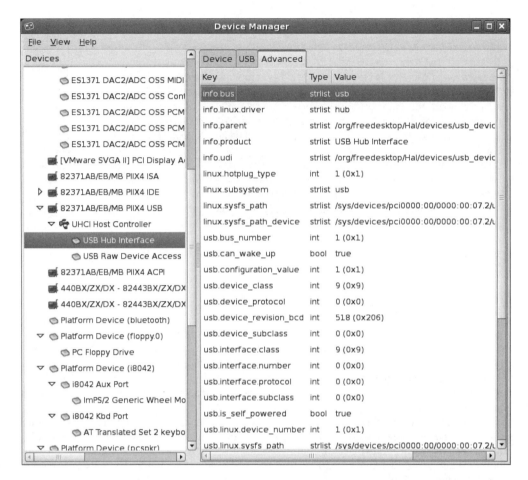

Figure 8-1. *Device Manager can display just about everything you need to know about attached hardware.*

Getting Online

Getting online is vital in our modern Internet age, and Fedora caters to all the standard ways of doing so. Linux was built from the ground up to be an online operating system, and is based on UNIX, which pioneered the concept of networking computers together to share data back in the 1970s. However, none of this is to say that getting online with Fedora is difficult! In fact, it's very easy.

Regardless of whether you use a modem, standard Ethernet card, or wireless card, the same program is used to configure your network settings under Fedora. Support for many makes and models of equipment is built in, so in most cases, all you need to do is enter a few configuration details.

■**Note** Linux actually runs around 60 percent of the computers that make the Internet work! Whenever you visit a web site, there's a strong chance that it's run using Linux. As your Linux skills increase, you'll eventually get to a stage where you, too, can run your own Internet servers. It sounds difficult, but it can be quite easy.

Using an Ethernet Card

Ethernet is one of the oldest and most established network technologies. When we talk of Ethernet, we refer to wired networks—all the computers on the network are connected by cabling to a central hub or router. (The other form of networking technology, which works without wires, is covered in the next section.)

You might go online via an Ethernet card in a variety of situations. If you have DSL or cable broadband service at your home or workplace, for example, you might use a DSL router. Your computer will then connect to this router via Ethernet, and all you need to worry about on your PC is getting your Ethernet card up and running.

■**Note** Using a DSL or cable modem router is the preferred way of going online via broadband. However, some people use USB-based DSL modems, which connect to and are operated by their PC. These are covered in the "Using a USB-Based DSL Modem" section later in this chapter.

If you're running Fedora on a PC in an office environment, it's likely that you will connect to the local area network using an Ethernet card. This lets your computer communicate with other computers, as well as with printers. In some offices in which an Internet connection is provided, this connection will allow you to go online.

Configuring a Network Card via DHCP

Most computers that connect to a broadband router or an office network receive their configuration data via the Dynamic Host Configuration Protocol (DHCP), which is to say that your computer receives its IP, gateway, subnet mask, and Domain Name Service (DNS) addresses automatically. However, you will need to configure your network card to work via DHCP. You can do this configuration with the Network Configuration applet, which can be found under the System ➤ Administration menu. Because you're going to configure hardware settings, you'll need to enter your password to proceed.

Follow these steps to configure your network card:

1. Select System ➤ Administration ➤ Network to open the Network Configuration dialog box.

2. You should find your Ethernet card at the top of the list. It will be identified as eth, followed by a number, such as eth0 or eth1. Fedora should indicate that the card isn't configured. Click the entry for your Ethernet card, and then click the Edit button.

■**Note** Listed beneath the Ethernet card will be any other networking devices you might have, such as a dial-up modem. If you don't want to use these, you can leave them unconfigured.

---

3. Under the General tab of the Ethernet Device dialog box, put a check in the "Activate device when computer starts" check box, and make sure the drop-down list next to "Automatically obtain IP address settings" reads DHCP. Also put a check in the "Automatically obtain DNS information from provider" check box. Then click OK.

4. In the main Network Configuration window, click Activate.

5. After a few seconds, your network card should be up and running. Test it by using the web browser to visit a site.

From this point on, your network card should automatically activate each time you boot, so you should not need to return to the Network Settings applet.

Configuring a Static IP Address

On some networks, you might have been assigned an IP address, which you must enter manually, along with a few other networking addresses. This is referred to as a *static IP address*.

You should speak to your system administrator or technical support person to determine these settings. Ask the administrator for your *IP address*, *DNS server addresses* (there are usually two or three of these), your *subnet mask*, and the *router address* (sometimes referred to as the *gateway address*). The settings you will get from your system administrator will usually be in the form of a series of four numbers separated by dots, something like 192.168.0.233.

Once you know your settings, proceed as follows:

1. Select System ➤ Administration ➤ Network to open the Network Configuration dialog box.

2. Find your network card in the list (it should be referred to as eth0), click its entry, and then click Edit.

3. In the dialog box that appears, make sure the "Statically set IP addresses" radio button is selected. In the Address, Subnet mask, and Default gateway address text boxes, fill in the relevant details. Figure 8-2 shows an example of a completed Ethernet Device dialog box. Click OK after filling in the information.

Figure 8-2. *You can configure Fedora to work with DHCP networks, or you can define a static IP address.*

4. In the Network Configuration dialog box, click the DNS tab.

   5. Type the first DNS address in the Primary DNS text box. Then enter the second DNS
      address, if you have been given one, in the Secondary DNS text box (and then enter a third
      if you have been given one).

■**Tip** If you're using a static IP address with a router, such as that provided by a DSL modem, the DNS address
will probably be the same as the router/gateway address.

---

   6. Click the Activate button.

   7. A message comes up informing you that you must save your settings before the device can
      be activated. Click Yes.

   A message will come up informing you that you should reboot your computer, or restart the
network if the network connection doesn't work.

   Your network connection should now work. You can test it by using the web browser to visit
a web site. However, if your system administrator mentioned that a proxy must also be configured,
you'll also need to follow the instructions in the "Working with a Proxy Server" section later in this
chapter.

Joining a Wireless Network

A wireless (also referred to as Wi-Fi) network is, as its name suggests, a network that does away
with cabling and uses radio frequencies to communicate. It's more common for notebooks and
handheld computers to use wireless connections, but some desktop computers also do too.

   Notebooks and PDAs typically use built-in wireless network cards, with an antenna built into
the case. However, some notebooks use PCMCIA cards, which have an external square antenna.

Configuring a Wireless Card

The process for configuring a wireless network card is quite similar to configuring a standard
Ethernet card, meaning that you can follow the instructions for configuring a network card in the
previous section, with the following differences:

   • The wireless card will be identified as *Wireless Connection*. If your computer also has a stan-
     dard Ethernet adapter in addition to wireless capabilities, you'll need to make sure you select
     the wireless card when choosing an adapter to configure.

   • You need to select the base station you wish to connect to in the Network Name (ESSID)
     drop-down list, or, if your base station is configured so that it doesn't broadcast its name,
     you should type it manually into the Network Name (ESSID) field (by selecting the Specified
     radio button under Network name). If you work in an office environment, you may need to
     speak to your network administrator to find out the base station name.

   • If the connection doesn't use Wired Equivalent Privacy (WEP) protection, you can leave the
     WEP Key field empty. If it does use WEP protection, continue reading for instructions on how
     to configure it.

   In most instances, wireless network cards are configured with DHCP so that they will grab a
network address automatically. The nature of a wireless network, in which many people might join
or leave the network at will, means that using static IP addresses is a bad idea.

Using WEP or WPA Encryption

Some wireless networks use the WEP or Wi-Fi Protected Access (WPA) system. These systems encrypt the data being transmitted on the network so it cannot be stolen by hackers with special equipment. Also, people can't join the wireless network unless they know the encryption key, which is basically an access code. This prevents unauthorized people from accessing the network.

Note At one time just a few years ago, people walking or driving past office blocks would be able to steal a business's Internet connection! This practice, known as *war driving*, became a hobby for some people. It's still possible today, although businesses have realized the dangers and usually protect their networks. Additionally, connecting to a wireless network connection without permission has been made illegal in some countries.

The encryption key normally takes the form of a string of letters and numbers, which you should get from your system administrator. Alternatively, your administrator may give you a passphrase, which might be a sentence in English, including spaces between words. You then enter that as a kind of long password.

WEP is by far the easiest choice when it comes to configuration. Although WEP has been found to be relatively easy to circumvent, for most home users, it offers sufficient protection.

SECURE SOCKETS LAYER (SSL)

The transfer of confidential or financial data across the Web—to and from online banking sites, for example—is nearly always protected by an additional layer of secure protection called Secure Sockets Layer (SSL) HTTP. You can tell if this is the case with any site because the address will begin with `https://`. Additionally, most browsers display a padlock symbol at the bottom of the screen. Accessing such sites should be safe, even if your wireless connection isn't protected with either WEP or WPA.

Similarly, although online shopping sites don't use SSL while you're browsing, when it's time to pay, they always use SSL. This ensures your credit card details are encrypted. If the store doesn't adopt an `https://` address when you click to visit the virtual checkout, you shouldn't shop there!

So, there's an argument to be made that you don't really need WEP or WPA protection if you simply use your wireless connection to browse the Internet. However, some web mail services transfer your username and password in the clear, which is to say without using SSL. This means that this information could be picked up by an eavesdropper. In the case of Hotmail and Yahoo Mail, you can select secure login, but it isn't activated by default. Google's Gmail appears to use SSL all the time for login, but after this, your e-mail messages are transmitted across the Internet in the clear and, in theory, can be eavesdropped on by anyone, anywhere.

Configuring WEP

WEP keys come in either hexadecimal (hex) or plain text (passphrase) varieties. Hex keys look like this in their 128-bit form: CB4C4189B1861E19BC9A9BDA59. In their 64-bit form, they will be shorter and may look similar to 4D9ED51E23. A passphrase will take the form of a single short sentence. Fedora can work with both 64- and 128-bit keys, as well as passphrases.

Follow these steps to configure WEP (these steps assume your network card has already been configured, as described previously):

1. Select System ➤ Administration ➤ Network to open the Network Settings dialog box.

2. Double-click the entry in the list corresponding to your wireless card.

3. If you have a hex key, just prepend **0x** before typing your hex key in the text box. Alternatively, you can just type in the passphrase.

4. In the Network Settings dialog box, click the entry in the list for your wireless card, as shown in Figure 8-3. Select Deactivate, and then click Activate. Then click OK.

5. Test your connection by attempting to browse to a web site.

If you find your card doesn't seem to work after you enter new WEP settings, try rebooting. Then open the Network Settings applet and make sure your card is activated.

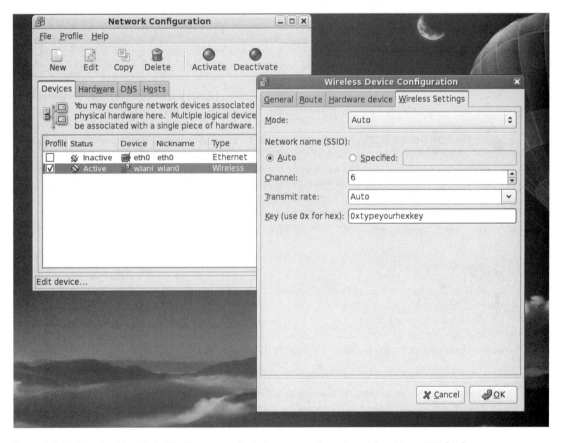

Figure 8-3. *Fedora is able to join WEP-protected wireless networks, using either 64- or 128-bit keys.*

THE NETWORKMANAGER TOOL

The NetworkManager tool provides automatic and pain-free network detection and configuration. It monitors the network interfaces and will automatically switch you to the best connection. For example, if you connect an Ethernet cable to your machine, depending on the connection speed, NetworkManager will switch to the Ethernet connection if it's faster.

NetworkManager also makes configuring WEP and WPA very easy. To enable NetworkManager, open a Terminal window (Applications ➤ System Tools ➤ Terminal) and type the following:

```
su -
[Enter password]
chkconfig NetworkManager on
chkconfig NetworkManagerDispatcher on
service NetworkManager start
service NetworkManagerDispatcher start
```

Running the chkconfig NetworkManager on command results in NetworkManager starting each time during boot. Similarly, you want the NetworkManagerDispatcher tool to also start during boot. The service NetworkManager start command will start NetworkManager.

Once this is done, you will find a new icon in the notification area. NetworkManager works best with the DHCP setting. When using NetworkManager, you don't need to provide any network settings in the System ➤ Administration ➤ Network tool.

When you click the NetworkManager icon in the notification area, you'll see a list of all available connections, both wired and wireless. To see the signal strength of the wireless connection, just hover the mouse over the NetworkManager icon. NetworkManager will also inform you of the connection speed, IP address, and other connection settings if you right-click the NetworkManager icon and select Connection Information.

To configure encryption for new connections, click the NetworkManager notification icon and select Create New Wireless Network. Then simply choose the type of encryption you wish to use—WEP or WPA.

Configuring WPA

It's possible to join networks using WPA—with a little work. This involves editing a couple of configuration files.

Perhaps it goes without saying that you should ensure your wireless card is compatible with WPA before you start. It's found on models of one or, at most, two years old. You can learn this information from the card's packaging or by visiting the manufacturer's web site.

Caution Some earlier wireless cards rushed to include WPA before it was fully certified and may feature buggy implementations. In such cases, it might be possible to update the firmware of the card, usually using a utility that runs in Windows. If you suspect your card has this fault, check the manufacturer's support site for details.

You'll also need to know if the card uses a driver module that's compatible with wpasupplicant, the software that handles WPA management under Fedora. As this book goes to press, wpasupplicant is compatible with the following wireless drivers: HostAP, Prism54, Madwifi, Atmel, wext, ipw2100, ipw2200, and NDISwrapper.

You can discover which driver your card uses through the Device Manager program discussed in the "Viewing Your Hardware" section. Open Device Manager (System ➤ Administration ➤ Hardware) and look for your wireless card in the list of hardware on the left side of the window. Once you find it, select it, and then click the Advanced tab on the right side of the window. Find the line that reads "info.linux.driver," and look in the Value column for the name of the driver. If what you discover isn't in the list of compatible drivers, then `wpasupplicant` won't work with your card. If it is present, make a note of the name of the driver, because you'll need to know it to complete the configuration.

Finally, you'll need to know how Fedora refers to your wireless card. Open the Network Settings applet (System ➤ Administration ➤ Network) and look for the entry in the list referring to your wireless card.

Note There's a chance that `wpasupplicant` will support more drivers than those we've listed by the time you read this. For a list of all the supported drivers, just type `wpa_supplicant` in a Terminal window and read the Drivers section of the help documentation that appears on the screen.

To enable WPA, you need to edit the `wpa_supplicant.conf` file:

1. Open a Terminal window (Applications ➤ System Tools ➤ Terminal) and type the following:

```
su -c 'gedit /etc/wpa_supplicant/wpa_supplicant.conf'
```

2. Add the following section to the existing file:

```
network={
ssid="network ssid"
key_mgmt=WPA-PSK
psk="write WPA passphrase"
}
```

3. The WPA service does not automatically start at bootup, so open the Service Configuration program (System ➤ Administration ➤ Services). Look for wpa_supplicant at the left of the window, and put a check in the check box alongside it. Now click the Start button.

4. You should now find that you are able to connect to the WPA-protected wireless network.

USING NDISWRAPPER

You might find that your wireless card is not supported under Fedora. While the people who write drivers for Linux endeavor to have the operating system work with all wireless cards, they often need to reverse-engineer wireless card technology, and this can mean that drivers take a while to appear. In cases such as this, it's sometimes possible to use NDISwrapper. This allows you to use Windows XP drivers for the wireless card. It's not a perfect solution, but it's certainly worth a try.

Sadly, although NDISwrapper is fundamentally simple to use, there are special considerations for each card and it's not possible to provide an all-encompassing guide here. The best policy if you wish to use NDISwrapper is to search the Fedora forums (`www.fedoraforum.org/`) for a guide to configuring your particular card. It's quite possible that someone has posted a how-to tutorial. However, you should first check `http://ndiswrapper.sourceforge.net/mediawiki/index.php/List` to see if your card is listed among those known to work.

Configuring Dial-Up Internet Access

At one time, nearly all home users (and even some workplaces) used dial-up modems across phone lines to access the Internet. But since the boom in broadband courtesy of DSL and cable television, dial-up access has declined in popularity.

Fedora has excellent support for dial-up connections but, unfortunately, only for certain modems. In simple terms, it supports many external serial modems and some internal models (including PCI and PCMCIA cards), but it doesn't directly support so-called winmodems, which are the most popular type of dial-up modem on the market today.

Winmodems rely on Windows taking care of the coding/decoding work, hence the name. This is done to save on component costs during manufacturing.

The companies that make the hardware behind winmodems aren't always helpful to the Linux kernel programmers, and it can be difficult for them to make the modems work under Linux. Yet more manufacturers provide the required drivers, but under a software license that's not compatible with the GNU Public License (GPL) used throughout the rest of Linux. This means that including the software with Linux brings with it ethical and even legal issues.

A project that works to bring support for most winmodems to Linux is called Linmodems. However, the Fedora developers have decided not to include its software within Fedora at the moment. If you would like to try to make your winmodem work under Fedora, visit the Linmodems project's web page, at `http://linmodems.org/`. You'll find a welcoming community of users who are dedicated to helping others get online. Alternatively, you can skip straight to the guide that's written for beginners who would like to make a winmodem work under Linux: `http://walbran.org/sean/linux/linmodem-howto.html`. Searching the Fedora forums (`www.fedoraforum.org/`) might also reveal useful information.

■**Note** The easiest solution if you have a winmodem and intend to use dial-up connections on your computer is to buy an external modem that connects to your computer via its serial port. These types of modems can be purchased for as little as $10 to $20, if you shop around. Auction sites like eBay (`www.ebay.com/`) are a particularly good place to look for external modems. Practically all external modems are guaranteed to work with Fedora.

Before you start configuring your dial-up modem, you'll need to know your dial-up username and password, and also the phone number to use in order to get online. You should ensure that your modem is plugged into the phone socket and powered up.

1. Right-click a blank spot on the Panel (at the top of the Fedora desktop) and select Add to Panel.

2. In the list of applets, scroll down and click Modem Lights. Then click the Add button.

3. Open the Network settings program (System ➤ Administration ➤ Network) and click New.

4. Select Modem connection and click Forward. Fedora will scan the system to determine the port to which the modem is connected. You will then be guided through the configuration steps.

5. You will be asked to enter the ISP's dial-up number as well as the area code or prefix. The prefix is the number that you might need to access an outside line if you're in an office. Alternatively, you might choose to enter the prefix you normally dial to activate a particular call plan. Otherwise, this box can be left empty.

6. In the Login name and Password fields, enter your dial-up username and password (*not* your Fedora login username and password).

7. Click Forward. You can choose to automatically obtain the IP address and the DNS settings or manually specify them. Click Forward when you are done. You will be informed of your settings. Click Apply to confirm all the values are correct.

8. Close the Network settings window.

After this setup, you can connect to your ISP by clicking the button on the left side of the Modem Lights icon on the Panel. You are asked if you want to connect, as shown in Figure 8-4.

Figure 8-4. *Going online with your dial-up modem is simply a matter of clicking a button on the Modem Lights icon.*

Using a USB-Based DSL Modem

Some people connect to broadband Internet services using a DSL modem that connects to the computer via USB. This is very common in the United Kingdom, where such modems are provided free of charge as part of ADSL broadband subscriptions.

Sadly, as with dial-up modems, support for the majority of USB-based DSL modems isn't included in Fedora. To get such modems working, you must download and install additional drivers, as well as configuration software. This can be rather complicated and, if you can afford it, by far the best policy is to upgrade to a router-based modem and connect via an Ethernet or wireless connection. Such modem routers are inexpensive nowadays, and most modern PCs have Ethernet ports built in. The popular HowStuffWorks site (`http://computer.howstuffworks.com/home-network.htm`) provides a good guide for beginners that explains home networking.

It is beyond the scope of this book to offer a step-by-step guide on configuring a DSL modem. There are far too many available, and even though with slight modification some basic steps can be adapted to work for a variety of modems based on a particular type of hardware, it would be impossible for us to offer a detailed guide.

Working with a Proxy Server

Some networks in offices require that you use a web proxy (often referred to as an *HTTP proxy*). A proxy is a server computer that does two things. First, it provides additional security by providing a single portal to all web pages. Second, it helps speed up Internet access by storing frequently accessed pages. This means that if ten people request the same web page, there's no need to get the same ten pieces of data from the Internet. The proxy computer can send them its own copies. For various reasons, proxies are becoming less popular nowadays, but larger organizations might still use them.

You'll need to speak to your system administrator to see if your office uses a proxy. If it does, your administrator will most likely give you an address, which may take the form of a web address or an IP address. Once you have this information, follow these steps to configure the proxy:

1. Click System ➤ Preferences ➤ Internet and Network ➤ Network Proxy.

2. In the Network Proxy Preferences dialog box, click Manual Proxy Configuration. You can now specify the DNS name or the IP address in the HTTP proxy text field.

3. To specify a username and password, click the Details button and click the Use Authentication check box. Enter a username and password. If your proxy doesn't use usernames and passwords, simply leave them out. You can specify the port number in the Port spin box.

FIREFOX AND PROXY SETTINGS

The Firefox web browser does not adhere to the system proxy settings just discussed. To configure the Proxy settings for Firefox, click Tools ➤ Options. In the Options dialog box, click the Advanced button, and then click the Network tab. Then click the Settings button.

Click the "Manual proxy configuration" radio button in the Connection Settings dialog box and fill in the proxy settings.

■**Tip** Some ISPs run proxy servers, too. However, unlike proxies in offices, it's normally up to you whether you choose to use them. You might find that using a proxy speeds up your connection, especially when you access popular sites, so it's worth trying out. To find out if your ISP offers a proxy, visit its technical support web pages or phone its technical support line.

Setting Up Online Software Repositories

Although you've installed Fedora from the DVD-ROM supplied with this book, you should download any additional software from the online Fedora software repositories. It might take a few minutes for the software to download, but you're almost certainly guaranteed the latest version of the program in question.

In addition, once the online software repositories are set up, your system will automatically upgrade any software you have to the newest supported versions. This makes for a more secure system, because many software updates fix critical bugs that can leave your system open to illicit interests.

The installation, removal, and updating of software under Fedora is handled by Pirut Package Manager. This is a little like the Add/Remove Programs applet within the Windows Control Panel, except that it will automatically search for, download, and install any new software you require. As is the Linux way, there's no charge for new software. What more could you ask?

■**Note** *Package* is Linux lingo for a complete file that contains everything you need to install a piece of software on your system.

You can find Pirut Package Manager under Applications ➤ Add/Remove Software. Depending on whether the Fedora installation program was able to get online, you might find that Pirut Package Manager is already set up to use the online repositories. Whatever the case, you should follow these steps to make sure:

1. Open a Terminal window (Applications ➤ System Tools ➤ Terminal) and run the following commands:

```
cd /etc/yum.repos.d/
ls
```

Here's what we got on our test system:

```
fedora.repo                    fedora-updates.repo
fedora-updates-testing.repo    fedora-development.repo
```

2. These are all the software repositories Fedora is currently set up to use. These are the official software repositories and you can trust them. You can look at each of these files by using `less` at the terminal:

```
less fedora.repo
```

3. Look at the line that says `enabled=1`. This determines whether Fedora should use this repository. If you look at some other repository, like `fedora-legacy`, you'll find that in it, `enabled` is set to `0`. This means that Fedora will not use the legacy repository when installing software.

There are certain third-party repositories that provide software for Fedora as well. These include `livna`, `atrpms`, and `freshrpms`. Because of the free nature of Fedora, you will not find any proprietary drivers in any of its repositories. Because of this, you might have to resort to these third-party repositories from time to time.

4. To set up the `livna` (`http://rpm.livna.org/`) repository, open a Terminal window (Applications ➤ System Tools ➤ Terminal) and type the following:

```
rpm -ivh http://rpm.livna.org/fedora/7/i386/livna-release-7-2.noarch.rpm
```

5. If you now look under the `/etc/yum.repos.d/` directory, you'll also find `livna-repo` along with all the other files.

You can similarly install the `freshrpms` repository (`http://freshrpms.net`).

■**Caution** Certain programs that are in both Fedora and the `livna` repository can cause problems. For example, the Mplayer program is available through both repositories and often conflicts with other programs. It is best to disable a repository if you will be installing software from some other repository.

Updating your system software is covered in Chapter 9, and you'll find a full introduction to the way Fedora handles software installation and removal in Chapter 28.

ADDITIONAL NOTEBOOK CONFIGURATION

Generally speaking, a notebook computer will not need any configuration above and beyond what's outlined in this chapter. For example, if you have a wireless PCMCIA card, you can simply follow the instructions in the "Configuring a Wireless Card" section. However, if you have a touchpad that needs to be configured or you want to adjust your CPU's frequency, this sidebar provides more information.

Touchpad Configuration

If your notebook has a Synaptics TouchPad, you may want to configure it to your liking. Many notebooks come equipped with Synaptics hardware, although there are also similar touchpads made by other manufacturers.

If your touchpad is a genuine Synaptics pad, Fedora will have installed the correct driver automatically. This should let you use the right edge of the pad to fast scroll through documents and web pages. Sadly, Fedora doesn't come with any way of configuring the touchpad (the Mouse applet under the System ➤ Preferences ➤ Hardware menu will have no effect). This means that you will be unable to adjust the sensitivity of the pad to your tastes.

However, you can download and use GSynaptics, which allows you to set touchpad preferences. Open Pirut (Applications ➤ Add/Remove Software) and search for "gsynaptics." Mark it for installation by putting a check in the check box, and then click Apply.

Before you can use GSynaptics, you need to add a line to your X.org configuration file. You can do this by editing the file in Gedit. Type `su -c 'gedit /etc/X11/xorg.conf'` in a GNOME Terminal window to open the configuration file. Look through the document for the line that reads `Identifier "Synaptics Touchpad"`, and then beneath it, insert a new line that reads `Option "SHMConfig" "true"`. Then save the file and reboot your system. Once Fedora is up and running, click System ➤ Preferences ➤ Touchpad to start GSynaptics.

CPU Frequency Scaling

Another handy notebook add-on is the GNOME CPU Frequency Scaling Monitor. If you have a compatible CPU in your notebook, this tool lets you adjust the speed of the chip to save battery power. Most modern mobile-oriented CPUs support this function. Unfortunately, because of its ability to slow down your system, the applet is considered a security risk. Before you use it, you must reconfigure your system to allow it to work.

Open a GNOME Terminal window (Applications ➤ System Tools ➤ Terminal) and type `yum install cpuspeed`. Once it is installed, right-click a blank spot on the Panel (at the top of the screen). Click Add to Panel, and then in the dialog box that appears, scroll down and select the CPU Frequency Scaling Monitor icon and click the Add button. To alter your CPU frequency, click the applet and choose the clock speed setting you desire.

Various cpufreq kernel options support modern laptops. So, they don't need to be adjusted for power saving. Also, the *cpuspeed* system service is installed automatically and should normally produce the best results without the need to tinker with any settings, other than turning off applications that are a huge drain on the power and turning down the brightness of the LCD display.

Configuring E-Mail and Instant Messaging

Being online is all about staying in touch, and Fedora is no slouch in this regard. Fedora offers a full-featured e-mail program, called Evolution, as well as an instant messaging client called Pidgin.

Unlike similar instant messaging clients, Pidgin supports a variety of Internet chat protocols, including ICQ, MSN, Yahoo, and IRC. This means you can chat with friends and colleagues on different networks using this one program.

Note Pidgin was formerly known as Gaim, but following a trademark settlement with AOL in early 2007, it was rechristened.

Evolution is able to work with both IMAP and the popular POP3 mail servers offered by ISPs and used within corporate environments. Additionally, it can work with the Microsoft Exchange protocol used by offices running the Outlook mail program and also Novell GroupWise. We'll look at using Evolution in Chapter 27. Here, you'll learn how to configure the e-mail client to receive and send mail.

Configuring E-Mail Access

Before starting, you'll need to find out the addresses of the mail servers you intend to use. In the case of POP3 and IMAP mail accounts, you'll need to know the incoming and outgoing server addresses (outgoing may be referred to as SMTP). In the case of Microsoft Exchange, you'll need to know the OWA URL and, optionally, the Active Directory/Global Address List server. You'll also need to install Evolution Connector—open a Terminal window and type `su -c 'yum install evolution-connector'`. With Novell GroupWise, you'll simply need to know the server name.

You'll also need to know your username and password details for the incoming and possibly outgoing mail servers.

After gathering the necessary information, follow these steps to configure Evolution:

1. Start the Evolution e-mail client by clicking its icon at the top of the screen, to the right of the menus. Alternatively, you can select Applications ➤ Internet ➤ Email.

2. When Evolution starts for the first time, you'll be invited to enter your configuration details via a wizard. The first screen will ask for your name and the e-mail address you wish to use within Evolution. These are what will appear in outgoing messages. Beneath this is a check box that you should leave checked if you want the account you're about to create to be the default account. In nearly all situations, this will be the correct choice. You can also fill in the Reply-To and Organization fields if you wish, but these can be left blank. They're not normally displayed by most e-mail clients. Click the Forward button to continue.

3. The next screen asks for details on the receiving (incoming) mail server that you want to use, as shown in Figure 8-5. First, select the server type from the drop-down list. If you don't know which option to go with, select POP. This is by far the most common type of incoming mail server currently in use.

4. In the Configuration section, enter the server address and username in the relevant fields. It's very likely that you'll need to select Always from the Use Secure Connection drop-down list, too. Most POP servers employ at least a password system, and some employ more elaborate protection. You can find out what system your mail server uses by clicking the Check for Supported Types button. Click Forward to continue.

5. You might need to enter your mail password, depending on which server type you chose. In some cases, you'll need to type this later when you download your mail for the first time. Click Forward to continue.

6. You're given the chance to choose between various additional options, such as how often you want Evolution to check for new mail or if you want to delete mail from the server after it has been downloaded. Unless you have been told otherwise or have special requirements, it should be OK to leave the default settings as they are. If you use a Microsoft Exchange server, you may need to enter the Active Directory/Global Address List server details here. Click Forward to continue.

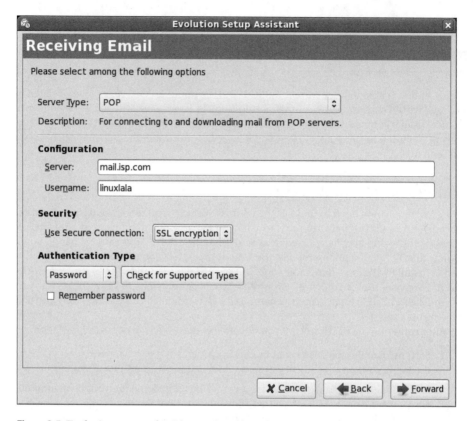

Figure 8-5. *Evolution can work with a variety of mail servers, including POP3, Microsoft Exchange, and IMAP.*

7. Depending on the server type you chose, you might now need to fill in the outgoing (SMTP) server address. Type this into the Server field. If your SMTP server requires authentication, put a check in the relevant box, and then enter your username. Again, unless you've been specifically told to use this option, you can leave it at its default (inactive) state. Click Forward to continue.

8. You're invited to enter a name for the account. This is the account name you will see when you use Evolution. The default is your e-mail address, but you can type something more memorable if you wish. Click Forward to continue.

9. Finally, choose your location, which will have the effect of automatically defining your time zone. This will ensure that e-mail messages are correctly time-stamped. Click Forward to continue, and then click the Apply button to finish the wizard.

Setting Up Instant Messaging

Instant messaging is a way of chatting with other people in real time. It's as if you were having a phone conversation, but you're typing instead of speaking. You can talk to one other person or a whole group of people, and sometimes share files with them.

The instant messaging program under Fedora, Pidgin, offers the same functions and works in an almost identical way to programs that you might have used under Windows. It supports virtually all the popular chat standards, such as ICQ/AOL and MSN (Hotmail/Passport). It assumes that you already have an account with each service, which will likely be the case if you've used instant messaging programs under Windows. You can have as many accounts as you wish and can select the one you want to use when you log in.

To transfer your instant messaging account over to Pidgin, you just need your screen name and password. As with other instant messaging clients, you'll be able to choose an onscreen alias.

Tip If you have questions about how Pidgin works, see the FAQ at `http://developer.pidgin.im/wiki/FAQ`. If you're interested in learning everything there is to know about Pidgin (formerly Gaim), consider reading *Open Source Messaging Application Development: Building and Extending Gaim*, written by Pidgin project leader Sean Egan.

Follow these steps to set up Pidgin:

1. Start Pidgin by clicking Applications ➤ Internet ➤ Internet Messenger. When the program starts for the first time, it will automatically open the Add Account dialog box, although it might be behind the main login window. If so, click to bring it to the front of the desktop.

2. In the Add Account dialog box, select the account type you want to set up from the Protocol drop-down list.

3. Enter your screen name, password, and alias details, as required.

4. If you don't want to type your password each time you run Pidgin, check Remember Password. However, be aware that someone else using the computer could abuse your account.

5. You can put a check in the Auto-Login check box if you want to log into your account as soon as Pidgin is launched. However, as with many other instant messaging clients, Pidgin adds an icon to the notification area, and you can click this to go online and offline.

6. You can put a check in the New Mail Notifications box if you want to be notified of any mail sent to you via the address registered with your instant messaging service.

7. If you want to use a buddy icon (the icon that others will see when they connect to you), click the Open button and browse to a picture.

8. If you wish to connect to a specific instant messaging server or if your network uses a proxy, click Show More Options and enter the details accordingly. In most cases, you won't need to do this.

9. When you've finished, click the Save button. Then, in the main Pidgin login window, click Sign On.

After this, you should find the program works just like any other instant messaging program. You can double-click each contact in your list to start a conversation. To sign off, right-click the icon in the notification area and select the option from the menu, as shown in Figure 8-6. To add another account, click the Accounts ➤ Add/Edit button in the login window, and then click the Add button in the Accounts window. Then follow the preceding step-by-step instructions.

Figure 8-6. *You can control Pidgin by right-clicking its notification area icon.*

Adding a Printer

Most people have a printer nowadays, and Fedora supports a wide variety of models—everything from laser printers to color ink-jet models, and even some of the very old dot-matrix printers.

If you work in an office environment, you'll probably be expected to access a shared printer. Sharing a printer is usually achieved by connecting the device directly to the network. The printer itself normally has special built-in hardware to allow this to happen. Alternatively, the printer might be plugged into a Windows computer, such as a Windows NT, 2000, or XP server (or even simply someone's desktop PC), and shared so that other users can access it. Fedora will work with network printers of both types.

Configuring a Local Printer

A *local printer* is one that's directly connected to your computer, normally via USB, although if the printer is a number of years old, it might connect via the parallel port. To set up a local printer, fol-low these instructions:

1. Click System ➤ Administration ➤ Printing. In the Printer configuration window, click the New Printer button.

2. In the New Printer dialog box, specify a name for the printer and click Forward. With any luck, your printer will be automatically detected. Select it from the list on the left of the dialog box. In case your printer is not listed, select USB Printer #1 for a USB printer, or LPT #1 for a parallel port–based printer. Click the Forward button to continue.

3. Select your printer manufacturer from the list on the left and click Forward. Now select the printer model from the list on the left. The printer will be referred to by its full title, rather than just its model number. This includes any prefixes, such as *Optra* or *Stylus Color*.

■**Tip** If you can't find your printer, or any mention of it, try visiting the manufacturer's web site and looking on its support pages for a Postscript Printer Driver (PPD) file. You might also take a look at `www.linuxprinting.org/download/PPD/` and `www.adobe.com/products/printerdrivers/winppd.html`, which offer many printer drivers available for download. If you find one, download it, and then click the Install Driver button to install it.

---

4. Once installation has finished, the printer will then appear in the Printer configuration window, as shown in Figure 8-7. To see whether it's working correctly, click the Print Test Page button on the Settings tab.

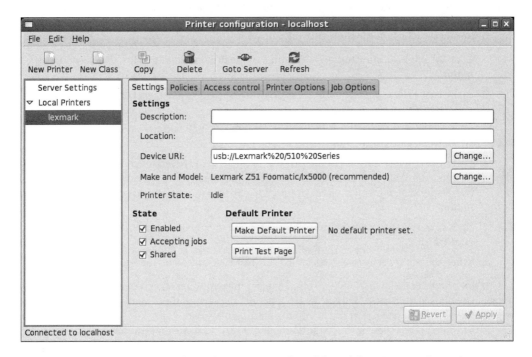

Figure 8-7. *Once the printer is configured, it appears in the sidebar of the Printer configuration window.*

If the printer is installed correctly, you should find yourself with a test page showing color gradations.

If the printer hasn't been installed correctly, it either won't work at all or will start spewing out page after page of junk text. If this is the case, turn off the printer, and then double-click the printer icon. In the window that appears, right-click the print job and select Cancel. You have either selected the wrong port or, more likely, installed incompatible printer drivers. Right-click the new printer's icon and select Remove. Then repeat the installation steps, this time trying different settings.

Configuring a Network Printer

A network printer is one that is not directly connected to any computer. Instead, it connects to the network via an Ethernet cable. In this way, all computers in the office will be able to use it. If the printer is directly connected to a computer, it will very probably be shared via Windows/SMB. In this case, follow the instructions in the next section.

Some printers have the required server hardware built in, but others might use a special print server module that attaches to the printer's USB or parallel printer port. Fedora can work with both types of hardware.

Fedora is compatible with UNIX (LPD), HP JetDirect, and Internet Printing Protocol (IPP) server types. These are the most ubiquitous types currently in use. Before beginning, you'll need to find out the printer's network address and, if relevant, the queue name or the port number. You should be able to find out these details by speaking to your network administrator or the person who configured the printer.

Follow these steps to configure a network printer:

1. Click System ➤ Administration ➤ Printing. In the Printers window, click the New Printer button.

2. In the New Printer dialog box, enter a name for the printer and click Forward.

3. Select the type of printer server from the list on the left of the dialog box. If you're unsure of which to choose, try Internet Printing Protocol (IPP). If you wish to connect to a Hewlett-Packard printer, select AppSocket/HP JetDirect.

4. Enter the network address of the printer. In the case of HP JetDirect, the default port number should be OK, unless you have been specifically told to enter a different number. Depending on which server option you chose, you may also need to enter the queue name.

5. Choose the printer make and model (see step 3 in the previous section for guidance). Then click Finish.

6. When the printer is installed, click the Print Test Page button on the Settings tab.

If the printer doesn't work, it's likely that you set the wrong server type. Try an alternative type; if you chose CUPS the first time, try HP JetDirect the second time. Many print servers can emulate a variety of modes, so trying a different setting may work.

If the printer starts spewing out page after page of text, it's likely that you selected an incorrect printer driver. Cancel the job at the printer. Then double-click the printer icon, right-click the job, and select Cancel. Then right-click the printer name, select Remove, and repeat the installation steps, this time trying an alternative driver.

Configuring a Windows/SMB Shared Printer

A Windows (or SMB) printer is one that's directly connected to a computer and then made available across the network. Effectively, the computer acts as the printer server. Often, in corporate environments, such printers are attached to server computers, but an individual may share the printer attached to a workstation.

In a home situation, a Windows/SMB share is an excellent and inexpensive way of sharing a printer among many computers. The printer is attached to one PC, and, as long as that computer is switched on, the printer will be available to the other computers in the household.

Assuming that the printer has been correctly set up to be shared on the host computer, connecting to a Windows/SMB printer share is easy. In most cases, Fedora will do the hard work for you.

Follow these steps to set up a Windows/SMB shared printer:

1. Click System ➤ Administration ➤ Printing. In the Printer configuration window, click the New Printer button.

2. In the New Printer dialog box, provide a name for the printer and click Forward.

3. From the list on the left of the dialog box, select Windows Printer (SMB). Enter the SMB address and the username and password (if applicable) for the shared printer, and click Forward.

4. Select your printer from the list on the left of the dialog box and click Forward. Select the exact model to install the printer driver (see Step 3 in the "Configuring a Local Printer" section for guidance). Then click Forward.

5. When the printer is installed, click the Print Test Page button on the Settings tab.

If the printer doesn't work at all, the username and password details may be wrong. Alternatively, if you entered the printer network address manually, you might have entered it incorrectly. Try repeating the installation steps and using alternative settings.

If the printer makes a noise as if to start printing, but then decides not to, you might need to change a setting *on the Windows machine*. Click Start ➤ Printers and Faxes, and then right-click the shared printer's icon. Select Properties, and then click the Ports tab in the window that appears. Remove the check from the Enable Bidirectional Support box and click OK. Then restart both the Windows and Fedora computers.

If the printer starts spewing out page after page of text instead of the test page, it's likely that you selected an incorrect printer driver. Cancel the job at the printer. Then double-click the printer icon in Fedora, right-click the job, and select Cancel. Next, right-click the printer and select Remove. Then repeat the installation steps, this time trying an alternative driver.

Setting Up Digital Imaging Devices

One of the ironies of computers is that they're ruthlessly logical yet allow people to pursue their creative hobbies. Photography is just one example. If you want to transfer your photos into your Fedora system, you can use one of the two usual ways: get them from your digital camera or scan them in using a scanner. We'll look at both methods here, starting with digital cameras.

Transferring Photos from a Digital Camera

Digital cameras have been around for a while now and offer a genuine alternative to traditional film photography. They store pictures on computer memory cards rather than on film, meaning that their images can quickly and easily be downloaded to a PC.

You can transfer your pictures from your digital camera to your computer via a direct cable connection into your USB or serial port, or by using a card reader. The latter requires buying an extra piece of hardware into which you insert the memory card from the camera so you can download images from it. Fedora supports both ways of transferring digital images.

■**Note** Very nearly all card readers are supported by Fedora. If you find that your camera doesn't work via a direct cable connection, consider buying a card reader.

Using a Card Reader

When you use a card reader, Fedora simply mounts the contents of the memory card into a folder on your hard drive. I'll describe how mounting works in Chapter 14, but basically it makes a virtual folder on your hard disk from which you can access the contents of the memory card. In most cases, you can read, delete, and even write new contents to the card in this way.

No extra software is necessary, and you can simply use Nautilus, the standard hard disk file browser under Fedora, to access the folder's contents.

■**Note** If there's no card in the reader, it probably won't be identified by Fedora when you plug it in. The reader will not be recognized until a card is present.

With a card reader, the setup procedure is simple: attach it to your PC, and then insert the memory card. Within seconds of doing so, you should see an icon for your card appear on the desktop. You'll also find that several card reader slots are accessible via the Places ➤ Computer menu, even if they don't have any cards in them. This can prove handy if, for whatever reason, the desktop icon doesn't appear. This behavior depends on the model of the card reader. Some card readers will only be visible when there's a memory card present in the slot.

Double-click the desktop icon to open the virtual folder containing the card contents, and you can then copy them to folders on your hard disk or otherwise manipulate the files.

A very important rule must be followed when accessing memory cards with Fedora: the card must be *unmounted* before you remove it from the card reader. This is quite simple to do. Just right-click the desktop icon and select Unmount Volume. Make sure that you save and close any files that you may have been working on before you unmount the card.

Following this, you can safely remove the card. Reinserting it will make it available once again.

■**Caution** Be very careful not to remove a memory card from a card reader while you're writing to or reading from it on your PC. This will most likely damage the card irreparably. At the very least, it will wipe the contents of the card, so you'll lose your photographs.

Using a Camera's Cable Connection

Setting up a digital camera cable connection is usually easy. In most cases, you can simply plug it in to your USB port, turn it on, and Fedora will recognize it and make its contents available in a folder (in a virtually identical way to that described in the previous section for a card reader).

Fedora comes complete with the gThumb software, which includes support for the vast majority of older cameras (those a few years old that directly connect to your PC by its serial or USB port). Because of the way these cameras work, they are not usually automatically configured by Fedora; hence the need for a separate software package.

To configure your camera through gThumb, follow these steps:

1. Select Applications ➤ Graphics ➤ gThumb Image Viewer.

2. Click File ➤ Import Photos. If you've already set up your camera in the program, skip to step 5.

3. The first time you use the program, you'll need to set up your camera. To do so, click the camera icon at the top left. In the Camera Model dialog box, select your model from the drop-down list. This should fill in the Port field automatically, but it's a good idea to check that this setting is correct. If your camera isn't listed, select the nearest match. (This might work for many camera models.) Click OK.

4. Close the Import Photos dialog box. Then open it again by clicking File ➤ Import. This time, your camera will be recognized, and thumbnails of the photos stored on the camera will be shown in the dialog box.

5. In the Import Photos dialog box, select the photos that you wish to import by clicking them (hold down the Ctrl key to select multiple photos). Then click the Import button. The pictures will transfer across to your PC. Bear in mind that this might take some time if you're using a serial connection! It might appear as if the program is doing nothing, even though it is in fact working.

6. After importing has finished, you should find your pictures available in your home directory. When gThumb imports the pictures, it creates a directory based on the date and time.

Configuring a Scanner

Although scanners have fallen out of favor recently with the advent of digital photography, they're vital for getting non-digital photos and old documents onto your PC.

A lot of flatbed scanners can be made to work under Fedora, but not all types are supported. You can check the list of currently supported scanners by visiting www.sane-project.org/sane-mfgs.html. Additional models are added to the list all the time, and this is another reason to make sure your system is completely up to date (see Chapter 9).

The best test of whether your scanner is supported under Fedora is simply to test if it works. Scanning within Fedora is handled by the XSane utility. This is a stand-alone program that operates like the TWAIN drivers that you might have used under Windows, except it's a lot more powerful.

■Tip XSane is even capable of optical character recognition! Simply use Pirut Package Manager to download and install the gocr program. Then select the OCR button on the toolbar of XSane's image preview window.

To configure a scanner and also scan images, follow these steps:

1. Select Applications ➤ Graphics ➤ XSane Image Scanning Program. On startup, the program will attempt to detect your scanner. If it finds a compatible model, you will then see its findings in a splash screen, on which you can click the OK button. If the scanner hasn't been detected, you'll be told that, and XSane won't start.

2. The main XSane program window is similar in appearance to the TWAIN scanner drivers you might have used under Windows. At the top of the window is the XSane mode drop-down list. Here, you can select from a variety of scanning modes, such as those to scan documents for faxing. However, in most cases, the Viewer setting is best. This lets you preview your scans and then save them to disk if you're happy with them.

3. Beneath this is the color/monochrome drop-down list. Here, you can select Binary (line-art), Gray (grayscale), or Color.

4. Below this, you'll find the drop-down list that sets the scanning type. You should select Full Color Range for scanning photographs or artwork. If you have a compatible scanner, you can select "Slide (transparency) and negative scanning."

5. Next is the "dots per inch (DPI)" setting. Generally speaking, 300 DPI is acceptable for scanned photos, while 150 DPI will be acceptable for artwork such as diagrams.

6. Beneath the DPI setting are the gamma, brightness, and contrast sliders (in that order). You can use these sliders to adjust the quality of the scan.

7. To scan a preview, click the Scan button.

8. When the scan is complete, the image viewer window will display the scan (note that XSane is clever enough to crop the picture and delete any space around it). Here, you can choose to manipulate the image by rotating it or applying cleaning filters (look in the Filters menu). Once you're happy with the results, click the Save button on the preview window's toolbar (the first button on the left).

9. If you wish, you can adjust the brightness/contrast settings and scan again. Just close the original preview and click the Scan button.

Using a USB Memory Stick

Although at one time the floppy disk drive ruled when it came to transferring small files between computers, the USB memory stick has since taken its place. These small devices, often incorporated into key rings, contain nonvolatile memory and retain their contents even when no power is applied.

The good news is that Fedora works with just about every make and model of memory stick. Simply insert the device, and then wait a few seconds while Fedora recognizes it. It will then make the contents of the stick available via a desktop icon. Alternatively, you can click Places ➤ Computer to access the device. The standard Nautilus file browser window is used to access the device, so you can copy, delete, and rename files as usual.

An important caveat is that when you're finished with the device, you *shouldn't* simply unplug it. Instead, you need to *unmount* it first. Make sure you've saved and closed any files on the memory stick. You might also need to close any Nautilus file browser windows that are browsing the stick. Then right-click its desktop icon and select Unmount Volume.

Installing 3D Graphics Card Drivers

Virtually all graphics cards are automatically supported and configured within Fedora, so you can stick with the default X.org drivers installed by Fedora. However, if you want to use their 3D functionality—usually to play 3D games or run 3D modeling software—then some extra steps may be necessary.

NVIDIA 3D cards are well supported under Fedora, including the Radeon series and the GeForce series. At the time of writing, there are some issues with ATI cards on Fedora 7. The situation will hopefully be resolved soon, so you should keep checking for updates.

Adding 3D graphics support involves downloading and installing special driver software from the third-party Fedora repositories via Pirut Package Manager. If you haven't yet configured Pirut Package Manager, see the "Setting Up Online Software Repositories" section earlier in the chapter. The drivers are provided by the manufacturer of the graphics card and are closed source (sometimes referred to as *binary only* or *proprietary*). The drivers that we install in the following sections are available from the livna software repository.

Installing an NVIDIA Driver

The NVIDIA driver supports practically all NVIDIA 3D cards produced in recent times—everything from the latest GeForce cards to the oldest TNT cards from the mid-1990s.

To install support for NVIDIA cards, follow these steps:

1. Select Applications ➤ Add/Remove Software.

2. Click the Search button and enter nvidia as a search term. In the list of results, click the check box next to kmod-nvidia. Then click Apply.

3. After the installation has completed, log out and then log in again. To test the drivers, open a Terminal window (Applications ➤ System Tools ➤ Terminal) and type su -c 'glxinfo | grep direct'.

4. If the output is direct rendering: Yes, then it is installed perfectly.

5. Certain machines may require that you reboot the computer for the new drivers to take effect.

Configuring Bluetooth

Bluetooth is the short-range networking facility that allows various items of hardware, usually those designed for mobile devices, to work with each other wirelessly. You can use Bluetooth for everything from transferring files between a mobile phone and a computer to employing a wireless keyboard with your desktop computer.

For Bluetooth to work, both devices need to have Bluetooth support. Many mobile phones come with Bluetooth nowadays, and an increasing number of notebook computers do, too. It's also possible to buy very inexpensive Bluetooth dongles that attach to the USB port of your computer.

Bluetooth hardware is automatically recognized under Fedora, and the low-level driver software is installed by default. Therefore, all you normally need to do is install the software that provides the Bluetooth functionality you require.

Pairing Bluetooth Devices

When two pieces of Bluetooth-compatible hardware need to communicate on a regular basis, they can *pair* together. This means that they trust each other, so you don't need to authorize every attempt at communication between the devices.

Pairing is very simple in practice and works on the principle of a shared personal ID number (PIN). The first Bluetooth device generates the PIN, and then asks the second Bluetooth device to confirm it. Once the user types in the PIN, the devices are paired.

Pairing is easily accomplished under Fedora and doesn't require any additional software. As an example, we paired our Fedora test PC to a Motorola A780 mobile phone. It's easiest to initiate pairing on the phone, which should then autosense the PC's Bluetooth connection. On the Motorola A780, the Bluetooth manager autosensed the Fedora PC, which was identified as `localhost.localdomain-0`. On clicking Bond on the phone, we were prompted to enter a PIN.

To make pairing work, you need to edit a couple of files, so let's begin.

1. Open a Terminal window and type the following:

   ```
   su -
   [Enter password]
   cd /etc/bluetooth/
   ```

2. Now type `gedit hcid.conf` at the terminal and look for the line that reads `passkey "BlueZ";`. This is the default PIN under Fedora. Many phones only allow numeric values to be used as PINs. This is the case with the Motorola A780, so we changed the PIN to 55555. The line now reads `passkey "55555";`.

3. Next you need to edit the `/etc/bluetooth/rfcomm.conf` file. Type `gedit rfcomm.conf` at the terminal and look for the line `# bind no;` Remove the # and replace `no` with `yes` such that the line now reads `bind yes;`.

You now have to restart the Bluetooth service, so type the command `service bluetooth restart` (you need to be root to run this command) and press Enter. This will restart Fedora's Bluetooth service to take into account your reconfiguration.

Using the Bluetooth Preferences dialog box (System ➤ Preferences ➤ Internet and Network ➤ Bluetooth Preferences), you can specify a name for your Bluetooth adapter.

Transferring Files Between Bluetooth Devices

If you own a Bluetooth-equipped camera phone, you might be used to transferring pictures to your computer using Bluetooth. It's by far the easiest way of getting pictures off the phone and avoids the need for USB cables or card readers.

In order to transfer files via Bluetooth, you'll need to install some additional software from the Fedora repositories. If you haven't yet configured Pirut Package Manager, see the "Setting Up Online Software Repositories" section earlier in this chapter. Then open Pirut Package Manager (Applications ➤ Add/Remove Software). Click the Search button and enter **gnome-bluetooth** as a search term. In the list of results, click the check box alongside the entry, and then click Apply.

You should now find a new entry on the Applications ➤ System Tools menu: Bluetooth File Sharing.

The following instructions detail how to transfer any kind of file to and from your PC using Bluetooth. Once again, we use a Motorola A780 in the examples, but the instructions should work with any phone, or even any Bluetooth device capable of sending and receiving files.

■**Note** Some phones refuse to transfer files unless the phone and computer are paired, so follow the instructions in the previous section first.

Sending Files to a Fedora PC

Follow these steps to send files from a Bluetooth device to your PC:

1. Select Applications ➤ System Tools ➤ Bluetooth File Sharing. Nothing will appear to have happened, but in fact a new icon will have been added to the notification area. This indicates that your computer is ready for incoming Bluetooth connections.

2. On the Bluetooth device from which you wish to send the file, start the file transfer.

3. When the file transfer is initiated, a dialog box will appear on your computer asking if you wish to accept the file. Click OK. (If the two devices are paired, the file transfer may happen instantly without the confirmation dialog box.) The file will be saved to your /home directory.

Sending Files from a Fedora PC to Another Device

The easiest way to send files from your PC to a Bluetooth device is to right-click the file you wish to transfer and click Send To ➤ Bluetooth. To send multiple files at once, you can select multiple files, right-click any one, and choose Send To ➤ Bluetooth.

Using a Bluetooth Keyboard or Mouse

You may find that your Bluetooth-equipped keyboard or mouse works automatically under Fedora. However, if not, you may find the following instructions useful:

1. Open a GNOME Terminal window (Applications ➤ System Tools ➤ Terminal) and type `hcitool scan`.

2. Your Bluetooth keyboard or mouse should be identified in the results (ignore any other devices that might appear in the list). If not, make sure it isn't in sleep mode. You might also have to press a button on the device for it to be made visible.

3. Alongside the entry for the keyboard or mouse will be a MAC address—a series of numbers like 00:12:62:A5:60:F7.

4. In the GNOME Terminal window, type the following:

   `hidd --connect xx:xx:xx:xx:xx:xx`

   Replace xx:xx:xx:xx:xx:xx with the series of numbers you discovered in the previous step.

5. You should now find that your keyboard or mouse works under Fedora. You now need to make sure your mouse or keyboard works every time you boot your computer, so you'll need to edit the Fedora Bluetooth configuration file. Type the following in the GNOME Terminal window to open the configuration file in Gedit:

   `su -c 'gedit /etc/default/bluez-utils'`

6. Search for the line that reads HIDD_ENABLED=0 and change it to HIDD_ENABLED=1.

7. Beneath this will be a line that begins `HIDD_OPTIONS=`. Change this so that it reads like this:

   `HIDD_OPTIONS="--connect xx:xx:xx:xx:xx:xx --server"`

   Once again, `xx:xx:xx:xx:xx:xx` should be replaced with the MAC number you discovered earlier.

8. If you find that the keyboard or mouse doesn't connect upon reboot, try step 7 again, but this time change the `HIDD_OPTIONS` line so that it reads like this (again replacing `xx:xx:xx:xx:xx:xx` with the MAC address you discovered earlier):

   `HIDD_OPTIONS="-i xx:xx:xx:xx:xx:xx --server"`

9. Save the file and reboot to see if the mouse or keyboard is working.

■**Tip** If you want to quickly connect a Bluetooth keyboard or mouse to your computer, but don't need to make it permanent, just open a GNOME Terminal window (Applications ➤ System Tools ➤ Terminal) and type `hidd --search`.

Configuring Sound Cards

Generally speaking, your sound card shouldn't require any additional configuration and should work immediately after you install Fedora. The icon for the volume control applet is located at the top right of the Fedora desktop, and it offers a quick way to control the master volume.

However, if your sound card offers more than stereo output, such as multiple-speaker surround sound, then it's necessary to take some simple steps to allow full control of the hardware:

1. Right-click the Volume Control icon (the one that looks like a speaker) and select Open Volume Control.

2. In the dialog box that appears, click Edit, and then click Preferences.

3. The Volume Control Preferences dialog box appears, as shown in Figure 8-8. Select the sliders that you wish to be visible.

4. When you've finished, click the Close button.

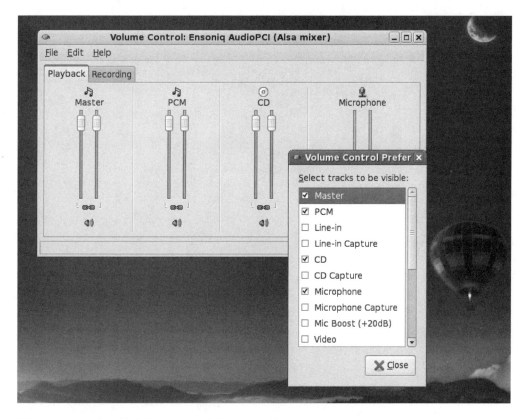

Figure 8-8. *You can add sliders to control all aspects of your sound card's output.*

Summary

In this chapter, you learned how to set up just about every piece of hardware you might have attached to your computer. Additionally, we looked at configuring various software components within your Fedora setup that are vital for its correct functioning.

We stepped through getting online with Fedora (including joining a wireless network), configuring e-mail, adding a printer, setting up online software repositories, setting up a digital camera, configuring a 3D graphics card, and much more.

In Chapter 9, we move on to look at how you can ensure that your system is secure and protected against attacks.

How to Secure Your Computer

Linux is widely considered one of the most secure operating systems around. On a basic level, Linux is built from the ground up to be fundamentally sound, and it forces users to work with security in mind. For instance, it enforces the system of ordinary users who are limited in what they can do, thus making it harder for virus infections to occur.

In addition, Linux contains a firewall that is hard-wired into the kernel. It's called iptables (www.netfilter.org/), and is considered among the best by practically all computer security experts. Not only that, but it can protect your home PC just as well as it can protect the most powerful supercomputer. But, as with many Linux kernel components, iptables is difficult to use. It requires in-depth knowledge of how networks operate and an ability to hack configuration files, both of which are beyond the skills of many ordinary computer users. Fortunately, several programs act as interfaces to iptables and make it simple to operate (or at least as simple as any equivalent Windows-based software firewall, such as Zone Labs's ZoneAlarm).

As we saw in the "Post-Install Configuration" section of Chapter 5, Fedora allows you to configure and install a firewall. Irrespective of whether you install the firewall and what settings you use, you can use Fedora's Security Level Configuration tool (System ➤ Administration ➤ Firewall and SELinux) to change the firewall settings. This tool is somewhat primitive, in that it doesn't allow for greater control on the various settings.

However, configuring the firewall with a program like Firestarter, which we examine later in this chapter, can be done so quickly and with such little effort that there's no reason *not* to make use of the Linux firewall.

In this chapter, you'll learn how to configure the Linux firewall, but first, you'll spend some time examining more basic security concepts. Following that, we'll look at some elementary steps that you can take to protect your system.

Windows Security vs. Linux Security

If you've switched to Fedora from Windows, there's a very good chance that the security failings of Windows featured in your decision. By any measure, Microsoft's record on security within its products is appalling. A new and serious security warning appears seemingly on an ongoing basis, and a new and devastating virus makes news headlines with similar frequency (usually described as "a PC virus" rather than what it actually is: a Windows virus).

One argument is that Windows is the target of so many viruses merely because it's so popular. Although it's true that some of the underground crackers who write viruses dislike Microsoft, there's also little doubt that Windows has more than its fair share of security issues.

The situation is certainly getting better but, even so, Microsoft's last operating system, Windows XP, provides many good examples of why it's an easy target. Upon installation, the default user is given root powers. True, a handful of tasks can be performed only by the genuine administrator, but the default user can configure hardware, remove system software, and even wipe every file from the hard disk if she pleases. Of course, you would never intentionally damage your own system, but computer attackers use various techniques to get you to run malicious software (by pretending it's a different file, for example) or by simply infecting your computer across the Internet without your knowledge, which is how most worms work. Microsoft Vista, the latest operating system offering from Microsoft, tries to curb some of these defects through improved security measures such as user account control.

Viruses and worms also usually take advantage of security holes within Windows software. As just one example, a famous security hole within Outlook Express allowed a program attached to an e-mail message to run when the user simply clicked a particular message to view it. In other words, infecting a Windows machine was as easy as sending someone an e-mail message!

It's a different story with Linux. Viruses and worms are far rarer than they are on Windows. In fact, the total number of viruses and worms that have been found in the wild infecting Linux systems number far less than 100 (one report published in 2003 put the number at 40, and the number is unlikely to have grown much since then). Compare that to Windows, where according to the Sophos antivirus labs (www.sophos.com/), approximately 1,000 new viruses are discovered *every month*! The Sophos antivirus product now guards against about 100,000 viruses.

■**Note**   The high number of Windows viruses may be due to the quantity of Windows PCs out there. After all, for a virus to spread, it needs computers to infect, and it won't have trouble finding other Windows computers.

But while we would love to say that security holes are not found on Linux, the sad truth is that they're a fact of life for users of every operating system. Many so-called rootkits are available, generated by members of underground cracking groups. These are specialized software toolkits that aim to exploit holes within the Linux operating system and its software.

The bottom line is that while writing a virus or worm for Linux is much harder than doing the same thing on Windows, all Linux users should spend time defending their system and *never* assume that they're safe.

Root and Ordinary Users

As we've mentioned in earlier chapters, Linux makes use of something called the *root* user account. This is sometimes referred to as the *superuser* account, and that gives you an idea of its purpose in life: the root user has unrestricted access to all aspects of the system. The root user can delete, modify, or view any file, as well as alter hardware settings.

Linux systems also have ordinary user accounts, which are limited in what they can do. Such users are limited to saving files in their own directory within the /home directory (although the system is usually configured so that an ordinary user can read files outside the /home directory, too). But an ordinary Fedora user cannot delete or modify files other than those that he created or for which he has explicitly been given permission to modify by someone else.

On most Linux systems, it's possible to type root at the login prompt and, after providing the correct password, actually log in as root and perform system maintenance tasks. Regular users can also borrow superuser powers whenever they're required. For this to happen, they still need to provide the root login password. With desktop programs, they are prompted to enter the root password, but at the command prompt, users need to use the su - command to inherit superuser privileges.

■**Note** Often, people associate the `su` command with *superuser*. The *su* actually stands for *switch user* or *substitute user*. The `su` command can be used to inherit any users' privileges.

Most key operating system files "belong" to root, which is to say that only someone with superuser powers or the root user can alter them. Ordinary users are simply unable to modify or delete these system files, as shown in Figure 9-1. This is a powerful method of protecting the operating system configuration from accidental or even deliberate damage.

■**Note** Along with the root and ordinary user accounts, there is a third type of Linux account, which is similar to a limited user account, except that it's used by the system for various tasks. These user accounts are usually invisible to ordinary users and work in the background. For example, the shutdown subsystem has its own user account that Fedora uses to shutdown Fedora. The concepts of users and files are discussed in more depth in Chapter 14.

ARE YOU A CRACKER OR A HACKER?

Linux users are often described as *hackers*. This doesn't mean they maliciously break into computers or write viruses. It's simply using the word *hacker* in its original sense from the 1970s, when it described a computer enthusiast who was interested in exploring the capabilities of computers. Many of the people behind multinational computing corporations started out as hackers. Examples are Steve Wozniak, a cofounder of Apple Computer, and Bill Joy, cofounder of Sun Microsystems.

The word *hacker* is believed to derive from model train enthusiasts who "hacked" train tracks together as part of their hobby. When computing became popular in the early 1970s, several of these enthusiasts also became interested in computing, and the term was carried across with them.

However, in recent years, the media has subverted the term *hacker* to apply to an individual who breaks into computer systems. This was based on ignorance, and many true hackers find the comparison extremely offensive. Because of this, the term *cracker* was invented to clearly define an individual who maliciously attacks computers.

So, don't worry if an acquaintance describes herself as a Linux hacker, or tells you that she has spent the night hacking. Many Linux types use the term as a badge of honor.

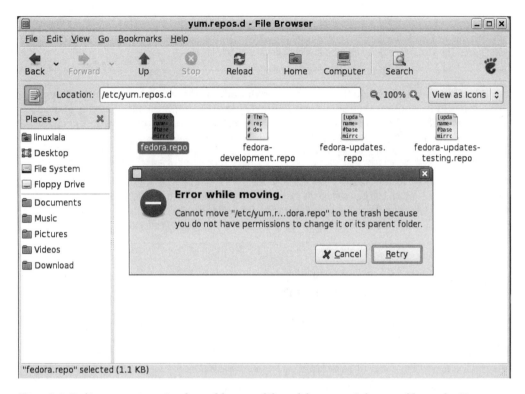

Figure 9-1. *Ordinary users are simply unable to modify or delete essential system files under Linux.*

Common-Sense Security

As you start to understand how Fedora works, you'll become more and more aware of common-sense methods that will protect your system. However, we'll outline a few of these now to get you started:

Entering your password: Be very wary if you're asked to enter the root password. You'll be asked to provide the root password when following many of the configuration steps within this book, for example, and this is acceptable and safe. But if you're asked to do so out of the blue, then you should be suspicious. If the root password prompt dialog box appears when you run a file that shouldn't really need root permissions, such as an MP3 or OpenOffice.org file, then you should treat the situation with caution. Each time the root password dialog appears (shown in Figure 9-2), you should read what it says carefully. It often informs you why the root password is required.

Installing new software: Be careful in choosing programs to download and install. Because Linux works on the basis of open source code, anyone can theoretically tamper with a program and then offer it for download to the unwary. This very rarely happens in real life. Even so, it's wise to avoid downloading programs from unofficial sources, such as web sites you find online via a search engine and whose authenticity you cannot totally trust. Instead, get software from the web site of the people who made it in the first place or, ideally, from the official Fedora software repositories or other trusted repositories (discussed in Chapter 8).

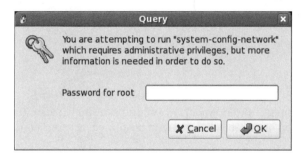

Figure 9-2. *Beware if you're asked to type your password out of the blue or for no apparent reason.*

Updating your system: Always ensure that your system software is completely up to date. As with Windows, many Fedora programs have bugs that lead to security holes. Crackers target such vulnerabilities. Downloading the latest versions of Fedora software ensures that you not only get the latest features, but also that any critical security holes are patched. As with most versions of Linux, updating Fedora is easy and, of course, it's also free of charge. You'll learn how to get online updates in the next section.

Locking up your PC: Limit who has physical access to your computer. Any Fedora system can be compromised by a simple floppy boot disk, by a LiveCD distribution, or from the GRUB boot loader. Booting a PC using such disks gives anyone complete root access to your system's files, with no limitations. This is for obvious reasons; the idea of a boot disk is to let you fix your PC should something go wrong, and you cannot do this if you're blocked from accessing certain files. When Linux is used on servers that hold confidential data, it's not uncommon for the floppy and CD-ROM drives to be removed, thus avoiding booting via a boot disk. Such computers are also usually locked away in a room or even in a cupboard, denying physical access to the machine.

Securing GRUB

The GRUB boot loader has a security feature that disallows people from using it to become the root user. The GRUB boot loader can be used to enter Fedora as the root user, without ever having to enter a password. To do this, at the GRUB menu, highlight the Fedora entry and press E. This allows you to edit the entry. Highlight the kernel entry using the arrow keys and press E again. Now type the word `single` at the end of the line, as follows:

```
rhgb quiet single
```

Now press Enter and then B to boot into Fedora. You will soon be dropped to the root shell. There will be no graphical desktop, but you will have complete access to the system.

To stop this from happening, you can password protect the GRUB boot loader such that you are prompted to enter a password to boot into Fedora, or even if you wish to edit the GRUB entries. Follow these steps to create a GRUB password:

1. Open a terminal (Applications ➤ System Tools ➤ Terminal).

2. Run the command `/sbin/grub-md5-crypt`.

3. You will be asked for a password. This will be used on the GRUB boot loader, so be careful of what you use.

4. You will be invited to enter the password again. This is to ensure that you didn't mistype the first time:

```
[root@localhost ~]# grub-md5-crypt
Password:
Retype password:
$1$diwIw1$I5iFKODj2Ve99FOLwr5.A/
```

5. The last line in the preceding listing is the encrypted form of the password typed in. The encrypted string might have a dot or a slash at the end, as in the preceding case. This is part of the encrypted password.

6. From the terminal, run the command gedit /boot/grub/grub.conf and enter the encrypted string under the initrd line, like so:

```
title Fedora Core (2.6.18-1.2798.fc6)
        root (hd0,0)
        kernel /vmlinuz-2.6.18-1.2798.fc6 ro root=/dev/VolGroup00/LogVol00 rhgb quiet
        initrd /initrd-2.6.18-1.2798.fc6.img
password --md5 $1$diwIw1$I5iFKODj2Ve99FOLwr5.A/
```

7. Save the file and close Gedit. Now whenever you boot into Fedora or try to edit the GRUB entry, you'll be asked to enter the password. Just type in the original password and press Enter. GRUB will then compare the password with the encrypted string, and if they match, you will be able to boot into Fedora.

■**Caution** Remember that anyone with physical access to your computer can still bypass the GRUB security with the aid of a LiveCD Linux distribution. A BIOS password, however, can render a LiveCD distribution useless for this purpose.

WHERE'S THE ANTIVIRUS?

At first glance, it may appear that there are very few Linux antivirus programs. Actually, many of these exist, but they're designed to work on server computers and primarily guard against Windows viruses, in addition to the handful of Linux viruses. The idea is that they protect Windows users who access the server.

Very few antivirus products are aimed at the Linux desktop. However, one example includes F-Secure's Anti-Virus for Linux Workstations. This costs around $60 dollars and is available from www.f-secure.com/products/fsavcsl.html. AVG (www.grisoft.com/) and Kaspersky (http://www.kaspersky.com/linux) also produce Linux workstation versions of their antivirus products.

The main issue with all of these programs is that they're not open source, as with most of the Linux software included in Fedora. If you absolutely must have your entire system running free software, consider ClamAV (www.clamav.net/). This is a product designed to work on Linux servers but is flexible enough to run on desktop computers, too. ClamAV is included in the Fedora software repository, and so is available via Pirut Package Manager. Be aware that ClamAV is a command-line program, however. You'll need to read its man page to learn how it works. In addition, you might choose to read the online documentation at www.clamav.net/doc/.

Online Updates

The Fedora notification area (the equivalent of the Windows system tray) contains a program called Puplet that automatically monitors the package repositories and tells you when updates are available.

Puplet runs each time you boot Fedora. If there are updates available, an icon appears in the notification area that informs you of available updates. In addition, each time you boot, you will see a speech bubble telling you whether updates are available.

You can apply all the updates by clicking the icon and selecting Apply. You can use the Pup package updater program to see a list of all the available updates, as shown in Figure 9-3, click Applications ➤ System Tools ➤ Software Updater (you'll be asked for the root password). After selecting a package, you can click Update Details to see details about the update—whether it is a bug fix, a feature upgrade, a new version of the software, or security fix. Additionally, Update Details informs you whether an update requires you to restart the computer.

By default, all updates are set to be installed. Remove the check from the check box if you don't want to apply an update. Clicking the Apply Updates button will install all the selected updates.

Figure 9-3. *You'll be informed if your system is in need of updates, and Pup can take care of everything for you.*

Be aware that some updates can be large and might take some time to download, particularly if you're doing it for the first time after installing Fedora.

Once the downloads have finished, you probably won't need to reboot unless the kernel file has been updated.

The Fedora Firewall

A *firewall* is a set of programs that protects your PC when it's online. It does this by watching what data attempts to enter your PC from the Internet and allowing in only what it is sure is secure (which usually is what you've asked for). It also attempts to close off various aspects of your Internet connection so that crackers don't have a way in should they target your system.

Although Fedora includes a powerful firewall in the form of iptables, you'll also need a program that can manage it. Here, we'll show you how to use Firestarter, available from the Fedora software repository, for this purpose. Together with the built-in firewall, this really does provide industrial-level protection.

The benefit of configuring the firewall is that even if your system has security vulnerabilities because of buggy software, crackers will find it a lot harder to exploit them across the Internet. When someone attempts to probe your system, it will appear to be virtually invisible.

■**Caution** Although software firewalls such as the one built into Linux offer a high level of protection, it's best to use them in concert with a hardware firewall, such as that provided by most DSL/cable broadband routers (curiously, some of these routers actually use Linux's iptables software as well). Many security experts agree that relying solely on a software firewall to protect a PC affords less than the best level of protection.

Installing Firestarter

Let's get started by downloading and installing Firestarter. Follow these steps:

1. Select System ➤ Applications ➤ Add/Remove Software. Click the Search button and enter **firestarter** as a search term. In the list of results, locate the program and click the check box. Then choose to install the package.

2. You'll find Firestarter under the Applications ➤ System Tools menu. Alternatively, you can start Firestarter from the command-line. Open a terminal and type **su -c 'firestarter'**. When you run Firestarter for the first time, it will walk you through a wizard.

3. Click the Forward button to continue the wizard beyond the introductory page.

4. The first step asks which network interface Firestarter should configure, as shown in Figure 9-4. If you use an Ethernet card, have a wireless card, or attach a broadband modem directly to your computer, the answer will probably be eth0 or wlan0. However, if you use a modem, the answer is ppp0.

5. Put a check in the "IP address is assigned via DHCP" check box, *unless you're using a modem*.

6. You're asked if you want to enable Internet connection sharing. This allows you to turn your computer into an Internet router and can be very useful in certain circumstances. You can activate this later on by running the wizard again (to rerun the wizard, simply click Firewall on Firestarter's main window, and then click Run Wizard).

7. Save your settings. The Firestarter main window then opens.

■**Note** If you haven't enabled your firewall, click System ➤ Administration ➤ Firewall and SELinux, and choose to enable the firewall.

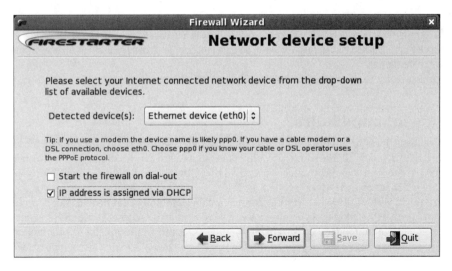

Figure 9-4. *Firestarter includes a wizard to walk you through the basics of firewall configuration.*

Configuring Firestarter

Firestarter works by controlling the data that goes in and out of your computer via your Internet or network connection. By default, it blocks every type of uninvited inbound connection but allows every type of outbound connection. This needs some explanation.

Whenever you click a link on a web page, your computer sends a request for data to the web server hosting the web page. Within a few milliseconds, that data will be sent to your computer. This is an *inbound* data connection. The Linux firewall is clever enough to realize that the data was requested by you, so it is allowed through. However, any uninvited connections are turned away. If, out of the blue, someone attempts to connect to your computer via the popular Secure Shell (SSH) tool, as just one example, he won't be allowed to make that connection. This is a good thing because it makes your computer secure. Crackers are turned away whenever they try to connect, no matter *how* they try to connect.

But in some circumstances, allowing uninvited connections is useful. For example, if you create a shared folder for other computers in your office to connect to, they will frequently make uninvited inbound connections to your computer. And if you want to make use of SSH to connect to your computer remotely, you will need to allow such incoming connections. Therefore, Firestarter lets you allow certain types of inbound connections.

Outbound traffic is any kind of data originating on your computer that is sent out on the network and/or Internet. By default, Firestarter allows out all data, no matter what it is. This is described as a *permissive* policy. But Firestarter can be configured to block all outgoing connections *apart from those you opt to allow through*. This is described as a *restrictive* policy and can be useful in blocking certain types of programs that "phone home" with personal data about you, such as spyware. It can also prevent certain types of viruses and worms from spreading. You are much safer on Linux than Windows considering that spyware is very rare in Linux.

The downside is that you must configure Firestarter to take into account every type of outgoing data connection, such as those for web browsers, instant messaging programs, and so on. You can configure Firestarter by clicking the Policy tab in the main program window. Click the Editing drop-down list and choose to configure either the inbound traffic policy or the outbound traffic policy.

■**Note** Firestarter is used only to configure the built-in firewall and doesn't need to be running for the firewall to work. Once you've finished configuration, you can quit the program. You'll need to use it again only if you wish to reconfigure the firewall.

Setting Inbound Rules

For most users, Firestarter's default inbound traffic policy will be perfectly acceptable. It configures the firewall to disallow all uninvited incoming data, apart from certain diagnostic tools, such as ping, traceroute, and so on. You can choose to disallow those as well, as described shortly in the "Turning Off Diagnostic Services" section.

You might wish to allow an incoming connection if you intend to connect to your computer via SSH from a remote location or if you have a shared folder created for other computers in your office. It's a must if you're running the BitTorrent file sharing application. Additionally, if you run a web, e-mail, or other type of server on your computer, you will need to allow the correct type of incoming connection here.

Here's how to set inbound connection rules:

1. In the Firestarter main window, click the Policy tab. Select Inbound Traffic Policy in the Editing drop-down list.

2. Right-click in the second box on the Policy tab (with the headings Allow Service / Port / For), and then select Add Rule.

3. The Add New Inbound Rule dialog box appears. In the Name drop-down list, select the type of outgoing connection you want to allow, as shown in Figure 9-5. To allow others to access shared folders on your computer, select Samba (SMB). To allow SSH or BitTorrent connections to your computer, select the relevant entry from the list. Selecting the service will automatically fill in the Port box, which you shouldn't alter unless you know exactly what you're doing.

4. If you know the IP address of the computer that's going to make the incoming connection, you can click the IP, Host or Network radio button, and then type in that address. However, the default of Anyone will allow anyone using any IP address to connect to your computer.

5. Click Add. Back in the main Firestarter window, click the Apply Policy button.

■**Note** You'll need to return to Firestarter whenever you activate new services on your computer. For example, in Chapter 12, we will look at accessing Windows shares across a network, and you'll need to enable SMB incoming and outgoing access for this to work. In Chapter 33, we will look at using the SSH service, which will have to be allowed through the firewall. In other words, securing your computer isn't something you can do once and then forget about. It's a continual process.

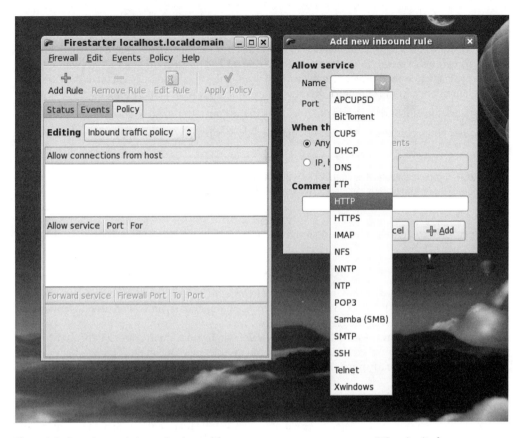

Figure 9-5. *Creating an inbound rule enables computers to connect to your PC uninvited.*

Setting Outbound Rules

By default, Firestarter allows all types of outgoing connections and, as with its incoming connections policy, this is by no means a bad choice for the average user. It's certainly the option that involves the least fuss. However, by opting to go with a restrictive traffic policy, you can completely control what kind of data leaves your computer. Any type of data connection that isn't authorized will be refused; as far as the program sending the data is concerned, it will be as if your computer did not have a network or Internet connection.

Here's how to set outbound connection rules:

1. In the Firestarter main window, click the Policy tab. Select Outbound Traffic Policy in the Editing drop-down list.

2. Click the Restrictive by Default, Whitelist Traffic radio button.

3. In the second empty box at the bottom of the Policy tab, right-click and select Add Rule.

4. The Add New Outbound Rule dialog box appears. Select the type of data connection you wish to allow. At the very least, you should select HTTP. This will allow your web browser to operate correctly (it's also needed to allow the Pirut Package Manager and Package Updater programs to work). You should also add a rule for POP3 and another for SMTP, without which your e-mail program won't work. Selecting the type of service will fill in the Port box automatically. You shouldn't alter this unless you know what you're doing.

5. Click the Add button to add the rule. Back in the Firestarter main window, click Apply Policy.

6. Test your settings with a program that uses the services you've just authorized.

■Caution If you created an inbound rule, you'll need to create a matching outbound rule. If you created an incoming rule for BitTorrent, for example, you'll need to create an outgoing rule for BitTorrent, too.

You can delete both incoming and outgoing rules by right-clicking their entries in the list.

Turning Off Diagnostic Services

Certain network tools can be misused by crackers in order to break into a computer or just cause it problems. In the past, the traceroute and ping tools, among others, have been used to launch denial-of-service (DoS) attacks against computers.

Fedora is set to allow these tools to operate by default. If you want to adopt a belts-and-braces approach to your computer's security, you can opt to disable them. If you don't know what ping and traceroute are, you're clearly not going to miss them, so there will be no harm in disallowing them. Here's how:

1. In the Firestarter main window, click Edit ➤ Preferences.

2. On the left side of the Preferences window, click ICMP Filtering. Then click the "Enable ICMP filtering" check box, as shown in Figure 9-6. *Don't* put a check in any of the boxes underneath, unless you specifically want to *permit* one of the services.

3. Click the Accept button to finish.

PARANOIA AND SECURITY

There's a fine line between security and paranoia. Using Firestarter gives you the opportunity to ensure your system is secure, without needing to constantly reassess your system for threats and live in fear.

When considering your system security, remember that most burglars don't enter a house through the front door. Most take advantage of an open window or poor security elsewhere in the house. In other words, when configuring your system's security, you should always select every option and extra layer of security, even if it might not appear to be useful. You should lock every door and close every window, even if you don't think an attacker would ever use them.

Provided a security setting doesn't impact your ordinary use of the computer, you should select it. For example, deactivating the ping response of your computer might sound like a paranoid action, but it's useful on several levels. First, it means your computer is less easy to detect when it's online. Second, and equally important, it means that if there's ever a security flaw in the ping tool (or any software connected with it), you'll be automatically protected.

This illustrates how you must think when configuring your system's security. Try to imagine every situation that might arise. Remember that you can never take too many precautions!

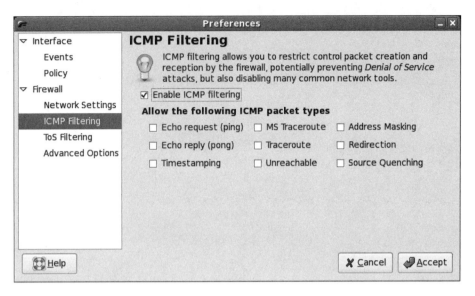

Figure 9-6. *By deactivating traceroute, ping, and other services, you can add extra protection to your PC.*

Summary

In this chapter, we've looked at what threats your system faces and how security holes can be exploited by malicious interests. You learned about measures you can take to protect your system, such as updating it online and configuring the system's firewall. We also discussed some common-sense rules you can follow to keep your system safe.

In the next chapter, we move on to looking at how your Fedora system can be personalized and how to set up everything to suit your own preferences.

■■■

Personalizing Fedora: Getting Everything Just Right

If you've read this book from Chapter 1, by this stage, you no doubt have become comfortable with Fedora. You've started to realize its advantages and are on the way to making it your operating system of choice.

But things might still not be quite right. For instance, you might find the color scheme is not to your tastes. Or perhaps the mouse cursor moves a little too fast (or too slowly). Maybe you simply want to stamp your own individuality on your system to make it your very own.

That's what this chapter is all about. We look at personalizing Fedora so that you're completely happy with your user experience.

Changing the Look and Feel

Fedora is similar to Windows in many ways, but the developers behind it introduced improvements and tweaks that many claim make the software easier to use. For example, Fedora offers multiple virtual desktops—long considered a very useful user interface feature that seems to have passed Microsoft by. It also moves the programs menu to the top of the screen, leaving the whole width of the screen at the bottom to display taskbar buttons. This is very sensible, because the buttons don't look cramped when more than a handful of applications are open. However, if you're not satisfied with Fedora's out-of-the-box look and feel, you can change it.

You might be used to changing the desktop colors or wallpaper under Windows, but Fedora goes to extremes and lets you alter the look and feel of the entire desktop. Everything from the styling of the program windows to the desktop icons can be altered quickly and easily.

Altering the Theme

Fedora refers to the look of the desktop as a *theme*. Because it's built on the GNOME desktop, Fedora allows you to radically personalize your desktop theme. Several different themes come with the distribution, and you can download many more themes. Each lets you change the way the windows look, including the buttons and the icon set (although some themes come without additional icons).

However, unlike Windows themes, most GNOME themes don't change the fonts used on the desktop, and the wallpaper and color scheme will probably remain broadly the same. You can change these manually, as described in the "Setting Font Preferences" and "Changing the Wallpaper" sections a bit later in this chapter.

To alter the theme, select System ➤ Preferences ➤ Look and Feel ➤ Theme. Then it's simply a matter of choosing a theme from the list in the Theme Preferences dialog box, as shown in

Figure 10-1. A useful hint is to open a Nautilus file browser window in the background (Places ➤ Desktop), so you can see how the changes will affect a typical window.

Note The default Fedora theme is called Fedora. It is based on the Clearlooks theme, which itself was based on the original Bluecurve Red Hat theme.

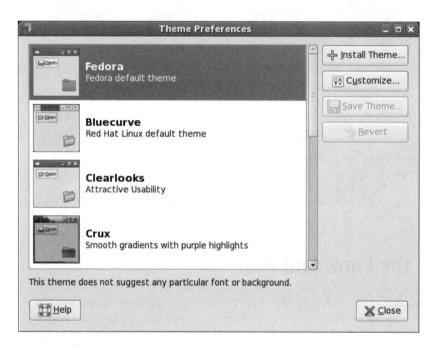

Figure 10-1. *Fedora comes with several theme choices.*

Clearlooks and Mist are two popular themes, largely because they're simple and uncompli-cated. Remember that you'll be working with the theme on a daily basis, so it should be practical and not too distracting. Those miniature close, minimize, and maximize buttons might look stylish, but they're useless if they're so small that you can't reliably click them with your mouse.

As well as changing the overall theme, you can also modify individual theme components, and even download more theme components.

Changing Individual Theme Components

You can alter the three aspects that constitute a GNOME theme: the *controls* (sometimes known as *widgets*), the *window borders*, and the *icons*. Controls are simply the elements you click within dialog boxes and windows: buttons, scroll bars, and so on. The window borders are, as seems obvious, the borders of program windows and dialog boxes, with particular attention paid to the top of the window, where the program name appears along with the minimize, maximize, and close buttons.

> **Note** To make matters a little confusing, some window borders have their own selection of close, minimize, and maximize controls, which can't be overridden with individual selections for controls.

To make changes to a theme, click the Theme Details button in the Theme Preferences dialog box (Figure 10-1), and then click each tab to see your choices, as shown in Figure 10-2. Unfortunately, there are no thumbnail previews of each style, but as soon as you click each option, it will be automatically applied to the currently open windows. To preview the effects fully, the best policy is to keep a Nautilus window open (Places ➤ Home Folder).

Figure 10-2. *You can create a theme by choosing you own controls, window borders, and icons.*

When you've made your choices, you can save the theme for further use. Simply click the Save Theme button in the Theme Preferences dialog box. You'll need to give the theme a name and, if you wish, a short description for future reference. If you don't save the theme, as soon as you select another one, the changes you've made will be lost.

Installing Additional Components

If you get tired of the built-in possibilities, you can download additional theme components, such as window borders and controls, to enhance your desktop experience. You have two ways of getting new themes:

- Download themes from the official Fedora repositories.
- Visit the GNOME Art web site (http://art.gnome.org/) and download items from there.

Downloading from the Fedora Repositories

To get theme components from the Fedora software repositories, use Pirut Package Manager. Setting up Pirut Package Manager to use the online repositories is described in Chapter 8.

Select System ➤ Administration ➤ Add/Remove Software, click the Search tab, and enter **gnome themes** as a search term. In the results, look for "gnome-theme-extras." This is a collection of some eye-catching metathemes for GNOME.

If you go this route, don't forget that you'll be downloading a theme component, not an entire theme. To use your new theme components, select System ➤ Preferences ➤ Look and Feel ➤ Theme, click the Theme Details button, and browse the various lists. You'd find several new options now available for you to use.

Downloading from the GNOME Art Web Site

Visiting the GNOME Art site (http://art.gnome.org), shown in Figure 10-3, gives you access to just about every theme ever created for GNOME. In fact, the site also contains wallpaper selections, icons, and much more besides. All of the offerings are free to use, and most of the packages are created by enthusiasts.

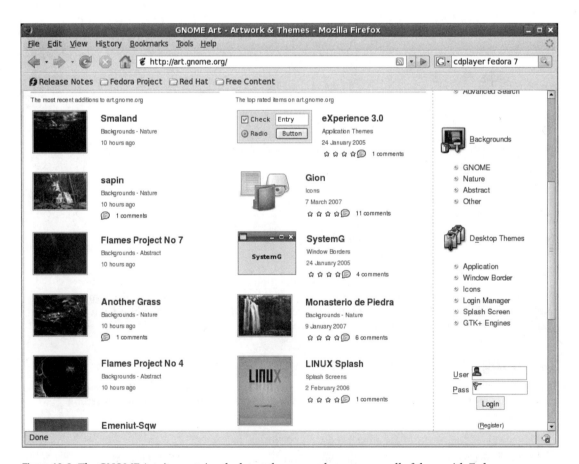

Figure 10-3. *The GNOME Art site contains the latest themes, and you can use all of them with Fedora.*

Installing new theme components is easy. If you wish to install a new window border, for example, click the link to browse the examples, and then when you find one you like, click to download it. It will be contained in a `.tar.gz` archive, but you don't need to unpack it. Simply select System ➤ Preferences ➤ Look and Feel ➤ Theme, and click the Install Theme button in the Theme Preferences dialog box. Then browse to the downloaded theme and click Open. You can delete the downloaded file when you're finished.

Note The same principle of sharing that underlines the GPL software license is also usually applied to themes. This means that one person can take a theme created by someone else, tweak it, and then release it as a new theme. This ensures constant innovation and improvement.

Changing the Wallpaper

The default Fedora wallpaper, Flying High, is a love-it-or-hate-it affair. There has been a lot of debate over the use of the dark colors, clouds, and balloons. Some believe that Fedora DNA, the wallpaper on Fedora's previous incarnation, was far more appropriate. But many have applauded the flying high metaphor, depicting Fedora's growth and evolution.

If you're one of those who prefer something different, it's easy to switch. Simply right-click the desktop and click Change Desktop Background. If you want to use a picture of your own as wallpaper, click the Add Wallpaper button, and then browse to its location.

In the Style drop-down list, you can select from the following choices:

Centered: This option places the wallpaper in the center of the screen. If the wallpaper is not big enough to fill the screen, a border appears around the edge. If it's bigger than the screen, the edges of the wallpaper are cropped off.

Fill Screen: This option forces the picture to fit the screen, including squashing or expanding it if necessary (known as *altering its aspect ratio*). If the wallpaper isn't in the same ratio as the screen, it will look distorted. Most digital camera shots should be OK, because they use the same 4:3 ratio as most monitors (although if you have a wide-screen monitor, a digital camera picture will be stretched horizontally).

Scaled: Like the Fill Screen option, this option enlarges the image if it's too small and shrinks it if it's too big, but it maintains the aspect ratio, thus avoiding distortion. However, if the picture is in a different aspect ratio than the monitor, it may have borders at the edges.

Zoom: Like the Fill Screen option, this option enlarges the images if it's too small. Unlike Scaled, it does not have any borders and it enlarges the images to the point that they fill up the entire screen. The image might get blurry because of the zoom.

Tiled: If the picture is smaller than the desktop resolution, this option simply repeats the picture (starting from the top left) until the screen is filled. This option is primarily designed for patterned graphics.

Don't forget that the GNOME Art web site (`http://art.gnome.org/`) offers many wallpaper packages for download.

Tip Looking for some good wallpaper? Visit Flickr (`www.flickr.com/`). This is a community photography site where many people make their pictures publicly available.

Setting Font Preferences

Fedora lets you change the fonts that are used throughout Fedora (referred to as *system fonts*). You can also alter how they're displayed.

To change a system font, select System ➤ Preferences ➤ Look and Feel ➤ Font. In the Font Preferences dialog box, shown in Figure 10-4, click the button next to the system font you want to change, and then choose from the list. You can also set the font point size so you can, for example, make the labels beneath icons easier to read.

By clicking the entries under the Font Rendering heading in the Font Preferences dialog box, you can change how fonts look on your monitor. This will alter the *antialiasing* and *hinting* of the font. Antialiasing softens the edges of each letter to make them appear less jagged. Hinting affects the spacing and shaping of the letters. Used together, they can make the onscreen text look more pleasant. Try each Font Rendering setting in sequence to see which looks best to you (the text in the dialog box will update automatically to show the changes). Nearly everyone with a TFT-based screen, including notebook users, finds the Subpixel smoothing option best.

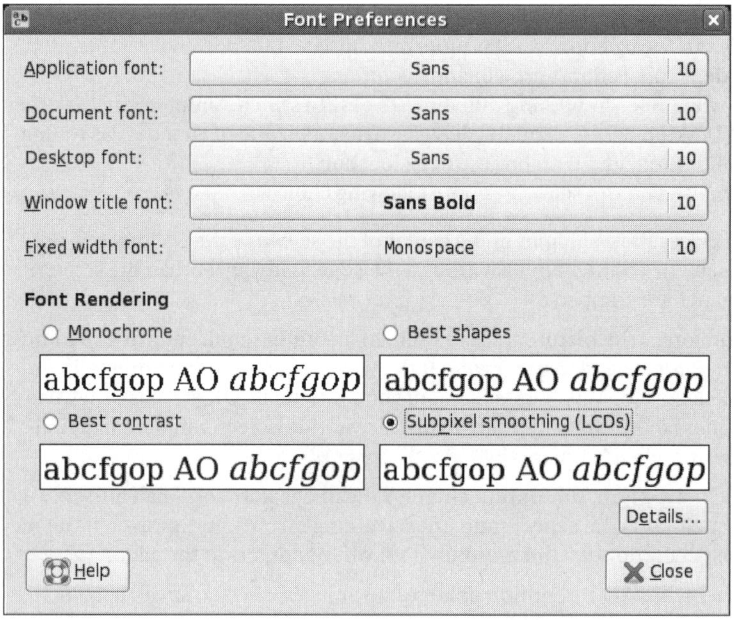

Figure 10-4. *You can alter the way fonts appear on the screen by using the Font Preferences dialog box.*

Configuring Input Devices

Mouse and key repeat speeds are personal to each user, and you may find the default Fedora settings not to your taste, particularly if you have a high-resolution mouse such as a gaming model. Fortunately, changing each setting is easy. You'll find the relevant options under the categorized System ➤ Preferences menu.

Configuring Mouse Options

Select System ➤ Preferences ➤ Hardware ➤ Mouse to open the Mouse Preferences dialog box, which has three tabs:

Buttons: This tab lets you set whether the mouse is to be used by a left-handed or right-handed person. Effectively, it swaps the functions of the right and left buttons. Beneath this is the double-click timeout setting. This is ideal for people who are less physically dexterous because the double-click speed can be slowed down. On the other hand, if you find yourself accidentally double-clicking items, you can speed it up.

Pointers: On this tab, you can select from any mouse cursor themes that are installed. You can also activate the Locate Pointer option, which causes a box to appear around the mouse cursor when you press the Ctrl key. This can help you find the cursor on a busy desktop.

Motion: This tab, shown in Figure 10-5, lets you alter the speed of the mouse pointer, as well as the drag-and-drop threshold. Changes are made as each setting is adjusted, so to test the new settings, simply move your mouse. Here's what the settings do:

- The Acceleration setting controls how fast the mouse moves. Whenever you move the mouse, the pointer on the screen moves a corresponding amount. However, the cursor actually increases in speed the more you move your hand (otherwise, you would need to drag your hand across the desk to get from one side of the screen to the other). This is referred to as *acceleration*. If you set the acceleration too high, the pointer will fly around the screen, seemingly unable to stop. If you set it too slow, you'll need to ramp the mouse several times to make it go anywhere.

- The Sensitivity setting controls how quickly the acceleration kicks in when you first move the mouse. Choosing a higher setting means that you can move the mouse relatively quickly before it starts to accelerate and cover more screen space. A low setting means that acceleration will begin almost as soon as you move the mouse. Higher sensitivity settings give you more control over the mouse, which can be useful if you use image-editing programs, for example.

- The Threshold setting determines the amount of mouse movement allowed in a click-and-drag maneuver before the item under the cursor is moved. This setting is designed for people who have limited dexterity and who might be unable to keep the mouse perfectly still when clicking or double-clicking an icon. In such cases, a large threshold value may be preferred.

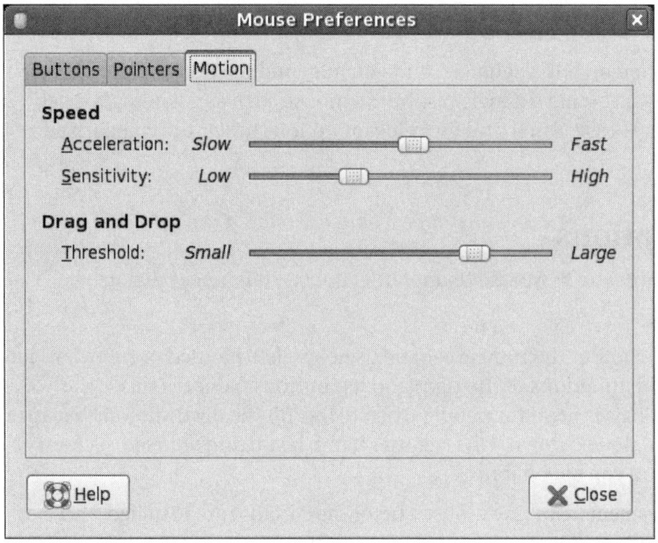

Figure 10-5. *The Mouse Preferences dialog box lets you tame that mouse.*

Changing Keyboard Settings

Select System ➤ Preferences ➤ Hardware ➤ Keyboard to open the Keyboard Preferences dialog box. This dialog box has four tabs:

Keyboard: Using the Keyboard tab, you can alter the rate of key repeat. This can be useful if you often find yourself holding down the Backspace key to delete a sentence; a shorter setting on the Delay slider and a faster setting on the Speed slider can help. However, if you get the settings wrong, you may find double characters creeping into your documents; typing an *f* may result in *ff*, for example. Beneath the Repeat Keys setting is the Cursor Blinking slider. Altering this may help if you sometimes lose the cursor in a document; a faster speed will mean that the cursor spends less time being invisible between flashes.

Layouts: On the Layouts tab, you can choose to add an alternative keyboard layout, as shown in Figure 10-6. For example, if you write in two different languages on your keyboard, it may be helpful to be able to switch between them. Click the Add button and select the second language from the list.

Layout Options: This tab lets you select from a variety of handy tweaks that affect how the keyboard works. For example, you can configure the Caps Lock key to act like a simple Shift key, or you can turn it off altogether. You can configure the Windows key so that it performs a different function, too. Put a check alongside the option you want after reading through the extensive list of options.

Typing Break: This tab features a function that can force you to stop typing after a predetermined number of minutes. It does this by blanking the screen and displaying a "Take a break!" message. Note that a notification area icon will appear before the break time to give you advanced warning of the lockout.

Figure 10-6. *You can have more than one language setting in place for a keyboard, which is handy if you need to type in a foreign language.*

Creating Keyboard Shortcuts

Fedora lets you define your own keyboard shortcuts for just about any action on the system. To create a shortcut, select System ➤ Preferences ➤ Personal ➤ Keyboard Shortcuts. In the dialog box, search through the list for the action you want to create a shortcut for, click it, and then press the key (or key combination) you want to use. For example, you might locate the Volume Up and Volume Down entries in the list, click each, and then press Ctrl+left arrow and Ctrl+right arrow. Then you will be able to turn the volume of your sound card up or down by holding down Ctrl and tapping the left or right arrow key, respectively.

■**Caution** Be careful not to assign a shortcut to a popular, frequently used key. It might be nice to make Totem Media Player appear when you hit the spacebar, for example, but that will mean that it will start up several times whenever you type a sentence in a word processor! Also be aware that some key combinations are used by applications. Within OpenOffice.org's Writer, for example, the Ctrl+left/right arrow key combination moves you from word to word in a paragraph. If you define those combinations as shortcuts, you will no longer have this functionality.

There are several excellent shortcuts that you can use, such as minimizing all open windows to show the desktop or bringing up your home folder at the stroke of a key.

Personalizing Login Options

You can even personalize the login screen under Fedora. This is known technically as the GNOME Display Manager, or GDM. To access its configuration options, select System ➤ Administration ➤ Login Screen. The dialog box has six tabs:

General: This tab lists the options that control the behavior of the login screen. For example, you can decide whether the password field should show circles or asterisks when you type, or choose to restart the X server with each login.

Local: In the Style drop-down list, you can choose the type of login screen: Themed Greeter, which includes the Fedora graphic; Plain Greeter, which is a basic login box into which you can type your details; or Plain with Face Browser, which allows users to click their photo, after which they're prompted to type in the password for their account. The Themed Greeter style is the default under Fedora, and it makes the standard login page appear. You can select from a couple of other themes from the list. Particularly handy is the Happy GNOME with Browser option, which shows a list of all users on your system during login. To log in, just click the appropriate entry and type the necessary password. You can even type your own welcome text by clicking the Custom radio button under Welcome Message. You can also activate the X Display Manager Control Protocol (XDMCP) for GDM (by clicking the Include Hostname Chooser menu item check box), which will let users log in graphically using GDM from a remote computer (this requires the remote system to be specially configured). Clicking the Add button lets you install a Themed Greeter theme from disk. You can download these from http://art.gnome.org/.

Remote: This tab offers you a drop-down list that lets you choose the type of greeter to be used for logging remotely into the machine.

Accessibility: You can customize sounds for various stages of login from here. You can specify sounds for successful login, for example.

Security: The Enable Automatic Login check box lets you do away with the login box completely and goes straight to the desktop from bootup. Simply put a check in the box and provide a username. This presents obvious security issues, but if you're the only person using the computer and if it's located in a secure location, you might want to choose this option. The Enable Timed Login option lets you select a user who will be logged in by default after a given period. This is useful if you want to present the opportunity to log in as a different user but also want to have the failsafe of logging in automatically, too. This tab lets you alter login settings that might present a security risk to your system.

Users: Here, you can specify which users are offered as choices within GDM if the Face Browser theme is activated. Bear in mind that Linux has many system user accounts that aren't designed to allow logins. By default, all users who have a password are displayed, which is the best way of working (the system accounts don't have passwords because they aren't login accounts). This raises a security issue. If the Happy GNOME with Browser theme is activated in the Local tab, you can enable the Face Browser, which will show a picture on the login screen. This is considered a security risk, because it removes the need for people to type in their usernames, thus potentially handing valuable information to hackers.

SETTING UP ASSISTIVE TECHNOLOGY SUPPORT

You might know about the Accessibility tools under Windows, which help people with special needs use the computer. It's possible to use an onscreen magnifier so that users can better see what they're typing or reading, for example.

Under the GNOME desktop, the Accessibility tools are referred to as Assistive Technology Support. To use them, you need to install additional software packages, and then enable them. Follow these steps:

1. Assuming the Pirut Package Manager is set up to use the online repositories (see Chapter 8), open the program (Applications ➤ Add/Remove Software).

2. Click the Search button and enter **gok** as a search term. In the list of results, click the check box alongside the **gok** entry, and then click Apply.

3. Click the Search button again and search for **festival**. Again, mark its entry for installation. Then click Apply.

4. Once the packages are installed, select System ➤ Preferences ➤ Personal ➤ Assistive Technology Support Preferences. Click the check box alongside Enable Assistive Technologies.

5. Choose from the list the features you would like to use. They will then start automatically the next time you log in. The options work as follows:

   • The Screenreader uses a speech synthesizer to announce whatever you click, as well as whatever you type.

   • The GNOME Onscreen Keyboard (GOK) can be used by a mouse, but is most useful when an alternative input device is used, such as a touch screen. As well as presenting a virtual keyboard, it shows the options on the screen as a large and easy-to-activate series of buttons. For more information, click the Help button when GOK starts.

   • The Magnifier divides the screen into two halves. The right side displays a magnified version of the left side.

Changing Your Login Picture

If you activate the Face Browser feature along with the Happy GNOME with Browser option, GDM will display a picture alongside your username on the login screen, as shown in Figure 10-7. You can then click this and type your password to log in. You might be familiar with a similar system under Windows XP.

You can choose your login picture by clicking System ➤ Preferences ➤ Personal ➤ About Me. Click the blank area to the left of your name to bring up the Select Image window. Fedora offers several pictures that you can choose from, or you can browse the file system to locate your own. Ideally, the image you choose should be square and 96 by 96 pixels, although if the picture is too large, it will be automatically scaled down.

Figure 10-7. *The Face Browser lets each user choose an icon to appear on the login screen.*

Adding and Removing Desktop Items

Virtually the entire Fedora desktop can be redesigned and restructured. You can move the Applications menu from the top of the screen to the bottom to be more like Windows, for example, or you can add numerous desktop shortcuts to popular applications and/or files.

Adding a Shortcut

Fedora's nearest equivalent to a Windows-style desktop shortcut is a *launcher*. An important difference, however, is that launchers are designed to run a certain command. Therefore, they can only point at programs (although you could create a launcher that contained a command chain required to run a particular program and file; to use The GIMP to open a picture, you might create a launcher that ran gimp picture.jpg, for example).

If you want to make a shortcut to a data file, such as a picture, you need to create a *link*. This is just as easy as creating a launcher.

Creating a Launcher

You can create a launcher two ways. One way is to simply click and drag an icon from one of the main menus to the desktop. This effectively copies the menu's launcher to the desktop, rather than creating a new launcher, but the effect is the same.

The other way to create a launcher is to right-click the desktop and select Create Launcher. In the Create Launcher dialog box, you need to fill in only the Name and Command fields; the others fields can be left blank. The Command field must contain a Linux executable program, command, or script. If you use a command-line program or script, you must select the Application in Terminal option from the Type drop-down list. This will open a GNOME Terminal window automatically and run the command or script within it. The terminal window will disappear as soon as the command has finished.

To choose an icon for your launcher, click the No Icon button in the Create Launcher dialog box. If you don't choose an icon, the stock GNOME one is used (the same icon used for unidentified and/or system files). You can select from several predefined icons or choose your own picture by clicking the Browse button, as shown in Figure 10-8.

Figure 10-8. *Creating a launcher is easy. Just fill in the Name and Command fields, and choose an icon.*

Creating a Link

Although you can create a link to a program, which will then work the same as a launcher, links are usually used to create shortcuts to files. If you then double-click the shortcut, the application associated with that file type will open the file. If you create a shortcut to a picture, for example, when you double-click it, the Eye of GNOME previewer will start.

To create a link, locate the file you want to create the link to, right-click it, and select Make Link. Then copy the new link to wherever you want it to appear, such as the desktop. You don't need to choose an icon, because the link inherits the icon of the original file. For example, if it's a picture link, it will inherit the thumbnail preview icon.

■**Note** If you find the Make Link option grayed out, it's likely that you don't have sufficient permissions to write the link to the directory in question.

Adding and Removing Menus

You can add either the Applications menu or the entire set of menus (Applications, Places, and System) to the bottom of the screen. This can help those who long for the Windows Start button approach to accessing programs.

Adding All the Menus to a Panel

To add the Application, Places, and System menus to the Panel at the bottom of the Fedora desktop, follow these steps:

1. Right-click a blank spot on the Panel and select Add to Panel.

2. In the dialog box that appears, click the Menu Bar option to add all three menus.

3. Click the Add button at the bottom of the dialog box.

Adding the Applications Menu to a Panel

When you add just the Applications menu, it appears as a single icon. To move it to the bottom-left side of the desktop, in the same location as the Windows Start menu, you need to first unlock the Show Desktop button and Window List and move them to the right. Here are the steps:

1. Right-click the Show Desktop button and remove the check from the Lock to Panel check box. Do the same for the Window List.

2. Right-click the Window List and select Move. You can now move the Window List, so move your mouse a little to the right. You don't have to click.

3. Right-click the Show Desktop button and select Move. Shift it slightly to the right as well.

4. Right-click the blank area at the bottom-left of the Panel and select Add to Panel.

5. In the dialog box that appears, select the Main Menu option and then click Add.

6. Right-click the new menu icon, select Move, and relocate it to the extreme left.

7. Right-click the Panel and select Add to Panel.

8. Select Separator in the dialog box and click Add.

9. Move the separator bar next to the Main Menu icon, right-click it, and put a check in the Lock to Panel check box.

10. Move the Show Desktop button and the Window List to the left, and lock them both to the Panel.

When you're finished, the Applications menu should appear as shown in Figure 10-9.

Figure 10-9. *If you just can't do without that Start button, you can re-create one on your Fedora desktop.*

Deleting a Menu

Creating new instances of the menus won't delete the old ones. If you create a new Applications menu at the bottom of the screen, for example, the old Applications menu will remain at the top of the screen. In fact, you can have as many instances of the menus on the desktop as you wish, although this won't be a good use of desktop space!

To delete any menu, simply right-click anywhere on that menu and select Remove from Panel.

Personalizing the Panels

Panels are the long strips that appear at the top and bottom of the Fedora screen and play host to a choice of applets and/or icons. You can add a new panel by simply right-clicking an existing one and selecting New Panel, or you can remove a panel by right-clicking it and selecting Delete This Panel.

■**Caution** If you delete a panel, the arrangement of applets it contains will be lost. Of course, you can always re-create the collection of applets on a different panel.

By right-clicking a panel and selecting Properties, you can change its size and dimensions. For example, by unchecking the Expand box, you can make the panel shrink to its smallest possible size. Then, when you add new applets (or, in the case of a panel containing the Window List, when a new program is run), the panel will expand as necessary. This can be a neat effect and also creates more desktop space.

Selecting the Autohide feature will make the panel slide off the screen when there isn't a mouse over it. Choosing Show Hide Buttons will make small arrows appear on either side of the panel so that you can click to slide it off the side of the screen when it's not in use.

Working with Applets

Almost everything you see on the desktop is an applet, with the exception of shortcut icons and the panels. A menu is a form of applet, for example, as is the Workspace Switcher.

Fedora provides many more applets that you can choose to add to the desktop to provide a host of useful or entertaining functionality. To add an applet, right-click the Panel and select Add to Panel. As shown in Figure 10-10, you have a wide choice of applets. Many require configuration when they've been created, so you may need to right-click them and select Properties. For example, you'll need to set your location in the Weather Report applet's properties so it can provide accurate forecasting.

To remove an applet, simply right-click it and select Remove from Panel.

Figure 10-10. *A wide variety of applets are available. Some are informative; others are just fun.*

Setting Power-Saving Features

Fedora includes a number of power-saving features for your computer, including the ability to switch off the monitor after a set period of inactivity. However, some quick configuration is necessary to set up the system just the way you want it.

Tip If your computer has a CPU that can adjust its clock speed on the fly, such as a mobile processor or an AMD chip with the PowerNow! function, Fedora will automatically install software that will make this work.

To see the speed of your processor, right-click the Panel, select Add to Panel, and choose the CPU Frequency Scaling Monitor.

Controlling Monitor Shutoff

You can configure the monitor to go into standby mode after a certain amount of time has passed. This can save a lot of electricity should you happen to leave your computer unattended for long periods.

To configure this aspect of Fedora, select System ➤ Preferences ➤ System ➤ Power Management. You can specify the time period after which your monitor should turn off in case of no activity, as shown in Figure 10-11.

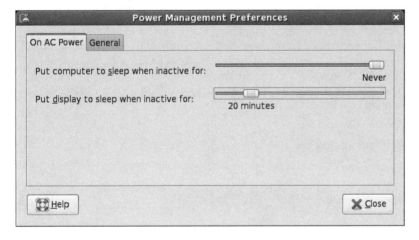

Figure 10-11. *You can configure your monitor to automatically switch itself off after a certain period.*

The General tab on the Power Management Preferences window lets you decide whether the computer should go into hibernation when inactive.

Spinning Down the Hard Disk

All modern hard disks come with the ability to spin down their motors to save energy. Then, when data is requested, the motors spin up again. There may be a slight delay while this happens, and some people dislike using disk spin-down because of this. However, on a notebook, it can lead to a substantial increase in battery life. On a desktop system, it's worth considering, because over the lifetime of a computer, it can save a lot of electricity (and therefore money!).

The spin-down settings are contained in the /etc/hdparm.conf file, which you'll need to edit by hand. Follow these steps to adjust the spin-down settings:

1. Open a GNOME Terminal window (Applications ➤ System Tools ➤ Terminal).

2. Type the following in the terminal window:

   ```
   su -c 'gedit /etc/rc.d/rc.local'
   ```

3. Write this command at the bottom of the file:

   ```
   hdparm -S 24 /dev/sda
   ```

   ```
   #!/bin/sh
   # This script will be executed *after* all the other init scripts.
   # You can put your own initialization stuff here if you don't
   # want to do the full Sys V style init stuff.

   touch /var/lock/subsys/local
   hdparm -S 24 /dev/sda
   ```

4. The -S command option tells the hdparm program that you wish to specify the spin-down value. You can alter the value to anything you want. Each time unit is 5 seconds, so 24 equates to 120 seconds (24 × 5 seconds), or 2 minutes. To set a time of 20 minutes, enter 240 (240 × 5 seconds). If you specify a number above 240, the time units are increased to 30 minutes. In other words, a value of 241 will equate to 30 minutes, a value of 242 will equate to 60 minutes, and so on.

5. When you've finished, save the file.

6. Reboot for the settings to take effect.

POWER SAVING—IS IT WORTH IT?

An average computer draws anywhere between 100 to 500 watts of power. An average lightbulb draws around 150 watts of power, so you can see that, relatively speaking, computers are low power consumers compared to many household devices. However, it's still worth considering employing power-saving techniques. You might not save yourself a lot of money, but if you switch on power saving, and your neighbor does too, and her neighbor does, then the cumulative effect will add up, and we can all contribute less toward global warming.

Try to avoid leaving your computer turned on overnight, or when you're away from it for long periods. As well as saving power, switching off your computer will avoid wear and tear on its components. Although the CPU can work 24/7 without trouble, it's cooled by a fan that's a simple mechanical device. There are other fans in your computer too, such as the graphics card fan and case fan. Each of these will eventually wear out. If your graphics card fan stops working, the card itself will overheat and might burn out. The same is true of the CPU fan. However, by shutting down your computer overnight, you can effectively double the life of the fans and radically reduce the risk of catastrophic failure. Isn't that worth considering?

Summary

In this chapter, you've learned how to completely personalize Fedora to your own tastes. We've looked at changing the theme so that the desktop has a new appearance, and we've examined how to make the input devices behave exactly as you would like.

In addition, you've learned how to add and remove applets from the desktop in order to add functionality or simply make Fedora work the way you would like.

Finally, we looked at the power-saving functions under Fedora and how you can prevent your computer from wasting energy.

In the next chapter, we will look at what programs are available under Fedora to replace those Windows favorites you might miss.

■ ■ ■

## CHAPTER 11

Fedora Replacements for Windows Programs

Fedora is a thoroughly modern operating system and, as such, includes a comprehensive selection of software for just about every day-to-day task. Regardless of whether you want to write letters, edit images, or listen to music, Fedora offers something for you.

This chapter introduces the software under Fedora that performs the tasks you might be used to under Windows. It's not a detailed guide to each piece of software; instead, it aims to get you up and running with the Fedora replacements as quickly as possible. The chapter will tell you the name of the software, where you can find it on Fedora's menus, and a few basic facts about how to use it. In many cases, these applications are covered in far more depth later in the book.

Available Software

Table 11-1 lists various popular Windows programs alongside their Fedora counterparts. You'll find most of the programs listed on the Applications menu. Table 11-1 also includes a number of other mainstream alternatives, most of which aren't installed by default under Fedora, but are available from the Fedora online software repositories. You might want to try these later on. As you might expect, they're all free of charge, so you have nothing to lose.

■**Note** Table 11-1 lists only a fraction of the programs available under Linux. There are quite literally thousands of others. The programs listed here are those that work like their Windows equivalents and therefore provide an easy transition.

Table 11-1. *Linux Alternatives to Windows Software*

Type of Program	Windows	Fedora	Alternative Choices
Word processor	Microsoft Word	OpenOffice.org Writer	AbiWord (www.abisource.com/), KOffice KWord (www.koffice.org/kword/)
Spreadsheet	Microsoft Excel	OpenOffice.org Calc	Gnumeric (www.gnome.org/projects/gnumeric/), KOffice KSpread (www.koffice.org/kspread/)
Presentation program	Microsoft PowerPoint	OpenOffice.org Impress	KOffice KPresenter (www.koffice.org/kpresenter/)
Drawing (vector art) program	Adobe Illustrator	OpenOffice.org Draw	Inkscape (www.inkscape.org/), KOffice Karbon14 (www.koffice.org/karbon/)
Database	Microsoft Access	OpenOffice.org Base	Rekall (www.rekallrevealed.org/)
Web page–authoring program	Microsoft FrontPage	OpenOffice.org Writer	Mozilla Composer (www.mozilla.com/), Amaya (www.w3.org/Amaya/), Nvu (www.nvu.com/)
E-mail application	Microsoft Outlook	Evolution	Mozilla Thunderbird (www.mozilla.com/thunderbird/), KMail (http://kontact.kde.org/kmail/)
Contacts manager/calendar	Microsoft Outlook	Evolution	Kontact (www.kontact.org/)
Web browser	Microsoft Internet Explorer	Mozilla Firefox	Epiphany (www.gnome.org/projects/epiphany/), Konqueror (www.konqueror.org/), Opera (www.opera.com/)[1]
CD/DVD burner	Nero	Nautilus[2]	Gnomebaker (http://gnomebaker.sourceforge.net/), X-CD-Roast (www.xcdroast.org/), K3b (www.k3b.org/)
MP3 player	Winamp	Rhythmbox	XMMS (www.xmms.org/), Banshee (http://banshee-project.org/)
CD player	Windows Media Player	CD Player	XMMS (www.xmms.org/), AlsaPlayer (www.alsaplayer.org/)
Movie/DVD player	Windows Media Player	Totem Media Player	VideoLan Client (VLC) (www.videolan.org/vlc/)
Image editor	Adobe Photoshop	The Gimp	KOffice Krita (www.koffice.org/krita/)
Zip file–management program	WinZip	Archive Manager	TkZip (www.woodsway.com/TkZip/)
MS-DOS prompt	cmd.exe/command.exe	GNOME Terminal	Xterm (www.x.org)[3]
Calculator	Calc	Gcalctool	Too many to mention!
Text editor/viewer	Notepad	Gedit	KWrite (www.kde-apps.org/content/show.php?content=9901)

Type of Program	Windows	Fedora	Alternative Choices
PDF viewer	Adobe Acrobat	Evince	Too many to mention!
Desktop games	Minesweeper/Solitaire	Mines/AisleRiot Solitaire	Too many to mention!

1. Opera is a proprietary project; it's not open source. However, it is free of charge.

2. Nautilus is the file manager within Fedora; to activate its CD/DVD burning mode, click Go ➤ CD/DVD Creator.

3. Xterm is part of the X.org package, so it is installed by default under Fedora. To use it, type **xterm** in a GNOME Terminal window. See Chapter 10 to learn how to create a permanent desktop launcher for Xterm.

LINUX HAS IT ALL

The Fedora software archives contain thousands of programs to cover just about every task you might wish to do on your computer. Diversity is vitally important within the Linux world. For example, rather than offering just one e-mail program, you'll find many available. They compete with each other in a gentle way, and it's up to you which one you settle down with and use.

Part of the fun of using Linux is exploring what's available. Of course, the added bonus is that virtually all this software is free of charge, so you can simply download, install, and play around. If you don't like a program, just remove it from your system. However, don't forget to revisit the program's home page after a few months; chances are the program will have been expanded and improved in that short period, and it might be better at meeting your needs.

A Quick Start with Common Linux Programs

The remainder of this chapter outlines a handful of the programs listed in Table 11-1. Our goal is to give you a head start in using each program, pointing out where most of the main functions can be found. You'll find more details about The GIMP image editor, multimedia tools, and office applications in Parts 5 and 6 of this book.

Keep in mind that Linux doesn't aim to be an exact clone of Windows. Some of the programs will work in a similar way to Windows software, but that's not true of all of them. Because of this, it's very easy to get frustrated early on when programs don't seem to work quite how you want, or respond in strange ways. Some programs might hide functions in what seem like illogical places compared with their Windows counterparts. Some patience is required, but it will eventually pay off as you get used to Linux.

Word Processing: OpenOffice.org Writer

OpenOffice.org is an entire office suite for Linux that was built from the ground up to compete with Microsoft Office. Because of this, you'll find that much of the functionality of Microsoft Office is replicated in OpenOffice.org, and the look and feel is also similar. The major difference is that OpenOffice.org is open source and therefore free of charge.

OpenOffice.org Writer (Applications ➤ Office ➤ Word Processor), shown in Figure 11-1, is the word processor component. As with Microsoft Word, it's fully WYSIWYG (what you see is what you get), so you can quickly format text and paragraphs. This means that the program can be used for elementary desktop publishing, and pictures can be easily inserted (using the Insert menu).

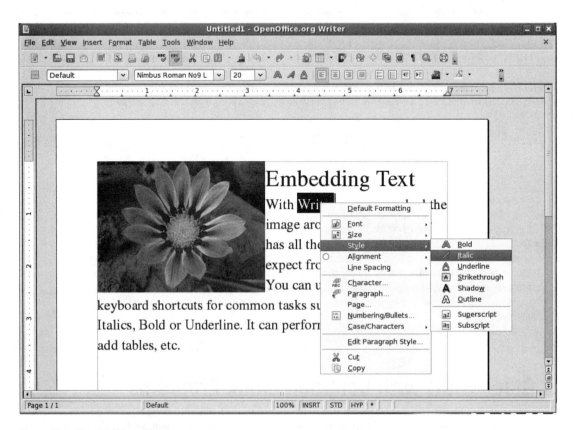

Figure 11-1. *OpenOffice.org Writer*

Writer's toolbars provide quick access to the formatting tools, as well as to other common functions. The vast majority of menu options match those found in Word. Right-clicking the text itself also offers quick access to text-formatting tools.

A number of higher-level functions are provided, such as mail merge and spell-checking, (found on the Tools menu). You can perform spell-checking on the fly, with incorrect words underlined in red as you type.

As with all OpenOffice.org packages, Writer is fully compatible with Microsoft Office files, so you can save and open .doc files. Just select the file type in the Save As dialog box. The only exception is with password-protected Word files, which cannot be opened. You can also export documents as PDF files (using File ➤ Export As PDF), so they can be read on any computer that has Adobe Acrobat Reader installed.

OpenOffice.org Writer is covered in more detail in Chapter 23.

Spreadsheet: OpenOffice.org Calc

As with most of the packages that form the OpenOffice.org suite, Calc (Applications ➤ Office ➤ Spreadsheet) does a good impersonation of its Windows counterpart, Microsoft Excel, both in terms of powerful features and the look and feel, as you can see in Figure 11-2.

However, it doesn't run Excel Visual Basic for Applications (VBA) macros. Instead, Calc (and all OpenOffice.org programs) uses its own macro language called OpenOffice.org Basic (for more information, see http://development.openoffice.org/).

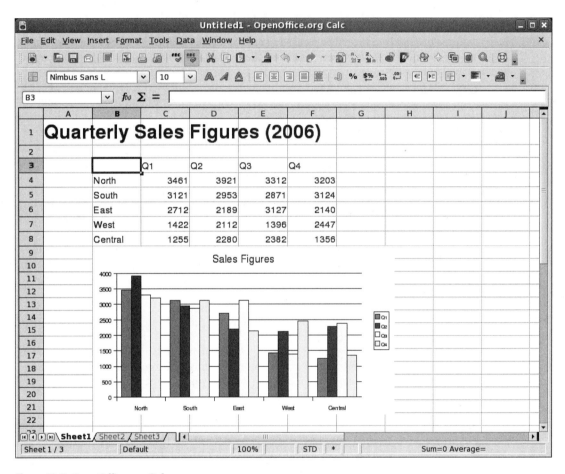

Figure 11-2. *OpenOffice.org Calc*

Calc has a vast number of mathematical functions. To see a list, choose Insert ➤ Function. The list includes a brief explanation of each function to help you get started. Just as with Excel, you can access the functions via the toolbar (by clicking the Function Wizard button), or you can enter them directly into cells by typing an equal sign and then the formula code. Calc is intelligent enough to realize when formula cells have been moved and to recalculate accordingly. It will even attempt to calculate formulas automatically and can work out what you mean if you type something like "sales + expenses" as a formula.

As you would expect, Calc also provides automated charting and graphing tools (under Insert ➤ Chart). In Figure 11-2, you can see an example of a simple chart created automatically by the charting tool.

You can format cells using the main toolbar buttons, or automatically apply user-defined styles (choose Format ➤ Styles and Formatting).

■**Tip** In all the OpenOffice.org applications, you can hover the mouse cursor over each button for one second to see a tooltip showing what it does.

If you're a business user, you'll be pleased to hear that you can import databases to perform serious number-crunching. Use Insert ➤ Link to External Data to get the data, and then employ the tools on the Data and Tools menu to manipulate it.

As with all OpenOffice.org programs, compatibility with its Microsoft counterpart—Excel files in this case—is guaranteed. You can also open other common data file formats, such as comma-separated values (CSV) and Lotus 1-2-3 files.

OpenOffice.org Calc is covered in more detail in Chapter 24.

Presentations: OpenOffice.org Impress

Anyone who has used PowerPoint will immediately feel at home with Impress, OpenOffice.org's presentation package (Applications ➤ Office ➤ Presentation), shown in Figure 11-3. Impress duplicates most of the common features found in PowerPoint, with a helping of OpenOffice.org-specific extras.

The program works via templates into which you enter your data. Starting the program causes the Presentation Wizard to appear. This wizard guides you through selecting a style of presentation fitting the job you have in mind. At this point, you can even select the type of transition effects you want between the various slides.

Once the wizard has finished, you can choose from the usual master and outline view modes (look under the View menu). Outline mode lets you enter your thoughts quickly, while master mode lets you type straight onto presentation slides.

You can format text by highlighting it and right-clicking it, by using the Text Formatting toolbar that appears whenever you click inside a text box, or by selecting an entry on the Format menu. Impress also features a healthy selection of drawing tools, so you can create even quite complex diagrams. These are available on the Drawing toolbar along the bottom of the screen. You can also easily insert pictures, other graphics, and sound effects.

You can open and edit existing PowerPoint (PPT) files and, as with all OpenOffice.org packages, save your presentation as a PDF file. Unique to Impress is the ability to export your presentation as an Adobe Flash file (SWF). This means that anyone with a browser and Adobe's Flash plug-in can view the file, either after it's put online or via e-mail. Simply click File ➤ Export, and then choose Macromedia Flash from the File Format drop-down list. Along with slide presentations, Impress also lets you produce handouts to support your work.

OpenOffice.org Impress is covered in more detail in Chapter 25.

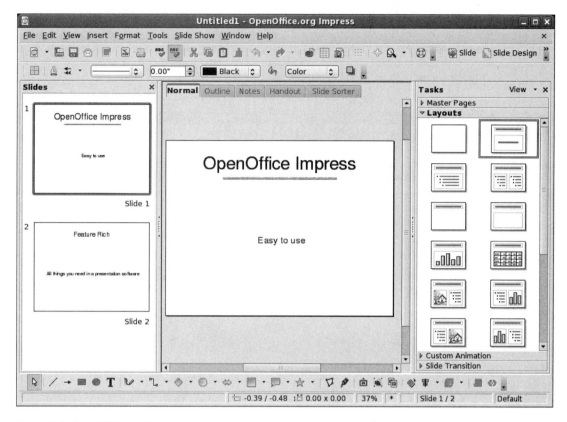

Figure 11-3. *OpenOffice.org Impress*

Database: OpenOffice.org Base

Base, shown in Figure 11-4, is the newest component of OpenOffice.org, introduced with version 2. Base allows you to create relational databases using a built-in database engine, although it can also interface with external databases. It's very similar to Microsoft Access in look and feel, although it lacks some of Access's high-end functions. For most database uses, it should prove perfectly adequate.

If you know the fundamentals of database technology, you shouldn't have any trouble getting started with Base immediately. This is made even easier than you might expect because, when the program starts, a wizard guides you through the creation of a simple database.

As with Access, Base is designed on the principles of tables of data, forms by which the data is input or accessed, and queries and reports by which the data can be examined and output. Once again, wizards are available to walk you through the creation of each of these, or you can dive straight in and edit each by hand by selecting the relevant option.

Each field in the table can be of various types, including several different integer and text types, as well as binary and Boolean values.

Forms can contain a variety of controls, ranging from simple text boxes to radio buttons and scrolling lists, all of which can make data entry easier. Reports can feature a variety of text formatting and can also rely on queries to manipulate the data. The queries themselves can feature a variety of functions and filters in order to sort data down to the finest detail.

You'll learn more about Base in Chapter 26.

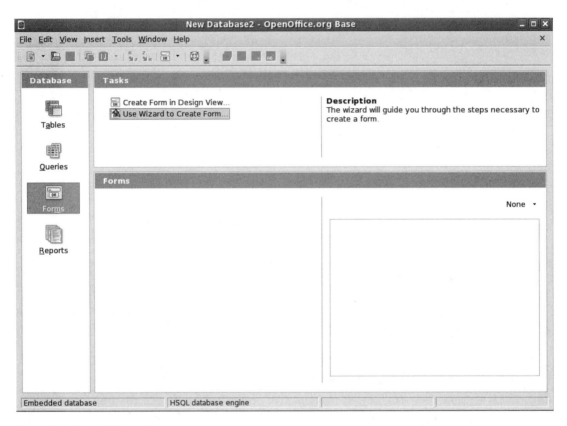

Figure 11-4. *OpenOffice.org Base*

E-Mail/Personal Information Manager: Evolution

Evolution is a little like Microsoft Outlook in that, in addition to being an e-mail client, it can also keep track of your appointments and contacts.

Before using the program, you'll need to set it up with your incoming and (if applicable) outgoing mail server settings, as detailed in Chapter 8. Evolution is compatible with POP/SMTP, IMAP, Novell GroupWise, and Microsoft Exchange servers.

Once the program is up and running, as shown in Figure 11-5, you can create a new message by clicking the New button on the toolbar. To reply to any e-mail, simply select it in the list, and then click the Reply or Reply To All button, depending on whether you want to reply to the sender or to all the recipients of the message.

To switch to Contacts view, click View ➤ Window and select Contacts. If you reply to anyone via e-mail, they're automatically added to this Contacts list. You can also add entries manually by either right-clicking someone's address in an open e-mail or right-clicking in a blank space in the Contacts view.

Clicking the Calendar view shows a day-and-month diary. To add an appointment, simply select the day, and then double-click the time you want the appointment to start. You can opt to set an alarm when creating the appointment, so that you're reminded of it when it it's scheduled.

Finally, by clicking the Tasks button, you can create a to-do list. To add a task, click the bar at the top of the list. Once an entry has been created, you can put a check in its box to mark it as completed. Completed tasks are marked with strike-through, so you can see at a glance what you still need to do.

In addition to the setup guide in Chapter 8, you'll find a full explanation of Evolution's features in Chapter 27.

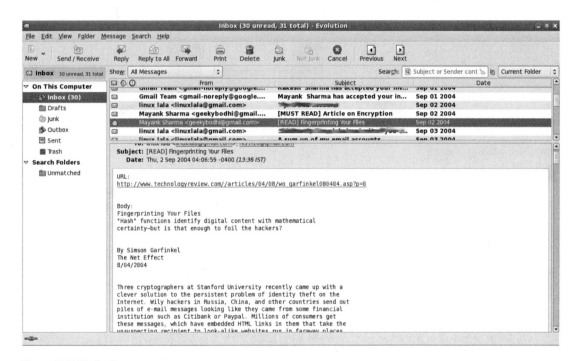

Figure 11-5. *Evolution*

Web Browser: Firefox

You might already know of Mozilla Firefox under Windows, where it's firmly established itself as the alternative browser of choice. The good news is that the Linux version of Firefox is nearly identical to its Windows counterpart.

When the program starts, as shown in Figure 11-6, you can type an address into the URL bar to visit a web site. If you wish to add a site to your bookmarks list, click Bookmarks ➤ Bookmark This Page. Alternatively, you can press Ctrl+D.

Figure 11-6. *Mozilla Firefox*

Searching is very easy within Firefox, using its search bar at the top right of the window. By default, Firefox uses Google for searches. To choose from other search engines, click the small down arrow on the left side of the search box. You can even enter your own choice of site if your favorite isn't already in the list.

The main benefit of Firefox over Internet Explorer is the principle of tabbed browsing, although newer versions of Internet Explorer offer this functionality as well, which means you can have more than one site open at once. To open a new tab, type Ctrl+T. You can move between the tabs by clicking each.

Tip   When Firefox starts, tabs aren't activated. If you would like to keep tabs in view all the time, click Edit ➤ Preferences, and then click the Tabs icon. Now put a check in the Always show the tab bar check-box.

Firefox is compatible with the same range of extensions you might have used under the Windows version of the browser. You can download new extensions from https://addons.mozilla.org/ extensions. In addition, Firefox under Fedora can work with Flash animations, although you'll need to download the Flash Player software first. See the instructions in Chapter 19 to learn more.

Audio Playback: Rhythmbox and CD Player

Fedora's multimedia software is basic but effective. It can play back the majority of audio files, as long as it's properly configured, which is to say after additional software has been installed. We'll describe how to set up this software in Chapter 18, and if you're thinking of playing audio files on your computer, you may want to read that chapter immediately.

Apart from being an audio file player, Rhythmbox is a music librarian, radio listener, and podcast catcher. It can even burn a playlist into a CD for you. We cover configuring Rhythmbox to tune into online radio stations in Chapter 18.

The simply titled CD Player application will automatically start whenever an audio CD is inserted into the drive. Figure 11-7 shows both of these applications.

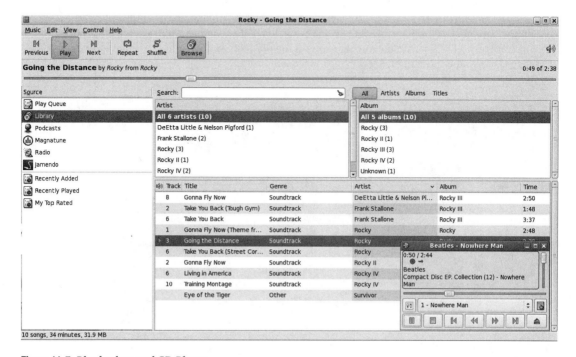

Figure 11-7. *Rhythmbox and CD Player*

When Rhythmbox is run for the first time, it will attempt to find and then catalog your music collection. You might be used to this kind of functionality with Windows utilities like iTunes. After the initial file search has taken place, whenever Rhythmbox runs, you will find your tracks listed by artist or name, providing they have the relevant tag information embedded in them (such as ID3 tags in MP3 music).

■**Note** Unlike iTunes, Rhythmbox can't play Digital Rights Management (DRM)-protected files.

To start playing a music track, double-click it in the list. To make the player smaller so that it doesn't dominate the screen, click View ➤ Small Display.

CD Player works just like virtually every other CD player application you might have used. It features tape recorder–like controls to stop and pause playback, and skip ahead/back buttons to change tracks. It is able to automatically look up the artist and track information about most CDs online, and then save the information for future reference.

You can control the output volume within the applications themselves or use the volume control applet, which is located at the top-right side of the Fedora desktop, near the clock. Simply click and then drag the slider to alter the volume.

Movie Playback: Totem Movie Player

Totem Movie Player is able to handle the majority of video files you might own, as long as some additional software is installed. Totem can also play back DVD movies, which, again, requires the installation of software. We'll cover setting up this software in Chapters 18 and 19, where we'll show you how to install a different version of Totem known as totem-xine; if you intend to play back videos and DVDs, these chapters should be your first port of call.

As with Rhythmbox and CD Player, Totem is a simple and uncomplicated application, as shown in Figure 11-8. The video file will play in the top left of the window. A playlist detailing movies you have queued appears in the top-right area of the program window. You can remove this, to give the video window more room, by clicking the Sidebar button.

Figure 11-8. *Totem Movie Player*

You can control video playback using the tape recorder–like controls at the bottom left. In addition, provided a compatible video format is being played, you can use the Time bar to move backward and forward within the video file. You can switch to full-screen playback by clicking View ➤ Fullscreen. To switch back, simply press the Escape key (labeled Esc on some keyboards). If you're watching a program that has been ripped from TV, you might want to use the Deinterlace feature on the View menu to remove any interference patterns.

Provided the software described in Chapter 19 is installed, DVD playback will start automatically as soon as a disc is inserted, and you should be able to use the mouse with any onscreen menus. In addition, you can skip between chapters on the disc using the Go menu, and also return to the DVD's main or submenu systems. To switch between the various languages on a DVD (if applicable), click Sound ➤ Languages and choose from the list.

CD/DVD Burning: Nautilus

As soon as you insert a blank writable disc, whether it's a CD or DVD, Fedora will detect it and create a relevant icon on your Desktop. It will also immediately ask you if you want to create a disk. When you double-click this icon, the Nautilus CD/DVD creator will open.

Using the Nautilus CD/DVD Creator, shown in Figure 11-9, is quite straightforward. Just drag and drop files onto the window to create shortcuts to the files. When it comes time to burn, Nautilus will take the files from their original locations. When you've finished choosing files, click the Write to Disc button on the toolbar. Unfortunately, you won't see a warning if the disc's file size has been exceeded until you try to write to the disc. However, by right-clicking an empty space in the Nautilus window and selecting Properties, you can discover the total size of the files. Remember that most CDs hold 700 MB, and most DVD+/-R discs hold around 4.3 GB (some dual-layer discs hold twice this amount; see the DVD disc packaging for details).

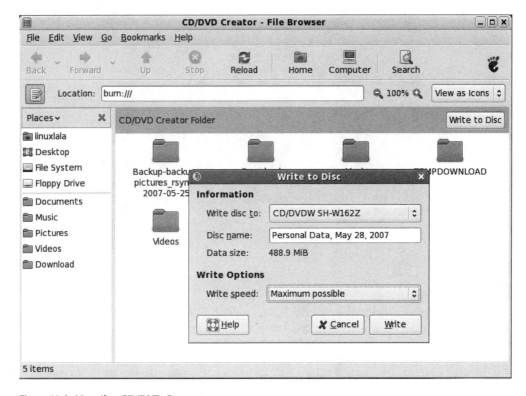

Figure 11-9. *Nautilus CD/DVD Creator*

Photo Editing: The GIMP

While many of the other programs introduced so far mirror the Windows look and feel in some way, The GIMP (Applications ➤ Graphics ➤ GIMP Image Editor) walks a different path. It has its own unique way of working, which takes a little getting used to. But it's very much worth the effort, because The GIMP offers photo-editing tools on par with professional products like Adobe Photoshop. It's certainly more than powerful enough for tweaking digital camera snapshots.

When you initially run The GIMP, it will install itself on your hard disk. Some of the questions it asks look complicated, but you can stick with the default choices throughout.

Once the program is running, you'll notice that it's actually little more than a large toolbar on the left side of the screen, as shown in Figure 11-10. Everything else that runs within The GIMP—whether it's a window containing the image you're editing or an additional configuration dialog box—uses its own program window. This also means that each program item that you activate gets its own button on the Panel at the bottom of the screen.

Figure 11-10. *The GIMP*

To open a picture, select File ➤ Open and select your image from the hard disk. Once an image file is opened, you can manipulate it using the tools on the toolbar (which are similar to those found in other image editors). On the bottom half of the main program window, you'll find the settings for each tool, which can be altered, usually via click-and-drag sliders.

To apply filters or other corrective changes, right-click anywhere on the image to bring up a context menu with a variety of options. Simple tools to improve brightness and contrast can be found on the Layer ➤ Colors submenu.

For an in-depth look at The GIMP package, see Chapter 20.

Other Handy Applications

Many additional applications might prove useful on a day-to-day basis. Here, we'll review some of the more common ones.

Calculator

The GNOME Calculator (also known as gcalctool) can be found on the Applications ➤ Accessories menu. In its default mode, shown in Figure 11-11, it shouldn't present any challenges to anyone who has ever used a real-life calculator, although the Bksp key might be new. This simply deletes the last number you typed (handy if you miskey during a calculation).

Figure 11-11. *GNOME Calculator*

Calculator also has three other modes that you can switch into using the View menu: Advanced, Financial, and Scientific. All offer calculator functions relevant to their settings. The Advanced mode is simply a more complicated version of the basic Calculator. It can store numbers in several memory locations, for example, and carry out less common calculations such as square roots and reciprocals.

Floppy Formatter

The Floppy Formatter is a small and simple program designed, as its name suggests, to format 3.5-inch floppy disks, as shown in Figure 11-12. By default it is not available on the Applications menu. You can edit the default menu layout using the Alacarte tool. Click System ➤ Preferences ➤ Look and Feel ➤ Main Menu. Under the Main Menu window, select System Tools from the Menus sidebar and put a check in the Floppy Formatter check box under the Items list.

You will now find the Floppy Formatter tool on the Applications ➤ System Tools menu. The program can format disks in Linux (ext2) or DOS format. The latter is the best option, bearing in mind you might be sharing disks with others who run Windows. There's also no harm in doing so, since DOS-formatted disks will work fine under Fedora, too.

You can choose between Quick, Standard, and Thorough formats. Quick simply wipes the disk's table of contents, Standard performs an actual disk format, and Thorough adds in a disk scan to mark up any bad data blocks.

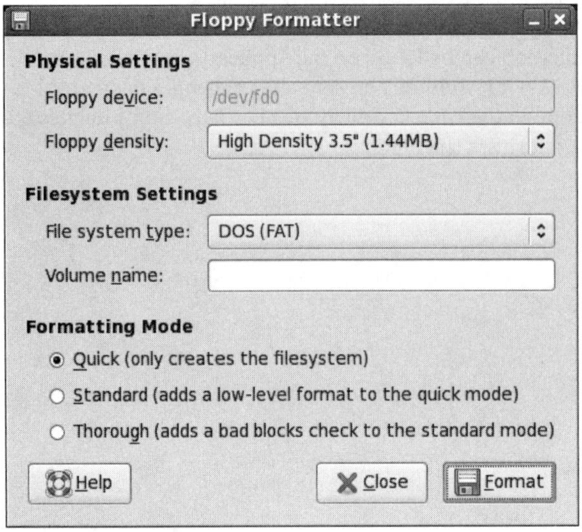

Figure 11-12. *Floppy Formatter*

Archive Manager

Archive Manager (also known as File Roller), shown in Figure 11-13, is Fedora's archive tool. It's the default program that opens whenever you double-click .zip files (or .tar, .gz, or .bzip2 files, which are the native archive file formats under Linux). If you want to start the program manually, click Applications ➤ Accessories ➤ Archive Manager.

To extract files from an archive, select them (hold down the Ctrl key to select more than one file), and then click the Extract button on the toolbar.

To create an archive, start Archive Manager and click the New button. Give the archive a name, and then drag and drop files onto the Archive Manager window. When you've finished, simply close the Archive Manager window.

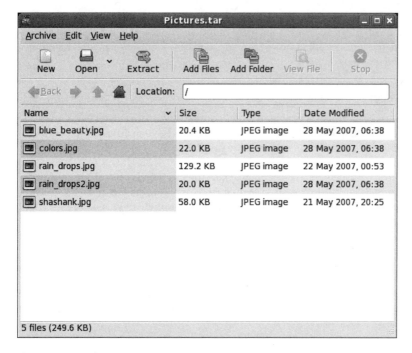

Figure 11-13. *Archive Manager*

Dictionary

The Dictionary tool, shown in Figure 11-14, will look up the definition of words from one of the several online dictionaries. You can see a list of all available dictionaries by clicking View ▶ Sidebar and selecting Available Dictionaries from the drop-down list.

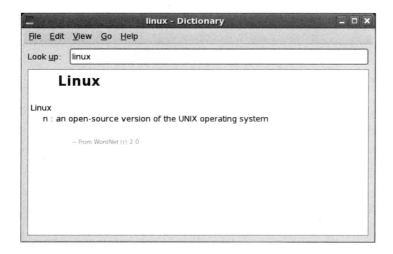

Figure 11-14. *Dictionary*

You'll find the Dictionary program on the Applications ➤ Accessories menu. As soon as you start typing, the program will begin to look up the word in the dictionary, which can cause a momentary delay before the letters appear on your screen. You can select any particular dictionary by double-clicking its name.

Pidgin Internet Messenger

Pidgin is the instant messaging software provided with Fedora. Unlike most other messaging programs, Pidgin isn't exclusive to one chat protocol. In other words, you can use it to connect to MSN, AOL/ICQ, Yahoo, and many other services. The program can be found on the Applications ➤ Internet menu.

Details for setting up Pidgin are given in Chapter 8. Once the program is up and running, you can chat with any of your buddies by double-clicking their icons, as shown in Figure 11-15. To set your status, click the Away icon at the bottom left and select an appropriate message.

You can administer the rest of the program by right-clicking the notification area icon that appears when the program starts. For example, you can initiate file transfers or sign off from there.

Note   As a result of a trademark settlement with AOL, the Gaim instant messenger was renamed Pidgin. You can still find lots of references to the Gaim Internet messenger on the Internet. If you're interested in learning more about Pidgin (formerly Gaim), check out *Open Source Messaging Application Development: Building and Extending Gaim*, authored by Pidgin project leader Sean Egan.

Figure 11-15. *Pidgin instant messenger*

Mines

Mines is the Fedora equivalent of Minesweeper and, in fact, is almost exactly the same as the Windows program, as you can see in Figure 11-16. The rules are identical, too: on each grid are several hidden mines, and it's your job to locate them. After you've clicked one square at random, you'll see a series of empty squares and several with numbers in them. Those with numbers indicate that a bomb is near. Your job is to use logic to work out where the bombs are, and then mark them by right-clicking them. Oh, and you have to do this as quickly as possible because you're being timed.

To change the grid size, click Settings ➤ Preferences. Your choices are Small, Medium, Large, and Custom.

Figure 11-16. *Mines*

Ekiga

If you want to conduct a video conference using Fedora, then Ekiga is for you. It's a very popular program and was earlier known as GnomeMeeting. It supports the commonly used H.323 protocol, as used by Microsoft's NetMeeting, and also lets you register to an Internet Locator Service (ILS) directory, as well as take part in multiple-user calls via a Multipoint Control Unit (MCU). In addition, by registering using the link provided, you can make PC telephone calls, although this requires paying a fee and setting up an account.

You'll find Ekiga listed under the Internet menu as IP Telephony, VoIP and Video Conferencing. When the program starts, it will walk you through setup via a wizard. Simply answer the questions with the details of your setup. Once the program is up and running, as shown in Figure 11-17, type the URL of the person you would like to call into the address bar, and click Call ➤ Call.

Figure 11-17. *Ekiga*

Summary

In this chapter, we've taken a look at some Fedora programs that provide vital functions that you might have used daily under Windows. The aim was to get you started with this software as quickly as possible by pointing out key features. You've seen how some programs mirror the look and feel of their Windows counterparts almost to the letter, while others resolutely strike out on their own path. It takes just a little time to become familiar with Fedora software, and then using these programs will become second nature.

In the next chapter, we'll move on to more fundamental Fedora tasks: manipulating files. However, once again, this is not too dissimilar from the Windows experience, which makes getting used to the system very easy.

CHAPTER 12

■ ■ ■

Managing Your Files

Files are what make the world of Linux go round. They're the currency of any kind of operating system, because every time you use your computer, you generate new files, even if they're only temporary.

How Linux views files, as well as the disks and partitions that contain them, varies somewhat from how Windows handles files. In many ways, the Linux system of file management is far simpler than that of Windows (which, ironically, was created as an attempt to make everything easy). The Linux system is also much more established.

In this chapter, we will explain how you can manage your files under Fedora. This isn't a definitive guide; you'll need to wait until Chapter 15 to learn the technical ins and outs of the file system. However, it provides enough information for you to understand how the system works, and where and how you should store your data.

Understanding File System Concepts

Just like Windows, Fedora has a file system that is shared among software components and your own personal data, which you generate within various applications, or perhaps download from the Internet. However, Fedora differs from Windows in a couple of important ways.

Drive References

Perhaps the most important differences in Linux are that it doesn't use drive letters and it uses a forward slash (/) instead of a backslash (\) in filename paths. In other words, something like /home/john/myfile is typical under Fedora, as opposed to C:\Documents and Settings\John\myfile under Windows. The root of the hard disk partition is usually referred to as C:\ under Windows. In Fedora, and all other Linux distributions, it's referred to simply with a forward slash (/).

If you have more than one drive, the drives are usually combined together into the one file system under Linux. This is done by *mounting*, which allows any additional drives to appear as virtual folders under the file system. In other words, you browse the other hard disks by switching to various directories within the main file system. We'll explain mounting in Chapter 15.

Case Sensitivity

Another important difference between Fedora and Windows is that filenames in Fedora are case-sensitive. This means that MyFile is distinctly different from myfile. Uppercase letters are vitally important. In Windows, filenames might appear to have uppercase letters in them but, actually, these are ignored when you rename or otherwise manipulate files.

Because of this case sensitivity of Linux, you could have two separate files existing in the same place, one called `MyFile` and another called `myfile`. In fact, you could also have `myFile`, `Myfile`, `MYFILE`, and so on, as shown in Figure 12-1.

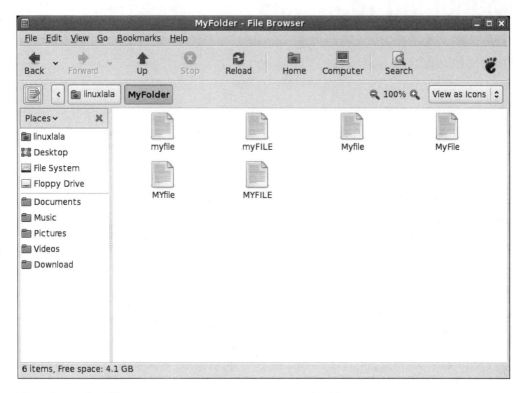

Figure 12-1. *Fedora filenames are case-sensitive, so many similar filenames can exist, differing only in which letters are capitalized.*

File Access and Storage

Under Windows on a desktop computer, you have access to the entire hard disk. You can write, read, or delete files anywhere (unless the system has specifically been configured otherwise). You can save your personal files in `C:\Windows`, for example. Under Fedora, ordinary users can browse most of the hard disk, but they aren't able to write files to the majority of folders (in some cases, they won't even be able to access files).

We'll cover the file system in much more depth in Chapter 15, but for the moment, it's enough to know that you've been given your own part of the hard disk in which to store your stuff. This is a directory located within the `/home` directory, and its name is taken from your username. If your login name is `frank`, your place for storing files will be `/home/frank`. Figure 12-2 shows an example of a user's home directory.

■**Note** Linux generally uses the terms *directory* and *subdirectory* for the places you put files, whereas Windows XP refers to them as *folders*. It's merely a matter of semantics. However, within the Nautilus file browser, directories are pictured as folders and are referred to as such, thus furthering the confusion!

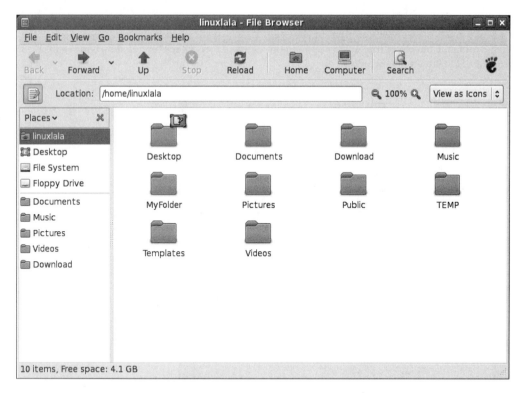

Figure 12-2. *Your personal area on the hard disk is in the /home directory; it's named after your username.*

Some programs might create subdirectories in your home directory in order to store and organize their output. For example, a digital camera program might create a Pictures directory within your /home directory. It's up to you whether you use these. The standard practice within the Linux community is to simply save everything into your /home subdirectory (e.g., /home/linuxlala) and sort it out later!

Files within Fedora remember who owns them. If user john creates a file, he can make it so that only he can read or write the file (the default setting is that other users will be able to read the file but not write any new data to it). Directories, too, are owned by people, and the owner can set access permissions. By default, a user can't access another user's /home directory.

■**Note** Any user with superuser powers has access to all of the system and can create, edit, and delete files in all directories. This is so that user can perform essential system maintenance.

Using Nautilus

Nautilus is the name of the default file browser in Fedora. You can use the File Browser tool (Applications ➤ System Tools ➤ File Browser) to browse through your system. You can alternatively use a regular Nautilus window (Places ➤ Home Folder).

The default Nautilus view might surprise some of you, as it's nothing like the File Browser. If you, like most users, prefer the "web" or "browser" view, just click Edit ➤ Preferences and select the Behavior tab. Then check the "Always open in browser window" check box, as shown in Figure 12-3, and close the Preferences window.

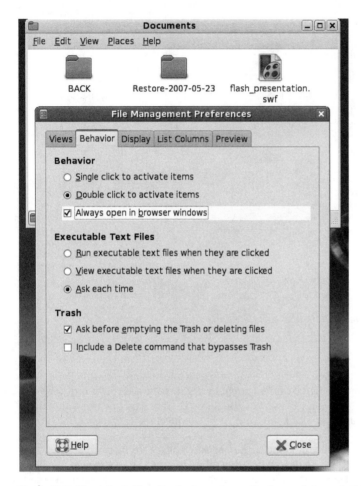

Figure 12-3. *The default Nautilus look can be easily changed through Edit ➤ Preferences.*

The view now (see Figures 12-1, 12-2, and 12-5) is not dissimilar to My Computer/Windows Explorer under Windows in that it presents a list of files on the right side of the window and a series of shortcuts to popular locations within the file system on the left side.

Starting Nautilus is simply a matter of clicking the Places menu and choosing a location, as shown in Figure 12-4. Alternatively, you can click Applications ➤ System Tools ➤ File Browser, which will open the default browsing location (your /home folder).

Figure 12-4. *You can open a file browser window by selecting a location under the Places menu.*

The Nautilus window consists of several elements:

Menu bar: The menus offer options for controlling the way files are displayed in the Nautilus window, as well as the look and feel of Nautilus itself. The Bookmarks menu lets you create web browser–like shortcuts to certain locations in your file system so that you can access them instantly.

Toolbar: As in a web browser, the toolbar allows you to quickly move backward and forward from place to place in your browsing history. In addition, you can reload the file listing, in order to reflect any changes that might have taken place since the Nautilus window opened, and quickly navigate to popular file system locations, such as your /home folder.

Location bar: This feature, located beneath the toolbar, is unique to Nautilus and lets you see where you are in your file system, as well as quickly and easily move through your file-browsing history. For example, if you to start in /home/linuxlala and then browse to /home/linuxlala/pics/flowers/garden, clicking the pics button will return you to /home/linuxlala/pics. The other folders listed on the location bar (flowers and garden in this example) won't disappear, so you can return to those as well. It's best demonstrated by example, so give it a try!

■**Tip** You can choose to have a more traditional location bar that displays the path instead of buttons (Figures 12-2 and 12-5). Simply click the button to the left of the location bar.

Zoom controls: To the right of the location bar are the zoom controls. These make the icons representing the files bigger or smaller. When you're browsing a lot of files at once, shrinking them will fit more in the window. On the other hand, when you're viewing photo thumbnails, it can be handy to increase the zoom setting so you can see more detail in the pictures. You can also use Ctrl+= or Ctrl+- to respectively increase or decrease the icon size. These shortcuts work in many places throughout GNOME and also across several applications (such as Firefox), where they affect the font size.

View As Icons/List option: To the right of the zoom controls is a drop-down list that switches between icon and list view. List view shows details about the files, such as file size, the type of file, its permissions, and so on. Icon view presents the files as a series of large icons. In many cases, the icons will give a clue as to the nature of the file; for example, MP3 files appear with speaker and musical note graphics. If the folder you're browsing contains image files (or certain document files, such as PDFs), these will be automatically thumbnailed—the icon will be a small version of the contents of the file, as shown in Figure 12-5. This is very handy when browsing pictures for printing or editing.

Figure 12-5. *Whenever you view a folder full of pictures in icon view, they will be automatically thumbnailed.*

Places pane: The Places pane on the left lists the most popular locations within the file system. Double-clicking each icon takes you to that location instantly. Clicking the File System entry takes you to the root of the file system (/).

As under Windows, you can right-click each file in the file browser window to see a context menu with options to rename the file, delete it, open it with particular applications, and so on. The Properties option on the context menu lets you view information about the file and alter certain aspects of it, such as its access permissions (discussed in Chapter 15). You can even add some text notes about the file if you wish!

■**Caution** You should never delete your /home folder. Doing so will most likely destroy all of your data and your personal Fedora setup, and prevent you from logging in.

File and Folder Icons

Files and folders can have *emblems* applied to them. These are smaller icons that are "tagged onto" the larger icons in both list view and icon view. Emblems are designed to give you quick clues about the nature of the file. To apply an emblem, right-click the file or folder, select Properties, and then click the Emblems tab. As shown in Figure 12-6, a range of icons is available; in fact, any file or folder can have several emblems applied at once. Simply put a check in the box beside the icons you wish to apply.

■**Note** Nautilus makes use of a handful of emblem icons for its own needs, too. For example, a file with a lock emblem attached to it indicates that you don't have the necessary file permissions to edit or delete that file. An X emblem means that you don't have permissions to access that file or folder at all, not even to view it. In most cases, the emblems are self-explanatory.

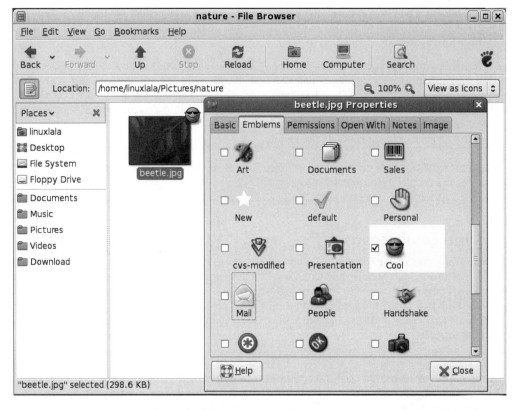

Figure 12-6. *A variety of miniature emblems can be applied to an icon to aid recognition of the file.*

Special Nautilus Windows

As well as letting you view your files, Nautilus has a number of *object modes*. This is a complicated way of saying that Nautilus lets you view things other than files.

The most obvious example of this is the computer view of your file system, which presents an eagle's eye view of your storage devices. To access this view, click Places ➤ Computer. If you have a card reader attached, it will appear here, as will any Windows partitions that may be on your hard disk. Double-clicking each item opens a standard Nautilus file browser window (for this to work with Windows partitions, they must be set up correctly, as described in the "Accessing Windows Files" section later in this chapter).

Another Nautilus object mode is the fonts view, which lets you see at a glance any fonts installed on your computer. To access fonts view, click Go ➤ Location in any open Nautilus window, and then type fonts://. You can just type this in the location bar, if you are not using the default "buttons" style.

Object modes come into their own when viewing network locations. Clicking Places ➤ Network Servers brings up the browsing network object view, for example. You can also browse to FTP sites by clicking Go ➤ Location in a file browser window and entering an FTP address (prefacing it with ftp://).

Note You might be used to dragging and dropping files onto program windows or taskbar buttons within Windows in order to open the file. This works with only some programs within Fedora, such as The GIMP, Firefox, Evince, Gedit, and VLC. Generally, the best policy is to try it and see what happens. If the program starts but your file isn't opened, it obviously didn't work.

HIDDEN FILES AND DIRECTORIES

When you view your /home directory via Nautilus, you're not seeing every file that's there. Several hidden files and directories relating to your system configuration also exist. You can take a look at them by clicking View ➤ Show Hidden Files in the Nautilus menu. Clicking this option again will hide the files and directories.

You might notice something curious about the hidden items: they all have a period before their filenames. In fact, this is all that's needed to hide any file or directory: simply place a period at the front of the filename. There's no magic involved above and beyond this.

For example, to hide the file picture.jpg, you could simply right-click it and rename it .picture.jpg. You'll need to click the Reload button on the toolbar for the file view to be updated and for the file to disappear. As you might expect, removing the period will unhide the file.

Files are usually hidden for a reason, and it's no coincidence that most of the hidden files are system files. In addition, every program that you install, or is installed by default, will usually create its own hidden folder for its system configuration data. Deleting such files by accident can be catastrophic.

Launching Files and Running Programs

As with Windows, most of the programs on your Fedora system automatically associate themselves with various file types that they understand. For example, double-clicking a picture will automatically open the Eye of GNOME viewer application, and double-clicking a .doc file will start OpenOffice.org Writer.

Fedora is automatically set up to view common file types. However, you might find Table 12-1 useful. It shows which programs are required for viewing certain types of documents.

Note Whenever you install new software from the installation CD or the official software repositories, it should add an entry to the Applications menu. If for some reason this doesn't happen, you can create a shortcut using the techniques explained in Chapter 10.

Table 12-1. *Common File Types*

File Type	File Extension	Viewer	Location on Applications Menu
Word processor document	`.odt,.doc, .rtf`	OpenOffice.org Writer	Office ➤ Word Processor
Spreadsheet	`.ods,.xls`	OpenOffice.org Calc	Office ➤ Spreadsheet
Presentation	`.odp,.ppt`	OpenOffice.org Impress	Office ➤ Presentation
PDF file	`.pdf`	Evince	Not on Applications menu*
Compressed file	`.zip, .tar, .gz, .bz2`, and others	File Roller	Accessories ➤ Archive Manager
Image file	`.jpg, .gif, .tif, .bmp`, and others	Eye of GNOME	Not on applications menu
HTML file	`.htm, .html`	Firefox	Internet ➤ Firefox Web Browser
Text file	`.txt, .log`	Gedit	Accessories ➤ Text Editor
Audio file	`.wav`	Rhythmbox	Sound & Video ➤ Rhythmbox Music Player
Video file	`.mpg, .mpeg, .avi`	Totem	Sound & Video ➤ Totem Movie Player

* *For some reason, Evince is not present on the Applications menu, although it is installed by default and associated with PDF files. If you wish, you can add your own shortcut, following the instructions in Chapter 10.*

If you want to change the program associated with a file type, right-click the file, select Open with Other Application, and choose the other program, as shown in Figure 12-7. From that point on, every time you right-click, you'll be offered the choice of the program to open the file.

Under Windows, you can use Windows Explorer to launch program executables by just browsing to their location within Program Files and double-clicking their .exe file. It's technically possible to run programs by browsing to their location using Nautilus, but this is discouraged. One reason is that Fedora doesn't store all of its programs in one central folder, as does Windows. However, most programs that are used on a daily basis can be found in /usr/bin. If the program itself isn't stored in /usr/bin, it will contain a symbolic link (effectively, a shortcut) to the program's genuine location on the hard disk.

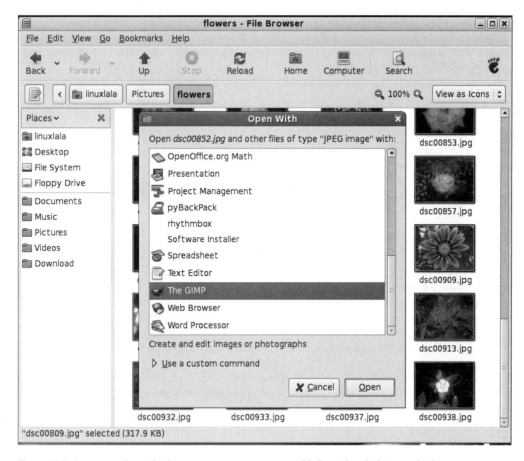

Figure 12-7. *You can select which program to use to open a file by right-clicking and selecting Open with Other Application.*

Accessing Windows Files

Running Fedora on your PC makes you a relative stranger in a world of Windows users. It's likely that you'll need to access Windows files on a regular basis. If you've chosen to dual-boot with Windows, you might want to grab files from the Windows partition on your own hard disk. If your PC is part of a network, you might want to access files on a Windows-based server or workstation on which a shared folder has been created.

Working with Files in Windows Partitions

Fedora may or may not make your Windows partitions available automatically. It depends on whether your Windows partition is FAT32, as used with Windows 95, 98, and Me; or NTFS, as used with Windows NT, 2000, and XP. FAT32 partitions will be instantly accessible, but making NTFS partitions accessible requires some work.

■**Note** It's possible for an installation of Windows 2000 or XP to use FAT32 instead of NTFS, but this requires the user to make a deliberate choice during setup. Unless you know your Windows 2000 or XP system has been formatted with FAT32, it's very likely that it is NTFS.

If the drive is available, an icon for it should appear on the desktop.

■**Note** You should be able to read and write to FAT32 partitions, but you cannot write to or edit files in an NTFS partition. Although it is *technically* possible, it's not advisable because of various technical limitations. Therefore, the NTFS partition is made read-only. If you have a desperate need to *write* files to your Windows NTFS partition from within Fedora, refer to Chapter 14, where we discuss how you can write to an NTFS partition.

Accessing Networked Files

The easiest way to access servers or shared folders on Windows workstations or servers over a network is to click Places ➤ Network. This will start Nautilus and attempt to search for Windows machines on your local network, just like Network Neighborhood and My Network Places on the various versions of Windows. However, if you've ever used either of these services under Windows, you might also know how unreliable they can be—some computers simply don't appear in the list, others appear eventually after a wait, and others appear but then prove to be mysteriously inaccessible.

A far quicker and more reliable method of accessing a Windows machine is to open a Nautilus file browser window (Places ➤ Home Folder), and then click Go ➤ Location. In the box, type the following:

```
smb://Windows computer's IP address/
```

As you can see, you'll need to know the IP address of the Windows computer. Ask your system administrator or the person in charge of that machine for this address. You may also be prompted to enter a username and/or password to access the shared folder.

■**Note** If you're accessing a Windows 95, 98, or Me shared folder, only password protection will have been set (these versions of Windows are unable to specify a username). However, when prompted by Nautilus, you still need to type *something* into the Username box to gain access—anything will do, as long as the password is correct. You cannot leave the Username box blank.

Accessing Removable Storage Devices

Fedora automatically makes available any CDs or DVDs you insert into your computer, and they'll appear instantly as icons on the desktop. The same is true of any card readers or USB memory devices that you use.

Alternatively, you can access the storage devices by clicking Places ➤ Computer. Here, you'll find icons for all of the storage devices attached to your computer, including the floppy disk drive, as shown in Figure 12-8. However, because of the way floppy disk drives work, Fedora isn't able to automatically detect if a floppy has been inserted. Instead, you'll need to double-click the icon, as with Windows.

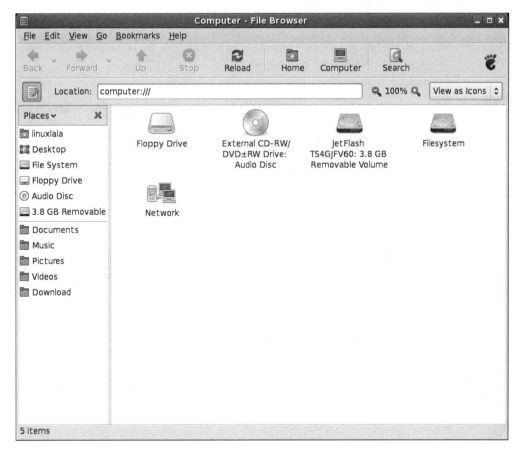

Figure 12-8. *Select Places ➤ Computer to access your removable storage drives.*

Whenever you double-click any entry in the Computer window, it will open a Nautilus file browser window. You can copy files by clicking and dragging, and right-clicking files offers virtually all the options you could need.

■Tip You don't need to use Places ➤ Computer each time to access your floppy, CD, or DVD drive. These drives are mounted in the /media folder on your hard disk. Just browse to /media/floppy and /media/cdrom.

Ejecting Media from Drives

Fedora isn't quite like Windows when it comes to ejecting or unplugging removable storage devices. In some cases, devices must be *unmounted*, which is to say that you need to tell Fedora that you're finished with the device in question and that you're about to unplug it.

In the case of CD or DVD discs, you can simply press the Eject button on the drive itself. Fedora is clever enough to realize that the disc is being ejected, so it will automatically unmount the drive. Alternatively, you can right-click the CD or DVD icon on your desktop and select Eject.

In the case of floppy disks, memory cards, and other USB storage devices, you'll need to right-click the icon and select Unmount Volume. You can then unplug and/or remove the device. This also applies when you're removing a memory card from a card reader—before pulling out the card from the reader, it needs to be unmounted.

Note It's necessary to close any files that were open on the device before unmounting, and even close any file browser windows that were accessing the device.

If you fail to unmount the device, Fedora will still believe the device is attached. This shouldn't cause too many problems to your system, but it could crash any programs that were accessing the device. If you remove a device without properly unmounting it, you run the risk of data loss or corruption. This can also reduce the lifespan of your USB devices.

Summary

This chapter has led you on your first steps in exploring the Linux file system. The file system is vitally important to how Linux works, and we'll go into it in much greater depth in upcoming chapters.

Here, you were introduced to elementary concepts, such as where personal files are stored and the basic rules that govern what you can and cannot do with files. We also looked at the principle method of accessing files via the GUI: the Nautilus file manager. Additionally, you learned how to run programs manually, as well as how to access any Windows partition or files that may exist on your hard disk or across a network.

In Part 4 of this book, starting in the next chapter, we will look at some of the underlying technology that makes Fedora work and how you can gain more control over your computer. Chapter 13 introduces the BASH shell—perhaps the most powerful piece of software offered by Fedora to control your system.

PART 4

■■■

The Shell and Beyond

CHAPTER 13

■ ■ ■

Introducing the BASH Shell

As you learned in Chapter 1, strictly speaking, the word *Linux* refers to just the kernel, which is the fundamental, invisible program that runs your PC and lets everything happen. However, on its own, the kernel is completely useless. It needs programs to let users interact with the PC and do cool stuff, and it needs a lot of system files (also referred to as *libraries*) to provide vital functions.

The GNU Project provides many of these low-level pieces of code and programs. This is why many people refer to the Linux operating system as GNU/Linux, giving credit to the fact that, without the GNU components, Linux wouldn't have gotten off the starting blocks.

The GNU Project provides various shell programs, too. Some of these offer graphical functionality, but most are text only. These text shell programs are also known as *terminal programs*, and they're often colloquially referred to as *command-line prompts*, in reference to the most important component they provide. This kind of shell lets you take control of your system in a quick and efficient way. Like a GUI, it's another way of interfacing with your computer, except that you type commands, rather than using a mouse.

By learning how to use the shell, you'll become the true master of your own system. In this part of the book, you'll learn all you need to know about using the shell. This chapter introduces the BASH shell, which is the default shell in Fedora.

What Is the BASH Shell?

The best way of explaining the BASH shell to a Windows user is to compare it to the DOS command prompt. It lets you issue commands directly to the operating system via the keyboard without needing to mess around with the mouse and windows (although it is sometimes possible to use the mouse within a BASH shell to copy and paste text, and sometimes to control simple text-based menus). The big difference is that the BASH shell has commands for just about everything you might do on your system, whereas the DOS command prompt is restricted to tools capable of manipulating and viewing files and directories, and on modern Windows machines, configuring certain system settings.

In the old days, the DOS command prompt was also the visible layer of an entire operating system in which DOS programs were designed to be run. However, the shell is merely one of the many ways of accessing the Linux kernel and subsystems. It's true that many programs are designed to run via the BASH shell, but technically speaking, most actually run on the Linux operating system, and simply take and show input via the BASH shell.

■**Note** Linux purists will point out another reason why the shell isn't exactly the same as a DOS command prompt within Windows: it doesn't run in virtual machine mode, a CPU trick by which part of the memory is subdivided to let programs run as if they had the PC all to themselves.

Linux finds itself with the BASH shell largely because Linux is a clone of UNIX. In the early days of UNIX, the text-based shell was all that was offered as a way of letting users control the computer. Typing commands in directly is one of the most fundamental ways of controlling any type of computer and, in the evolutionary scale, comes straight after needing to set switches and watch blinking lights in order to run programs.

That the BASH shell can trace its history back to the early days of UNIX might sound like a tacit indication that the BASH shell is somehow primitive—far from it. It's one of the most efficient and immediate ways of working with your computer. Many people consider the command-line shell to be a way of using a computer that has yet to be superseded by a better method.

■**Note** When you run a shell on a Linux system, the system refers to it as a `tty` device. This stands for tele-typewriter, a direct reference to the old system of inputting data on what were effectively electronic typewriters connected to mainframe computers. These, in turn, took their names from the devices used to automate the sending and receiving of telegrams in the early part of the twentieth century.

Most Linux distributions come with a choice of different kinds of shell programs. However, the default shell is BASH, as is the case in Fedora. BASH stands for Bourne Again Shell. This is based on the Bourne shell, a tried-and-tested program that originated in the early days of UNIX.

The other shells available include PDKSH (Public Domain Korn Shell, based on the Korn shell, another early UNIX shell), and ZSH (Z Shell), a more recent addition. These are usually used by people who want to program Linux in various ways, or by those who simply aren't happy with BASH.

The BASH shell is considered by many to be the best of all worlds in that it's easy enough for beginners to learn, yet is able to grow with them and offer additional capabilities as necessary. BASH is capable of scripting, for example, which means you can even create your own simple programs.

■**Note** Technically speaking, a *shell* refers to any type of user interface. The windowing system offered by Windows and Macintosh operating systems are a type of shell. However, many people in the Linux and UNIX worlds use the word *shell* as shorthand for a shell that offers a command line.

Why Bother with the Shell?

You might have followed the instructions in Part 2 of this book and by now consider yourself a proficient Linux user. But the real measure of a Linux user comes from your abilities at the shell.

In our modern age, the GUI is mistakenly considered "progress." For instance, users of the Microsoft and Apple-based operating systems are quite used to using a mouse to navigate and perform various tasks. While it's handy in certain situations—it would be difficult to imagine image editing without a mouse, for example—in many other situations, such as when manipulating files, directly typing commands is far more efficient.

Most modern Linux distributions prefer you to use the GUI to do nearly everything. This is because they acknowledge the dominance of Windows and realize they need to cater to mouse users who might not even know the shell exists (and, of course, programs like web browsers would be unusable without a GUI!). To this end, they provide GUI tools for just about every task you might wish to undertake. Fedora is strong in this regard, and you can configure a lot of things from the desktop.

However, it's well worth developing at least some command-line shell skills, for a number of reasons:

It's simple and fast. The shell is the simplest and fastest way of working with Fedora. As just one example, consider the task of changing the IP address of your network card. You could click the Systems menu, then the Administration option, then the Network option, and then double-click the entry in this list relating to your network card. That will take at least a minute or two if you know what you're doing, and perhaps longer if it's new to you. Alternatively, you could simply open a shell and type this:

```
ifconfig eth0 192.168.0.15 up
```

It's versatile. Everything can be done via the shell—from deleting files, to configuring hardware, to creating MP3s. A lot of GUI programs actually make use of programs you can access via the shell.

It's consistent among distributions. All Linux systems have shells and understand the same commands (broadly speaking). However, not all Linux systems will have Fedora's graphical configuration programs. SUSE Linux uses its own GUI configuration tool, as does Mandriva Linux. Therefore, if you ever need to use another system, or decide to switch distributions, a reliance on GUI tools will mean learning everything from scratch. Knowing a few shell commands will help you get started instantly.

It's crucial for troubleshooting. The shell offers a vital way of fixing your system should it go wrong. Your Linux installation might be damaged to the extent that it cannot boot to the GUI, but you'll almost certainly be able to boot into a shell. A shell doesn't require much of the system other than the ability to display characters on the screen and take input from the keyboard, which most PCs can do, even when they're in a sorry state. This is why most rescue floppies offer shells to let you fix your system.

It's useful for remote access. One handy thing about the shell is that you don't need to be in front of your PC to use it. Programs like ssh let you log into your PC across the Internet and use the shell to control your PC (as described in Chapter 33). For example, you can access data on a remote machine, or even fix it when you're unable to attend the machine's location. This is why Linux is preferred on many server systems when the system administrator isn't always present on the site.

It's respected in the community. Using a shell earns you enormous brownie points when speaking to other Linux users. It separates the wheat from the chaff and the men from the boys (or women from the girls). If you intend to use Linux professionally, you will most certainly need to be a master at the shell.

Seen in this light, learning at least a handful of shell commands is vital to truly mastering your PC.

The drawback when using a command-line shell is that it's not entirely intuitive. Take, for instance, the command to change the network card's IP address:

```
ifconfig eth0 192.168.0.15 up
```

If you've never used the shell before, it might as well be Sanskrit. What on earth does ifconfig mean? And why is there the word up at the end?

Learning to use the shell involves learning terms like these. Hundreds of commands are available, but you really need to learn only around 10 or 20 for everyday use. The comparison with a new language is apt because, although you might think it daunting to learn new terminology, with a bit of practice, it will all become second nature. Once you've used a command a few times, you'll know how to use it in the future.

The main thing to realize is that the shell is your friend. It's there to help you get stuff done as quickly as possible. When you become familiar with it, you'll see that it is a beautiful concept. The shell is simple, elegant, and powerful.

When Should You Use the Shell?

The amount of use the Linux shell sees is highly dependent on the user. Some Linux buffs couldn't manage without it. They use it to read and compose e-mail, and even to browse the Web (usually using the Mutt and Lynx programs, respectively).

However, most people simply use it to manage files, view text files (like program documentation), and run programs. All kinds of programs—including GUI and command-line—can be started from the shell. As you'll learn in Chapter 28, unlike with Windows, installing a program on Fedora doesn't necessarily mean the program will automatically appear on the Applications menu. In fact, unless the installation routine is specifically made for the version of Linux you're running, this is unlikely. Therefore, using the shell is a necessity for most people.

Note Unlike with DOS programs, Fedora programs that describe themselves as "command-line" are rarely designed to run solely via the command-line shell. All programs are like machines that take input at one end and output objects at the other. Where the input comes from and where the output goes to is by no means limited to the command line. Usually, with a command-line program, the input and output are provided via the shell, and the programmer makes special dispensation for this, but this way of working is why GUI programs often make use of what might be considered shell programs. You'll often find that a GUI program designed to, for example, burn CDs, will also require the installation of a command-line program that will actually do the hard work for it.

There's another reason why the shell is used to run programs: you can specify how a particular program runs before starting it. For example, to launch the Totem Movie Player in full screen mode playing the `myvideofile.mpg` file, you could type this:

```
totem --fullscreen myvideofile.mpg
```

This saves the bother of starting the program, loading a clip, and then selecting the full screen option. After you've typed the command once or twice, you'll be able to remember it for the next time. No matter how much you love the mouse, you'll have to admit that this method of running programs is more efficient.

When you get used to using the shell, it's likely you'll have it open most of the time behind your other program windows.

Getting Started with the Shell

You can start the shell in a number of ways. The most common is to use a terminal emulator program. As its name suggests, this runs a shell inside a program window on your desktop.

You can start GNOME Terminal, the built-in GNOME shell emulator, by clicking Applications ➤ System Tools ➤ Terminal, as shown in Figure 13-1.

You'll see the terminal window—a blank, white window that's similar to a simple text editor window. It will show what's referred to as a *command prompt*: a few words followed by the dollar symbol: $. On our test system, this is what we see:

```
linuxlala@localhost:~$
```

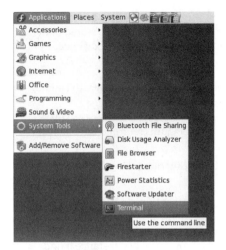

Figure 13-1. *Start the GNOME Terminal program from the Accessories submenu.*

The first part is the username—the user account we created during installation and use to log into the PC. After the @ sign is the name of the PC, which was also chosen when installing Fedora. Actually, localhost is the default name, but you can choose any other name as well. The name of the PC isn't important on most desktop PCs; it's a legacy from the days of UNIX. After the colon is the current directory you're browsing. In this example, the ~ symbol appears instead of an actual path or directory name. This is merely Linux shorthand for the user's home directory. In other words, wherever we see a ~ on the test PC, we read it as /home/linuxlala. After this is the dollar symbol ($), which indicates that an ordinary user is logged in. Finally, there is a cursor, and this is where you can start typing commands!

■**Note** If you were to log in as root, a hash (#) would appear instead of the dollar prompt. This is important to remember because often in magazines and some computer manuals the use of the hash symbol before a command indicates that it should be run as root. In addition, if you use the rescue function of the install CD, you'll be running as root, and a hash will appear at the prompt. See Chapter 14 for more information about the root user.

Running Programs

When we refer to *commands* at the shell, we're actually talking about small programs. When you type a command to list a directory, for example, you're actually starting a small program that will do that job. Seen in this light, the shell's main function is to simply let you run programs—either those that are built into the shell, such as ones that let you manipulate files, or other, more complicated programs that you've installed yourself.

The shell is clever enough to know where your programs are likely to be stored. This information was given to it when you first installed Fedora and is stored in a system variable.

■**Note** A *variable* is what Linux uses to remember things like names, directory paths, and other data. There are many system variables that are vital for the running of Fedora.

The information about where your programs are stored, and therefore where Fedora should look for commands you type in, as well as any programs you might want to run, is stored in the PATH variable. You can take a look at what's currently stored there by typing the following:

```
echo $PATH
```

Don't forget that the difference between uppercase and lowercase letters matters to Fedora, unlike with Windows and DOS.

The echo command merely tells the shell to print something on screen. In this case, you're telling it to "echo" the PATH variable onto your screen. On our test PC, this returned the following information:

```
/usr/kerberos/bin:/usr/local/bin:/usr/bin:/bin:/usr/X11R6/bin:/home/linuxlala/bin
```

Several directories are in this list, each separated by a colon.

Don't worry too much about the details right now. The important thing to know is that whenever you type a program name, the shell looks in each of the listed directories in sequence. In other words, when you type ls, the shell will look in each of the directories stored in the PATH variable, starting with the first in the list, to see if the ls program can be found. The first instance it finds is the one it will run. (The ls command gives you a directory listing, as described in the "Listing Files" section later in this chapter.)

But what if you want to run a program that is not contained in a directory listed in your PATH? In this case, you must tell the shell exactly where the program is. Here's an example:

```
/home/linuxlala/myprogram
```

This will run a program called myprogram in the /home/linuxlala directory. It will do this regardless of the directory you're currently browsing, and regardless of whether there is anything else on your system called myprogram.

If you're already in the directory where the program in question is located, you can type the following:

```
./myprogram
```

So, just enter a dot and a forward slash, followed by the program name.

Getting Help

Each command usually has help built in, which you can query (a little like typing /? after a command when using DOS). This will explain what the command does and how it should be used. In most cases, you'll see an example of the command in use, along with the range of command options that can be used with it. For example, you can get some instant help on the ifconfig command by typing this:

```
/sbin/ifconfig --help
```

You'll see the help screen shown in Figure 13-2.

The --help option is fairly universal, and most programs will respond to it, although sometimes you might need to use a single dash. Just type the command along with --help to see what happens. You'll be told if you're doing anything wrong.

In addition, most commands have manuals that you can read to gain a fairly complete understanding of how they work. Virtually every Fedora setup has a set of these man pages, which can be accessed by typing this:

```
man <command>
```

However, man pages are often technical and designed for experienced Linux users who understand the terminology.

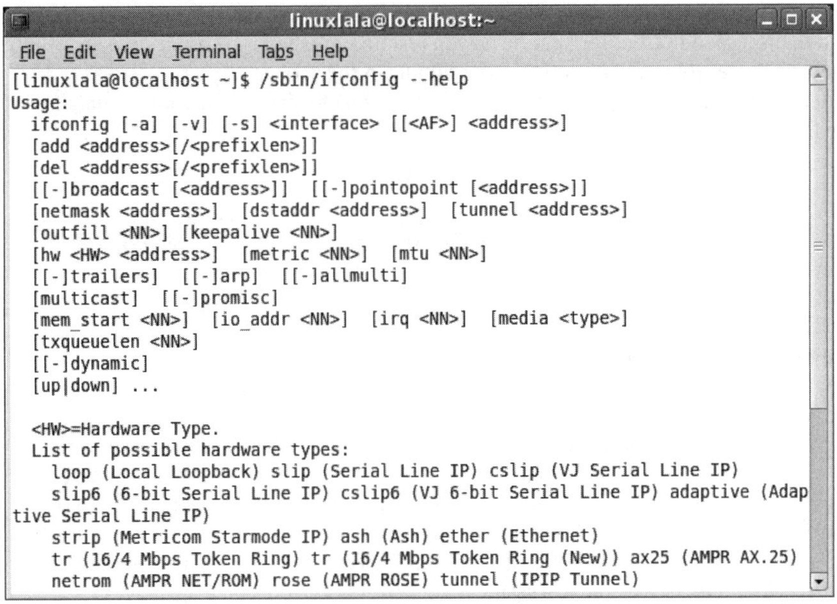

```
                          linuxlala@localhost:~                        _ □ x
File  Edit  View  Terminal  Tabs  Help
[linuxlala@localhost ~]$ /sbin/ifconfig --help
Usage:
  ifconfig [-a] [-v] [-s] <interface> [[<AF>] <address>]
  [add <address>[/<prefixlen>]]
  [del <address>[/<prefixlen>]]
  [[-]broadcast [<address>]]  [[-]pointopoint [<address>]]
  [netmask <address>]  [dstaddr <address>]  [tunnel <address>]
  [outfill <NN>] [keepalive <NN>]
  [hw <HW> <address>]  [metric <NN>]  [mtu <NN>]
  [[-]trailers]  [[-]arp]  [[-]allmulti]
  [multicast]  [[-]promisc]
  [mem_start <NN>]  [io_addr <NN>]  [irq <NN>]  [media <type>]
  [txqueuelen <NN>]
  [[-]dynamic]
  [up|down] ...

  <HW>=Hardware Type.
  List of possible hardware types:
    loop (Local Loopback) slip (Serial Line IP) cslip (VJ Serial Line IP)
    slip6 (6-bit Serial Line IP) cslip6 (VJ 6-bit Serial Line IP) adaptive (Adap
tive Serial Line IP)
    strip (Metricom Starmode IP) ash (Ash) ether (Ethernet)
    tr (16/4 Mbps Token Ring) tr (16/4 Mbps Token Ring (New)) ax25 (AMPR AX.25)
    netrom (AMPR NET/ROM) rose (AMPR ROSE) tunnel (IPIP Tunnel)
```

Figure 13-2. *Most commands contain built-in help to give you a clue as to how they're used.*

■**Note** Some commands, like `ifconfig`, are not in an ordinary user's `$PATH`. This is why you need to type `/sbin/ifconfig` to run it, or `/sbin/ifconfig --help` to get help. While you can run some programs like this, you need to be the root user to execute any system changes. Refer to Chapter 30 for more about `root` and the other users.

Some commands also have info pages, which offer slightly more down-to-earth guides. You can read these by typing this:

`info <command>`

If a command isn't covered by the info system, you'll be shown the default screen explaining basic facts about how the `info` command works.

Note that both `man` and `info` have their own man and info pages, explaining how they work. Just type `man man` or `info info`.

Running the Shell via a Virtual Console

As noted earlier, you can start the shell in a number of ways. The most common way among Linux diehards is via a virtual console. To access a virtual console, press Ctrl+Alt, and then press one of the function keys from F1 through F6 (the keys at the top of your keyboard).

Using a virtual console is a little like switching desks to a completely different PC. Pressing Ctrl+Alt+F1 will cause your GUI to disappear, and the screen to be taken over by a command-line prompt (don't worry; your GUI is still there and running in the background). You'll be asked to enter your username and your password.

Any programs you run in a virtual console won't affect the rest of the system, unless they're system commands. (As discussed in Chapter 16, one way to rescue a crashed GUI program is to switch to a virtual console and attempt to terminate the program from there.)

You can switch back to the GUI by pressing Ctrl+Alt+F7. Don't forget to quit your virtual console when you're finished with it, by typing exit.

BOOTING INTO THE SHELL

If you're really in love with the shell, you can choose to boot into it, avoiding the GUI completely (although you can later start the GUI by typing startx at the command line).

Booting into the shell is done by defining a custom run level. A *run level* is how the operating mode that Fedora is currently running in is described. For example, one particular run level might start a GUI, while another might start only a command prompt.

There are usually seven run levels under Linux, numbered from 0 to 6. Not all of them do something interesting. On Fedora, run level 5 runs the GUI. Run level 1 runs a command prompt, so it might seem ideal for booting into the shell, but it also shuts down a few essential services. This means it isn't suitable for day-to-day use. Run levels 2 and 3, just like run level 1, don't run a GUI either.

By default, Fedora boots into run level 5—that is, it runs a GUI. To change this behavior, you'll need to tell Fedora to boot straight to run level 3, rather than the default of 5. You do this by editing the /etc/inittab file, which is one of the first configuration files Fedora reads when booting. Issue the following commands at the shell to open the file in the Gedit text editor:

```
$ su -
[Password]
# gedit /etc/inittab
```

Then look for the following line, which will be near the top of the file:

```
id:5:initdefault
```

And edit it so that it reads:

```
id:3:initdefault
```

Then save the file. From now on, you'll always boot to a text-based virtual console, where you can log in and use the shell. To restore things to the way they were, simply restore the line in the /etc/inittab file to the way it appeared originally.

Working with Files

So let's start actually using the shell. If you've ever used DOS, then you have a head start over most shell beginners, although you'll still need to learn some new commands. Table 13-1 shows various DOS commands alongside their Fedora equivalents. This table also serves as a handy guide to some BASH commands, even if you've never used DOS. In Appendix B, you'll find a comprehensive list of useful shell commands, together with explanations of what they do and examples of typical usage.

Table 13-1. *DOS Commands and Their Shell Equivalents*

Command	DOS Command	Linux Shell Command	Usage
Copy files	COPY	cp	cp <filename> <new location>
Move files	MOVE	mv	mv <filename> <new location>
Rename files	RENAME	mv	mv <old filename> <new filename>[1]
Delete files	DEL	rm	rm <filename>[2]
Create directories	MKDIR	mkdir	mkdir <directory name>
Delete directories	DELTREE/RMDIR	rm	rm -rf <directory name>
Change directory	CD	cd	cd <directory name>
Edit text files	EDIT	vi	vi <filename>
View text files	TYPE	less	less <filename>[3]
Print text files	PRINT	lpr	lpr <filename>
Compare files	FC	diff	diff <file1> <file2>
Find files	FIND	find	find -name <filename>
Check disk integrity	SCANDISK	fsck	fsck[4]
View network	IPCONFIG	ifconfig	ifconfig settings
Check a network	PING	ping	ping <address> connection
View a network route	TRACERT	tracepath	tracepath <address>
Clear screen	CLS	clear	clear
Get help	HELP	man	man <command>[5]
Quit	EXIT	exit	exit

1. *The BASH shell offers a rename command, but this is chiefly used to rename many files at once.*

2. *To avoid being asked to confirm each file deletion, you can add the -f option. Be aware that the rm command deletes data instantly, without the safety net of a recycle bin, as with the GNOME desktop.*

3. *Use the cursor keys to move up and down in the document. Type Q to quit.*

4. *This is a system command and can be run only on a disk that isn't currently in use. To scan the main partition, you'll need to boot from the installation CD and select the rescue option. Then issue the fsck command.*

5. *The info command can also be used.*

CREATING ALIASES

If you've ever used DOS, you might find yourself inadvertently typing DOS commands at the shell prompt. Some of these will actually work, because most distribution companies create command aliases to ease the transition of newcomers to Linux.

Aliases mean that whenever you type certain words, they will be interpreted as meaning something else. However, an alias won't work with any of the command-line switches used in DOS. In the long run, you should try to learn the BASH equivalents.

You can create your own command aliases quickly and simply. Just start a BASH shell and type the following:

```
alias <DOS command>'<Linux shell command>
```

For example, to create an alias that lets you type del instead of rm, type this:

```
alias del='rm'
```

Note that the Fedora command must appear in single quotation marks.

Listing Files

Possibly the most fundamentally useful BASH command is ls. This will list the files in the current directory, as shown in Figure 13-3. If you have a lot of files, they might scroll off the screen. If you're running GNOME Terminal, you can use the scroll bar on the right side of the window, or Shift+Page Up/Page Down, to view the list.

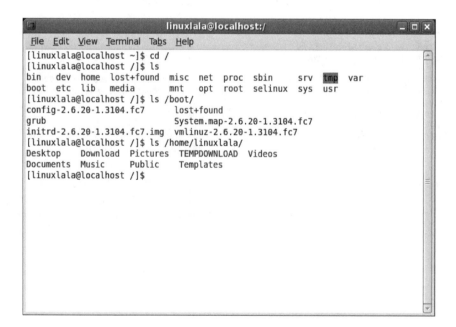

Figure 13-3. *The ls command lists the files in the current directory.*

Having the files scroll off the screen can be annoying, so you can cram as many as possible onto each line by typing the following:

```
ls -m
```

The dash after the command indicates that you're using a command option. These are also referred to as command-line *flags* or *switches*. Nearly all shell commands have options like this. In fact, some commands won't do anything unless you specify various options. In the case of the ls command, only one dash is necessary, but some commands need two dashes to indicate an option.

You can see a list of all the command options for ls by typing the following (itself a command option):

```
ls --help
```

Once again, the output will scroll off the screen, and you can use the window's scroll bars to examine it. (In Chapter 17, you'll learn a trick you can use to read this output without needing to fiddle around with the scroll bars, even if there's screen after screen of it.)

With most commands, you can use many command options at once, as long as they don't contradict each other. For example, you could type the following:

```
ls -lh
```

This tells the ls command to produce "long" output and also to produce "human-readable" output. The long option (-l) lists file sizes and ownership permissions, among other details (permissions are covered in Chapter 14). The human-readable option (-h) means that rather than listing files in terms of bytes (such as 1029725 bytes), it will list them in kilobytes and megabytes. Notice that you can simply list the options after the dash; you don't need to give each option its own dash.

■**Caution** We've said it before, and we'll say it again: don't forget that case-sensitivity is vitally important in Fedora! Typing ls -L is not the same as typing ls -l. It will produce different results.

Copying Files

Another useful command for dealing with files is cp, which copies files. You can use the cp command in the following way:

```
cp myfile /home/linuxlala/
```

This will copy the file to the location specified.

One important command-line option for cp is -r. This stands for "recursive" and tells BASH that you want to copy a directory and its contents (as well as any directories within this directory). Most commands that deal with files have a recursive option.

■**Note** Only a handful of BASH commands default to recursive copying. Even though it's extremely common to copy folders, you still need to specify the -r command option most of the time.

One curious trick is that you can copy a file from one place to another but, by specifying a filename in the destination part of the command, change its name. Here's an example:

```
cp myfile /home/linuxlala/myfile2
```

This will copy `myfile` to `/home/linuxlala`, but rename it `myfile2`. Be careful not to add a final slash to the command when you do this. In the example here, doing so would cause BASH to think that `myfile2` is a directory.

This way of copying files is a handy way of duplicating files. By not specifying a new location in the destination part of the command, but still specifying a different filename, you effectively duplicate the file within the same directory:

```
cp myfile myfile2
```

This will result in two identical files: one called `myfile` and one called `myfile2`.

Moving Files

The `mv` command is similar to `cp`, except that rather than copying the file, the old one is removed. You can move files from one directory to another, for example, like this:

```
mv myfile /home/linuxlala/
```

As shown in Figure 13-4, you can also use the `mv` command to quickly rename files:

```
mv myfile myfile2
```

■**Note** Getting technical for a moment, moving a file in Linux isn't the same as in Windows, where a file is copied and then the original deleted. Under Fedora, the file's absolute path is rewritten, causing it to simply appear in a different place in the file structure. However, the end result is the same.

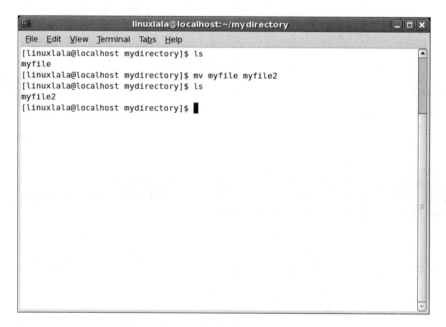

Figure 13-4. *You can also use the mv command to rename files.*

Deleting Files

But how do you get rid of files? Again, this is relatively easy, but first a word of caution: the shell doesn't operate any kind of recycle bin. Once a file is deleted, it's gone forever. (There are utilities you can use to recover files, but these are specialized tools and aren't to be relied on for day-to-day use.)

Removing a file is achieved by typing something like this:

```
rm myfile
```

It's as simple as that.

You'll be asked to confirm the deletion after you issue the command. If you want to delete a file without being asked to confirm it, type the following:

```
rm -f myfile
```

The f stands for force (i.e., force the deletion).

If you try to use the rm command to remove a directory, you'll see an error message. This is because the command needs an additional option:

```
rm -rf mydirectory
```

As noted earlier, the r stands for recursive and indicates that any folder specified afterward should be deleted, in addition to any files it contains. You must exercise caution when using the rm -rf command, because files once deleted cannot be easily recovered.

■**Note** You might have used wildcards within Windows and DOS. They can be used within Fedora, too. For example, the asterisk (*) can be used to mean any file. So, you can type rm -f * to delete all files within a directory, or type rm -f myfile* to delete all files that start with the word myfile. But remember to be careful with the rm command. Keep in mind that you cannot salvage files easily if you accidentally delete them!

Changing and Creating Directories

Another handy command is cd, which stands for change directory. This lets you move around the file system from directory to directory. Say you're in a directory that has another directory in it, named mydirectory2. Switching to it is easy:

```
cd mydirectory2
```

But how do you get out of this directory once you're in it? Try the following command:

```
cd ..
```

The .. refers to the *parent* directory, which is the one containing the directory you're currently browsing. Using two dots to indicate this may seem odd, but it's just the way that Fedora (and UNIX before it) does things. It's one of the many conventions that UNIX relies on and that you'll pick up as you go along.

You can create directories with the mkdir command:

```
mkdir mydirectory
```

Summary

This chapter has introduced the command-line shell, considered by many to be the heart of Linux. We discussed its similarities to MS-DOS, and showed that these are only cursory; knowledge of DOS doesn't equate to skill within BASH. In the long run, you should work to polish your BASH skills.

This chapter also introduced some elementary commands used within BASH, such as those used to provide directory listings and to copy files. We looked at how you can use command-line options to control BASH tools. In many cases, these are mandatory, so we covered how the BASH shell itself can be used to investigate a command and find out vital information about how it works.

At this point, your newfound knowledge will have no doubt caused you to venture into the Fedora file system itself, which can be a confusing, if not terrifying, place for the inexperienced. But don't worry. The next chapter explains everything you need to know about the file system and what you'll find in it.

Understanding Linux Files and Users

Most of us are used to dealing with files—the things that live on our hard disks, floppies, and CD-ROMs and contain data and program code. It should come as no surprise that Linux has its own file structure that is different from Windows in terms of where data is stored and also the underlying technology.

Taking a page from UNIX, Fedora takes the concept of the file system to an extreme. To Fedora, almost everything is treated as a file: your PC's hardware, network computers connected to your PC, information about the current state of your computer . . . almost everything finds a home within the Linux file system.

Linux places an equal emphasis on the users of the system. They own the various files and can decide who can and cannot access various files they create.

In this chapter, we'll delve into users, files, and permissions. You'll be introduced to how Fedora handles files and how files are tied into the system of user accounts.

Real Files and Virtual Files

Linux sees virtually everything as a series of files. This might sound absurd and certainly requires further explanation.

Let's start with the example of plugging in a piece of hardware. Whenever you attach something to a USB socket, the Linux kernel finds it, sees if it can make the hardware work, and, if everything checks out OK, it will usually make the hardware available as a file under the /dev directory on your hard disk (dev is short for "devices"). Figure 14-1 shows an example of a /dev directory.

The file created in the /dev directory is not a real file, of course. It's a file system shortcut plumbed through to the input and output components of the hardware you've just attached.

■Note As a user, you're not expected to delve into the /dev directory and deal with this hardware directly. Most of the time, you'll use various software packages that will access the hardware for you, or use special BASH commands or GUI programs to make the hardware available in a more accessible way for day-to-day use.

Here's another example. Say you're working in an office and you want to connect to a central file server. To do this under Linux, you must *mount* the file system that the server offers, making it a part of the Fedora file system. Doing this involves creating an empty directory (or using one that already exists) and using the mount command at the BASH shell to make the server's contents magically appear whenever that directory is accessed. We'll discuss how this is done later in this chapter, in the "Mounting" section (but remember that Fedora may do this automatically, as discussed in Chapter 12).

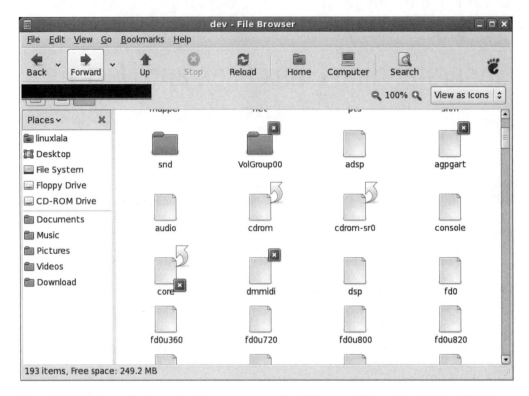

Figure 14-1. *Hardware devices under Linux are accessed as if they were files and can be found in the /dev folder.*

Once the network server is mounted, it is treated exactly like a directory on your hard disk. You can copy files to and from it, just as you would normally, using the same tools as you use for dealing with any other files. In fact, less knowledgeable users won't even be aware that they're accessing something that isn't located on their PC's hard disk (or, technically speaking, within their Fedora partition and file system).

By treating everything as a file, Linux makes system administration easier. To probe and test your hardware, for example, you can use the same tools you use to manipulate files. So how do you know which files are real and which are virtual? One method is to use the following command, which was introduced in the previous chapter:

```
ls -l
```

The -l option tells the ls command to list nearly all the details about the files. If you do this in GNOME Terminal, you'll see that the listing is color-coded. Table 14-1 shows what each color indicates. The command returns a lot of additional information, including who owns which file and what you and others can do with it. This requires an understanding of users and file permissions, which we'll discuss next.

■**Note** The command ls -la will give you even more information—perhaps too much for general use. In most instances, ls -l should show enough information.

Table 14-1. *Color-Coding Within GNOME Terminal*

Color	Type of File
Black text	Standard file
Light-blue text	Directory
Black outline with yellow text	Virtual device[1]
Green text	Program or script[2]
Cyan text	Symbolic link to another file[3]
Pink text	Image file
Red text	Archive[4]

1 This is found only in the /dev directory.

2 Technically speaking, green text indicates a program or script that has merely been marked as being executable.

3 This is similar to a Windows desktop shortcut.

4 Installation files are also marked red because they're usually contained in archives.

Users and File Permissions

The concept of users and permissions is as important to Fedora as the idea of a central and all-encompassing file system. In fact, the two are implicitly linked.

When initially installing Linux, you should have created at least one user account. By now, this will have formed the day-to-day login that you use to access Linux and run programs.

Although you might not realize it, as a user, you also belong to a group. In fact, every user on the system belongs to a group. Under Fedora, ordinary users belong to a group based on their username (under other versions of Linux, you might find that you belong to a group called "users").

■**Note** Groups are yet another reminder of Fedora's UNIX origins. UNIX is often used on huge computer systems with hundreds or thousands of users. By putting each user into a group, the system administrator's job is a lot easier. When controlling system resources, the administrator can control groups of users rather than hundreds of individual users. On most home-user PCs, the concept of groups is a little redundant, because there's normally a single user, or at most, two or three. However, the concept of groups is central to the way that Linux handles files.

A standard user account under Fedora is normally limited in what it can do. As a standard user, you can save files to your own private area of the disk, located in the /home directory, as shown in Figure 14-2, and in /tmp (the system-wide shared directory for temporary files), but almost nowhere else. You can move around the file system, but some directories are strictly out of bounds. In a similar way, some files can be opened as read-only, so you cannot save changes to them. All of this is achieved using file permissions.

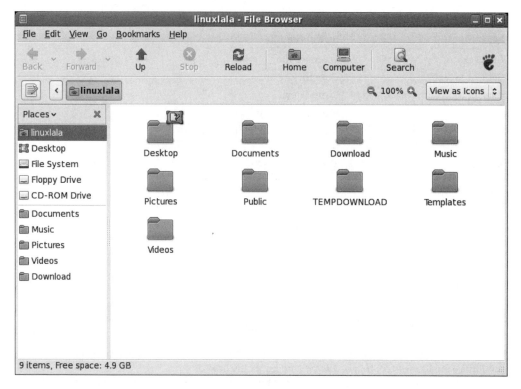

Figure 14-2. *Your personal directory within home is your area on the hard disk. This is enforced via file permissions.*

Every file and directory is owned by a user. In addition, files and directories have three separate settings that indicate who within the Linux system can read them, who can write to them, and, if the file in question is *runnable* (usually a program or a script), who can run it (*execute* it). In the case of directories, it's also possible to set who can browse them, as well as who can write files to them. If you try to access a file or directory for which you don't have permission, you'll be turned away with an "access denied" error message.

ROOT VS. USER

Fedora, like most versions of Linux, has two types of user accounts: standard and root. Standard users are those who can run programs on the system but are limited in what they can do. Root users have complete run of the system, and as such, are often referred to as *superusers*. They can access and delete whatever files they want. They can also configure hardware, change settings, and so on.

Most versions of Linux create a user account called root and let users log in as root to perform system maintenance. However, for practical as well as security reasons, most of the time the user is logged in as a standard user.

The command `su -` will drop you to the root shell. This means that you now have the root user's permissions.

Viewing Permissions

When you issue the ls -l command, each file is listed on an individual line. Here's an example of one line of a file listing from our test PC:

```
-rw-r--r-- 1 linuxlala linuxlala 40917 Oct 18 09:48 myfile
```

The r, w, and - symbols on the very left of the listing indicate the file permissions. The permission list usually consists of the characters r (for read), w (for write), x (for execute), or - (meaning none are applicable).

They're followed by a number indicating the link count, which you can ignore. After this is listed the owner of the file (linuxlala in the example) and the group that he belongs to (linuxlala). This is followed by the file size (in bytes), then the date and time the file was last accessed, and finally the filename itself.

The file permissions part of the listing might look confusing, but it's actually quite simple. To understand what's going on, you need to split it into groups of four, as illustrated in Figure 14-3.

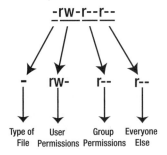

Figure 14-3. *The file permissions part of a file listing can be broken down into four separate parts.*

The four groups are as follows:

- *Type of file*: This character represents the file type. A standard data file is indicated with a dash (-). Most files on your system fall into this category. A d shows that the entry is not a file, but a directory. Table 14-2 lists the file type codes.

- *User permissions*: Next come the permissions of the person who owns the file. The three characters indicate what the person who owns the file can do with it. The owner of a file is usually the user who created it, although it's also possible to change the owner later on. In this example, you see rw-. This means that the owner of the file can read (r) and write (w) the file. In other words, she can look at it and also save changes to it. However, there's a dash following it, and this indicates that the user cannot execute the file. If this were possible, there would be an x in this spot instead.

- *Group permissions*: After the owner's permissions are the permissions given to members of that user's group. This is indicated by another three characters in the same style as those for user permissions. In the example, the group's permission is r--, which means that the group members can read the file but don't have permission to write to it, since there's a dash where the w would normally appear. In other words, as far as they're concerned, the file is read-only.

- *Everyone else's permissions*: The last set of permissions indicates the permissions of everyone else on the system (other users in other groups). In the example, they can only read the file (r); the two dashes following it indicate that they cannot write to the file nor execute it.

Table 14-2. *File Type Codes*

Code	File Type
-	Standard file
d	Standard directory
l	Symbolic link (a shortcut to another file)
p	Named pipe (a file that acts as a conduit for data between two programs)
s	Socket (a file designed to send and receive data over a network)
c	Character device (a hardware device driver, usually found in /dev)
b	Block device (a hardware device driver, usually found in /dev)

As you might remember from Windows, programs are stored as files on your hard disk, just like standard data files. On Linux, program files need to be explicitly marked as being executable. This is indicated in the permission listing by an x. Therefore, if there's no x in a file's permissions, it's a good bet that the file in question isn't a program or script (although this isn't always true for various technical reasons).

To make matters a little more confusing, if the entry in the list of files is a directory (indicated by a d), then the rules are different. In this case, an x indicates that the user can browse that directory. If there's no x, then the user's attempts to browse to that directory will be met with an "access denied" message.

File permissions can be difficult to understand, so let's look at a few real-world examples. These examples assume that you're logged into Linux as the user linuxlala.

LESS COMMON FILE TYPES

Instead of the x in the list of permissions for a directory, you might sometimes see a t. This means that the only people who can delete or alter a file in that directory are the users who created the file in the first place. This is a useful option to have in some circumstances, and is sometimes called the "sticky bit."

You might sometimes see a set of permissions like rws. The s stands for *setuid*. Like x, it indicates that the file is executable, except, in this case, it means that the file will be run with the permissions of the person who owns it, rather than the user who is executing it. In other words, if user frank tries to run a program owned by linuxlala that has the execute permission set as s, that program will be run as if linuxlala were running it. This is very useful, because it can make programs that require root powers usable by ordinary users, although this brings with it security risks, since this can give an unauthorized user privileges to sensitive system areas.

Typical Data File Permissions

Here's an example to understand basic file permissions:

```
-rw-rw---- 2 linuxlala linuxlala 4096 Dec 15 19:36 myfile2
```

You see immediately that this file is owned by user linuxlala because that username appears directly after the permissions. You also see that this user is a member of the group linuxlala.

Reading the file permissions from left to right, you see that the initial character is a dash. That indicates that this is an ordinary file and has no special characteristics. It's also not a directory.

After that is the first part of the permissions, rw-. These are the permissions for the owner of the file, linuxlala. You're logged in as that user, so this file belongs to you, and these permissions apply to you. You can read and write the file, but not execute it. Because you cannot execute the file, you can infer that this is a data file rather than a program (there are certain exceptions to this rule, but we'll ignore them for the sake of simplicity).

Following this is the next part of the file permissions, rw-. This tells you what other members of your group can do with the file. It's fairly useless information if you're the only user of your PC, but for the record, you're told that anyone else belonging to the group called linuxlala can also read and write the file, but not execute it. If you're not the only user of a computer, group permissions can be important. The "Altering Permissions" section, coming up shortly, describes how to change file permissions to control who can access files.

Finally, the last three characters tell you the permissions of everyone else on the system. The three dashes (---) mean that they have no permissions at all regarding the file. There's a dash where the r normally appears, so they cannot even read it. The dashes following it tell you they cannot write to the file or execute it. If they try to do anything with the file, they'll get a "permission denied" error.

Permissions on a User's Directory

Let's see how permissions for a directory are different from a regular file:

```
drwxr-xr-x 4 linuxlala linuxlala 824 Dec 27 14:37 mydirectory
```

The list of permissions starts with d, which tells you that this isn't a file but a directory. After this is the list of permissions for the owner of the directory (linuxlala), who can read files in the directory and also create new ones there. The x indicates that you can access this directory, as opposed to being turned away with an "access denied" message. You might think being able to access the directory is taken for granted if the user can read and write to it, but that's not the case.

Next are the permissions for the group members. They can read files in the directory but not write any new ones there (although they can modify files already in there, provided the permissions of the individual files allow this). Once again, there's an x at the end of their particular permission listing, which indicates that the group members can access the directory.

Following the group's permissions are those of everyone else. They can read the directory and browse it, but not write new files to it, as with the group users' permissions.

Permissions on a Directory Owned by Root

In the following example, we'll decipher permissions of a directory owned by root:

```
drwx------ 25 root root 1000 Dec 21 22:31 root
```

You can see that the file is owned by root. Remember that in this example, you're logged in as linuxlala and your group is linuxlala.

The list of permissions starts with a d, so you can tell that this is actually a directory. After this, you see that the owner of the directory, root, has permission to read, write, and access the directory.

Next are the permissions for the group: three dashes. In other words, members of the group called root have no permission to access this directory in any way. They cannot browse it, create new files in it, or even access it.

Following this are the permissions for the rest of the users. This includes you, because you're not the user root and don't belong to its group. The three dashes means you don't have permission to read, write, or access this directory.

SWITCHING USERS

If you have more than one user set up on your system, it's possible to switch users on the fly while you're working at the shell. On our test PC, there's an additional user account called FC. While logged in as any user, you can temporarily switch to user FC by typing the following command, which stands for *substitute user*:

```
su - FC
```

You'll then be asked for user FC's password. Once this is typed, you will effectively have logged in as user FC. Any files you now create will be saved with FC's ownership.

To return to your own account from any other account, type exit.

You can use the User Switcher applet to log into other user account without signing out of the current account. To learn how to use the User Switcher refer to Chapter 29.

Altering Permissions

You can easily change permissions of files and directories by using the chmod command. For example, if you want to change a file so that everyone on the system can read and write to it, type the following:

```
chmod a+rw myfile
```

In other words, you're adding read and write (rw) permissions for all users (a). Here's another example:

```
chmod a-w myfile
```

This tells Linux that you want to take away (-) the ability of all users (a) to write (w) to the file. However, you want to leave the other permissions as they are. You can substitute a with g to change group permissions instead.

The most useful function of chmod is in making a program file that you've downloaded executable. Due to the way the Internet works, if you download a program to install on your computer, it can lose its executable status while in transit. In this case, issue the following command:

```
chmod +x myprogram
```

Because nothing is specified before the +x, the shell assumes that the changes to be applied to the file are for everyone: user, group, and other.

To change the owner of a file, use the chown command. For security reasons, the chown command must be preceded with the su - command, which is to say that chown (and chgrp, to change the group) requires superuser powers.

For example, to set the owner of myfile as frank, type the following commands:

```
$ su -
[Enter Password]
# chown frank myfile
```

You can also change the owner *and* the group of a file using chown. Simply type each separated by a period:

```
chown frank.mygroup myfile
```

This will change myfile so that its owner is frank and its group is mygroup.

To change the group of a file, you can use the chgrp command in exactly the same way as chown:

```
chgrp mygroup myfile
```

■**Note** A user can change the group of any file he owns to any group he belongs to without using the su - command.

The File System Explained

Now that you understand the principles of files and users, we can take a bird's-eye view of the Linux file system and start to make sense of it.

You might already have ventured beyond the /home directory and wandered through the file system. You no doubt found it thoroughly confusing, largely because it's not like anything you're used to. The good news is that it's not actually very hard to understand. If nothing else, you should be aware that nearly everything can be ignored during everyday use.

■**Note** The Fedora file system is referred to as a *hierarchical* file system. This means that it consists of a lot of directories that contain files. Windows also uses a hierarchical file system. Fedora refers to the very bottom level of the file system as the root. This has no connection with the root user.

You can switch to the root of the file system by typing the following shell command:

```
cd /
```

When used on its own, the forward slash is interpreted as a shortcut for root.

We got the following result when we did this on our test PC, and then asked for a long file listing (ls -l):

```
total 152
drwxr-xr-x    2 root root  4096 Jan  1 01:29 bin
drwxr-xr-x    3 root root  4096 Dec 21 18:07 boot
drwxr-xr-x   11 root root  4020 Jan 10 00:43 dev
drwxr-xr-x  103 root root 12288 Jan 10 00:43 etc
drwxr-xr-x    3 root root  4096 Dec 21 22:41 home
drwxr-xr-x   14 root root  4096 Jan  3 00:32 lib
drwx------    2 root root 16384 Dec 21 22:16 lost+found
drwxr-xr-x    2 root root  4096 Jan 10 00:43 media
drwxr-xr-x    2 root root     0 Jan 10 00:42 misc
```

```
drwxr-xr-x    2 root root  4096 Dec 21 18:28 mnt
drwxr-xr-x    2 root root     0 Jan 10 00:42 net
drwxr-xr-x    2 root root  4096 Oct 11 03:36 opt
dr-xr-xr-x  126 root root     0 Jan 10  2007 proc
drwxr-x---   21 root root  4096 Jan 10 01:05 root
drwxr-xr-x    2 root root 12288 Jan  1 01:30 sbin
drwxr-xr-x    2 root root  4096 Dec 21 22:16 selinux
drwxr-xr-x    2 root root  4096 Oct 11 03:36 srv
drwxr-xr-x   11 root root     0 Jan 10  2007 sys
drwxrwxrwt   13 root root  4096 Jan 10 01:05 tmp
drwxr-xr-x   14 root root  4096 Dec 21 22:19 usr
drwxr-xr-x   26 root root  4096 Dec 21 22:30 var
```

The first thing you'll notice from this is that the root of the file system contains largely directories and that all files and directories are owned by root.

Only users with administrative powers can write files to the root of the file system. That means if you wanted to write to the root of the file system or otherwise access those files, you would need to use the su - command. This is to prevent damage, since most of the directories in the root of the file system are vital to the correct running of Linux and contain essential programs or data.

Caution It's incredibly easy to slip up when using the command-line shell and thereby cause a lot of damage. For example, simply mistyping a forward slash in a command can mean the difference between deleting the files in a directory and deleting the directory itself. This is just another reason why you should always be careful when working at the command line, especially if you use the su - command.

As you can see from the file permissions of each directory in the root of the file system, most directories allow all users to browse them and access the files within (the last three characters of the permissions read r-x). You just won't be able to create new files there or delete the directories themselves. You might be able to modify or execute programs contained within the directory, but this will depend on the permissions of each individual file.

Table 14-3 provides a brief description of what each directory and file in the Fedora root file system contains. This is for reference only; there's no need for you to learn this information. The Fedora file system broadly follows the principles in the Filesystem Hierarchy Standard, as do most versions of Linux, but it does have its own subtleties.

Table 14-3. *Directories and Files in the Fedora Root File System*

Directory	Contents
bin	Vital tools necessary to get the system running, or for use when repairing the system and diagnosing problems
boot	Boot loader programs and configuration files (the boot loader is the menu that appears when you first boot Linux)
dev	Virtual files representing hardware installed on your system
etc	Central repository of configuration files for your system
home	Where each user's personal directory is stored
lib	Shared system files used by Linux as well as the software that runs on it
lost+found	Folder where salvaged scraps of files are saved in the event of a problematic shutdown and subsequent file system check
media	Where the directories representing various mounted storage systems are made available (including Windows partitions on the disk)

Directory	Contents
mnt	Directory in which external file systems can be temporarily mounted
net	Mount point for remote file systems
opt	Software that is theoretically optional and not vital to the running of the system (many software packages you use daily can be found here)
proc	Virtual directory containing data about your system and its current status
root	The root user's personal directory
sbin	Programs essential to administration of the system
selinux	Configuration files for selinux
srv	Data files for any network servers you might have running on your system
sys	Mount point of the sysfs file system, which is used by the kernel to administer your system's hardware
tmp	Temporary files stored by the system
usr	Programs and data that might be shared with other systems (such as in a large networking setup with many users)[1]
var	Used by the system to store data that is constantly updated, such as printer spooling output

1 *The usr directory contains its own set of directories that are full of programs and data. Many system programs, such as the X11 GUI software, are located within the /usr directory. Note that the /usr directory is used even if your system will never act as a server to other systems.*

TYPES OF FILE SYSTEMS

Linux is all about choice, and this extends to the technology that makes the file system work. Unlike with Windows, where you can choose between just NTFS and FAT32 (with the emphasis being on NTFS), Linux offers many different types of file system technology. Each is designed for varying tasks. Most are scalable, however, which means that they will work just as happily on a desktop PC as on a massive cluster of computers.

Fedora uses the ext3 file system. This is a popular choice among distros, although the SUSE distro uses the reiserfs system. People are constantly arguing about which file system is best. The principal measuring stick is performance. Your computer spends a lot of time writing and reading files, so the faster a file system is, the faster your PC will be overall (although, in reality, the hardware is of equal importance).

Note that what we're talking about here is the underlying and invisible technology of the file system. In day-to-day use, the end user won't be aware of any difference between ext3, reiserfs, or another file system technology (although when things go wrong, different tools are used to attempt repairs; their selection is automated within Fedora).

Here are the various types along with notes about what they offer:

- *ext2*: Fast, stable, and well established, ext2 was once the most popular type of file system technology used on Linux. It has now been eclipsed by ext3.

- *ext3*: An extension of ext2, ext3 allows *journaling*, a way of recording what has been written to disk so that a recovery can be attempted when things go wrong.

- *reiserfs*: This is another journaling file system.

- *jfs*: This is a journaling file system created by IBM. It's used on industrial implementations of UNIX.

- *xfs*: This is a 64-bit journaling file system created by Silicon Graphics, Inc. (SGI) and used on its own version of UNIX, as well as Linux.

Mounting

Described in technical terms, mounting is the practice of making a file system available under Linux. This can take the form of a partition on your hard disk, a CD-ROM, a network server, or many other things.

Mounting drives might seem like a strange concept, but it actually makes everything much simpler than it might be otherwise. For example, once a drive is mounted, you don't need to use any special commands or software to access its contents. You can use the same programs and tools that you use to access all of your other files. Mounting creates a level playing field on which everything is equal and can therefore be accessed quickly and efficiently.

Using the mount Command

Mounting is usually done via the mount command. Under Fedora, you must have administrator powers to use the mount command, which means preceding it with the su - command and providing the root password.

With most modern versions of Linux, mount can be used in two ways: by specifying all the settings immediately after the command, or by making reference to an entry within the fstab file. fstab is a configuration file stored in the /etc directory that contains details of all file systems on the PC that can be mounted.

■**Note** The root file system is itself mounted automatically during bootup, shortly after the kernel has started and has all your hardware up and running. Every file system that Linux uses must be mounted at some point.

Let's say that you insert a CD or DVD into your computer's DVD-ROM drive. To mount the CD or DVD and make it available to Linux (something that is actually done automatically as soon as you put a disk in the drive—so this example is for demonstration purposes only), you would type the following (become root first by using the su - command):

```
mount /media/cdrom
```

The mount command first looks in your fstab file in the etc directory to find what you're referring to. Figure 14-4 shows an example of the contents of that file. (The example in the figure uses the cat command, which is discussed in Chapter 15). Using this information, the mount command attempts to make the contents of the CD available in a directory that's called a *mount point*. In this case, the content of the CD can be accessed through the /media/cdrom directory. Note that this is done in a virtual way; the files are not literally copied into the directory. The directory is merely a magical conduit that allows you to read the CD's contents.

There aren't any special commands used to work with mounted drives. The shell commands discussed in Chapter 13 should do everything you need.

The mount command doesn't see widespread usage by most users nowadays, because most removable storage devices like CDs, and even memory card readers, are mounted automatically under Fedora and an icon for them appears on the Desktop. This is because Fedora uses udev, which provides a dynamic device directory for actually present devices. So, when you plug in your USB drive or put a CD into your CD-ROM drive, it automatically gets mounted, whether or not there's an entry in your /etc/fstab file. However, there may be occasions when you need to mount a drive manually.

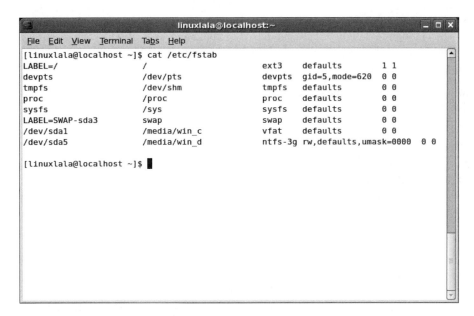

```
                            linuxlala@localhost:~                              _ □ x
 File  Edit  View  Terminal  Tabs  Help
[linuxlala@localhost ~]$ cat /etc/fstab
LABEL=/                   /                   ext3    defaults      1 1
devpts                    /dev/pts            devpts  gid=5,mode=620  0 0
tmpfs                     /dev/shm            tmpfs   defaults      0 0
proc                      /proc               proc    defaults      0 0
sysfs                     /sys                sysfs   defaults      0 0
LABEL=SWAP-sda3           swap                swap    defaults      0 0
/dev/sda1                 /media/win_c        vfat    defaults      0 0
/dev/sda5                 /media/win_d        ntfs-3g rw,defaults,umask=0000  0 0

[linuxlala@localhost ~]$ █
```

Figure 14-4. *Details of all frequently mounted file systems are held in the /etc/fstab file.*

Mounting a Drive Manually

Let's look at an example of when you might need to mount a drive manually. Suppose that you've just added a second hard disk to your PC that has previously been used on a Windows system. This has been added as the primary slave.

In the past, you'd have to create a mount point, which is an empty directory that will act as a location where you can tell the mount command to make the disk accessible. But the gnome-mount command bypasses these steps, in that it automatically creates mount points under the /media directory.

Here's what you need to do to mount a USB pen drive:

```
gnome-mount -d /dev/disk/by-id/usb-SanDisk_Cruzer_Mini
```

This will mount the USB drive under /media as disk/. An icon will appear on the Desktop once the disk is ready for use. The advantage with gnome-mount is that you don't need to know annoying device names.

To unmount the drive, use the gnome-umount command:

```
gnome-umount -p disk
```

Mounting Partitions

The first thing to do is create a mount point. You can create this directory anywhere, but under Linux, the convention is to create it in the /media directory. Therefore, the following command should do the trick (note that you need to use the su - command because writing to any directory other than your /home directory requires administrator privileges):

```
su -
[Enter Password]
mkdir /media/windows
```

You now need to know what kind of partition type is used on the disk, because you need to specify this when mounting. To find this out, use the `fdisk` command. Type the following exactly as it appears:

```
fdisk -l /dev/hdb
```

This will list the partitions on the second disk drive (assuming an average PC system). With most hard disks used under Windows, you should find a single partition that will be either NTFS or FAT32. The examples here assume that this is hdb1.

■**Caution**   Be aware that `fdisk` is a dangerous system command that can damage your system. The program is designed to partition disks and can wipe out your data if you're not careful!

With this information in hand, you're now ready to mount the disk. For a FAT32 disk, type the following:

```
mount -t vfat -o umask=0000 /dev/hdb1 /media/windows
```

The -t command option is used to specify the file system type. The -o flag indicates that you're going to specify some more command options, and you do so in the form of umask, which tells mount to ensure that the directory is readable and writable. After this, you specify the relevant file in the /dev directory (this file is only virtual, of course, and merely represents the hardware), and then specify the directory that is acting as your mount point.

Now when you browse to the /media/windows directory, by typing cd /media/windows, you should find the contents of the hard disk accessible. For more information about the mount command, read its man page (type man mount).

For an NTFS disk, you need to follow this procedure:

1. The first step is to install NTFS support. You need the kmod-ntfs package:

   ```
   yum install kmod-ntfs
   ```

2. To mount the disk, use this command:

   ```
   mount -t ntfs -o umask=0222 /dev/hdb1 /media/windows
   ```

You can even add an entry in the /etc/fstab file, so that the disk gets mounted automatically.

```
/dev/sda5     /media/windows    ntfs      ro,defaults,umask=0222    0 0
```

To read as well as write to a NTFS disk, you will need to install some other packages, apart from kmod-ntfs:

```
yum install fuse fuse-libs ntfs-3g
```

You can now mount the disk with this command:

```
mount -t ntfs-3g -o umask=0000 /dev/hdb1 /media/windows
```

In the /etc/fstab file, replace ntfs with ntfs-3g, and use the new umask value. You can now read and write to your NTFS disk!

■**Note**   Please refer to Chapter 28 for more information about yum.

Removing a Mounted System

To unmount a system, you use the special command umount (notice there's no n after the first u). Here's an example of using the command to unmount the CD-ROM drive (remember to become root by using su - before issuing this command):

```
umount /media/cdrom
```

You need to tell the umount command where to find the mounted contents. You can specify either the mount directory, as in the example, or the file in the /dev directory that refers to mounted resource (this is a little complicated, so in most cases, it's better to simply specify the file system location of the mount).

Note Sometimes you can automatically unmount a CD-ROM by hitting the eject button. This is because Fedora is clever enough to automatically unmount the CD if the button is pressed. However, if a program is accessing the CD, or if the CD is being browsed, the button won't work until all access to the CD has ceased.

If you're currently browsing the mounted directory, you'll need to leave it before you can unmount it, no matter whether you choose to do this manually or by hitting an eject button. The same is true of all kinds of access to the mounted directory. If you're browsing the mounted drive with Nautilus or if a piece of software is accessing it, you won't be able to unmount it until you've quit the program and closed the Nautilus window (or browsed to a different part of the file system).

File Searches

Files frequently get lost. Well, technically speaking, they don't actually get lost. We just forget where we've put them. But because of this, the shell includes some handy commands to search for files.

Using the find Command

Like the Search option on the Windows XP Start menu, the find command manually searches through all the files on the hard disk. It's not a particularly fast way of finding a file, but it is reliable. Here's an example:

```
find /home/linuxlala -name "myfile"
```

This will search for myfile using /home/linuxlala as a starting point (which is to say that it will search all directories within /home/linuxlala, and any directories within those directories, and so on, because it's recursive).

You can search the entire file system by leaving out the initial path. In this case, find will assume you want the search to start from /, the root of the file system.

If the file is found, you'll see it appear in the output of the command. The path will be shown next to the filename.

Period punctuation symbols have interesting meanings within file listings and therefore within the output of the find command. As you learned in Chapter 13, .. refers to the parent directory of the one you're currently browsing. In a similar way, a single . refers to the directory you're in at the moment; it's shorthand for "right here." So, if find returns a result like ./myfile, it means that myfile is right here in the current directory.

However, when a single period is used *at the beginning of a filename*, such as in .bashrc, it has the effect of hiding the file. In other words, that file won't appear when you type ls (although you can type ls -a to see all files, even those that are hidden).

If you give find a try, you'll see that it's not a particularly good way of searching. Apart from being slow, it will also return a lot of error messages about directories it cannot search. This is because, when you run the find command, it takes on your user permissions. Whenever find comes across a directory it cannot access, it will report it to you, as shown in the example in Figure 14-5. There are frequently so many of these warnings that the output can hide the instances where find actually locates the file in question!

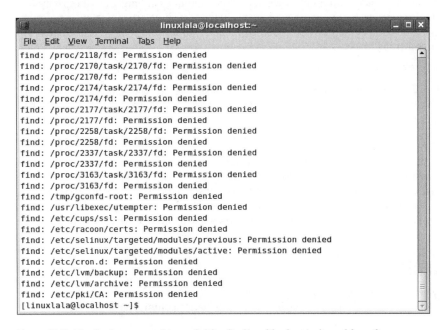

Figure 14-5. *The find command is useful for finding files but isn't problem-free.*

You can avoid these error messages in various ways, but perhaps the quickest solution is to precede the find command with su - to invoke superuser powers. In this way, you'll have access to every file on the hard disk, so the find command will be unrestricted in where it can search and won't run into any directories it doesn't have permission to enter.

■Caution Using the su - command with find may represent an invasion of privacy if you have more than one user on your system. The find command will search other users' /home directories and report any instances of files found there, too.

However, an even better solution for finding files is to use the locate command.

Using the locate Command

The alternative to using find is to use the locate command. This is far quicker than find because it relies on a central database of files, which is periodically updated. In other words, it doesn't literally search the file system each time.

The problem is that if you've saved a file recently and are hoping to find it, there's a chance that it won't yet appear in locate's database, so it won't turn up in the list of results.

Using locate is easy. You can use the following command to search for a file:

```
locate myfile
```

It's possible to update the locate database manually, although this might take a few minutes to work through. Simply issue the command updatedb. You need superuser powers to run this command.

After this, all files in the system should be indexed, making your search results more accurate.

Using the whereis Command

One other command worth mentioning in the context of searching is whereis. This locates where programs are stored and is an excellent way of exploring your system. Using it is simply a matter of typing something like this:

```
whereis cp
```

This will tell you where the cp program is located on your hard disk. It will also tell you where its source code and man page are located (if applicable). However, the first path returned by the search will be the location of the program itself.

File Size and Free Space

Often, it's necessary to know how large files are and to know how much space they're taking up on the hard disk. In addition, it's often handy to know how much free space is left on a disk.

Viewing File Sizes

Using the ls -l command option will tell you how large each file is in terms of bytes. Adding the -h option converts these file sizes to kilobytes, megabytes, and even gigabytes, depending on how large they are.

In order to get an idea of which are the largest files and which are the smallest, you can add the -S command option. This will order the files in the list in terms of the largest and smallest files.

The following will return a list of all the files in the current directory, in order of size (largest first), detailing the sizes in kilobytes, megabytes, or gigabytes:

```
ls -Slh
```

There's another more powerful way of presenting this information: using the du command, which stands for "disk usage." When used on its own without command switches, du simply presents the size of directories alongside their names (starting in the current directory). It will show any hidden directories (directories whose names start with a period) and will also present a total at the end of the list. This will probably be quite a long list. Once again, you can add the -h command option to force the du command to produce human-readable measurements of kilobytes and megabytes.

If you specify a file or directory when using the du command, along with the -s command option, you can find out its total file size:

```
du -sh mydirectory
```

This will show the size taken up on the disk by mydirectory, adding to the total any files or subdirectories it contains.

However, du is limited by the same file permission problems as the find tool, as shown in Figure 14-6. If you run du as an ordinary user, it won't be able to calculate the total for any directories you don't have permission to access. Therefore, you might consider using the su - command before using du.

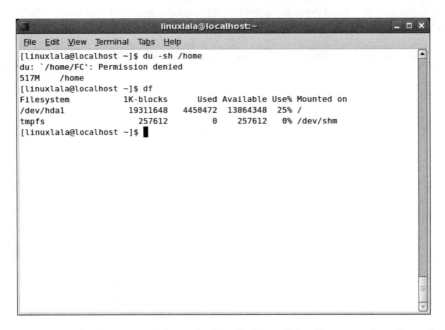

Figure 14-6. *The du command shows the size of a file, and the df command can be used to gauge the amount of free space on the disk.*

Finding Out the Amount of Free Space

What if you want to find out how much free space is left on the disk? In this case, you can use the df command. This command is also demonstrated in Figure 14-6.

The df command works on a partition-by-partition basis. Typing it at the command prompt will show you how much space is free on the entire disk. Once again, you can add the -h option to the df command to have the file sizes returned in megabytes and gigabytes (and even terabytes if your hard disk is big enough!).

The df command also returns information about something called tmpfs. These are temporary file stores, and you can ignore them.

■**Note** There is as much space free in any directory as there is space on the disk, which is why df displays data about the entire partition. If you're using a system managed by a system administrator within a business environment, you might find that quotas have been used to limit how much disk space you can take up. However, if you're using a desktop PC and are the only user, this won't be activated.

Summary

In this chapter, we examined how the Fedora file system lies at the heart to understanding how the operating system works. We also discussed how the file system and user accounts go hand in hand and are inextricably linked. This involved discussing the concept of file ownership and usage permissions, plus how these can be manipulated using command-line shell tools.

We also discussed the overall structure of the Fedora file system and how external file systems can be mounted and made available within Fedora. Finally, we looked at how to find files and how to gauge how much free space there is within the file system.

In the next chapter, we'll look at how the BASH shell can be used to view and otherwise manipulate text files, which are also important to the way Fedora works.

CHAPTER 15

■ ■ ■

Working with Text Files

Windows views text files as just another file type, but to Fedora, they can be essential components that make the system work. Configuration files are stored as plain text, and program documentation is also stored as text. This is clearly different from Windows, where it's very likely any information you're supposed to read will be contained in a Windows Help file, a rich text format (RTF) file, or even a Microsoft Word document.

Because of the reliance on text files, the shell includes several commands that let you display, edit, and otherwise manipulate text files in various ways. Learning to use the shell, and therefore learning how to administer your Fedora system, involves having a good understanding of these text tools. You'll use text tools for editing configuration files and viewing log files, as just two examples.

Viewing Text Files

You can easily view files using command-line tools, including `cat`, `less`, `head`, and `tail`. The simplest command for dealing with text files is `cat`.

Using the cat Command

When followed with a filename, the `cat` command will display the text file on the screen:

```
cat mytextfile
```

`cat` is short for "concatenate," and it isn't designed just to display text files. That it can do so is simply a side effect of its real purpose in life, which is to join two or more files together. `cat tmpfile2.txt tmpfile.txt > thirdfile.txt` will append the content of `tmpfile.txt` to the bottom of `tmpfile2.txt`. However, when used with a single file, it simply displays its contents on the screen.

If you try to use `cat`, you'll realize that it's good for only short text files; large files scroll off the screen.

Using the less Command

Because `cat` works well only with short files, and to give you more control when viewing text files, the `less` and `more` commands were created. The `more` command came first but was considered too primitive, so someone came up with `less`, which is preferred by many Linux users. However, both are usually available on the average Linux installation.

Let's look at using `less` to read the OpenOffice.org README file, which contains information about the current release of the office suite. The file is located at `/var/lib/openoffice.org2.0/README`, so to use `less` to read it, type the following:

```
less /usr/lib/openoffice.org2.0/README
```

In case you did not install OpenOffice.org, you can try to read some other file with `less`. Try the command `less /etc/services`. You can scroll up and down within the `less` display by using the cursor keys. If you want to scroll by bigger amounts of text, you can use the Page Up and Page Down keys. Alternatively, you can use the spacebar and B key, both of which are commonly used by old-hand Linux users for the same function. In addition, the Home and End keys will take you to the start and end of the document, respectively.

When using `less`, keep an eye on the bottom part of the screen, where you'll see a brief status bar. Alongside the filename, you'll see how many lines the document has and which line you're currently up to. In addition, you'll see as a percentage the amount of document you've already read through, so you'll know how much is left to go.

`less` lets you search forward through the file by typing a slash (/), and then entering your search term. Any words that are matched will be highlighted on the screen. To repeat the search, type n. To search backward in a file from your current point, type a question mark (?). To quit `less`, simply type q.

Although it's supposedly a simple program, `less` is packed with features. You can see what options are available by reading its man page or by typing `less --help`.

Using the head and tail Commands

A couple of other handy commands that you can use to view text files are `head` and `tail`. As their names suggest, these let you quickly view the beginning (head) of a file or the end (tail) of it.

Using the commands is simple:

```
tail mytextfile
```

or

```
head mytextfile
```

By default, both commands will display ten lines of the file. You can override this by using the `-n` command option followed by the number of lines you want to see. For example, the following will show the last five lines of `mytextfile`:

```
tail -n5 mytextfile
```

These two commands are very useful when viewing log files that might contain hundreds of lines of text. The most recent information is always at the end, so `tail` can be used to see what's happened last on your system, as shown in Figure 15-1.

Although they're powerful, none of these shell commands let you do much more than view text files. If you want to edit files, you'll need to use a text editor such as vi.

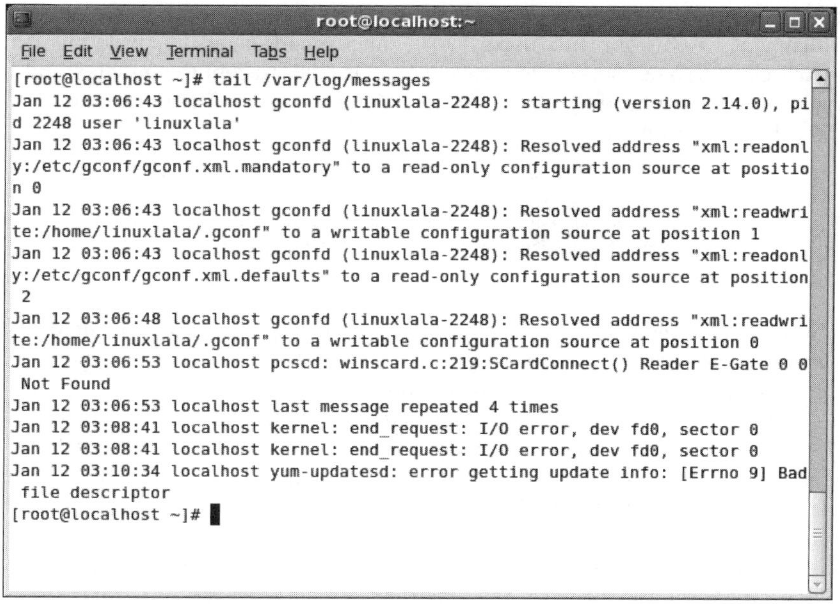

Figure 15-1. *The tail command can be very useful for viewing the last few lines of a log file.*

STANDARD INPUT AND OUTPUT

If you've read any of the Fedora man pages, you might have seen references to *standard input* and *standard output*. Like many things in Fedora, this sounds complicated but is merely a long-winded way of referring to something that is relatively simple.

Standard input is simply the device that Fedora normally takes input from. In other words, on the majority of desktop PCs when you're using the command-line shell, standard input refers to the keyboard. However, it's important to note that it could also feasibly refer to the mouse or any other device on your system capable of providing input; even some software can take the role of providing standard input.

Standard output is similar. It refers to the device to which output from a command is usually sent. In the majority of cases at the command line, this refers to the monitor screen, although it could feasibly be any kind of output device, such as your PC's sound card and speakers.

The man page for the `cat` command says that it will "concatenate files and print on the standard output." In other words, for the majority of desktop Fedora installations, it will combine (concatenate) any number of files together and print the results on the screen. If you specify just one file, it will display that single file on your screen.

In addition to hardware devices, input can also come from a file containing commands, and output can also be sent to a file instead of the screen, or even sent directly to another command. This is just one reason why the command-line shell is so flexible and powerful.

Using a Command-Line Text Editor

A variety of text editors can be used within the shell, but three stand out as being ubiquitous: ed, vi, and Emacs. The first in that list, ed, is by far the simplest. That doesn't necessarily mean that it's simple to use or lacks powerful features, but it just doesn't match the astonishing power of both vi and Emacs. To call vi and Emacs simple text editors is to do them a disservice, because both are extremely powerful interactive environments. In particular, Emacs is considered practically an operating system in itself, and some users of Linux treat it as their shell, executing commands and performing everyday tasks, such as reading and sending e-mail from within it. There are entire books written solely about Emacs and vi.

■**Note** Another shell-based text editor found on many Linux systems is nano. This offers many word processor–like features that can be helpful if you've come to Linux from a Windows background.

The downside of all the power within Emacs and vi is that both packages can be difficult to learn to use. They're considered idiosyncratic by even their most ardent fans. Both involve the user learning certain unfamiliar concepts, as well as keyboard shortcuts and commands.

Although there are debates about which text editor is better and which is best, it's generally agreed that vi offers substantial text-editing power but isn't too all-encompassing. It's also installed by default on Fedora. On Fedora, Emacs must be installed as an optional extra. Both text editors are normally available on virtually every installation of Linux or UNIX. We'll concentrate on using vi here.

It's important to understand that there are many versions of vi. The original vi program supplied with UNIX is rarely used nowadays. The most common version of vi is a clone called vim, for *vi improved*, and this is the version supplied with Fedora. There are still other versions, such as Elvis. Most work in a virtually identical way.

■**Note** There's always been a constant flame war between advocates of vi and Emacs, as to which is better. This could be quite a vicious and desperate debate, and the text editor you used was often taken as a measure of your character! Nowadays, the battle between the two camps has softened, and the Emacs vs. vi debate is considered an entertaining cliché of Linux and UNIX use. Declaring online which text editor a user prefers is often followed by a smiley symbol to acknowledge the once-fevered emotions.

Understanding vi Modes

The key to understanding how vi works is to learn the difference between the various modes. Three modes are important: Command mode, Insert mode, and Command-Line mode.

Command Mode

Command mode is vi's central mode. When the editor starts up, it's in Command mode, as shown in Figure 15-2. This lets you move around the text and delete words or lines of text. vi returns to Command mode after most operations. In this mode, the status bar at the bottom of the screen shows information such as the percentage of progress through the document. Although you cannot insert text in this mode, you can delete and otherwise manipulate words and lines within the file. You can also move through the text using the cursor keys and the Page Up and Page Down keys.

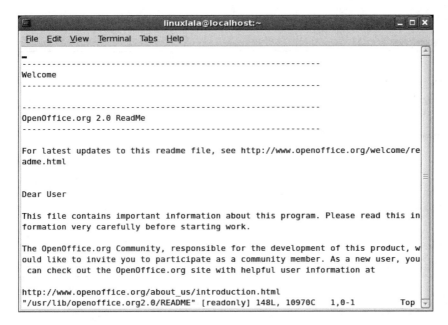

Figure 15-2. *In vi, the main mode is Command mode.*

Table 15-1 shows a list of the commands you can use in Command mode (consider photocopying it and sticking it to the side of your monitor as a handy reference).

Table 15-1. *Command Mode Commands in vi*

Command	Description
Delete Text	
dd	Delete the current line.
*n*dd	Delete *n* number of lines (e.g., 5dd will delete five lines).[1]
dw	Delete to the end of the current word under the cursor.[2]
db	Delete to the start of the word before the cursor.[2]
D	Delete everything from the cursor to the end of the line.[1]
Search	
/	Search forward (type the search text directly after the slash).
?	Search backward.
n	Repeat search in a forward direction.
N	Repeat search in a backward direction.
Cut and Paste	
yy	Copy the current line.[3]
*n*yy	Copy *n* number of lines into the buffer from the cursor downward (e.g., 5yy copies five lines of text).
p	Paste the contents of the clipboard.[3]

Continued

Table 15-1. *Continued*

Command	Description
Insert Text	
i	Switch to Insert mode at the cursor.
o	Switch to Insert mode, placing the cursor in a new line below current line.
O	Switch to Insert mode, placing the cursor in a new line above current line.
A	Append text to end of line.
Navigation[4]	
$	Move the cursor to the end of the current line.
w	Move the cursor to the next word.
b	Move the cursor to the previous word.
Miscellaneous	
.	Repeat the last command.
u	Undo the last command.

1. *A line ends where a line-break control character occurs in the file. Because of this, a line of text may actually take up several lines of the onscreen display.*

2. *This will delete the remainder of current word before/after the cursor if the cursor is in the middle of a word.*

3. *The standard documentation refers to copying as "yanking" and the clipboard as the "buffer."*

4. *You can also use the cursor keys to move around the file, and the Page Up and Page Down keys to move up and down a page at a time. Additionally, press 0 (zero) on the main keyboard, not the numeric keypad, to move the cursor to the start of the current line, or Shift+0 to move forward one sentence (until the next full stop).*

Insert Mode

To type your own text or edit text, you need to switch to Insert mode. This is normally done by typing i, but you can also type 0 or o to change to Insert mode, which is indicated by the word *INSERT* appearing at the bottom of the screen, as shown in Figure 15-3. The difference between the commands required to switch into Insert mode is that some let you insert before or after the cursor. Generally, i is most useful, because what you type will appear before the character under the cursor, as with most word processors. The commands that activate Insert Mode are listed in Table 15-1, under "Insert Text."

■**Tip** By typing A (i.e., Shift+A), you can add text to the end of the line on which the cursor currently resides.

In Insert mode, you can still move around the text using the cursor keys. Anything you type will appear at the point of the cursor. To quit this mode, press the Esc key. This will return you to Command mode.

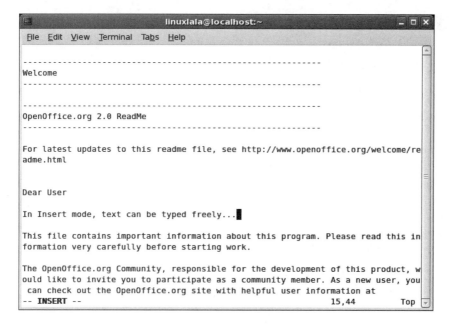

Figure 15-3. *Use vi's Insert mode to add and edit text.*

Command-Line Mode

The third mode you should be aware of is Command-Line mode (note that, irritatingly, this is not the same as the Command mode). As its name suggests, this is the mode in which you can enter commands to save and load files, as well as perform other fundamental tasks to control vi or to quit the program. You can enter Command-Line mode by typing a colon (:), although if you're in Insert mode, you'll first need to leave it by pressing the Esc key. You can identify when vi is in this mode because the cursor will be at the bottom of the screen next to a colon symbol, as shown in Figure 15-4. To quit Command-Line mode, press the Esc key. You'll be returned to Command mode. Note that you'll automatically leave Command-Line mode after each command you issue has completed.

For a list of basic Command-Line mode commands, see Table 15-2.

Table 15-2. *Some vi Command-Line Mode Commands*

Command	Description
:w	Save the file.
:w!	Save the file and ignore errors such as an existing file with the same filename.
:q	Quit vi.
:q!	Quit vi and ignore errors such as an unsaved file.
:s/word/replacement/	Search from the cursor downward and replace any instances of the word with the replacement.[1]
:help	View the help documentation.

1. *The search tool is very powerful and uses a number of command options for additional flexibility. Read the vi help file to learn more.*

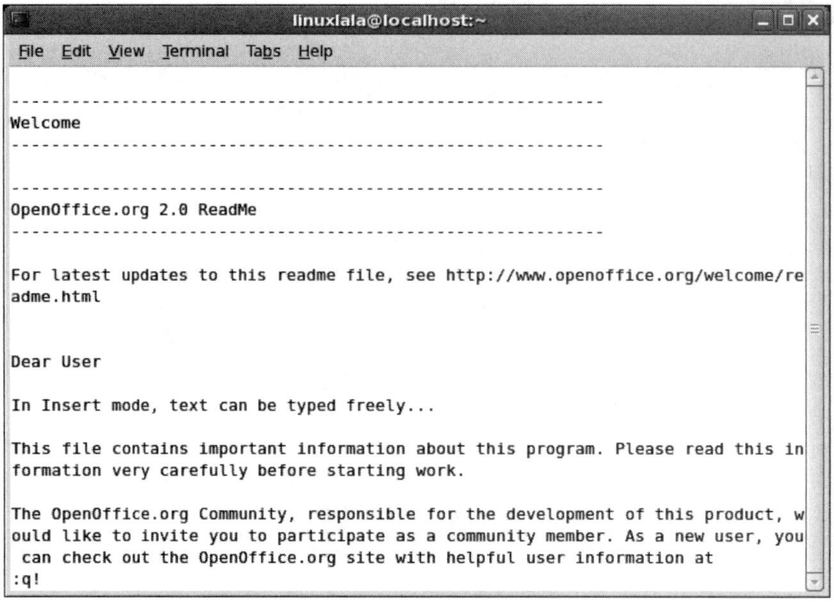

Figure 15-4. *Use vi's Command-Line mode to issue commands.*

Using vi to Edit a File

As an example, let's use vi to edit the /etc/services file. You don't want to actually alter this file, so start by making a copy of it in your home directory:

```
cp /etc/services ~
```

This will copy the file to your /home directory, which you indicate using the ~ symbol.

Then fire up vi with the file, like this:

```
vi services
```

■ Note Windows makes a lot of use of file extensions in order to recognize files and therefore know what program to use to run them. By default, a file with a .doc extension tells Windows that it should use Microsoft Word to open the file, for example. Linux uses a different system based on the first few bytes of each file. Because of this, file extensions are used within Linux simply to let the users know what type of file they're dealing with. Often, they're not used at all. If a file is called README, you can be fairly certain that it's a text file, for example.

Once the file is opened, you'll find yourself automatically in Command mode and will be able to move around the file using the cursor keys. Altering the text is achieved using various commands (see Table 15-1). For example, typing dd will delete the line of text that the cursor is currently within. Typing x will delete the letter under the cursor. Typing dw will delete to the end of the current word under the cursor. Try some of these to see how they work.

To actually edit a file and type text, you'll need to switch to Insert mode. Type i to do this. Insert mode is fairly easy to understand. You can move around the text using the cursor keys, and then simply start typing wherever you want. The Backspace key will delete text behind the cursor, and the Delete key will delete text in front of the cursor.

When you're finished, press the Esc key to return to Command mode. Once back in Command mode, you can page through the text. The Page Up and Page Down keys will move a screenful of text at a time. Pressing the up and down cursor keys will cause the screen to scroll when the cursor reaches the top or bottom.

After you're finished editing, you'll need to save the file. This is done in Command-Line mode. You can enter this mode by typing a colon (:). You'll see a colon appear at the bottom of the screen, and this is where you type the commands. Note that after you type a command, you'll immediately exit Command-Line mode, so if you want to issue another command, you'll need to type a colon again.

To save a file, in Command-Line mode, type :w (which stands for "write"). If you want to save the current file with a different name, you'll need to enter a filename after the w command, like this:

```
:w mytextfile
```

To quit vi, type :q. However, if you've edited a file, you won't be able to quit until the file has been saved. If you want to save the file and then quit, you can type :wq. If you don't want to save the file, type :q!. The exclamation point tells vi to override any objections it might have. You can also use it with the save command :w! to force the overwriting of a file that already exists.

Note If you don't have the correct permissions to write a file, vi might tell you that you can use :w! to override. In this case, it's wrong. The only way to write to a file for which you don't have permissions is to change its permissions.

Creating a New Text File Using vi

Creating and editing a new file with vi is easy. From any command-line shell, simply type this:

```
vi myfile
```

This will start vi and give your new file a name. However, the file won't be saved until you manually issue the save command (:w) in vi. This means that if your computer crashes before you save, the file will be lost!

Note The version of vi provided with Fedora, vim, includes some elementary file-save protection. If, for any reason, vim is not shut down properly, there's a chance you'll be able to recover a version of file the next time vim starts. However, as with all such protection in any kind of program, you shouldn't rely on this. You should use the :w command to save your file periodically.

As always with vi, you start out in the default Command mode. To start typing immediately, enter Insert mode by typing i. You'll notice when typing that although the text is wrapped on each line, words are not carried over, and they often break across lines in an ugly way. This is because vi is primarily a text editor, not a word processor. For people who create text files, like programmers, having line breaks shown in this way can be useful.

When you're finished typing a sentence or paragraph, you can press the Enter key as usual to start a new line. You should then be able to move between lines using the up and down cursor keys. You'll notice an odd thing when you try to do this, however: unlike with a word processor, moving up a line of text that spreads across more than one line on the screen will take the cursor to the start of the line, rather than into the middle of it. This again relates to vi's text editor focus, where such a feature is useful when editing documents such as program configuration files.

When you're finished, press the Esc key to switch to Command mode. Then type a colon to enter Command-Line mode. Type :w to save the file using the filename you gave it earlier. If you started vi without specifying a filename, you'll need to specify a filename with the save command, such as :w myfile.

USING GEDIT TO EDIT TEXT FILES

If all this talk of vi sounds like too much hard work, don't forget that the GNOME desktop includes an excellent text editor in the form of Gedit. In fact, to describe Gedit as merely a text editor is to do it something of a disservice because it includes many handy word processor–like features.

You can call Gedit and open a file in it from the command-line prompt as follows:

gedit *<filename>*

If you need to adopt superuser powers to edit the likes of configuration files, simply use the su - command before running Gedit.

You'll find Gedit fairly straightforward to use.

Searching Through Files

You can search for particular words or phrases in text files by loading the file into less or vi (see Table 15-1). The maneuverability offered by both programs lets you leap from point to point in the text, and their use is generally user-friendly.

However, using vi or less can take precious seconds. There's a quicker command-line option that will search through a file in double-quick speed: grep.

Using grep to Find Text

grep stands for Global Regular Expression Print. grep is an extremely powerful tool that can use pattern-based searching techniques to find text in files. Pattern-based searching means that grep offers various options to loosen the search so that more results are returned.

The simplest way of using grep is to specify some brief text, followed by the name of the file you want to search. Here's an example:

grep 'helloworld' myfile

This will search for the phrase helloworld within myfile. If it's found, the entire line that helloworld is on will be displayed on the screen.

If you specify the * wildcard instead of a filename, grep will search every file in the directory for the text. Adding the -r command option will cause grep to search all the files, and also search through any directories that are present:

grep -r 'helloworld' *

Another handy command option is -i, which tells grep to ignore differences between upper-case and lowercase letters when it's searching. Figure 15-5 shows an example of using grep.

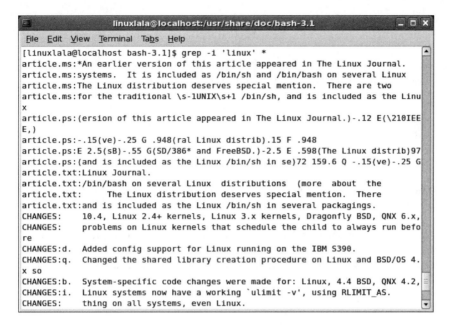

Figure 15-5. *grep is a powerful tool that can search for text within files.*

■Note You might never choose to use grep for searching for text within files, but it can prove very handy when used to search through the output of other commands. This is done by "piping" the output from one command to another, as explained in Chapter 17.

Using Regular Expressions

The true power of grep is achieved by the use of search patterns known as *regular expressions*, or *regexes* for short. Put simply, regexes allow you to be vague rather than specific when searching, meaning that grep (and many similar tools that use the system of regexes, such as the find command discussed in Chapter 14) will return more results.

For example, you can specify a selection or series of characters (called a *string* in regex terminology) that might appear in a word or phrase you're searching for. This can be useful if you're looking for a word that might be spelled differently from how you anticipate, for example.

The most basic form of regex is the bracket expansion. This is where additional search terms are enclosed in square brackets within a search string. For example, suppose you want to find a file that refers to several drafts of a document you've been working on. The files are called myfile_1draft.doc, myfile_2draft.doc, and so on. To find any document that mentions these files, you could type this:

```
grep 'myfile_[1-9]draft\.doc' *
```

The use of square brackets tells grep to fill in details within the search string based on what's inside the square brackets. In this case, 1-9 means that all the numbers from 1 to 9 should be applied to the search string. It's as if you've told grep to search for myfile_1draft.doc, and then told it to search for myfile_2draft.doc, and so on. Notice that the example has a backslash before the period separating the file extension from the filename. This indicates to grep that it should interpret the period as an element of the string to be searched for, rather than as a wildcard character, which is how grep usually interprets periods.

You don't need to specify a range of characters in this way. You can simply enter whatever selection of characters you want to substitute into the search string. Here's an example:

```
grep 'myfile[12345]\.doc' *
```

This will attempt to find any mention of myfile1.doc, myfile2.doc, myfile3.doc, and so on, in any file within the directory.

Here's another example:

```
grep '[GgNn]ome' *
```

This will let you search for the word *Gnome* within files, but takes into account any possible misspelling of the word by people who forget to use the silent *G*, and any use of uppercase or lowercase.

This is only scratching the surface of what regexes can do. For example, many regexes can be combined together into one long search string, which can provide astonishing accuracy when searching. Table 15-3 contains some simple examples that should give you an idea of the power and flexibility of regexes.

Table 15-3. *Some Examples of Regular Expressions*

Search String	Description
'document[a-z]'	Returns any lines containing the string "document" followed by any single letter from the range *a* through *z*.
'document[A-Za-z]'	Returns any lines containing the string "document" followed by the letters *A* through *Z* or *a* through *z*. Note that no comma or other character is needed to separate possibilities within square brackets.
'document.'	Returns any lines containing the string "document" followed by any other character. The period is used as a wildcard signifying any single character.
'document[[:digit:]]'	Returns any lines containing the string "document" followed by any number.
'document[[:alpha:]]'	Returns any lines containing the string "document" followed by any alphabetic character.
'^document'	Returns any lines that have the string "document" at the beginning. The caret symbol (^) tells grep to look only at the beginning of each line.
'document$'	Returns any line that has the string "document" at the end of the line. The dollar sign symbol ($) tells grep to look for the string only at the end of lines.
'document[^1-6]'	Returns lines that have the string "document" in them, but not if it's followed by the numbers 1 through 6. When used in square brackets, the caret character (^) produces a nonmatching list—a list of results that don't contain the string.

grep is very powerful. It can be complicated to master, but it offers a lot of scope for performing extremely precise searches that ensure you find only what you're seeking. It's well worth reading through its man pages. You can also refer to books on the subject, of which there are many. A good example is *Regular Expression Recipes: A Problem-Solution Approach* by Nathan A. Good.

Comparing Text Files

If you want to compare the differences between two text files, one way to do this is to use the `diff` command. This is designed primarily to uncover small changes in otherwise identical documents, such as revisions made by another person. Of course, it can also be used to prove that two files are identical. If you run the files through `diff`, and it shows no output, it has been unable to spot any differences.

`diff` is ordinarily used like this:

```
diff mytextfile1 mytextfile2
```

If `diff` spots any differences between the files, the results are a little more complicated than you might be used to. Any lines that are different within the files will appear on the screen. Those lines that are identical won't be displayed. Lines preceded with a left angle bracket (<) are from the first file, while those with a right angle bracket (>) are from the second file.

For a different display, you could type something like this:

```
diff -y mytextfile1 mytextfile2
```

This places the two lists side by side and highlights lines that are different with a pipe symbol (|). However, it requires a lot more screen space than using `diff` without the -y option.

■Note When you use the -y command option with `diff`, it will struggle to fit the output in a standard GNOME Terminal window. If it is maximized on a 17-inch screen (1024 × 768 resolution), it should be just large enough to fit the information in, depending on the complexity of the files being compared.

By specifying the -a command option, you can make `diff` process binary files, too. This is a handy way of comparing virtually any kind of files, including program files, to see if they're identical. If there's no output from `diff`, then the two files are identical. If your screen fills with gibberish, then the files are clearly different.

Incidentally, if you want to compare three documents, you can use a very similar command: `diff3`. Check the command's man page to learn more about how it works.

Summary

In this chapter, we examined how text files can be manipulated. In many ways, the BASH shell is built around manipulating text, and we explored various tools created with this goal in mind. We started with the commands that can display text files (or part of them).

We then looked at how the vi text editor can be used to both edit and create documents. Next, we explored how regexes can be used with the `grep` command to create sophisticated search strings, which can uncover any text within documents. Finally, you saw how to compare text files.

In the next chapter, we'll look at how you can use various command-line tools to take control of your system.

CHAPTER 16

■■■

Taking Control of the System

By now, you should be starting to realize that the shell offers an enormous amount of power when it comes to administering your PC. The BASH shell commands give you quick and efficient control over most aspects of your Linux setup. However, the shell truly excels in one area: controlling the processes on your system.

Controlling processes is essential for administration of your system. You can tidy up crashed programs, for example, or even alter the priority of a program so that it runs with a little more consideration for other programs. Unlike with Windows, this degree of control is not considered out of bounds. This is just one more example of how Linux provides complete access to its inner workings and puts you in control.

Without further ado, let's take a look at what can be done.

Viewing Processes

A process is something that exists entirely behind the scenes. When the user runs a program, one or many processes might be started, but they're usually invisible unless the user specifically chooses to manipulate them. You might say that programs exist in the world of the user, but processes belong in the world of the system.

Processes can be started not only by the user, but also by the system itself to undertake tasks such as system maintenance, or even to provide basic functionality, such as the GUI system. Many processes are started when the computer boots up, and then they sit in the background, waiting until they're needed (such as programs that send mail). Other processes are designed to work periodically to accomplish certain tasks, such as ensuring system files are up to date.

You can see what processes are currently running on your computer by running the top program. Running top is simply a matter of typing the command at the shell prompt.

As you can see in Figure 16-1, top provides very comprehensive information and can be a bit overwhelming at first sight. However, the main area of interest is the list of processes (which top refers to as *tasks*).

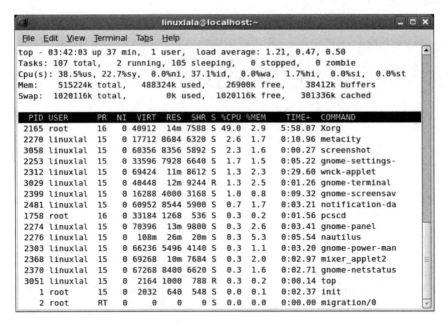

Figure 16-1. *The top program gives you an eagle-eye view of the processes running on your system.*

Here's an example of a line taken from top on our test PC, shown with the column headings from the process list:

```
PID USER PR NI VIRT RES SHR S %CPU %MEM TIME+ COMMAND
5499 root 15 0 78052 25m 60m S 2.3 5.0 6:11.72 Xorg
```

A lot of information is presented here, as described in Table 16-1.

Table 16-1. *The top Program Process Information*

Column	Description
PID	The first number is the process ID (PID). This is the unique number that the system uses to track the process. The PID comes in handy if you want to kill (terminate) the process (as explained in the next section of this chapter).
USER	This column lists the owner of the particular process. As with files, all processes must have an owner. A lot of processes will appear to be owned by the root user. Some of them are system processes that need to access the system hardware, which is something only the root user is allowed to do. Other processes are owned by root for protection; root ownership means that ordinary users cannot tamper with these processes.
PR	This column shows the priority of the process. This is a dynamic number, showing where the particular process is in the CPU queue at the present time.

Column	Description
NI	This column shows the "nice" value of the process. This refers to how charitable a process is in its desire for CPU time. A high figure here (up to 19) indicates that the process is willing to be interrupted for the sake of other processes. A negative value means the opposite: the process is more aggressive than others in its desire for CPU time. Some programs need to operate in this way, and this is not necessarily a bad thing.
VIRT	This column shows the amount of virtual memory used by the process.[1]
RES	This column shows the total amount of physical memory used.[1]
SHR	This column shows the amount of shared memory used. This refers to memory that contains code that is relied on by other processes and programs.
S	This column shows the current status of the task. Generally, the status will either be sleeping, in which case an *S* will appear, or running, in which case an *R* will appear. Most processes will be sleeping, even ones that appear to be active. Don't worry about this; it just reflects the way the Linux kernel works. A *Z* in this column indicates a zombie process (a child of a process that has been terminated).
%CPU	This column shows the CPU use, expressed as a percentage.[2]
%MEM	This column shows the memory use, again expressed as a percentage.[2]
TIME+	This column shows a measure of how long the process has been up and running.
COMMAND	This shows the actual name of the process itself.

1. *Both VIRT and RES are measured in kilobytes, unless an* m *appears alongside the number; in which case you should read the figure as megabytes.*

2. *The %CPU and %MEM entries tell you in easy-to-understand terms how much of the system resources a process is taking up.*

This list will probably be longer than the screen has space to display, so top orders the list of processes by the amount of CPU time the processes are using. Every few seconds, it updates the list. You can test this quite easily. Let your PC rest for a few seconds, without touching the mouse or typing. Then move the mouse around for a few seconds. You'll see that the process called Xorg leaps to the top of the list (or appears very near the top). Xorg is the program that provides the graphical subsystem for Linux, and making the mouse cursor appear to move around the screen requires CPU time. When nothing else is going on, moving the mouse causes Xorg to appear as the number one user of CPU time on your system.

■**Note** Typing d while top is running lets you alter the update interval, which is the time between screen updates. The default is three seconds, but you can reduce that to one second or even less if you wish. However, a constantly updating top program starts to consume system resources and can therefore skew the diagnostic results you're investigating. Because of this, a longer, rather than shorter, interval is preferable.

It's possible to alter the ordering of the process list according to other criteria. For example, you can list the processes by the quantity of memory they're using, by typing M while top is up and running. You can switch back to CPU ordering by typing P.

RENICING A PROCESS

You can set how much CPU time a process receives while it's actually running. This is done by *renicing* the process. This isn't something you should do on a regular basis, but it can prove very handy if you start a program that then uses a lot of system resources and makes the system unbearably slow.

The first thing to do is to use top to spot the process that needs to be restrained and find out its PID number. This will be listed on the left of the program's entry on the list. Once you know this, type r, and then type in the PID number. You'll then be asked to specify a renice value. The scale goes from –20, which is considered the highest priority, to 19, which is considered the lowest. Therefore, you should type 19. After this, you should find some responsiveness has returned to the system, although how much (if any) depends on the nature of the programs you're running.

You might be tempted to bump up the priority of a process to make it run faster, but this may not work because of complexities in the Linux kernel. In fact, it might cause serious problems. Therefore, you should renice with care and only when you must.

Controlling Processes

Despite the fact that processes running on your computer are usually hidden away, Linux offers complete, unrestricted, and unapologetic control over them. You can terminate processes, change their properties, and learn every item of information there is to know about them.

This provides ample scope for damaging the currently running system, but in spite of this, even standard users have complete control over processes that they personally started (one exception occurs with zombie processes, described a bit later in this section). As you might expect, the root user (or any user who adopts superuser powers) has control over all processes that were created by ordinary users, as well as those processes started by the system itself.

The user is given this degree of control over processes in order to enact repairs when something goes wrong, such as when a program crashes and won't terminate cleanly. It's impossible for standard users to damage the currently running system by undertaking such work, although they can cause themselves a number of problems.

■**Note** This control over processes is what makes Linux so reliable. Because any user can delve into the workings of the kernel and terminate individual processes, crashed programs can be cleaned up with negligible impact on the rest of the system.

Killing Processes

Whenever you quit a program, or in some cases, when it completes the task you've asked of it, it will terminate itself. This means ending its own process and also that of any other processes it created in order to run. The main process is called the *parent*, and the ones it creates are referred to as *child* processes.

■**Note** You can see a nice graphical display of which parent owns which child process by typing pstree at the command-line shell.

While this should mean your system runs smoothly, badly behaved programs sometimes don't go away. They stick around in the process list. Alternatively, you might find that a program crashes and so isn't able to terminate itself. In very rare cases, some programs that appear otherwise healthy might get carried away and start consuming a lot of system resources. You can tell when this happens because your system will start slowing down for no reason, as less and less memory and/or CPU time is available to run actual programs.

In all of these cases, the user usually must kill the process in order to terminate it manually. This is easily done using top.

The first task is to track down the crashed or otherwise problematic process. In top, look for a process that matches the name of the program, as shown in Figure 16-2. For example, the Firefox web browser generally runs as a process called firefox-bin.

```
TIME+   COMMAND
7:01.58 Xorg
0:06.44 firefox-bin
0:13.05 metacity
0:30.74 wnck-applet
0:06.15 gnome-settings-
0:00.22 screenshot
0:10.61 gnome-screensav
0:03.86 notification-da
0:00.42 pdflush
0:01.14 kjournald
0:00.28 gpm
0:00.18 gdm-binary
0:05.93 nautilus
```

Figure 16-2. *You can normally identify a program by its name in the process list.*

Caution You should be absolutely sure that you know the correct process before killing it. If you get it wrong, you could cause other programs to stop running.

Because top doesn't show every single process on its screen, tracking down the trouble causing process can be difficult. A handy tip is to make top show only the processes created by the user you're logged in under. This will remove the background processes started by root. You can do this within top by typing u, and then entering your username.

Once you've spotted the crashed process, make a note of its PID number, which will be at the very left of its entry in the list. Then type k. You'll be asked to enter the PID number. Enter that number, and then press Enter once again (this will accept the default signal value of 15, which will tell the program to terminate).

With any luck, the process (and the program in question) will disappear. If it doesn't, the process you've killed might be the child of another process that also must be killed. To track down the parent process, you need to configure top to add the PPID field, for the parent process ID, to its display. To add this field, type f, and then b. Press Enter to return to the process list. The PPID column will appear next to the process name on the right of the window. It simply shows the PID of the parent process. You can use this information to look for the parent process within the main list of processes.

The trick here is to make sure that the parent process isn't something that's vital to the running of the system. If it isn't, you can safely kill it. This should have the result of killing the child process you uncovered prior to this.

■**Caution** If the PPID field in `top` displays a value of 1, that means the process doesn't have a parent process. In both the PPID and PID fields, you should always watch out for low numbers, particularly one-, two-, or three-digit numbers. These are usually processes that started early on when Linux booted and that are essential to the system.

Controlling Zombie Processes

Zombie processes are those that are children of processes that have terminated. However, for some reason, they failed to take their child processes with them. Zombie processes are rare on most Linux systems.

Despite their name, zombie processes are harmless. They're not actually running and don't take up system resources. However, if you want your system to be spick-and-span, you can attempt to kill them.

In the top-right area of `top`, you can see a display that shows how many zombie processes are running on your system, as shown in Figure 16-3. Zombie processes are easily identified because they have a Z in the status (S) column within `top`'s process list. To kill a zombie process, type k, and then type its PID. Then type 9, rather than accept the default signal of 15.

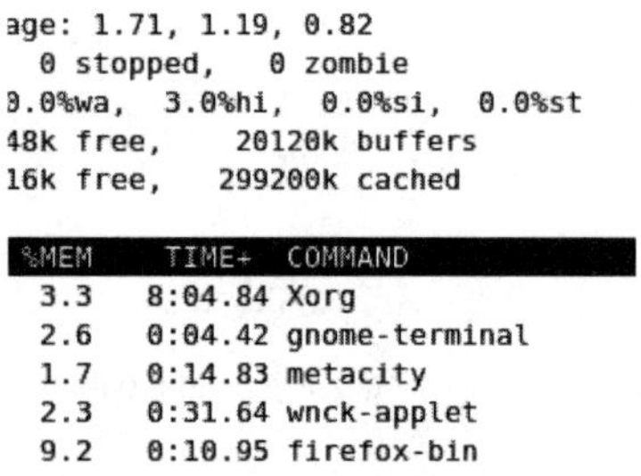

```
age: 1.71, 1.19, 0.82
   0 stopped,   0 zombie
9.0%wa,  3.0%hi,  0.0%si,  0.0%st
48k free,    20120k buffers
16k free,   299200k cached

%MEM    TIME+  COMMAND
 3.3  8:04.84 Xorg
 2.6  0:04.42 gnome-terminal
 1.7  0:14.83 metacity
 2.3  0:31.64 wnck-applet
 9.2  0:10.95 firefox-bin
```

Figure 16-3. *You can see at a glance how many zombie processes are on your system by looking at the top right of top's display.*

■**Note** No magic is involved in killing processes. All that happens is that `top` sends them a "terminate" signal. In other words, it contacts them and asks them to terminate. By default, all processes are designed to listen for commands such as this; it's part and parcel of how programs work under Linux. When a program is described as *crashed*, it means that the user is unable to use the program itself to issue the terminate command (such as Quit). A crashed program might not be taking input, but its *processes* will probably still be running.

In many cases, zombie processes simply won't go away. When this happens, you have two options. The first is to restart the program that is likely to be the zombie's owner, in the hope that it will reattach with the zombie, and then quit the program. With any luck, it will take the zombie child with it this time. Alternatively, you can simply reboot your PC. But it's important to note that zombie processes are harmless and can be left in peace on your system!

Using Other Commands to Control Processes

You don't always need to use top to control processes. A range of quick and cheerful shell commands can diagnose and treat process problems.

The first of these is the ps command. This stands for Process Status and will report a list of currently running processes on your system. This command is normally used with the -aux options:

```
ps -aux
```

This will return a list something like what you see when you run top.

If you can spot the problematic process, look for its PID and issue the following command:

```
kill <PID number>
```

For example, to kill a process with a PID of 5122, you would type this:

```
kill 5122
```

If, after this, you find the process isn't killed, then you should use the top program, as described in the previous sections, because it allows for a more in-depth investigation.

Another handy process-killing command lets you use the actual process name. The killall command is handy if you already know from past experience what a program's process is called. For example, to kill the process called firefox-bin, which is the chief process of the Firefox web browser, you would use the following command:

```
killall firefox-bin
```

■**Caution** Make sure you're as specific as possible when using the killall command. Issuing a command like killall bin will kill all processes that have the word bin in them!

CLEARING UP CRASHES

Sometimes a crashed process can cause all kinds of problems. The shell you're working at may stop working, or the GUI itself might stop working properly.

In cases like this, it's important to remember that you can have more that one instance of the command-line shell up and running at any one time. For example, if a process crashes and locks up GNOME Terminal, simply start a new instance of GNOME Terminal (Applications ➤ System Tools ➤ Terminal). Then use top within the new window to kill the process that is causing trouble for the other terminal window.

If the crashed program affects the entire GUI, you can switch to a virtual console by pressing Ctrl+Alt+F1. Although the GUI disappears, you will not have killed it, and no programs will stop running. Instead, you've simply moved the GUI to the background while a shell console takes over the screen. Then you can use the virtual console to run top and attempt to kill the process that is causing all the problems. When you're ready, you can switch back to the GUI by pressing Ctrl+Alt+F7.

Controlling Jobs

Whenever you start a program at the shell, it's assigned a job number. *Jobs* are quite separate from processes and are designed primarily for users to understand what programs are running on the system.

You can see which jobs are running at any one time by typing the following at the shell prompt:

```
jobs
```

When you run a program, it usually takes over the shell in some way and stops you from doing anything until it's finished what it's doing. However, it doesn't have to be this way. Adding an ampersand symbol (&) after the command will cause it to run in the background. This is not much use for commands that require user input, such as vi or top, but it can be very handy for commands that churn away until they're completed.

For example, suppose you want to run the find command on your user account. This will take a long time, during which the shell would be unusable. However, you can type the following to retain use of the shell:

```
find /home/linuxlala > tmpfile.txt &
```

When you do this, you'll see something similar to the following, although the four-digit number will be different:

```
[1] 7483
```

This tells you that find is running in the background and has been given job number 1. It also has been given process number 7483 (although bear in mind that when some programs start, they instantly kick off other processes and terminate the one they're currently running, so this won't necessarily be accurate).

■**Note** If you've ever tried to run a GUI program from the shell, you might have realized that the shell is inaccessible while it's running. Once you quit the GUI program, the control of the shell will be returned to you. By specifying that the program should run in the background with the & (ampersand symbol), you can run the GUI program and still be able to type away and run other commands.

You can send several jobs to the background, and each one will be given a different job number. In this case, when you wish to switch into a running job, you can type its number. For example, the following command will switch you to the background job assigned the number 3:

```
%3
```

You can exit a job that is currently running by pressing Ctrl+Z. It will still be there in the background, but it won't be running (officially, it's said to be *sleeping*). To restart it, you can switch back to it, as just described. Alternatively, you can restart it but still keep it in the background. For example, to restart job 2 in the background, leaving the shell prompt free for you to enter other commands, type the following:

```
%2 &
```

You can bring the command in the background into the foreground by typing the following:

```
fg
```

When a background job has finished, something like the following will appear at the shell:

```
[1]+ Done find /home/linuxlala > tmpfile.txt
```

Using jobs within the shell can be a good way of managing your workload. For example, you can move programs into the background temporarily while you get on with something else. If you're editing a file in vi, you can press Ctrl+Z to stop the program. It will remain in the background, and you'll be returned to the shell, where you can type other commands. You can then resume vi later on by typing fg or typing % followed by its job number.

Summary

This chapter has covered taking complete control of your system. We've looked at what processes are, how they're separate from programs, and how they can be controlled or viewed using programs such as top and ps. In addition, we explored job management under BASH. You saw that you can stop, start, and pause programs at your convenience.

In the next chapter, we'll take a look at several tricks and techniques that you can use with the BASH shell to finely hone your command-line skills.

CHAPTER 17

■■■

Cool Shell Tricks

The BASH shell is the product of many years of development work by a lot of people. It comes from the old days of UNIX and was an important step in computer software evolution. It's a program that retains complete simplicity, yet packs in more features than most users could ever hope to use.

One of the best things about the shell is its sheer power. If you ever wonder if you can do a task differently (and more efficiently), you'll probably find that one of the many BASH developers has implemented a method to do so. Once you learn these techniques, you'll find you can whiz around the shell at blinding speed. It's just a matter of exploring the far reaches of the shell, and that's what you'll do in this chapter. Hold onto your hats, because it's an exciting ride!

Using Autocompletion

The Tab key is your best friend when using the shell because it will cause BASH to automatically complete whatever you type. For example, if you want to run Fedora's web browser, you can enter firefox at the command line. However, to save yourself some time, you can type fir, and then press Tab. You'll then find that BASH fills in the rest for you. It does this by caching the names of the programs you might run according to the directories listed in your $PATH variable (see Chapter 13).

Of course, autocompletion has some limitations. On our Fedora test system, typing loc didn't autocomplete locate. Instead, it caused BASH to beep. This is because on a default Fedora installation, there is more than one possible match. Pressing Tab again shows those matches. Depending on how much you type (how much of an initial clue you give BASH), you might find there are many possible matches.

In this case, the experienced BASH user simply types another letter, which will be enough to distinguish the almost-typed word from the rest, and presses Tab again. With any luck, this should be enough for BASH to fill in the rest.

Autocompletion with Files and Paths

Tab autocompletion also works with files and paths. If you type the first few letters of a folder name, BASH will try to fill in the rest. This also obviously has limitations. There's no point in typing cd myfol and pressing Tab if there's nothing in the current directory that starts with the letters *myfol*. This particular autocomplete function works by looking at your current directory and seeing what's available.

Alternatively, you can specify an initial path for BASH to use in order to autocomplete. Typing cd /ho and pressing Tab will cause BASH to autocomplete the path by looking in the root directory (/). In other words, it will autocomplete the command with the directory home. In a similar way, typing cd myfolder/myfo will cause BASH to attempt to autocomplete by looking for a match in myfolder.

If you want to run a program that resides in the current directory, such as one you've just down-loaded, for example, typing ./, followed by the first part of the program name, and then pressing Tab should be enough to have BASH autocomplete the rest. In this case, the dot and slash tell BASH to look in the current directory for any executable programs or scripts (programs with X as part of their permissions) and use them as possible autocomplete options.

BASH is clever enough to spot whether the command you're using is likely to require a file, directory, or executable, and it will autocomplete with only relevant file or directory names.

Viewing Available Options

The autocomplete function has a neat side effect. As we mentioned earlier, if BASH cannot find a match, pressing Tab again causes BASH to show all the available options. For example, typing ba at the shell and then pressing Tab twice will cause BASH to show all the possible commands starting with the letters *ba*. On our test PC, this produces the following list of commands:

bamstex	base64	bash	batch
baobab	basename	bashbug-32	

This can be a nice way of exploring what commands are available on your system. You can then use each command with the --help command option to find out what it does, or browse the com-mand's man page.

When you apply this trick to directory and filename autocompletion, it's even more useful. For example, typing cd in a directory, and then pressing the Tab key twice will cause BASH to show the available directories, providing a handy way of retrieving a brief directory listing. Alternatively, if you've forgotten how a directory name is spelled, you can use this technique to find out prior to switching into it.

Figure 17-1 shows a few examples of using this technique with BASH.

Figure 17-1. *Autocompletion makes using BASH much easier.*

Using Keyboard Shortcuts

Your other good friends when using BASH are the Ctrl and Alt keys. These keys provide shortcuts to vital command-line shell functions. They also let you work more efficiently when typing by providing what most programs call keyboard shortcuts.

Shortcuts for Working in BASH

Table 17-1 lists the most common keyboard shortcuts in BASH (there are many more; see BASH's man page for details). If you've explored the Emacs text editor, you might find these shortcuts familiar. Such keyboard shortcuts are largely the same across many of the software packages that originate from the GNU Project. Often, you'll find an option within many Fedora software packages that lets you use Emacs-style navigation, in which case, these keyboard shortcuts will most likely work equally well.

Table 17-1. *Keyboard Shortcuts in BASH*

Shortcut	Description
Navigation	
Left/right cursor key, Ctrl+B/Ctrl+F	Move left/right in text
Ctrl+A	Move to beginning of line
Ctrl+E	Move to end of line
Ctrl+right arrow, Alt+F	Move forward one word
Ctrl+left arrow, Alt+B	Move left one word
Editing	
Ctrl+U	Delete everything behind cursor to start of line
Ctrl+K	Delete from cursor to end of line
Ctrl+W	Delete from cursor to beginning of word
Alt+D	Delete from cursor to end of word
Ctrl+T	Transpose characters on left and right of cursor
Alt+T	Transpose words on left and right of cursor
Miscellaneous	
Ctrl+L	Clear screen (everything above current line)
Ctrl+_	Undo everything since last command[1]
Alt+R	Undo changes made to the line[2]
Ctrl+Y	Undo deletion of word or line caused by using Ctrl+K, Ctrl+W, and so on[3]
Alt+L	Lowercase current word (from the cursor to the end of the word)

1. *In most cases, this has the effect of clearing the line.*

2. *This is different from Ctrl+_, because it will leave intact any command already on the line, such as one pulled from your command history.*

3. *This allows primitive cutting and pasting. Delete the text and then immediately undo, after which the text will remain in the buffer and can be pasted with Ctrl+Y.*

Shortcuts for System Control

In terms of the control over your system offered by keyboard commands, as mentioned in Chapter 16, pressing Ctrl+Z has the effect of stopping the current program. It suspends the program until you switch back into it or tell it to resume in another way, or manually kill it.

In the same style, pressing Ctrl+C while a program is running will quit it. This sends the program's process a termination signal, a little like killing it using the top program. Ctrl+C can prove handy if you start a program running by accident and quickly want to end it, or if a command takes longer than you expected to work and you cannot wait for it to complete. It's also a handy way of attempting to end crashed programs. Some complicated programs don't take too kindly to being quit in this way, particularly those that need to save data before they terminate. However, most should be OK.

Ctrl+D is another handy keyboard shortcut. This sends the program an end-of-file (EOF) message. In effect, this tells the program that you've finished your input. This can have a variety of effects, depending on the program you're running. For example, pressing Ctrl+D on its own at the shell prompt when no program is running will cause you to log out (if you're using a GUI terminal emulator like GNOME Terminal, the program will quit). This happens because pressing Ctrl+D informs the BASH shell program that you've finished your input. BASH then interprets this as the cue that it should log you out. After all, what else can it do if told there will be no more input?

While it might not seem very useful for day-to-day work, Ctrl+D is vital for programs that expect you to enter data at the command line. You might run into these as you explore BASH. If ever you read in a man page that a program requires an EOF message during input, you'll know what to press.

Using the Command History

The original hackers who invented the tools used under UNIX hated waiting around for things to happen. After all, being a hacker is all about finding the most efficient way of doing any particular task.

Because of this, the BASH shell includes many features designed to optimize the user experience. The most important of these is the *command history*. BASH remembers every command you enter (even the ones that don't work!) and stores them as a list on your hard disk.

During any BASH session, you can cycle through this history using the up and down arrow keys. Pressing the up arrow key takes you back into the command history, and pressing the down arrow key takes you forward.

The potential of the command history is enormous. For example, rather than retype that long command that runs a program with command options, you can simply use the cursor keys to locate it in the history and press Enter.

■**Note** Typing !-3 will cause BASH to move three paces back in the history file and run that command. In other words, it will run what you entered three commands ago.

On our Fedora test system, BASH remembers 1,000 commands. You can view all of the remembered commands by typing history at the command prompt. The history list will scroll off the screen because it's so large, but you can use the scroll bars of the GNOME Terminal window to read it.

Each command in the history list is assigned a number. You can run any of the history commands by preceding their number with an exclamation mark (!), referred to as a *bang*, or sometimes a *shriek*. For example, you might type !923. On our test system, command number 923 in the BASH history is cd .., so this has the effect of switching into the parent directory.

Command numbering remains in place until you log out (close the GNOME Terminal window or end a virtual console session). After this, the numbering is reordered. There will still be 1,000 commands, but the last command you entered before logging out will be at the end of the list, and the numbering will work back 1,000 places until the first command in the history list.

Note One neat trick is to type two bangs: ! !. This tells BASH to repeat the last command you entered.

Rather than specifying a command number, you can type something like !cd. This will cause BASH to look in the history file, find the last instance of a command line that started with cd, and then run it.

Pressing Ctrl+R lets you search the command history from the command prompt. This particular tool can be tricky to get used to, however. As soon as you start typing, BASH will autocomplete the command based on matches found in the history file, starting with the last command in the history. What you type appears before the colon, while the autocompletion appears after it.

Because BASH autocompletes as you type, things can get a little confusing when you're working with the command history, particularly if it initially gets the match wrong. For example, typing cd will show the last instance of the use of cd, as in the example in Figure 17-2. This might not be what you're looking for, so you must keep typing the command you want until it autocompletes correctly.

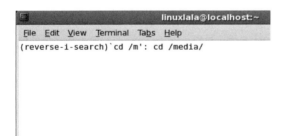

Figure 17-2. *BASH history completion is very useful, but can also be confusing.*

Piping and Directing Output

It's not uncommon for a directory listing or output from another command to scroll off the screen. When using a GUI program like GNOME Terminal, you can use the scroll bars to view the output; but what if you are working at the bare command-line prompt?

By pressing Shift+Page Up and Shift+Page Down, you can "scroll" the window up to take a look at some of the old output, but very little is cached in this way, and you won't see more than a few screens. A far better solution is to pipe the output of the directory listing into a text viewer. Another useful technique is to redirect output to a file.

Piping the Output of Commands

Piping was one of the original innovations provided by UNIX. It simply means that you can pass the output of one command to another, which is to say the output of one command can be used as input for another.

This is possible because shell commands work like machines. They usually take input from the keyboard (referred to technically as *standard input*) and, when they've done their job, usually show their output on the screen (known as *standard output*).

The commands don't need to take input from the keyboard, and they don't need to output to the screen. Piping is the process of diverting the output before it reaches the screen and passing it to another command for further processing.

Let's assume that you have a directory that is packed full of files. You want to do a long directory listing (ls -l) to see what permissions various files have. But doing this produces reams of output that fly off the screen. Typing something like the following provides a solution:

```
ls -l | less
```

The | symbol between the two commands is the pipe. It can be found on most US keyboards next to the square bracket keys (above the Enter key; you'll need to hold down the Shift key to get it).

What happens in the example is that ls -l is run by the shell, but rather than sending the output to the screen, the pipe symbol (|) tells BASH to send it to the command that follows—to less. In other words, the listing is displayed within less, where you can read it at your leisure. You can use Page Up and Page Down or the arrow keys to scroll through it. Once you quit less, the listing evaporates into thin air; the piped output is never actually stored as a file.

In the previous section, you saw how you can use the history command to view the command history. At around 1,000 entries, its output scrolls off the screen in seconds. However, you can pipe it to less, like so:

```
history | less
```

Figure 17-3 shows the result on our test PC.

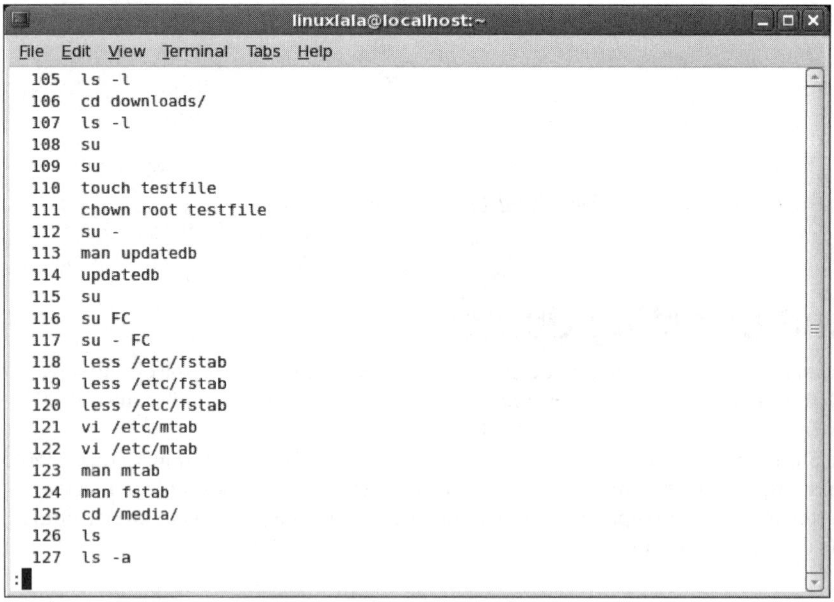

Figure 17-3. *Piping the output of the history command into the less command lets you read the output fully.*

You can pipe the output of any command. One of the most common uses is when searching for a particular string in the output of a command. For example, let's say you know that, within a crowded directory, there's a file with a picture of some flowers. You know that the word *flower* is in the filename, but can't recall any other details. One solution is to perform a directory listing, and then pipe the results to grep, which is able to search through text for a user-defined string (see Chapter 15):

```
ls -l | grep -i 'flower'
```

In this example, the shell runs the ls -l command, and then passes the output to grep. The grep command then searches the output for the word *flower* (the -i option tells it to ignore uppercase and lowercase). If grep finds any results, it will show them on your screen.

The key point to remember is that grep is used here as it normally is at the command prompt. The only difference is that it's being passed input from a previous command, rather than being used on its own.

You can pipe more than once on a command line. Suppose you know that the filename of the picture you want involves the words *flower* and *daffodil*, yet you're unsure of where they might fall in the filename. In this case, you could type the following:

```
ls -l | grep -i flower | grep -i daffodil
```

This will pass the result of the directory listing to the first grep, which will search the output for the word *flower*. The second pipe causes the output from grep to be passed to the second grep command, where it's then searched for the word *daffodil*. Any results are then displayed on your screen.

Redirecting Output

Redirecting is like piping, except that the output is passed to a file rather than to another command. Redirecting can also work the other way: the contents of a file can be passed to a command.

If you wanted to create a file that contained a directory listing, you could type this:

```
ls -l > directorylisting.txt
```

The angle bracket (>) between the commands tells BASH to direct the output of the ls -l command into a file called directorylisting.txt. If a file with this name exists, it's overwritten with new data. If it doesn't exist, it's created from scratch.

You can add data to an already existing file using two angle brackets:

```
ls -l >> directorylisting.txt
```

This will append the result of the directory listing to the end of the file directorylisting.txt, although, once again, if the file doesn't exist, it will be created from scratch.

Redirecting output can get very sophisticated and useful. Take a look at the following:

```
cat myfile1.txt myfile2.txt > myfile3.txt
```

As you learned in Chapter 15, the cat command joins two or more files together. If the command were used on its own without the redirection, it would cause BASH to print myfile1.txt on the screen, immediately followed by myfile2.txt. As far as BASH is concerned, it has joined myfile1.txt to myfile2.txt, and then sent them to standard output (the screen). By specifying a redirection, you have BASH send the output to a third file. Using cat with redirection is a handy way of combining two files.

It's also possible to direct the contents of a file back into a command. Take a look at the following:

```
sort < textfile.txt > sortedtext.txt
```

The sort command simply sorts words in alphanumeric order (it actually sorts them according to the ASCII table of characters, which places symbols and numbers before alphabetic characters).

Directly after the sort command is a left angle bracket, which directs the contents of the file specified immediately after the bracket into the sort command. This is followed by a right angle bracket, which directs the output of the command into another file.

■**Note** To see a table of the ASCII characters, type `man 7 ascii` at the command-line prompt.

There aren't many instances in day-to-day usage where you'll want to use the left angle bracket. It's mostly used with the text-based mail program (which lets you send e-mail from the shell), and in shell scripting, in which a lot of commands are combined together to form a simple program.

REDIRECTING STANDARD ERROR OUTPUT

Standard input and standard output are what BASH calls your keyboard and screen. These are the default input and output methods that programs use unless you specify something else, such as redirecting or piping output and input.

When a program goes wrong, its error message doesn't usually form part of standard output. Instead, it is output via *standard error*. Like standard output, this usually appears on the screen.

Sometimes, it's very beneficial to capture an error message in a text file. This can be done by redirecting the standard error output. The technique is very similar to redirecting standard output:

```
cdrecord --scanbus 2> errormessage.txt
```

The cdrecord command is used to burn CDs, and with the --scanbus command option, you tell it to search for CD-R/RW drives on the system, something that frequently results in an error message if your system is not properly configured.

After the initial command, you see the redirection. To redirect standard error, all you need to do is type 2>, rather than simply >. This effectively tells BASH to use the second type of output: standard error.

You can direct both standard output and standard error to the same file. This is done in the following way:

```
cdrecord --scanbus > error.txt 2>&1
```

This is a little more complicated. The standard output from cdrecord --scanbus is sent to the file error.txt. The second redirect tells BASH to include standard error in the standard output. In other words, it's not a case of standard output being written to a file, and then standard error being added to it. Instead, the standard error is added to standard output by BASH, and then this is written to a file.

Summary

In this chapter, we've looked at some tricks and tips to help you use the BASH shell more effectively. You've seen how BASH can help by autocompleting commands, filenames, and directories. You also learned about keyboard shortcuts that can be used to speed up operations within the shell.

This chapter also covered the command history function and how it can be used to reuse old commands, saving valuable typing time. Finally, we looked at two key functions provided by BASH: redirection and piping. This involved the explanation of standard input, output, and error.

In Part 5 of the book, starting with the next chapter, we move on to discuss the multimedia functionality within Fedora.

CHAPTER 18

■■■

Digital Music

Today's PC is a multimedia powerhouse, and it's hard to come across a home computer that doesn't have at least a set of speakers attached. Some people take this to extremes and have surround-sound speakers on their computers, as well as large monitors for crystal-clear video playback.

The people behind Fedora aren't blind to this and include not only an audio player, but also a video player with the distribution. In this chapter, you'll learn how to listen to MP3s, CDs, and Internet radio on your Fedora system. In the next chapter, you'll learn how to manage video playback.

Understanding the Legalities of Playback

As you might have read in the press, multimedia playback on computer devices, and Linux in particular, is hindered by a number of issues, including the following:

Software patents: Audio and video playback technologies such as MP3 and MPEG are patented in countries that allow software to be patented, such as the United States. A *patent* protects the implementation of an idea, as opposed to *copyright*, which protects the actual software. Patents are designed to restrict use of the technology unless permission is granted, usually via a payment to the license holder. Because Linux is based on the sharing of computing technology and knowledge, organizations like Fedora are fundamentally and philosophically opposed to any kind of software patenting. While this doesn't make playback of popular music and video files impossible under Fedora, it does mean that extra software must be downloaded and installed. Furthermore, depending on where you live in the world, there may be legal issues surrounding using such patented software.

Digital Rights Management (DRM): Much more devastating than patenting is DRM, a technology tied into audio or video playback software. It's designed to control how, where, when, and on what device you can play certain media. For example, Apple's iTunes DRM scheme means you can play back MP3s bought from iTunes only on their iPod range of devices (including the Motorola Rokr phone) or using the iTunes software. DVD movie players include a form of DRM called Content Scrambling System (CSS), which prevents users from playing DVDs on computers unless special software is purchased. Perhaps it goes without saying that the Linux community, including the Fedora project, is also fundamentally opposed to DRM. Because of this, practically no DRM software has been officially ported to Linux, so you can't, for example, play music purchased via the iTunes or Napster online stores.

Linux and other open source programmers are very resourceful and are often able to reverse-engineer technology formats in order to get around DRM or patent issues. But the laws in many countries—with the United States as a particularly strident example—prohibit reverse engineering in this way. In addition, the laws in some countries seek to prohibit use of software resulting from this process.

■**Note** You may be wondering why music and movie corporations are so intent on enforcing DRM and patenting if these schemes give their customers such a hard time. To learn more, and to find out what you can do to help halt the progress of such technology, visit the Electronic Frontier Foundation's web site, at `www.eff.org`.

Programmers have also come up with *free software* alternatives to proprietary formats. Examples include the Ogg Vorbis media format, which is every bit as good as MP3, but is unencumbered by patent issues. We'll look at using Ogg Vorbis later in this chapter, in the "Choosing a Format" section. There's also Ogg Theora, an extremely competitive open source video format. Refer to Chapter 19 for more details about Ogg Theora.

As you'll probably want to add support for MP3 and other popular music file formats, throughout this and the next chapter we'll examine installing media playback software, some of which may have issues surrounding patenting. In one case, the software is designed to bypass the DRM scheme that protects DVD movie discs.

■**Note** The United States and Japan both have laws allowing software to be patented. Most other countries, including those within the European Union, do not currently allow software patents.

Playing Music Files

Music playback under Fedora is handled by the Rhythmbox player. Like many modern music players, Rhythmbox can also manage your music collection, arranging it into a library so you can locate songs easily.

But before using Rhythmbox, you need to add support for MP3 and other popular music file formats.

Installing Codecs

The piece of software that handles the decoding (and also encoding) of digital music files is called a *codec*. The word is a shortened version of *coder-decoder*. For any digital multimedia file type you want to play back on your computer, you'll need an appropriate codec. This includes both audio and video files. In addition, if you wish to create your own multimedia files, you might need to download an additional codec that allows the *encoding* of files.

The necessary audio and video codec software for playback can be found in unofficial online software repositories such as `livna`. (See Chapter 8 for details on setting up Pirut Package Manager to access these repositories.) To obtain them, open Pirut Package Manager (Applications ➤ Add/Remove Software), click the Search button, and then type **gstreamer**. In the list of results, look for the following packages:

- gstreamer
- gstreamer-ffmpeg

- gstreamer-plugins-bad

- gstreamer-plugins-ugly

Click the check box alongside each and click the Apply button. You'll be told that each package needs additional software. Don't worry—this is why we recommend these particular packages! This set of packages contains support for just about every form of audio playback possible on a PC (with the exception of DRM technology like the iTunes M4P files).

Once Pirut Package Manager is through installing the selected packages and dependencies, quit the program.

Using Rhythmbox

You'll find the Rhythmbox music player on the Applications ➤ Sound & Video menu. The first time you run the program, it will ask you where your music files are stored. Simply click the Browse button, and then double-click the folder that holds those files. Then click OK.

When the program starts, your music files are listed at the bottom of the program window. At the top left of the program window, you'll find a listing of the artists behind the MP3s in your collection, and on the right, you'll see the album that the music track is taken from (provided that information is included in the music file itself, such as the MP3 ID3 tags). Figure 18-1 shows an example of a Rhythmbox window.

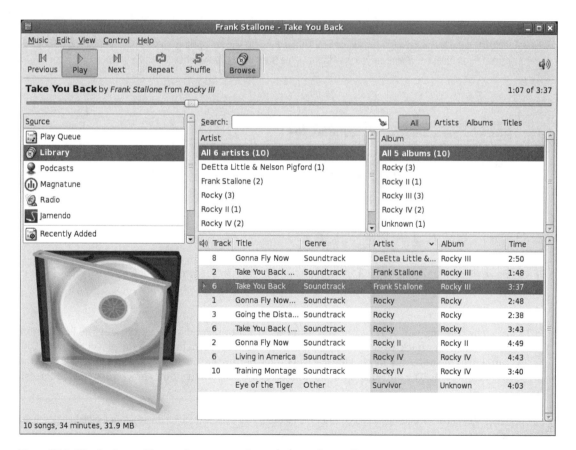

Figure 18-1. *Rhythmbox will organize your music tracks by artist or album.*

Playing a track is simply a matter of double-clicking it in the list. Once the track is finished, Rhythmbox will play the next track in the MP3 file list.

To create a playlist, click Music ➤ Playlist and select New Playlist. You'll be prompted to type its name. To add tracks to the playlist, click Library, and then drag and drop files onto your new playlist entry. To start the playlist, click the first track in its list.

Note You will find that whenever you double-click an MP3 file in a Nautilus window, Fedora will try to start Totem Movie Player rather than Rhythmbox. This is easy to fix: right-click any MP3 file, select Properties, and click the Open With tab. In the list of applications that appears, select Rhythmbox, and ensure that the radio button alongside its entry in the list is selected. Click the Close button, and you're all done!

Listening to Audio CDs

Playing back audio CDs is simple. Just insert the CD, and then click Applications ➤ Sound & Video ➤ CD Player. This will start Fedora's simple but effective CD playback application, as shown in Figure 18-2. If you're online, the application will immediately attempt to look up the CD artist and track listing information from an online repository. This means that it should show the names of the tracks being played.

Note If the online lookup results in several entries for a CD you are playing, choose the one that you think is correct. From then on, whenever you play that CD, the track listing you've chosen will be used.

Figure 18-2. *Fedora's CD Player application is simple but effective, and can look up artist and track information online.*

The controls work in the same way as those on any other audio player. Clicking the Play button plays the current track, which you can select from the drop-down list above the player controls. You can skip to the next track by clicking the Next Track button and cue backward and forward using the relevant buttons. The time display in the top left of the program window shows the track's progress.

Tip As with all GNOME applications, hover the mouse cursor over each button to display a tooltip that describes what it does.

If you find the track listing information is incorrect, you can correct it by clicking the Track Editor button on the right side of the program window. In the window that appears, double-click the track entry with the incorrect information and edit it as you see fit.

Tuning In to Online Radio Stations

You can listen to online radio stations (which play streaming audio) by downloading the Streamtuner application. This isn't an actual audio player, but is instead a kind of digital listings program that lets you search for stations to match just about any musical taste. It relies on external music player programs to actually allow you to listen to the streams.

To obtain Streamtuner, open Pirut Package Manager (Applications ➤ Add/Remove Software), search for the streamtuner package, and install it.

Using Streamtuner

Using Streamtuner is easy. But let's first configure it to use Rhythmbox. To do this, click Edit ➤ Preferences. Now, click the command next to "Listen to a .m3u file" and type **rhythmbox %q**. Do the same for the command next to "Listen to a stream," as shown in Figure 18-3.

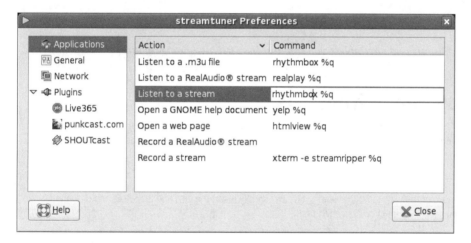

Figure 18-3. *Configuring Streamtuner to use Rhythmbox*

When Streamtuner launches, click one of the tabs to browse through the stations. In addition, some tabs have subcategories of stations on the left. The Shoutcast tab probably contains the most comprehensive selection; Live365 and Xiph, shown in Figure 18-4, are quite popular as well.

Whenever you double-click a stream, it will start playing. Most streams will play in Rhythmbox, which will start automatically; however, some are RealAudio streams, in which case you'll need to have RealPlayer installed to play them. See Chapter 19 for instructions on installing RealPlayer.

You can add any radio station to Rhythmbox by clicking the New Internet Radio Station button.

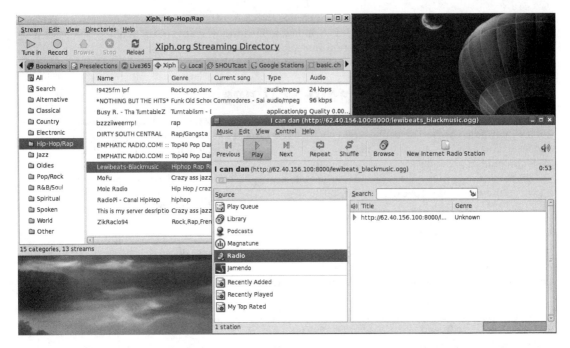

Figure 18-4. *With Streamtuner and Rhythmbox, you can tune in to a massive range of Internet radio stations.*

Ripping Music from CDs

Converting audio tracks on a CD to digital music files you can store on your hard disk for personal use is informally known as *ripping*. It's handled under Fedora using the Sound Juicer application, which can be found on the Applications ➤ Sound & Video menu.

■**Note** Because of the way audio CDs work, you can't simply insert the disc and then drag and drop the tracks onto your hard disk. They must be converted first.

Before you start to rip CDs, however, you'll need to decide the format in which you wish to store the audio files.

Choosing a Format

You have three basic choices for audio file formats: Ogg Vorbis, FLAC, and MP3. Let's look at what each has to offer:

Ogg Vorbis: This is the free software alternative to MP3. Unless you have a trained ear, you won't be able to tell the difference between Ogg and MP3 files (if you *do* have a trained ear, then you'll find Ogg better!). The two technologies generate files of around the same size, an average of 4 MB to 5 MB per song. The downside of Ogg is that not many portable audio players support it (although this situation is slowly changing), and other operating systems like Windows won't be able to play back Ogg files unless some additional software is installed (see www.vorbis.com/setup/).

FLAC: This stands for Free Lossless Audio Codec, and it's the choice of the audiophile. Ogg and MP3 are lossy formats, which means that some of the audio data is lost in order to significantly shrink the file. FLAC doesn't lose any audio data but still manages to compress files to a certain degree (although they're still much larger than an equivalent MP3 or Ogg file). FLAC scores points because it's free software, like Ogg, but you'll face the same lack of support in portable audio players and other operating systems (unless additional software is installed; see `http://flac.sourceforge.net/download.html`).

MP3: This is by far the most ubiquitous music file format, and practically everyone who owns a computer has at least a handful of MP3 tracks. This means software support for MP3 playback is strong and, of course, portable audio players are built around the MP3 format. The only problem for you, as a Linux user, is the issue surrounding patents, as explained at the beginning of this chapter. Using the MP3 format is to go against a lot of what the free software movement stands for. But in the end, the choice is up to you.

Adding MP3 Support to Sound Juicer

Support for Ogg and FLAC is built into Fedora, but if you wish to encode CD tracks as MP3s, you'll need to enter some configuration details into Sound Juicer.

■**Note** The software that's required to encode MP3s is installed with the gstreamer packages. If you didn't already download them, follow the instructions earlier in the chapter, in the "Installing Codecs" section.

Follow these steps to configure MP3 support:

1. Select Applications ➤ Sound & Video ➤ Sound Juicer to start the program.

2. Click Edit ➤ Preferences. In the dialog box that appears, click the Edit Profiles button.

3. Click New, and then type **MP3**. Then click Create.

4. Select the new MP3 entry in the list and click Edit.

5. In the Profile Name box, type **MP3**.

6. In the Profile Description box, type **MP3**.

7. In the GStreamer Pipeline box, type the following:

    audio/x-raw-int,rate=44100,channels=2 ! lame name=enc

8. In the File Extension box, type **mp3**.

9. Put a check in the Active? box.

10. Click OK.

11. Restart Sound Juicer.

12. Click Edit ➤ Preferences again, and select your new MP3 entry from the Output drop-down list.

Ripping Tracks

When you're ready to rip some music, insert the audio CD, and then start Sound Juicer. If the CD isn't read immediately, click Disc ➤ Re-read. As with CD Player, Sound Juicer will automatically look up the artist and track information for the CD.

Click Edit ➤ Preferences. In the Format part of the dialog box, choose the type of audio files you want to create. In addition, you can select where you would like the files to be saved to by clicking the drop-down list under the Music Folder heading.

Any track in the listing with a check in its box will be ripped. When you insert a CD, Sound Juicer assumes that all the tracks are to be ripped, as shown in Figure 18-5. If this isn't the case, remove the checks from the tracks you don't want to rip. By selecting a track and clicking the Play button, you'll be able to audition the track. This can be helpful if you're deciding on exactly which tracks to rip. Finally, check that the Title and Artist information is correct.

Figure 18-5. *Audio tracks can be ripped from CDs using the Sound Juicer program.*

To begin the process, click the Extract button. It will take up to a minute or so to rip each track, so ripping an entire CD may take some time. However, it's safe to leave Sound Juicer working in the background.

MAKING MUSIC AND RECORDING AUDIO

Most PCs come with sound cards that are capable of making music. You can use many open-source programs, designed for both amateurs and professionals alike, to create music or record and edit audio.

In terms of musical sequencers, Muse (www.muse-sequencer.org/), Rosegarden (www.rosegardenmusic.com/), and Jazz++ (www.jazzware.com/zope) are well worth investigating. Like all modern MIDI sequencers, all three programs let you record audio tracks, effectively turning your PC into a recording studio.

It's also possible to run virtual synthesizers on your PC, which effectively turn even the most basic sound card into a powerful musical instrument. Examples include Bristol (www.slabexchange.org/) and FluidSynth (www.nongnu.org/fluid/).

If you're interested in only audio recording and processing, Sweep (`www.metadecks.org/software/sweep/`) and Audacity (`http://audacity.sourceforge.net`) are worth a look. In addition to audio recording and playback, both feature graphical waveform editing and powerful filters.

Another program worthy of attention is Jokosher (`www.jokosher.org/`). A simple yet powerful audio studio, it can be used to create your own music, podcasts, and more.

Most of the packages mentioned here are available from the Fedora software repositories, and you can download them with Pirut Package Manager.

Creating Your Own CDs

You can create audio CDs by using the Rhythmbox player. Rhythmbox lets you burn your playlists, so you need to create a playlist of your favorite songs before you can burn them onto a disk.

To create a playlist, select the songs from the library. To select multiple songs, you can either use Shift or the Ctrl keys. If you click the first song and then click on the sixth while pressing the Shift key, all songs from the first to the sixth will be selected. Similarly, if you click several songs with the Ctrl key pressed, each of those particular songs will be selected. Right-click and select Add to Playlist ➤ New Playlist. You will be invited to give a name to the playlist. Press Enter after typing the name.

Once your playlist is ready, right-click its name and select Create Audio CD. You can specify the write speed in the dialog box that comes up. Click Create to burn your CD.

Tip You can also create a playlist by selecting Music ➤ Playlist ➤ New Playlist. To add songs to a playlist, right-click the selected songs from the library and choose Add to Playlist ➤ *yourplaylist*.

Summary

This chapter has covered the audio functions built into Fedora, and how, by downloading a few extra system files, you can play back the majority of audio files in existence. We started by discussing the moral and legal dilemmas associated with multimedia playback on a computer. Then we moved on to look at how to install the necessary codec files on your computer, before discussing how you can listen to music files, CDs, and online radio stations. We examined how you can convert CDs into music files, and then the inverse of this: how you can create CDs using audio files.

In Chapter 19, we'll look at how you can play back movies and online animations using Fedora.

Movies and Multimedia

Movie playback on computers is becoming increasingly popular. Modern PCs come equipped with DVD-ROM drives, and coupled with the right software, these can play movies on DVD. In addition, many web sites feature streaming movie clips or offer them for download.

Fedora provides support for movie playback, but as with audio support, you'll need to install additional codecs in order to enjoy the broadest range of playback options. This chapter explains how to set up Fedora for watching videos, DVDs, and TV on your computer, as well as playing online Flash animations.

Watching Videos

You use the Totem Movie Player application to play back video under Fedora. Like the other multimedia software provided with Fedora, it's basic but effective and does the job well. However, because of licensing issues, it doesn't support all video formats out of the box. In fact, it supports very few of those you might be used to using under Windows.

If you wish to play back the most common video file types, such as those listed in Table 19-1, you must install additional software. This software contains codecs that allow you to play Windows Media Player, RealPlayer, QuickTime, and DivX movie files under Fedora. In addition, you'll need to make some updates to Totem.

■**Caution** The codecs are quite literally lifted straight from a Windows installation. Therefore, you should install them only if you own a license for Windows and have also installed the relevant media player applications under Windows and agreed to their license agreements.

After following the instructions in this section, you will be able to play video files on your hard disk and also stream video from web sites within Firefox.

If you don't wish to install codes, the other option is to install VideoLan Client (discussed in the next section).

Table 19-1. *Popular Movie File Formats*

Format	Typical File Extensions	Web Site	Notes
Windows Media Player 9	.wmv, .wma, .asx, .asf	www.microsoft.com/windows/windowsmedia	Default format for Windows Media Player and, therefore, for most Windows users. Although it's possible to play Windows Media Player files under Fedora, you won't be able to play DRM-restricted files (those that rely on the download and installation of a certificate).
RealVideo	.rm, .ram	www.real.com/	By downloading the Win32 codec pack, you can play back RealVideo files in Totem. Alternatively, you can download a Linux version of Real-Player. Both approaches are described in this chapter.
QuickTime	.mov, .qt	www.quicktime.com	QuickTime is Apple's default media format and has gained ground on both Windows and Macintosh computers. As with Windows Media Player, you won't be able to play DRM-restricted files.
DivX	.avi, .divx	www.divx.com	The DivX format is one of the most popular formats for those in the Internet community who like to encode their own movies. It's renowned for its ability to shrink movies to very small sizes.

Installing VLC Media Player

www.videolan.org/vlc/ is the home of VideoLan Client, or VLC, a great media player that can handle just about any video and audio format. To install VLC, open a terminal (Application ➤ System Tools ➤ Terminal) and run the following command as root (use su -):

```
yum install videolan-client
```

Let yum work on determining the dependency list. Agree to install the dependencies, and when yum is done, you will find VLC, shown in action in Figure 19-1, under the Applications ➤ Sound & Video menu.

We recommend you use VLC to play all kinds of multimedia files. It works seamlessly with almost all of the popular multimedia file formats listed in Table 19-1, and you don't need to bother about codecs.

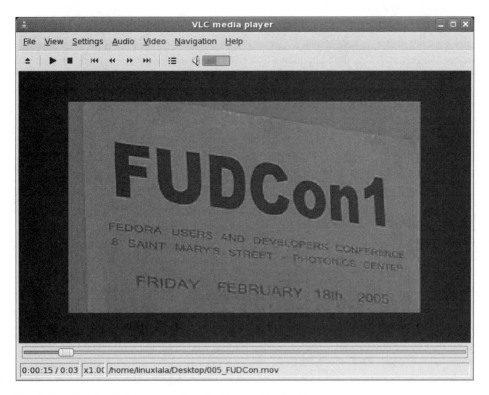

Figure 19-1. *VLC Media Player can handle almost all video formats.*

Installing Codecs

For video playback in Totem, you need the codecs described in the previous chapter, as well as a few more. If you haven't followed the instructions in the previous chapter and downloaded the various packages mentioned there, do that first.

We will now show you how to install the totem-xine package, which is a better variant of the Totem Movie Player installed by default by Fedora. Open a terminal window (Applications ➤ System Tools ➤ Terminal), and run this command as root (use su -):

```
rpm -e -no-deps totem
```

This will remove the default Totem player. The -no-deps command option is important because without it, this command would also remove Rhythmbox. Next, install totem-xine:

```
yum install totem-xine
```

Next, you need to install some codecs:

```
yum install libdvdcss libdvddread libdvdnav xine-lib-extras-nonfree
```

You will now be able to play DVDs in Totem Media Player (Applications ➤ Sound & Video ➤ Movie Player).

Installing RealPlayer

If you wish to install RealPlayer, head over to www.real.com/linux and follow the download links for the latest free Linux player. Download it, open a GNOME Terminal window (Applications ➤ System Tools ➤ Terminal), and type the following (replacing *filename* with the name of the RealPlayer file):

```
chmod +x filename
su -c './filename'
[Enter Password]
```

During installation, you'll be asked various questions. When asked where you would like to install RealPlayer, type /usr/bin/RealPlayer (don't agree to using the default path!). Answer yes to creating symbolic links, and agree to the default location for the links.

Playing Back Video

To play a movie file on your hard disk, simply double-click its icon. This will automatically start Totem. Double-clicking a DVD icon on your desktop has the same outcome. To make VLC the default player, right-click the file, move the mouse to Open With, and then click Other. Choose VLC from the list of applications.

■**Note** By default, all video files will play in Totem, including RealMedia. To change this so that RealPlayer handles them, right-click any RealPlayer movie file, select Open With, and select RealPlayer from the list. Make sure the radio button alongside RealPlayer is selected.

Using VLC is easy. At the top of the screen are the transport controls that allow you to pause, play, or move forward and backward in the video file. Alternatively, you can right-click the video window and select the controls from there.

Under the video window is the time bar. With certain types of video, you can drag and drop this to move through the video, but not all files support this function.

You can queue several video files to be played in sequence by simply dragging and dropping movies from a Nautilus file browser window. To view the playlist, click View ➤ Playlist.

To play the video full-screen, press the F key. This might not work for all types of video, so you can alternatively click View ➤ Fullscreen. To return to the program window, press the F key. In full-screen mode, you can start and pause the video by pressing the spacebar.

OPEN SOURCE MOVIE FILE FORMATS

A number of promising open source movie file formats are in development. Some are more mature than others, but few see widespread use at the moment. All promise much for the future. Many consider the following three formats as the chief contenders:

- Xvid (www.xvid.org/) is a reworking of the popular DivX MPEG-4-based file format. As such, it is able to encode movies to relatively small files sizes (a 90-minute movie can fit on a CD). Despite small file sizes, it can maintain good image and sound quality. In theory, it should also be possible to play Xvid movies using any MPEG-4 codec, such as DivX or QuickTime. Unfortunately, Xvid uses technology covered by patents in some parts of the world, so the project exists in a legal gray area. Additionally, it's only possible to download a Windows version of the codec, although if you follow the instructions at the beginning of this chapter, you will be able to download the ported Windows version of the codec so that you can play Xvid files under Fedora.

- Ogg Theora (www.theora.org/) is being developed by the Xiph.Org Foundation, the people behind the Ogg Vorbis audio codec project that's a favorite among Linux users. As such, it promises to be a completely open source project. Although the technology is covered by patents, Xiph.Org has promised never to enforce them, meaning that anyone in the world can use Theora without charge. At the time of writing, Theora is still in the alpha development phase, but it will almost certainly become the open source video codec of choice in the future. Both the VLC player as well as Totem can play Ogg Theora videos without requiring any codecs.

- The British Broadcasting Corporation (www.bbc.co.uk/), the UK's largest public service broadcaster, is sponsoring development of the Dirac codec (see http://dirac.sourceforge.net). Dirac is less mature than both Theora and Xvid, and it is aimed more at the broadcast/enthusiast market. For example, it is designed to support HDTV (high-definition television). However, it's certainly one to watch.

Watching DVDs

DVD movie discs are protected by a form of digital rights management (DRM) called Content Scrambling System (CSS). This forces anyone who would like to create DVD playback software or hardware to pay a fee to the DVD Copy Control Association, an industry organization set up to protect DVD movie technology.

Nearly all Linux advocates are scornful of any kind of DRM system. It isn't possible to buy licensed DVD playback software for Linux, and even if it were, few would be willing to support what they see as prohibitive software technology.

Some open source advocates reverse-engineered DVD and came up with the DeCSS software. This bypasses the CSS system and allows the playback of DVD movies under practically any operating system. Sadly, DeCSS is caught in a legal quagmire. The Motion Picture Association of America (MPAA) has attempted to stop its distribution within the United States but has failed. Some experts suggest that distributing DeCSS breaks copyright laws, but there has yet to be a case anywhere in the world that categorically proves this.

Fedora doesn't come with DeCSS installed by default, but you can download and install the software by issuing a simple command, as discussed in the "Installing Codecs" section.

So, just insert a DVD, and Totem will automatically start playing it. Alternatively, if Totem is already open, you can play the DVD by clicking its entry on the Movie menu.

Playing a DVD is not dissimilar to watching movie files on your hard disk. The only difference is that you can now navigate from chapter to chapter on the DVD by clicking the relevant entry under the Go menu, as shown in Figure 19-2. You can also return to the DVD's main menu this way. You can use your mouse to click entries in DVD menus.

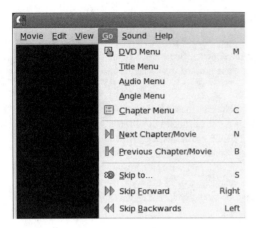

Figure 19-2. *Use the Go menu to access the DVD's menus and to skip forward or backward.*

■**Tip** If you find you have problems with video playback in Totem, such as Totem showing an error message about another application using the video output, try the following: click System ➤ Preferences ➤ More Preferences ➤ Multimedia Systems Selector. Click the Video tab, and in the Default Output drop-down list, select Xwindows (No Xv). Click Test. If this doesn't work, try the other Xwindow option instead.

Playing Flash Animations

Flash Player is a standard fixture on most modern browsers. It allows access to not only animations, but also to interactive web sites and games. Macromedia makes a player especially for Linux, and you can download it from their web site.

Flash Player enables you to enjoy online animations and games.

To install Flash Player, download the yum repository from `http://macromedia.mplug.org/ macromedia-i386.repo` into the `/etc/yum.repos.d/` directory. Here are the steps:

```
cd /etc/yum.repos.d/
su -c "wget http://macromedia.mplug.org/macromedia-i386.repo"
su -c "rpm -import http://macromedia.mplug.org/FEDORA-GPG-KEY
su -c "yum install flash-plugin"
```

Once installation has finished, log out and then back in again. Configuration is automatic, and you should now be able to visit any Flash site with Firefox.

Sadly, there isn't a Linux version of the Shockwave Director browser plug-in. If you really need to have access to Shockwave sites under Linux, consider using CrossOver Office (`www.codeweavers.com/`) to install the Windows version. But be aware that CrossOver Office is a commercial product, and you'll need to pay for it.

Installing Java

Some sites use Java to present interaction, animation, and even movies. You can install the Java Runtime program by downloading the Java Runtime Environment (JRE) package from `http:// java.sun.com/javase/downloads/index.jsp`. Click the download button. You'll have to agree to the license (click the Accept radio button). Then download the self-extracting Linux file. If you are going to develop Java applications, you should download the Java Development Kit (JDK). Its approximately 60 MB download includes the JRE.

When the download is complete, open a terminal (Applications ➤ System Tools ➤ Terminal). If the `compat-libstdc++-33` library is not installed on your system, run the command `yum install compat-libstdc++-33`. You'll then need to run a series of commands to install Java:

```
su -
[Enter password]
cd /opt
sh /home/linuxlala/downloads/jre-6u1-linux-i586.bin
```

The Java license will be displayed. You can scroll through the license by pressing the spacebar. You need to accept the license, so type yes to proceed. The installer will now install the software and create a `jre.1.6.0_01/` directory under `/opt`.

This next step installs the browser plug-in for Java. In the terminal, run the following command:

```
ln -s /opt/jre1.6.0/plugin/\
i386/ns7/libjavaplugin_oji.so\ /usr/lib/\
mozilla/plugins/libjavaplugin_oji.so
```

There is still some work left. You now need to tell Fedora to use Sun Java. By default, Fedora picks up GNU Java whenever you run a Java application:

```
/usr/sbin/alternatives --install usr/bin/java java\ /opt/jre1.6.0/bin/java 2
```

To see a list of all installations of Java, run the following command:

```
/us/sbin/alternatives --config java
```

You need to choose the one corresponding to the `/opt` path, as shown in the following output:

```
There are 2 programs which provide 'java'.
  Selection    Command
-----------------------------------------------
*+  1          /usr/lib/jvm/jre-1.4.2-gcj/bin/java
    2          /opt/jre1.6.0_01/bin/java

Enter to keep the current selection[+], or type selection number: 2
```

Press 2 to select Sun Java. The + represents the currently active version of Java. If you now run the `/usr/sbin/alternatives --config java` command, you'll find that the + is adjacent to 2.

You can now run the command `/usr/sbin/alternatives --display java` to test the installation. That's it! Close Firefox and restart it for the plug-in to work.

■**Note** Fedora ships with libgcj webplugin, a free software variant of the Java browser plug-in. If you wish to use this, run the command `ln -s /usr/lib/gcj-4.1.1/libgcjwebplugin.so /usr/lib/mozilla/plugins` instead of using the preceding method. Restart Firefox, and you'll find the free version installed. In fact, Sun has actually decided to release Java as free software under the GPL. Java Standard Edition, Micro Edition, and Enterprise Edition will all be available under the GPL.

MOVIE EDITING

The field of Linux movie-editing software is still young, and only a handful of programs are available for the nonprofessional user. One of the best is Kino (www.kinodv.org/), which is available in the unofficial Fedora software archives. Although far from being a professional-level program, Kino allows competent users to import and edit videos, apply effects, and then output in either MPEG-1 or MPEG-2 format.

If you're looking for something more powerful, but also more complicated, then Cinelerra is well worth a look (http://heroinewarrior.com/cinelerra.php3). To quote the web site, Cinelerra is "the same kind of compositing and editing suite that the big boys use," except it's made for Linux!

MainActor (www.mainconcept.com/) is the Linux version of a commercial Windows project. Although it's not free, most people agree that it's one of the most comprehensive video editors available for Linux at the moment, and possibly the easiest to use, too.

Incidentally, professional moviemakers use Linux all the time, particularly when it comes to adding special effects to movies. Movies like *Shrek 2*, *Stuart Little*, and the *Harry Potter* series all benefited from the CinePaint software running under Linux! For more details, see http://cinepaint.org/.

None of these applications are available from official Fedora repositories, but if you installed all the unofficial repositories mentioned in Chapter 8, you should be able to install them using Pirut Package Manager.

Watching TV

If you have a TV card, you may be able to use it to watch TV under Fedora. Fedora doesn't come with a TV tuner application by default, but you can download the tvtime program from the software repositories using Pirut Package Manager.

Checking for Video Input

Fedora includes the Video for Linux project, an extension to the Linux kernel that allows many popular TV and video capture cards to work. You can find out if yours is compatible by using the Multimedia System Selector. Unfortunately, it is not listed under the Preferences menu by default, so you need to customize the Preferences menu first.

Click System ➤ Preferences ➤ Look and Feel ➤ Main Menu. In the window that comes up, select System ➤ Preferences ➤ Hardware from the list on the left. Put a check in the check-box against Multimedia Systems Selector and click Close. Launch Multimedia Systems Selector (System ➤ Preferences ➤ Hardware ➤ Multimedia Systems Selector). In the dialog box that appears, click the Video tab, and then click the Test button in the Default Source part of the window. If you see a video window without an error message, then your TV card is compatible. If you receive an error message, try a different input setting from the drop-down list and click Test again.

Installing Tvtime

To download and install tvtime, open Pirut Package Manager (Applications ➤ Add/Remove Software), click the Search button, and enter **tvtime** as a search term. In the list of results, click the entry for tvtime and select it. Then click Apply.

When the download has completed, you'll be asked a number of questions during the configuration process. First, you need to choose your TV picture format. Users in the United States should choose NTSC. Users in the United Kingdom, Australia, and certain parts of Europe should choose PAL. To find out which TV system your country uses, look up your country at www.videouniversity.com/standard.htm. You also need to choose your geographical area from the list so that tvtime can set the correct radio frequency range for your TV card.

Once the program is installed, you'll find it on the Applications ➤ Sound & Video menu. Using the program is straightforward, but if you need guidance, visit the program's web site at `http://tvtime.sourceforge.net/`.

Summary

In this chapter, we looked at how you can watch movies on your PC. You've seen how you can update Fedora to work with the most popular digital video technologies, such as Windows Media Player and QuickTime.

In addition, we looked at how you can view online multimedia such as Flash animations on your computer, and discussed how you can watch TV on your PC.

In the next chapter, we'll take a look at image editing under Fedora. You'll learn about one of the crown jewels of the Linux software scene: the GIMP.

CHAPTER 20

■■■

Image Editing

The PC has become an increasingly useful tool in the field of photography. In fact, these days it's hard to imagine a professional photographer who doesn't use a computer in some way, whether to download digital camera images or to scan in images taken using traditional film-based cameras.

Fedora includes a sophisticated and professional-level image-editing program called The GIMP. The title stands for GNU Image Manipulation Program. This chapter introduces this jewel in the crown of Linux software.

Getting Pictures onto Your PC

Before you can undertake any image editing, you need to transfer your images to your PC. Depending on the source of the pictures, there are a variety of ways of doing this. We have already looked at transferring images to your PC in Chapter 8, but let's briefly recap the procedure here.

Most modern cameras use memory cards to store the pictures. If you have such a model, when you plug the camera into your PC's USB port, you should find that Fedora instantly recognizes it. An icon should appear on the desktop, and double-clicking it should display the memory card in a Nautilus window. Technically speaking, the memory card has been *mounted* (see Chapter 14 for an explanation of mounting).

If your camera doesn't appear to be recognized by Fedora, you should consider buying a USB card reader. These devices are typically inexpensive and can read a wide variety of card types, making them a useful investment for the future. Some new PCs even come packaged with card readers. Most generic card readers should work fine under Linux, as will most new digital cameras.

If your camera isn't recognized, however, or if it's a few years old and uses the serial port to connect to your PC, you can try using the gThumb software (Applications ➤ Graphics ➤ gThumb Image Viewer), as explained in Chapter 8.

If you're working with print photos, negative film, or transparencies, you can use a scanner to scan them in using the XSane image scanning program, also covered in Chapter 8. This works in a virtually identical way to the TWAIN modules supplied with Windows scanners, in that you need to set the dots per inch (DPI) figures, as well as the color depth. Generally speaking, 300 DPI and 24-bit color should lead to a true-to-life representation of most photos (although because of their smaller size, transparencies or negative film will require higher resolutions, on the order of 1,200 or 2,400 DPI).

Introducing The GIMP

The GIMP is an extremely powerful image editor that offers the kind of functions usually associated with top-end software like Adobe Photoshop. Although it's not aimed at beginners, those new to image editing can get the most from of it, provided they put in a little work.

The program relies on a few unusual concepts within its interface, which can catch many people off guard. The first of these is that each of the windows within the program, such as floating dialog boxes or palettes, gets its own panel entry. In other words, The GIMP's icon bar, image window, settings window, and so on have their own buttons on the panel alongside your other programs, as if they were separate programs.

■**Note** The GIMP's way of working is referred to as a Single Document Interface, or SDI. It's favored by a handful of programs that run under Linux and seems to be especially popular among programs that let you create things.

Because of the way that The GIMP runs, it's a wise idea to switch to a different virtual desktop (virtual desktops are discussed in Chapter 7), which you can then dedicate entirely to the program.

Click Applications ➤ Graphics ➤ GIMP Image Editor to run The GIMP. When the program starts for the first time, it will run through its setup routine. Usually, you can use the default answers to the various questions asked by the wizard.

After program has been set up, you'll be greeted by what appears to be a complex assortment of program windows. Now you need to be aware of a second unusual aspect of the program: its reliance on right-clicking. Whereas right-clicking usually brings up a context menu offering a handful of options, within The GIMP, it's the principal way of accessing the program's functions. Right-clicking an image brings up a menu offering access to virtually everything you'll need while editing. Fedora includes the latest version of The GIMP, 2.2, which features a menu bar in the main image-editing window. This is considered sacrilege by many traditional users of The GIMP, although it's undoubtedly useful for beginners. However, the right-click menu remains the most efficient way of accessing The GIMP's tools.

The main toolbar window, shown in Figure 20-1, is on the left. This can be considered the heart of The GIMP because, when you close it, all the other program windows are closed, too. The menu bar on the toolbar window offers most of the options you're likely to use to start out with The GIMP. For example, File ➤ Open will open a browser dialog box in which you can select files to open in The GIMP. It's even possible to create new artwork from scratch by choosing File ➤ New. To create original artwork, a better choice is a program like OpenOffice.org Draw (on the Applications ➤ Office menu).

Beneath the menu bar in the main toolbar window are the tools for working with images. Their functions are described in Table 20-1, which lists the tools in order from left to right, starting at the top left.

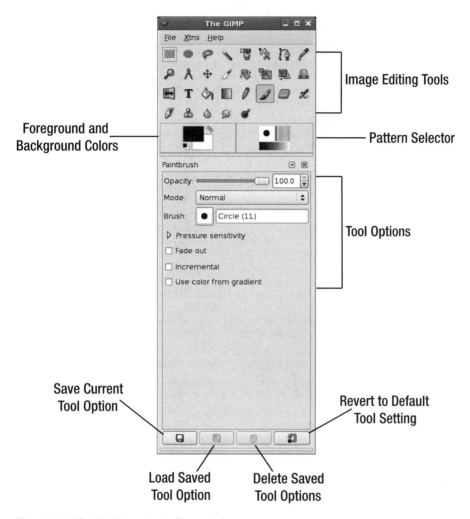

Figure 20-1. *The GIMP's main toolbar window*

Table 20-1. *The GIMP's Image-Editing Tools*

Tool	Description of Use
Rectangular selection tool	Click and drag to select a rectangular area within the image. This selected area can then be copied and pasted into a different part of the image or turned into a new layer.
Elliptical selection tool	This tool creates an oval or circular selection area within the image, which you can then copy and paste.
Hand-drawn selection tool	Click and draw with the mouse to create a hand-drawn selection area. Your selection should end where it started. If not, The GIMP will draw a straight line between the start and end of the selection.

Continued

Table 20-1. *Continued*

Tool	Description of Use
Contiguous regions selection tool	Known as the "magic wand" in other image editors, this tool creates a selection area based on the color of the pixels where you click. For example, clicking a red car hood will select most, if not all, of the hood, because it is mostly red.
Color region selection tool	This tool works like the contiguous region selection tool, but will create a selection across the entire image based on the color you select. In other words, selecting a black T-shirt will also select a black signpost elsewhere in the picture if the shades are similar.
Shape selection tool	Another "magical" tool, the shape selector lets you create a selection by clicking various points within an image, with the program joining the points together based on the color differences between the two points. This means that you can select the outline of a car by clicking a few points around the edge of the car and, provided the color of the car is different from the background, The GIMP will work out the color differences and select the car's shape automatically.
Path creation tool	This tool draws Bezier curves in order to create paths. Paths are akin to selections and can be saved for use later on in the image-editing process. Creating a Bezier curve is not too hard to do: just click and drag to draw a curve. Each extra click you make will define a new curve, which will be joined to the last one. To turn the path into a selection, click the button at the bottom of the toolbar.
Color picker	This lets you see the RGB, HSV, or CMYK values of any color within the image. Simply click the mouse within the image.
Zoom tool	Click to zoom into the image, right-click to see various zoom options, and hold down the Alt key while clicking to zoom out.
Measurer	This tool measures distances between two points (in pixels) and also angles. Just click and drag to use it. The measurements will appear at the bottom of the image window.
Move tool	Click and drag to move any selection areas within the image, as well as rearrange the positioning of various layers.
Crop tool	Click and drag to define an area of the image to be cropped. Anything outside the selection area you create will be discarded.
Rotate tool	This tool rotates any selections you make and can also rotate entire layers. It opens a dialog box in which you can set the rotation manually. Alternatively, you can simply click and drag the handles behind the dialog box to rotate by hand.
Scale tool	Known in some other image editors as "transform," this tool lets you resize the selection area or layer. It presents a dialog box where you can enter numeric values, or you can click and drag the handles to resize by hand.
Shear tool	This tool lets you transform the image by shearing it. Slant a selection by clicking and dragging the corners of the selection area (if the selection area isn't square, a rectangular grid will be applied to it for the purposes of transformation).
Perspective tool	This tool lets you transform a selection by clicking and dragging its four corners and independently moving them without affecting the other corners. In this way, a sense of perspective can be emulated.
Flip tool	This tool flips a selection or image so that it is reversed on itself, either horizontally (click) or vertically (hold down Ctrl and click).
Text tool	Click the image to add text.

Tool	Description of Use
Fill tool	This tool fills a particular area with solid color, according to the color selected in the color box below it.
Gradient fill	Click and drag to create a gradient fill based on the foreground and background colors.
Pencil tool	This tool lets you draw individual pixels when zoomed in, or hard-edge lines when zoomed out. Simply click and drag to draw freehand, and hold down Shift to draw lines between two points.
Brush tool	This tool lets you draw on the picture in a variety of brush styles to create artistic effects. A brush can also be created from an image, allowing for greater versatility.
Erase tool	Rather like the Brush tool in reverse, this tool deletes whatever is underneath the cursor. If layers are being used, the contents of the layer beneath will become visible.
Airbrush tool	This tool is also rather like the Brush tool, in that it draws on the picture in a variety of styles. However, the density of the color depends on the length of time you press the mouse button. Tap the mouse button, and only a light color will appear. Press and hold the mouse button, and the color will become more saturated.
Ink tool	This tool is like the Brush tool except that, rather like an ink pen, the faster you draw, the thinner the brush stroke is.
Pattern stamp	Commonly known as the clone tool, this is a popular image-editing tool. It is able to copy one part of an image to another via drawing with a brush-like tool. The origin point is defined by holding down Ctrl and clicking.
Blur/Sharpen tool	Clicking and drawing on the image will spot blur or sharpen the image, depending on the settings in the tool options area in the lower half of the toolbar.
Smudge tool	As its name suggests, clicking and drawing with this tool will smudge the image, rather like rubbing a still-wet painting with your finger (except slightly more precise).
Burn and Dodge tool	This tool lets you spot lighten and darken an image by clicking and drawing on the image. The results depend on the settings in the tool options part of the window.

Directly beneath the image-editing tool icons, on the right, is an icon that shows the foreground and background colors that will be used when drawing with tools such as the Brush. To define a new color, double-click either the foreground (top) or background (bottom) color box. To the left is the pattern selector, which lets you choose which patterns are used with tools such as the Brush.

Beneath these icons, you'll see the various options for the selected tool. By using the buttons at the bottom of the window, you can save the current tool options, load tool options, and delete a previously saved set of tool options. Clicking the button on the bottom right lets you revert to the default settings for the tool currently being used (useful if you tweak too many settings).

Next to the toolbar window is the Layers dialog box. This can be closed for the moment, although you can make it visible again later, if you wish.

Editing Images with The GIMP

After you've started The GIMP (and assigned it a virtual desktop), you can load an image by selecting File ➤ Open. The browser dialog box offers a preview facility on the right of the window.

You will probably need to resize the image window so that it fits within the remainder of the screen. You can then use the Zoom tool (see Table 20-1) to ensure that the image fills the editing window, which will make working with it much easier.

You can save any changes you make to an image by right-clicking it and selecting File ➤ Save As. You can also print the image from the same menu.

Before you begin editing with The GIMP, you need to be aware of some essential concepts that are vital to understand in order to get the most from the program:

Copy, cut, and paste buffers: Unlike Windows programs, The GIMP lets you cut or copy many selections from the image and store them for use later. It refers to these saved selections as *buffers*, and each must be given a name for future reference. A new buffer is created by selecting an area using any of the selection tools, and then right-clicking within the selection area and selecting Edit ➤ Buffer ➤ Copy Named (or Cut Named). Pasting a buffer back is a matter of right-clicking the image and selecting Edit ➤ Buffer ➤ Paste Named.

Paths: The GIMP paths are not necessarily the same as selection areas, although it's nearly always possible to convert a selection into a path and vice versa (right-click within the selection or path and look for the relevant option on the Edit menu). In general, the tools used to create a path allow the creation of complex shapes rather than simple geometric shapes, as with the selection tools. You can also be more intricate in your selections, as shown in the example in Figure 20-2. You can save paths for later use. To view the Paths dialog box, right-click the image and select Dialogs ➤ Paths.

■**Tip** Getting rid of a selection or path you've drawn is easy. In the case of a path, simply click any other tool. This will cause the path to disappear. To get rid of a selection, either choose Select ➤ None, or select any selection tool and quickly click once on the image, being careful not to drag the mouse while doing so.

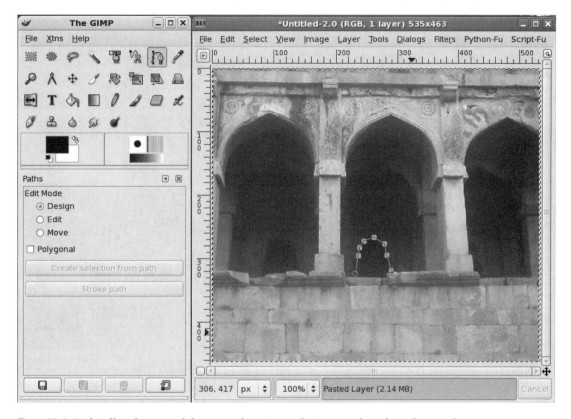

Figure 20-2. *Paths allow for more elaborate and intricate selections, such as those that involve curves.*

Layers: In The GIMP (along with most other image-editing programs), layers are like transparent sheets of plastic that are placed on top of the image. Anything can be drawn on each individual transparent sheet, and many layers can be overlaid in order to create a complicated image. Layers also let you cut and paste parts of the image between them. It's also possible to apply effects and transformations to a single layer, rather than to the entire image. The Layers dialog box, shown in Figure 20-3, appears by default, but if you closed it earlier, you can open it again by right-clicking the image and selecting Dialogs ➤ Layers. The layers can be reordered by clicking and dragging them in the dialog box. In addition, the blending mode of each layer can be altered. This refers to how it interacts with the layer below it. For example, its opacity can be changed so that it appears semitransparent, thereby showing the contents of the layer beneath.

Figure 20-3. *Set the opacity of various layers by clicking and dragging the relevant slider in the Layers dialog box.*

Making Color Corrections

The first step when editing most images is to correct the brightness, contrast, and color saturation. This helps overcome some of the deficiencies that are inherent in digital photographs or scanned-in images. To do this, right-click the image and select Layers ➤ Colors. You'll find a variety of options to let you tweak the image, allowing you a lot of control over the process.

For trivial brightness and contrast changes, selecting the Brightness/Contrast menu option will open a dialog box where clicking and dragging the sliders will alter the image. The changes you make will be previewed on the image itself, so you should be able to get things just right.

Similarly, the Hue/Saturation option will let you alter the color balance and also the strength of the colors (the saturation) by clicking and dragging sliders. By selecting the color bar options at the top of the window, you can choose individual colors to boost. Clicking the Master button will let you once again alter all colors at the same time.

The trouble with clicking and dragging sliders is that it relies on human intuition. This can easily be clouded by a badly calibrated monitor, which might be set too dark or too light. Because of this, The GIMP offers another handy option: levels.

To access the Levels feature, right-click the image and select Layer ➤ Colors ➤ Levels. This presents a chart of the brightness levels in the photo and lets you set the dark, shadows, and highlight points, as shown in Figure 20-4. Three sliders beneath the chart represent, from left to right, the darkest point, the midtones (shadows), and the highlights within the picture. The first step is to set the dark and light sliders at the left and right of the edges of the chart. This will ensure that the range of brightness from the lightest point to the darkest point is set correctly. The next step is to adjust the middle slider so that it's roughly in the middle of the highest peak within the chart. This will accurately set the midtone point, ensuring an even spread of brightness across the image.

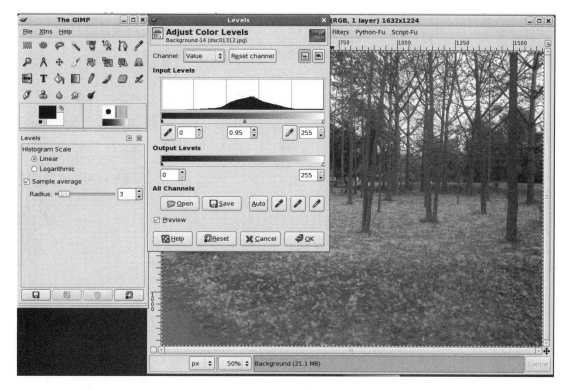

Figure 20-4. *The Levels function can be used to accurately set the brightness levels across an image.*

A little artistic license is usually allowed at this stage, and, depending on the effect on the photo, moving the midtone slider a little to the left or right of the highest peak might produce more acceptable results. However, be aware that the monitor might be showing incorrect brightness/ color values.

Cropping and Cloning

After you've adjusted the colors, you might want to use the Crop tool (see Table 20-1) to remove any extraneous details outside the focus of the image. For example, in a portrait of someone taken from a distance, you might choose to crop the photo to show only the person's head and shoulders, or you might separate a group of people from their surroundings, as shown in Figure 20-5.

You might also want to use the Clone tool to remove facial blemishes. Start by using the Zoom tool to close in on the area. If the blemish is small, you might need to zoom in quite substantially. Then try to find an area of skin that is clear and from which you can copy. Hold down Ctrl and click in that area. Then click and draw over the blemish. The crosshair indicates the area from which you're copying.

Figure 20-5. *You can use the Crop tool to remove any irrelevant details surrounding the subject of your photo.*

Sharpening

One final handy trick employed by professional image editors to give their photos a shot in the arm is to use the Sharpen filter. This has the effect of adding definition to the image and negating any slight blur caused by things such as camera shake and poor focusing. To apply the Sharpen filter, right-click the image and select Filters ➤ Enhance ➤ Sharpen.

As shown in Figure 20-6, a small preview window will show the effect of the sharpening on the image (you might need to use the scroll bars to move to an appropriate part of the image). Clicking and dragging the slider at the bottom of the dialog box will alter the severity of the sharpening effect. Too much sharpening can ruin a picture, so be careful. Try to use the effect subtly.

The Sharpen filter is just one of many filters you can apply in The GIMP, as explained in the next section.

Figure 20-6. *Sharpening an image can give it a professional finish by adding definition.*

Applying Filters

Like other image-editing programs, The GIMP includes many filters to add dramatic effects to your images with little, if any, user input. Filters are applied either to the currently selected layer or to a selection within the layer. To apply a filter, right-click the image and choose the relevant menu option. If you don't like an effect you've applied, you can reverse it by selecting Edit ➤ Undo, or by pressing Ctrl+Z.

The submenus offer filters grouped by categories, as follows:

Blur: These filters add various kinds of blur to the image or selection. For example, Motion Blur can imitate the effect of photographing an object moving at speed with a slow shutter. Perhaps the most popular blur option is Gaussian Blur, which has the effect of applying a soft and subtle blur.

Color: This option includes many technical filters, mostly of interest to image technicians or those who want to uncover and otherwise manipulate the color breakdown within an image. However, Filter Pack might appeal to the general user. This filter can quickly adjust the hue, saturation, and other values within the image. Also of interest is Colorify, which can tint the image to any user-defined color. Figure 20-7 shows an example of using the Colorify filter.

Figure 20-7. *The Colorify filter can be used to add a sepia-like effect to a picture.*

Noise: This collection of filters is designed to add speckles or other types of usually unwanted artifacts to an image. These filters are offered within The GIMP for their potential artistic effects, but they can also be used to create a grainy film effect—simply click Scatter RGB.

Edge Detect: This set of filters can be used to automatically detect and delineate the edges of objects within an image. Although this type of filter can result in some interesting results that might fall into the category of special effects, it's primarily used in conjunction with other tools and effects.

Enhance: The Enhance effects are designed to remove various artifacts from an image or otherwise improve it. For example, the Despeckle effect will attempt to remove unwanted noise within an image (such as flecks of dust in a scanned image). The Sharpen filter discussed in the previous section is located here, as is Unsharp Mask, which offers a high degree of control over the image-sharpening process.

Generic: In this category, you can find a handful of filters that don't seem to fall into any other category. Of particular interest is the Convolution Matrix option, which lets you create your own filters by inputting numeric values. According to The GIMP's programmers, this is designed primarily for mathematicians, but it can also be used by others to create random special effects. Simply input values and then preview the effect.

Glass Effects: As the name suggests, these filters can apply effects to the image to imitate the effects that come about when glass is used to produce an image. For example, the Apply Lens filter will apply the same kind of distortion caused by various wide-angle lenses used on cameras, as shown in Figure 20-8.

Figure 20-8. *The Glass Effects ➤ Apply Lens filter can be used to imitate a fish-eye lens.*

Light Effects: Here, you will find filters that imitate the effects that light can have on a picture, such as adding sparkle effects to highlights or imitating lens flare caused by a camera's lens.

Distorts: As the name of this category of filters suggests, the effects here distort the image in various ways. For example, Whirl and Pinch allow you to tug and push the image to distort it (to understand what is meant here, imagine that the image is printed on rubber and the surface is pinched or pushed). This category also contains other special effects, such as Pagecurl, which imitates the curl of a page at the bottom of a picture.

Artistic: These filters allow you to add painterly effects to the image. For example, you can make it appear as if it has been painted in impressionistic brushstrokes, or as if it has been painted on canvas. The GIMP does so by overlaying the texture of canvas onto the picture. Figure 20-9 shows an example of applying a filter for a cartoonish effect, such that the image appears to be hand drawn and then colored.

Map: These filters aim to manipulate the image by treating it like a piece of paper that can be folded in various ways and also stuck onto 3D shapes (a process referred to as *mapping*). Because the image is treated as if it were a piece of paper, it can also be copied, and the copies placed on top of each other to create various effects.

Render: Here, you'll find filters designed to create new images from scratch, such as clouds or flame effects. They obliterate anything that was previously underneath them on that particular layer or within that selection. The original image has no bearing on what is generated by the filter.

Figure 20-9. *The artistic effects can be used to give images a cartoon effect.*

Web: Here, you can create an image map for use in a web page. An *image map* is a single image broken up into separate hyperlinked areas, typically used on a web page as a sophisticated menu. For example, an image map is frequently used for a geographical map on which you can click to get more information about different regions.

Animation: These filters aim to manipulate and optimize GIF images, which are commonly used to create simple animated images for use on web sites.

Combine: Here, you'll find filters that combine two or more images into one.

Toys: These are so-called Easter Eggs, which aren't designed to manipulate the image, but are present in the program as harmless animations for the user to enjoy. They're created by the programmers of The GIMP as a way of thanking you for using their program.

■**Tip** The GIMP also includes Script-Fu and Python-Fu, scripting languages that can be used to daisy-chain several commands together to produce a particular effect or to automate a particular image-editing process. For more information, search for "script-fu" or "python-fu" using your favorite web search engine.

Summary

In this chapter, we took a look at image editing in Fedora. This involved an examination of one of the best programs available for the task under any operating system: The GIMP.

You learned how to start The GIMP and about some of the basic principles behind it. Next, we discussed some of the functions contained within The GIMP, including the image filters provided with the program.

In the next part of the book, we move on from multimedia to another core component of Fedora: the OpenOffice.org suite, which provides word processing, spreadsheet, presentation, and other functions.

PART 6

■ ■ ■

Office Tasks

CHAPTER 21

■■■

Making the Move to OpenOffice.org

You might be willing to believe that you can get a complete operating system for no cost. You might even be able to accept that this offers everything Windows does and much more. But one stumbling block many people have is in believing a Microsoft Office–compatible office suite comes as part of the zero-cost bundle. It's a step too far. Office costs hundreds of dollars—are they expecting us to believe that there's a rival product that is free?

Well, there is, and it's called OpenOffice.org. It is available for Fedora, as well as most other Linux distributions, making it the Linux office suite of choice. It's compatible with most Microsoft Office files, too, and even looks similar and works in a comparable way, making it easy to learn. What more could you want?

Office Similarities

OpenOffice.org started life as a proprietary product called StarOffice. Sun Microsystems bought the company behind the product and released its source code in order to encourage community development. This led to the creation of the OpenOffice.org project, a collaboration between open source developers and Sun. This project has released several new versions of OpenOffice.org, and at the time of writing, has just released version 2.2. This is the version included with Fedora.

■**Note** For what it's worth, Sun still sells StarOffice. This is based on the OpenOffice.org code, so it's effectively the same program. However, in addition to the office suite itself, Sun includes several useful extras such as fonts, templates, and the all-important technical support, which you can contact if you get stuck trying to undertake a particular task.

OpenOffice.org features a word processor, spreadsheet program, presentation package, drawing tool (vector graphics), web site–creation tool, database program, and several extras. As such, it matches Microsoft Office almost blow for blow in terms of core functionality. See Table 21-1 for a comparison of core packages.

Table 21-1. *How the Microsoft Office and OpenOffice.org Suites Compare*

Microsoft Office	OpenOffice.org	Function
Word	Writer	Word processor
Excel	Calc	Spreadsheet
PowerPoint	Impress	Presentation software
Visio	Draw[1]	Technical drawing/charting software
FrontPage	Writer[2]	Web site–creation software
Access	Base[3]	Database

1 *Draw is a vector graphics–creation tool akin to Adobe Illustrator. Creating flowcharts and organizational diagrams is one of many things it can do.*

2 *Writer is used for word processing and HTML creation; when switched to Web mode, its functionality is altered appropriately.*

3 *Writer and Calc can be coupled to a third-party database application such as MySQL or Firebird; however, OpenOffice.org also comes with the Base relational database.*

You'll find that the functionality within the packages is duplicated, too, although some of the very specific features of Microsoft Office are not in OpenOffice.org. But OpenOffice.org also has its own range of tools not yet found in Microsoft Office!

OpenOffice.org does have a couple of omissions. Perhaps most notably, it doesn't offer a directly comparable Outlook replacement. However, as discussed in Chapter 27, the Evolution application offers an accurate reproduction of Outlook, with e-mail, contacts management, and calendar functions all in one location. In Fedora, you'll find Evolution on the Applications ➤ Internet menu, listed as Email. Evolution isn't directly linked to OpenOffice.org, but it retains the overall Fedora look, feel, and way of operating.

OpenOffice.org Key Features

Key features of OpenOffice.org, apart from the duplication of much of what you find in Microsoft Office, include the ability to export documents in Portable Document Format (PDF) format across the entire suite of programs. PDF files can then be read on any computer equipped with PDF display software, such as Adobe Acrobat Reader.

In addition, OpenOffice.org features powerful accessibility features that can, for example, help those with vision disabilities use the programs more effectively. For those who are technically minded, OpenOffice.org can be extended very easily with a variety of plug-ins that allow the easy creation of add-ons using many different programming languages.

Although OpenOffice.org largely mirrors the look and feel of Microsoft Office, it adds its own flourishes here and there. This can mean that some functions are located on different menus, for example. However, none of this poses a challenge for most users, and OpenOffice.org is generally regarded as very easy to learn.

File Compatibility

In addition to its core feature compatibility, OpenOffice.org is also able to read files from Microsoft Office versions up to and including Office 2007, the latest version of Office at the time of writing. When a new version of Office comes out with a new file format, future versions of OpenOffice.org will support it. This is just one more reason why you should regularly update Fedora online in order to make sure you're running the very latest versions of each program.

■Note Many people still use the older Office file formats, even if they're using the latest version of Office. This is done to retain compatibility with other users who may not yet have upgraded.

Although file compatibility problems are rare, two issues occasionally crop up when opening Microsoft Office files in OpenOffice.org:

VBA compatibility: OpenOffice.org isn't compatible with Microsoft Office Visual Basic for Applications (VBA). It uses a similar but incompatible internal programming language. This means that Microsoft macros within a document probably won't work when the file is imported to OpenOffice.org. Such macros might be used in Excel spreadsheets designed to calculate timesheets, for example. In general, however, only high-end users use VBA.

Document protection: OpenOffice.org is unable to open any Office files that have a password, either to protect the document from changes or to protect it from being viewed. Theoretically, it would be easy for OpenOffice.org's developers to include such functionality, but the laws of many countries make creating such a program feature illegal (it would be seen as a device to overcome copy protection). The easiest solution is to ask whoever sent you the file to remove the password protection. For what it's worth, OpenOffice.org has its own form of password protection.

If you find that OpenOffice.org isn't able to open an Office file saved by your colleagues, you can always suggest that they, too, make the switch to OpenOffice.org. They don't need to be running Fedora to do so. Versions are available to run on all Windows platforms, as well as on the Apple Macintosh. As with the Fedora version, they're entirely free of charge. Indeed, for many people who are running versions of Office they've installed from "borrowed" CDs, OpenOffice.org offers a way to come clean and avoid pirating software. For more details and to download OpenOffice.org, visit `www.openoffice.org/`.

Once your colleagues have made the switch, you can exchange files using OpenOffice.org's native format, or opt to save files in the Office file format. Figure 21-1 shows the file type options available in OpenOffice.org's word processor component's Save dialog box.

■Note OpenOffice.org also supports RTF text documents and comma-separated value (CSV) data files, which are supported by practically every office suite program ever made.

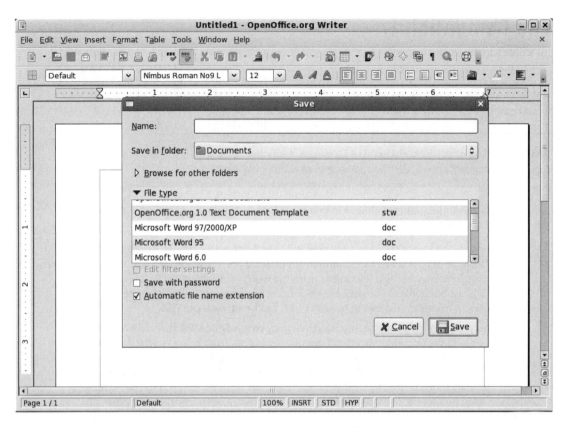

Figure 21-1. *All the OpenOffice.org components are fully compatible with Microsoft Office file formats.*

When it comes to sharing files, there's another option: save your files in a non-Office format such as PDF or HTML. OpenOffice.org is able to export documents in both formats, and most modern PCs equipped with Adobe Acrobat or a simple web browser will be able to read them. However, while OpenOffice.org can open and edit HTML files, the only action it can take with PDF files is to export them, so this format is best reserved for files not intended for further editing.

OPENDOCUMENT FORMAT

One of the principles behind all open source software is the idea of open file formats. This means that if someone creates a new open source word processor, he also makes sure that the technology behind the file format is explained so that other people can adapt their programs to read and/or save in that file format.

Compare this to Microsoft's approach, which is to not only attempt to keep its file formats secret, but also to patent the formats so that no one else can use them without permission. The only way for Office competitors like OpenOffice.org to understand Office file formats is to reverse-engineer them—to try to figure out how they work by taking them apart. This is a time-consuming process and, increasingly, resides in a legal gray area in many countries.

To meet the goals of open source software, the OpenDocument Format (ODF) was created. This is a completely open and free-to-use office document file format that all software suites can adopt. The idea is that ODF will make swapping files between all office suites easy.

Sadly, Microsoft has decided not to support ODF and is sticking with its own proprietary file formats. However, the OpenDocument Foundation, a nonprofit organization, was created to support and promote the ODF. The foundation is working on a plug-in that would enable Microsoft Office users to work with ODF.

However, Massachusetts has recently adopted ODF, as have several other local governments in countries all around the world. The National Archive of Australia has decided to use ODF, and the Belgian federal administration has announced that from September 2008, it will exchange all documents in ODF. There's little doubt that it won't be long before ODF becomes one of the main ways of disseminating and sharing documents online.

Perhaps it goes without saying that OpenOffice.org fully supports ODF (as shown in the following illustration). In fact, ODF was originally based on OpenOffice.org file formats.

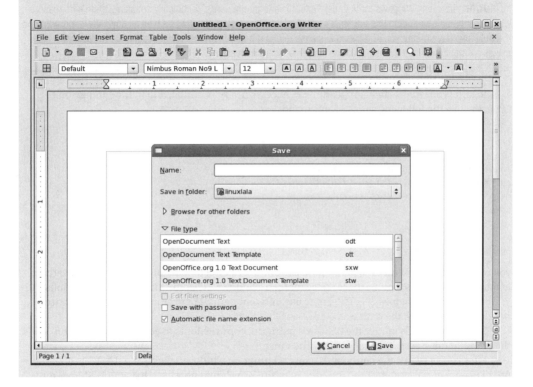

The Right Fonts

One key to compatibility with the majority of Microsoft Office files is ensuring you have the correct fonts. This is an issue even when using Windows. It's very common to open an Office document to find the formatting incorrect because you don't have the fonts used in the construction of the document.

Although most Windows systems have many fonts, most people tend to rely on a handful of core fonts, which are by default on most Windows installations: Arial, Tahoma, Verdana, Trebuchet MS, and Times New Roman (MS Comic Sans might also be included in that list, although it isn't often used within business documents).

You can obtain these fonts and install them on your Fedora system in several ways. Here, we'll cover two methods: copying your fonts from Windows and installing Microsoft's TrueType core fonts. The latter method is by far the easier way of undertaking this task.

Copying Windows Fonts

If you dual-boot Fedora with Windows, you can delve into your Windows partition's font folder and copy across every font you have available under Windows. This involves not only copying the files across, but also rebuilding several system files, which adds an extra level of complication. This method is useful if you wish to copy across *all* the fonts you use under Windows. If you wish to get just Arial and Times New Roman, you might want to skip ahead to the next section.

■**Caution** Installing Windows fonts under Fedora is a legal gray area. Technically speaking, there's no reason why you shouldn't be able to use the fonts under Fedora. Purchasing Windows as well as any software running on it should also have meant you purchased a license to use the fonts. But the license document for Windows XP makes no mention of font licensing, so the matter is far from clear-cut.

To copy your fonts, click Applications ➤ Accessories ➤ Terminal, and in the window that appears, type the following series of commands:

```
su -
[Password]
mkdir /usr/share/fonts/ttfonts
mount /dev/hda1 /media/win -o umask-0222
cp /media/win/Fonts/*.ttf /ust/share/fonts/ttfonts
mkfontdir /ust/share/fonts/ttfonts
umount /media/win
```

Regarding the line

```
cp /media/win/Fonts/*.ttf /ust/share/fonts
```

you may need to substitute the path to the Windows font directory, taking into account lowercase and uppercase letters. This path was relevant for a Windows XP Home machine; other versions of Windows, such as Windows 98 or Me, may use different paths. For example, on a machine with Windows 98 installed, the path was `/media/windows/fonts/`.

These commands mount the Windows partition, copy the fonts to your Fedora partition, and then rebuild the system file that catalogs the fonts.

After you've issued the commands, close all program windows, click System ➤ Log Out, and opt to log out of the system. Then log back in again. You should now find that your Windows fonts are available in all applications, including OpenOffice.org.

This is a highly irregular method for installing Windows fonts in Fedora. It is recommended that you follow the steps in the next section to make Windows fonts available under Fedora.

Installing TrueType Core Fonts

If you don't want to undertake the font-copying maneuver, you can download and install Microsoft's TrueType core fonts. This package contains common Windows fonts, including Arial, Courier, and Times New Roman.

This process of installing fonts might seem tedious at first, but it is fairly easy:

1. Make sure to install the rpm-build, rpmdevtools, and cabextract packages:

   ```
   su -c "yum install rpm-build cabextract rpmdevtools"
   ```

Note By default, Fedora will create rpms in the /usr/src/redhat directory. Since normal users don't have permission to use that directory, use rpmdevtools to install the build environment within the user's home directory.

---

2. Run the command rpmdev-setuptree.

3. Download the latest spec file from the core fonts project page (http://corefonts.sourceforge.net/):

   ```
   wget -c http://corefonts.sourceforge.net/msttcorefonts-2.0-1.spec
   ```

4. You now need to build the core fonts package. Make sure you are in the directory where you downloaded the spec file. The following command will create an rpm package:

   ```
   rpmbuild -ba msttcorefonts-2.0-1.spec
   ```

5. You can now install this rpm package with the following command:

   ```
   su -c "rpm -ivh /home/linuxlala/rpmbuild/\
   RPMS/noarch/msttcorefonts-2.0-1.noarch.rpm"
   ```

6. Close all OpenOffice program windows, and in a terminal (Applications ➤ Accessories ➤ Terminal), run the command fc-cache -f. You should now find that your Windows fonts are available in all applications, including OpenOffice.org. Figure 21-2 shows the new fonts available in OpenOffice.org as compared to the original fonts.

Microsoft TrueType fonts available under OpenOffice.org   The original fonts under OpenOffice.org

Figure 21-2. *The newly installed Windows fonts are available in all OpenOffice.org components.*

The preceding procedure installs the fonts in the /usr/share/fonts/msttcorefonts/ directory.

OTHER LINUX OFFICE SUITES

OpenOffice.org is widely regarded as one of the best Linux office suites, but it's not the only one. Its main open source competitor is KOffice. KOffice tightly integrates into the KDE desktop and mirrors much of its look and feel. It includes a word processor, spreadsheet, presentation package, flowchart tool, database access tool, and much more. As with OpenOffice.org, in most cases you can load and save Microsoft Office files. For more details, see its home page at www.koffice.org/. It's available with Fedora, too. Just use Pirut Package Manager to search for and install it.

In addition, there are several open source office applications that aren't complete office suites. AbiWord, for example, is considered an excellent word processor; it packs in a lot of features but keeps the user interface very simple. It's partnered with Gnumeric, a spreadsheet application that is developed separately). For more details, see www.abisource.com/ and www.gnome.org/projects/gnumeric/, respectively. You can also find both of these programs in the Fedora software repositories (use Pirut Package Manager to search for them).

In fact, AbiWord and Gnumeric, along with GNOME-DB, are considered the GNOME office suite. It's not as complete as either OpenOffice.org or KOffice, but it too has a large user base. See www.gnome.org/gnome-office/.

Summary

This chapter has given a general introduction to OpenOffice.org, providing an overview of what you can expect from the programs within the suite. In particular, we focused on the extent of the suite's similarities with Microsoft Office and discussed issues surrounding file compatibility with Microsoft Office. We also looked at how Windows fonts can be brought into Fedora, which aids in successfully importing and creating compatible documents.

In the next chapter, you'll learn about the configuration options globally applicable to the suite, as well as common functions provided across all the programs.

CHAPTER 22

■■■

OpenOffice.org Overview

All the programs in the OpenOffice.org suite rely on a common interface, and therefore look and operate in a similar way. They are also configured in an identical way, and all rely on central concepts such as wizards, which guide you through the creation of particular types of documents. In addition, many components within the suite are shared across the various programs. For example, the automatic chart-creation tool within Calc can also be used within Writer.

In this chapter, we'll look at the OpenOffice.org suite as a whole, and explain how it's used and configured. In the following chapters, we'll examine some specific programs in the suite.

Introducing the Interface

If you've ever used an office suite, such as Microsoft Office, you shouldn't find it too hard to get around in OpenOffice.org. As with Microsoft Office, OpenOffice.org relies primarily on toolbars, a main menu, and separate context-sensitive menus that appear when you right-click. In addition, OpenOffice.org provides floating palettes that offer quick access to useful functions, such as paragraph styles within Writer.

Figure 22-1 provides a quick guide to the OpenOffice.org interface, showing the following components:

- *Menu bar*: The menus provide access to most of the OpenOffice.org functions.
- *Standard toolbar*: This toolbar provides quick access to global operations, such as saving, opening, and printing files, as well as key functions within the program being used. The Standard toolbar appears in all OpenOffice.org programs and also provides a way to activate the various floating palettes, such as the Navigator, which lets you easily move around various elements within the document.
- *Formatting toolbar*: As its name suggests, this toolbar offers quick access to text formatting functions, similar to the type of toolbar used in Microsoft Office applications. Clicking the B icon will boldface any selected text, for example. This toolbar appears in Calc, Writer, and Impress.
- *Ruler*: The ruler lets you set tabs and alter margins and indents (within programs that use rulers).
- *Status bar*: The status bar shows various aspects of the configuration, such as whether Insert or Overtype mode is in use.
- *Document area*: This is the main editing area.

Most of the programs rely on the Standard and Formatting toolbars to provide access to their functions, and some programs have additional toolbars. For example, applications such as Impress (a presentation program) and Draw (for drawing vector graphics) have the Drawing toolbar, which provides quick access to tools for drawing shapes, adding lines, and creating fills (the blocks of color within shapes).

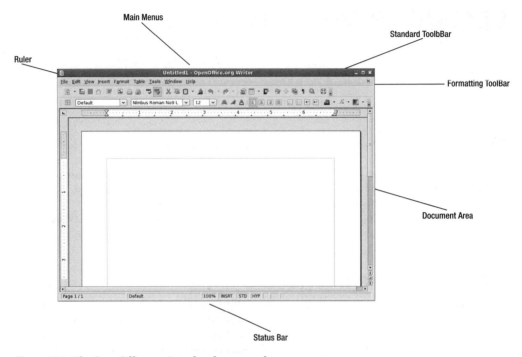

Figure 22-1. *The OpenOffice.org interface has several components.*

Customizing the Interface

You can select which toolbars are visible on your screen, as well as customize those that are already there. You can also add new toolbars and customize the OpenOffice.org menus.

Adding Functions to Toolbars

The quickest way to add icons and functions to any toolbar is to click the two small arrows at the right of a toolbar and select the Visible Buttons entry on the menu that appears. This will present a list of currently visible icons and functions, along with those that might prove useful on that toolbar but are currently hidden. Any option already visible will have a check next to it.

Additionally, you can add practically any function to a toolbar, including the options from the main menus and many more than those that are ordinarily visible. Here are the steps:

1. Click the small arrow to the right of a toolbar and select the Customize Toolbar option.

2. In the Customize dialog box, click the Add button in the Toolbar Contents section to open the Add Commands dialog box, as shown in Figure 22-2.

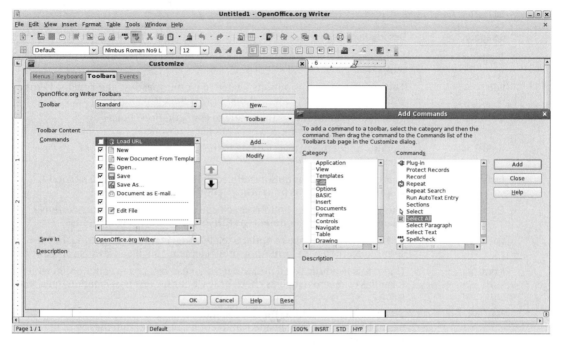

Figure 22-2. *Adding a new function to the toolbar is very easy within OpenOffice.org.*

3. Choose a category from the list on the left to see the available commands in the list on the right. The categories of functions are extremely comprehensive. For example, under the Format category, you'll find entries related to specific functions, such as shrinking font sizes or setting a shadow effect behind text. Table 22-1 provides brief descriptions of each of the categories listed in the Add Commands dialog box.

4. Select the function you want to add on the right side of the Add Commands dialog box, and then click the Add button.

5. Click the Close button. You'll then see your new function in the list of icons in the Customize dialog box.

6. Click and drag to move the new function left or right on the toolbar itself (you'll see the toolbar update when you release the mouse button). Alternatively, you can highlight the icon and click the up and down arrows next to the list.

Table 22-1. *OpenOffice.org Toolbar Customization Categories*

Category	Description
Application	These options relate to the specific OpenOffice.org application you're using. For example, if you select to customize a toolbar within Writer, the Application category menu will offer functions to start AutoPilots (effectively wizards) that will build word processing documents.
View	This category offers options related to the look and feel of the suite, such as which items are visible within the program interface.

Continued

Table 22-1. *Continued*

Category	Description
Templates	In this category, you'll find options related to the creation and use of document templates.
Edit	This category contains options related to cutting, pasting, and copying items within the document, as well as updating elements within it.
Options	These are various options that relate to configuration choices in OpenOffice.org, allowing you to control how it works.
BASIC	Options under this category relate to the creation and playback of OpenOffice.org macros.
Insert	This category includes options related to inserting objects, such as sound, graphics, and elements from other OpenOffice.org documents.
Documents	This category provides options specific to document control, such as those related to exporting documents as PDF files or simply saving files.
Format	Here, you'll find a range of options related largely to text formatting, but also some concerned with formatting other elements, such as drawings and images.
Controls	Under this heading, you'll find widgets that can be used in conjunction with formulas or macros, such as check boxes, buttons, text box–creation tools, and so on.
Navigate	This category offers tools that let you move around a document quickly—for example, to quickly edit headers and footers, or move from the top of the page to the end very quickly.
Table	Here, you'll find options related to the creation of tables.
Drawing	Here, you'll find tools related to drawing objects, such as shapes and lines, and also tools for creating floating text boxes.
Graphic	This category presents a handful of options related to manipulating bitmap graphics that are inserted into the document.
Data	Here, you'll find a couple of options related to working with information sources, such as databases.
Frame	These options relate to any frames inserted into the document, such as how elements within the frame are aligned and how text is wrapped around the frame.
Numbering	These are various options related to creating automatic numbered or bulleted lists.
Modify	These options relate to the drawing components within OpenOffice.org and let you manipulate images or drawings in various ways by applying filters.
OpenOffice.org BASIC Macros	Here you can select from various ready-made macros, which provide some of OpenOffice.org's functions.

Many functions that can be added are automatically given a relevant toolbar icon, but you can choose another icon for a function by selecting the icon in the list in the Customize dialog box, clicking Modify, and then selecting Change Icon. You can also use this method to change an icon that already appears on a toolbar.

Note To delete an icon from a toolbar, click the two small arrows to the right of a toolbar and select the Customize Toolbar option. Select the icon you want to remove, click the Modify button, and choose to delete it.

Adding a New Toolbar

If you want to add your own new toolbar to offer particular functions, you'll find it easy to do. Here are the steps:

1. Click the two small arrows to the right of any toolbar and select Customize Toolbar from the list of options. Don't worry—you're not actually going to customize that particular toolbar!

2. In the Customize dialog box, click the New button at the top right.

3. Give the toolbar a name. The default entry for the Save In field is correct, so you don't need to alter it.

4. Populate the new toolbar, following the instructions in the previous section.

5. Once you've finished, click the OK button.

You should see your new toolbar beneath the main toolbars. To hide it, click View ➤ Toolbars, and then remove the check alongside the name of your toolbar.

Customizing Menus

You can also customize the OpenOffice.org menus. Here are the steps:

1. Select Tools ➤ Customize from the menu bar.

2. In the Customize dialog box, select the Menus tab.

3. Choose which menu you wish to customize from the Menu drop-down list.

4. Select the position where you want the new function to appear on the menu by selecting an entry on the menu function list, and then click the Add button.

5. Add commands to the menu, as described earlier in the "Adding Functions to Toolbars" section.

The up and down arrows in the Customize dialog box allow you to alter the position of entries on the menu. You could move those items you use frequently to the top of the menu, for example.

You can remove an existing menu item by highlighting it in the Customize dialog box, clicking the Modify button, and then clicking Delete.

If you make a mistake, simply click the Reset button at the bottom right of the Customize dialog box to return the menus to their default state.

Configuring OpenOffice.org Options

In addition to the wealth of customization options, OpenOffice.org offers a range of configuration options that allow you to make it work exactly how you wish. Within an OpenOffice.org program, select Tools ➤ Options from the menu to open the Options dialog box, as shown in Figure 22-3.

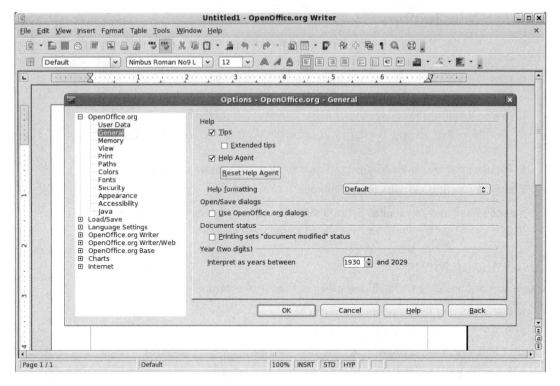

Figure 22-3. *You can access OpenOffice.org's main configuration options by selecting Tools ➤ Options.*

Most of the configuration options offered within each program apply across the suite, but those under the heading of the program's name apply only to the program in use. In other words, to set the options for Writer, you need to use the Writer Options dialog box. But to set global options for the entire suite, you can use any program's Options dialog box.

A variety of options are offered, allowing you to tweak everything from the default file format to the colors used by default within the software. Table 22-2 briefly describes each of the OpenOffice.org configuration options.

Table 22-2. *OpenOffice.org Configuration Options*

Option	Description
OpenOffice.org	
User Data	This is the personal data that will be added to the documents you create. You can leave this area blank if you wish.
General	This offers a handful of miscellaneous options, such as how to handle two-digit dates, when the help system should step in to offer tips, how the help system should be formatted (such as in high resolution for people with vision problems), and whether printing a document is interpreted by OpenOffice.org as modifying it.
Memory	This entry relates to how much system memory OpenOffice.org can use. You can limit the number of undo steps, for example, and alter the cache memory used for holding graphical objects.

Option	Description
View	Here, you can alter the look, feel, and operation of OpenOffice.org. You can define whether the middle mouse button performs a paste operation (which is consistent with how Fedora works), or whether it should perform a scrolling function, as with Windows. You can also alter elements such as whether icons appear in menus and if fonts are previewed in the toolbar menu.
Print	This option lets you adjust how printing is handled within OpenOffice.org. The functions relate to those that can stop documents from printing incorrectly, such as reducing any transparency effects within the documents so on-page elements don't appear faint or completely disappear in the final output. (Note that specific print functions are handled within the Print dialog box when you actually print a document.)
Paths	This is where the file paths for user-configured and vital system tools are handled. Generally, there's little reason to edit this list, although you might choose to alter the default location where your documents are saved (simply double-click the My Documents entry to do this).
Colors	Here, you can define the default color palette that appears in the various programs in the suite.
Fonts	By creating entries here, you can automatically substitute fonts within documents you open for others on your system. If you don't have the Microsoft core fonts installed, this might prove useful. For example, you might choose to substitute Arial, commonly used in Microsoft Office documents, for Luxi Sans, one of the sans serif fonts used under Fedora.
Security	This option controls which types of functions can be run within OpenOffice.org. For example, you can choose whether macros created by third parties should be run when you open a new document.
Appearance	Here, you can alter the color scheme used within OpenOffice.org, in a similar way to how you can alter the default Fedora desktop color scheme. Individual elements within documents and pages can be modified, too.
Accessibility	This option relates to features that might help people with vision disabilities to use OpenOffice.org. For example, you can define whether animated graphics are shown on the screen.
Java	This option lets you control whether you use the Java Runtime Environment (JRE), which may be necessary to use some of OpenOffice.org's features.
Load/Save	
General	Options here relate to how files are saved. You can select whether the default is to save in OpenOffice.org or Microsoft Office format. Choosing the latter is useful if you share a lot of documents with colleagues who are not running OpenOffice.org.
VBA Properties	This option relates to how Visual Basic for Applications (VBA) code is handled when Microsoft Office documents are opened. Specifically, it ensures that the code isn't lost when the file is saved again.
Microsoft Office	This option provides functions specifically needed to convert or open Microsoft Office files within OpenOffice.org.
HTML Compatibility	Here, you can set options that affect the compatibility of HTML files saved within OpenOffice.org.

Continued

Table 22-2. *Continued*

Option	Description
Language Settings	
Languages	Here, you can set your local language so that documents are spell-checked correctly. In addition, Asian language support can be activated, which allows for more complex document layout options.
Writing Aids	Under this option, you can activate or deactivate various plug-ins designed to help format documents, such as the hyphenator or the spell-checking component. In addition, you can alter how the spell-checker works, such as whether it ignores capitalized words.
OpenOffice.org Writer	
General	Here, you can alter various options related to the editing of word processing documents, such as which measurements are used on the ruler (centimeter, inches, picas, etc.).
View	Under this option, you can configure the look and feel of the Writer program, such as which scroll bars are visible by default. You can also turn off the display of various page elements, such as tables and graphics.
Formatting Aids	This option lets you choose which symbols appear for "invisible" elements (such as the carriage return symbol or a dot symbol to indicate where spaces have been inserted) in Writer.
Grid	This controls whether page elements will snap to an invisible grid. You can also define the dimensions and spacing of the grid cells here.
Basic Fonts (Western)	This controls which fonts are used by default in the various text styles, such as for the default text and within lists.
Print	This option offers control over printing options specific to Writer, such as which page elements are printed (e.g., you might choose to turn off the printing of graphics).
Table	Here, you can control how tables are created and how you interact with them within Writer. For example, you can control what happens when a table is resized, such as whether the entire table responds to the changes or merely the cell you're resizing.
Changes	This option lets you define how changes are displayed when the track changes function is activated.
Compatibility	Here, you can set specifics of how Writer handles the import and export of Microsoft Word documents.
AutoCaption	This offers settings for the AutoCaption feature within Writer.
Mail Merge E-Mail	This option lets you control the sending of e-mail mail merge messages.
OpenOffice.org Writer/Web	
View	Here, you can control the HTML editor component of OpenOffice.org (effectively an extension of Writer). You can control the look and feel of the HTML editor, including which elements are displayed on the screen.
Formatting Aids	As with the similar entry for Writer under Text Document, this option lets you view symbols in place of usually hidden text elements.
Grid	This lets you define a grid that onscreen elements are able to "snap to" in order to aid accurate positioning.
Print	Here, you can define how HTML documents created within OpenOffice.org are printed.
Table	Similar to the Tables entry under Text Document, this controls how tables are created and handled within HTML documents.
Background	This lets you set the default background color for HTML documents.

Option	Description
OpenOffice.org Calc	
General	Here, you can modify miscellaneous options related to Calc, such as which measurement units are used within the program and how the formatting of cells is changed when new data is input.
View	This option relates to the look and feel of Calc, such as the color of the gridlines between cells and which elements are displayed on the screen. For example, you can configure whether zero values are displayed, and whether overflow text within cells is shown or simply truncated at the cell boundary.
Calculate	This option relates to how numbers are handled during certain types of formula calculations, such as those involving dates.
Sort Lists	This option lets you create lists that are applied to relevant cells when the user chooses to sort them. Several lists are predefined to correctly sort days of the week or months of the year.
Changes	This option relates to the onscreen formatting for changes when the track changes function is activated.
Grid	This option lets you configure an invisible grid that stretches across the sheet, and also which page objects can be set to snap to the grid for correct alignment.
Print	This option relates to printing specifically from Calc, such as whether Calc should avoid printing empty pages that might occur within documents.
OpenOffice.org Impress	
General	This option refers to miscellaneous settings within the Impress program, such as whether the program should always start with a wizard and which units of measurement should be used.
View	This option relates to the look and feel of Impress and, in particular, whether certain onscreen elements are displayed.
Grid	This controls whether an invisible grid is applied to the page and whether objects should snap to it.
Print	This option controls how printing is handled within Impress and, in particular, how items in the document will appear on the printed page.
OpenOffice.org Draw	
General	This option relates to miscellaneous settings within Draw (the vector graphics component of OpenOffice.org).
View	Here, you can set specific preferences with regard to which objects are visible on the screen while you're editing with Draw.
Grid	This option relates to the invisible grid that can be applied to the page.
Print	This option lets you define which onscreen elements are printed and which are not printed.
OpenOffice.org Base	
Connections	This option lets you control how any data sources you attach to are handled.
Databases	Here, you can configure which databases are registered for use within Base.

Continued

Table 22-2. *Continued*

Option	Description
Charts	
Default Colors	Here, you can set the default color palette that should be used when creating charts, usually within the Calc program.
Internet	
Proxy	Here, you can configure network proxy settings specifically for OpenOffice.org, if necessary.
Search	Certain functions within various OpenOffice.org programs let you search the Internet. Here, you can configure how these search functions work.
E-mail	This option lets you specify which program you wish OpenOffice.org to use for e-mail.
Mozilla Plug-in	This function allows integration of OpenOffice.org into the Mozilla and/or Netscape browsers to allow the viewing of OpenOffice.org documents within the browser window.

Using OpenOffice.org Core Functions

Although the various programs within OpenOffice.org are designed for very specific tasks, they all share several core functions that work in broadly similar ways. In addition, each program is able to borrow components from other programs in the suite.

Using Wizards

One of the core functions you'll find most useful when you're creating new documents is the wizard system, which you can access from the File menu. A wizard guides you through creating a new document by answering questions and following a wizard-based interface. This replaces the template-based approach within Microsoft Office, although it's worth noting that OpenOffice.org is still able to use templates.

A wizard will usually offer a variety of document styles. Some wizards will even prompt you to fill in salient details, which they will then insert into your document in the relevant areas.

Getting Help

OpenOffice.org employs a comprehensive help system, complete with automatic context-sensitive help, called the Help Agent, which will appear if the program detects you're performing a particular task. Usually, the Help Agent takes the form of a lightbulb graphic, which will appear at the bottom-right corner of the screen. If you ignore the Help Agent, it will disappear within a few seconds. Clicking it causes a help window to open. Alternatively, you can access the main searchable help file by clicking the relevant menu entry.

Inserting Objects with Object Linking and Embedding

All the OpenOffice.org programs are able to make use of object linking and embedding (OLE). This effectively means that one OpenOffice.org document can be inserted into another. For example, you might choose to insert a Calc spreadsheet into a Writer document.

The main benefit of using OLE over simply copying and pasting the data is that the OLE item (referred to as an *object*) will be updated whenever the original document is revised. In this way, you can prepare a report featuring a spreadsheet full of figures, for example, and not need to worry about updating the report when the figures change. Figure 22-4 shows an example of a spreadsheet from Calc inserted into a Writer document.

Whenever you click inside the OLE object, the user interface will change so that you can access functions specific to that object. For example, if you had inserted an Impress object into a Calc document, clicking within the object would cause the Calc interface to temporarily turn into that of Impress. Clicking outside the OLE object would restore the interface back to Calc.

You can explore OLE objects by selecting Insert ➤ Object ➤ OLE Object. This option lets you create and insert a new OLE object, as well as add one based on an existing file.

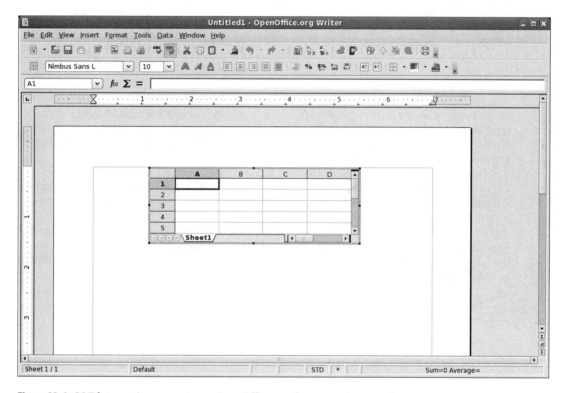

Figure 22-4. *OLE lets you incorporate one OpenOffice.org document into another.*

Creating Macros

OpenOffice.org employs a powerful BASIC-like programming language, which you can use to create your own functions. Although this language is called BASIC, it is several generations beyond the BASIC you might have used in the past. OpenOffice.org's BASIC is a high-level, object-oriented environment designed to appeal to programmers who wish to quickly add their own functions to the suite.

However, it's possible for any user to record a series of actions as a macro, which is then automatically turned into a simple BASIC program. This can be very useful if you wish to automate a simple, repetitive task, such as the insertion of a paragraph of text, or even something more complicated, such as searching and replacing text within a document.

To record a macro, select Tools ➤ Macro ➤ Record Macro. After you've selected this option, any subsequent actions will be recorded. All keyboard strokes and clicks of the mouse will be captured and turned automatically into BASIC commands. To stop the recording, simply click the button on the floating toolbar. After this, you'll be invited to give the macro a name (look to the top left of the dialog box). Once you've done so, click Save. You can then run your macro in the future by choosing Tools ➤ Macro ➤ Run Macro. Simply expand the My Macros and Standard entries at the top left of the dialog box, select your macro in the list, and then click Run.

Saving Files

As mentioned in Chapter 21, OpenOffice.org uses the OpenDocument range of file formats. The files end with an .ods, .odt, .odp, or .odb file extension, depending on whether they've been saved by Calc, Writer, Impress, or Base, respectively. The OpenDocument format is the best choice when you're saving documents that you are likely to further edit within OpenOffice.org. However, if you wish to share files with colleagues who aren't running Fedora or OpenOffice.org, the solution is to save the files as Microsoft Office files. To save in this format, just choose it from the Save As drop-down list in the Save As dialog box. If your colleague is running an older version of OpenOffice.org or StarOffice, you can also save in those file formats.

Alternatively, you might wish to save the file in one of the other file formats offered in the Save As drop-down list. However, saving files in an alternative format might result in the loss of some document components or formatting. For example, saving a Writer document as a simple text file (.txt) will lead to the loss of all of the formatting, as well as any of the original file's embedded objects, such as pictures.

To avoid losing document components or formatting, you might choose to output your OpenOffice.org files as PDF files, which can be read by the Adobe Acrobat viewer. The benefit of this approach is that a complete facsimile of your document will be made available, with all the necessary fonts and onscreen elements included within the PDF file. The drawback is that PDF files cannot be loaded into OpenOffice.org for further editing, so you should always save an additional copy of the file in the native OpenOffice.org format. To save any file as a PDF throughout the suite, select File ➤ Export As PDF. Then choose PDF in the File type drop-down box, as shown in Figure 22-5.

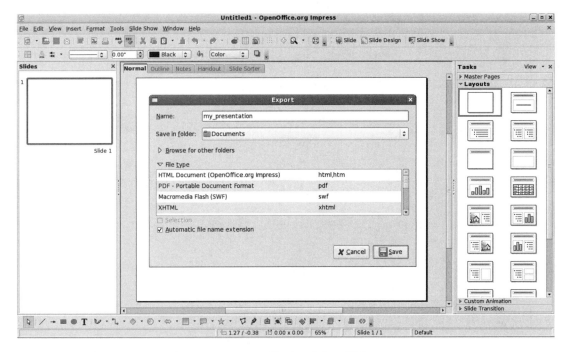

Figure 22-5. *All the programs in the suite can export files in Adobe PDF format.*

Summary

In this chapter, we looked at the configuration options provided with OpenOffice.org. You were introduced to the user interface, which is shared across all the programs within the suite, and learned how it can be customized. We also examined some common tools provided across the suite of programs, such as macro generation.

Over the following chapters, we will look at each major component of the suite, starting with Writer.

CHAPTER 23

■ ■ ■

In Depth: Writer

The word processor is arguably the most popular application within any office suite. That said, you'll be happy to know that OpenOffice.org's Writer component doesn't skimp on features. It offers all of the text-editing and formatting functionality you'd expect, along with powerful higher-level features such as mail merge.

In this chapter, we'll take a look at some of Writer's most useful features. As with all of the components in the OpenOffice.org suite, describing the features within Writer could easily fill an entire book. You should do some exploring on your own by clicking around to discover new features, as well as make judicious use of the help system.

Formatting Text

You can format text within Writer using several methods. Here, we'll look at using the Formatting toolbar, the context menu, and the Style and Formatting palette.

The Formatting Toolbar

Formatting text is easy to do via the Formatting toolbar, which is just above the ruler and main document area. Using the toolbar buttons, you can select the type of font you wish to use, its point size, and its style (normal, bold, italics, etc.). The range of fonts can be previewed in the Font drop-down list, making it easy to select the right typeface.

In addition, the Formatting toolbar lets you justify text so that it's aligned to the left or right margin, centered, or fully justified. You can also indent text using the relevant icons. As is the case almost everywhere in Fedora, a tooltip will appear over an icon when you hover the mouse cursor over it, as shown in Figure 23-1. To the right of the indentation buttons are tools to change the text background and foreground colors, and also a tool to create highlighter pen–style effects.

Figure 23-1. *When you hover your mouse over an icon, a tooltip appears to explain what it does.*

The Context Menu

Rather than use the Formatting toolbar, you can format text using the context menu. Right-click the text you want to format, and a context menu will present options for the font, size, style, alignment, and line spacing. The context menu also allows you to change the case of the highlighted characters—from uppercase to lowercase, and vice versa.

By selecting the Character option from the context menu, you get ultimate control over the font formatting. This will present a dialog box that includes every possible option, such as rotating the text and altering the individual character spacing.

■**Tip** The Character dialog box lets you create interesting typographical effects. The Paragraph dialog box has many options for formatting paragraphs. These tools open up the possibility of using Writer for simple desktop publishing work.

Selecting Paragraph from the context menu displays the Paragraph dialog box, as shown in Figure 23-2. This gives you control over paragraph elements, such as line spacing, indentation, and automatic numbering. Here, you will also find an option to automatically create drop caps, so you can start a piece of writing in style!

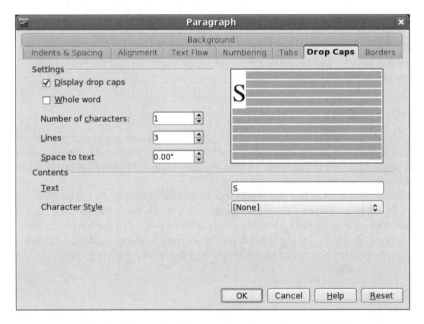

Figure 23-2. *Writer includes many elements found in desktop publishing packages, such as the ability to create drop caps.*

The Style and Formatting Palette

The Style and Formatting palette offers a variety of predefined formatting styles that you can apply to selected text or enable before you begin adding text. To make it appear, click Formatting ➤ Styles and Formatting, or press F11. You can simply click the palette's close button to get rid of it. You can easily add your own text styles to the Style and Formatting palette. Simply select some text that has the formatting applied, click the top-right button (denoted by a paragraph symbol next to a block of text), and then select New Style from Selection in the list. You'll be invited to give the style a name, and when you click OK, it will appear in the list.

Spell-Checking

Writer is able to automatically spell-check as you type. Any words it considers misspelled will be underlined in red. You can choose from a list of possible corrections by right-clicking the word and selecting from the context menu. If you're sure the word is spelled correctly but it doesn't appear to be in the dictionary, you can select Add ➤ Standard.dic from the context menu, as shown in Figure 23-3. This will add the word to your own personal dictionary extension (other users won't have access to your dictionary and will need to create their own list of approved words).

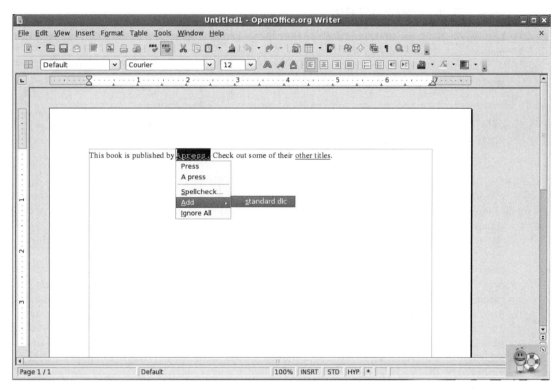

Figure 23-3. *Any words you're going to use frequently, but that Writer doesn't recognize, can be added to your personal dictionary.*

■**Tip** You might find that the spell-checker is set for US English. If you live outside the United States, or need to create documents for readers in other countries, you can choose a dictionary tailored to your locality or needs. To change the language, select Tools ➤ Options. In the list on the left, select Language Settings, and then Languages. In the Default Languages for Documents list, select your local variation. This will then become the default for all new documents.

If you find live spell-checking invasive or distracting, you can deactivate it by selecting Tools ➤ Spellcheck, clicking the Options button, and removing the check next to Check Spelling As You Type.

You can manually spell-check the document at any time by clicking Tools ➤ Spellcheck. This will scan through the document and prompt you for corrections for words the program considers misspelled.

Inserting Pictures

Writer includes quite substantial desktop publishing–like functions, such as the ability to insert pictures into text documents and to have text flow around pictures.

Inserting any kind of graphic—a graph, digital camera photo, drawing, or any other type of image—is easy. Simply choose Insert ➤ Picture ➤ From File.

■**Tip** If you have a scanner, you can also scan pictures directly into Writer documents. Simply click Insert ➤ Picture ➤ Scan ➤ Select Source.

After you've inserted a picture, you can place it anywhere on the page. When you select the picture, a new toolbar appears. This toolbar contains various simple image-tweaking tools, such as those for altering the brightness, contrast, and color balance of the image. Additionally, by clicking and dragging the blue handles surrounding the image, you can resize it.

Graphics that are imported into Writer must be anchored in some way. In other words, they must be linked to a page element so that they don't move unexpectedly. By default, they're anchored to the nearest paragraph, which means that if that paragraph moves, the graphic will move, too. Alternatively, by right-clicking the graphic, you can choose to anchor it to the page, paragraph, or character it is on or next to, as shown in Figure 23-4. Selecting to anchor it to the page will fix it firmly in place, regardless of what happens to the contents of the surrounding text. The As Character option is slightly different from the To Character option. When you choose As Character, the image will be anchored to the character it is next to, and it is actually inserted in the same line as that character, as if it were a character itself. If the image is bigger than the line it is anchored in, the line height will automatically change to accommodate it.

As you can see in Figure 23-4, the context menu also includes a Wrap option, which lets you set the type of text wrap you want to use. By default, Optimal Page Wrap is selected. This causes the text to wrap down just one side of the picture—the side on which the picture is farthest from the edge of the page. Alternatives include No Wrap, which means that the graphic will occupy the entire space on the page; no text is allowed on either side of it. However, Page Wrap is the best option if you're looking for a desktop publishing–style effect, because the text will wrap around both sides of the picture. Alternatively, if you wish the image to appear in the background of the page with text flowing across it, you can select the relevant option from the context menu.

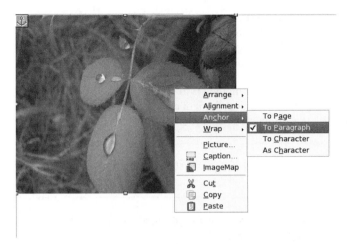

Figure 23-4. *A picture can be "anchored" to the page, a paragraph, or a character. This affects how it responds to the paragraphs surrounding it.*

As always within OpenOffice.org, ultimate control is achieved by opening the relevant dialog box. You can set up how graphics are treated on the page by right-clicking the image and selecting Picture. In the dialog box that appears, you can select the wrap effect, specify the invisible border around the wrap (which governs how close the text is to the image), and give the image a border frame.

Working with Tables

Often, it's useful to present columns of numbers or text within a word processor document. To make it easy to align the columns, OpenOffice.org offers the Table tool, which lets you quickly and easily create a grid in which to enter numbers or other information. You can even turn tables into simple spreadsheets, and tally rows or columns via simple formulas.

To insert a table, click and hold the Table icon on the Standard toolbar (which runs across the top of the screen beneath the menu). Then simply drag the mouse in the table diagram that appears until you have the desired number of rows and columns, and release the mouse button to create the table, as shown in Figure 23-5.

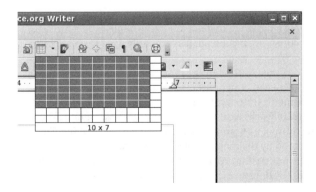

Figure 23-5. *Just select the Table icon on the main toolbar and drag the mouse to define the size of the table. Release the mouse button when you're finished.*

Whenever your cursor is inside the table, a new toolbar will appear, offering handy options. Once again, simply hover your mouse over each button to find out what it does via a tooltip.

As with spreadsheets, tables consist of cells arranged into rows (running horizontally) and columns (running vertically). Altering the size of a column is easy. Just hover the mouse over the edge of a cell until it changes to a resizing cursor, and then click and drag. You can do the same on a horizontal bar to alter a cell's height, but a far better method is to right-click within the cell, select Row ➤ Height, and enter a value. This will ensure that subsequent cells are shifted down to make space for the newly enlarged cell, which doesn't happen when you click and drag the cell's border.

■Tip An alternative way of resizing cells is to click in a cell and press the Enter key, which inserts a carriage return. Cells expand in size to fit their contents.

Once the cursor is within a table, you can move from cell to cell using the Tab key. Alternatively, you can move backward through the cells by pressing Shift+Tab.

To add more rows or columns, click the relevant icon on the Table toolbar (the fourth and fifth buttons on the bottom row). To split an existing cell, ensure your cursor is inside it and right-click. Select Cell from the menu, and then click Split.

If you want to total figures within a table, click in an empty cell, and then click the Sum icon on the Table toolbar (the Greek sigma symbol on the right side of the bottom row). This is similar to inserting a function in a spreadsheet. The cell holds the formula for the sum; clicking additional cells, or a range of cells, adds them to the sum.

■Note Only correctly formatted cells can be summed using the Sum icon on the Table toolbar. Cells with spaces or text within them cannot be added to the formula.

You can alter the styling of any cell using various icons on the Table toolbar, as well as the standard text formatting tools on the Formatting toolbar. The Table toolbar allows you to add borders to the cells and change the background colors. Alternatively, you can choose to remove all borders from the cells by clicking the Borders icon and then the No Borders option (note that gray borders will remain in place, but these are only for your convenience and won't appear in printouts).

Mail Merging

Mail merging refers to automatically applying a database of details, such as names and addresses, to a document, so that many personalized copies are produced. It's ordinarily used to create form letters for mailings.

OpenOffice.org makes the procedure very easy, but it requires source data that will be merged into the document. As with Microsoft Word, you can either enter this data within Writer itself or choose to import data from a separate document. Unless you have enough knowledge of databases to connect one to OpenOffice.org (the program works with dBase and MySQL files, among others), you may want to input existing data in the form of a comma-separated value (CSV) text file. This is the simplest form of data file that is understood by the majority of office programs and databases.

Here, we're going to look at entering the data within Writer, which is the best policy for smaller mail merge operations. You can then output the data as a CSV file, so you can use it again later. Here are the steps for using mail merge:

1. Select Tools ➤ Mail Merge Wizard to start the wizard, as shown in Figure 23-6.

2. Specify your starting document, which is the document in which the merged data will appear. You can opt to use the current document, create a new document, open a document from file, or use a template as the basis for your file.

3. Choose the mail merge type. You can choose to create a merged e-mail (for sending to multiple recipients) or a merged letter.

4. You're asked to tell Writer about your data. Writer needs to know where to find the addresses that will be merged into the document. Click the Select Different Address List button.

5. In the window that appears, you have a number of options. You can raid your Evolution e-mail address book for the data, click Add to select an already existing data source (such as a database or CSV file), or create a data source from scratch. Choose to create a data source to enter the data in Writer.

■**Note** The third option for choosing a mail merge data source, Filter, allows you to filter the database source you select after clicking Add so that you can import only specific data. To learn more about this technique, browse the OpenOffice.org Help file (click Help ➤ OpenOffice.org Help) and search for Filtering ➤ Data in Databases.

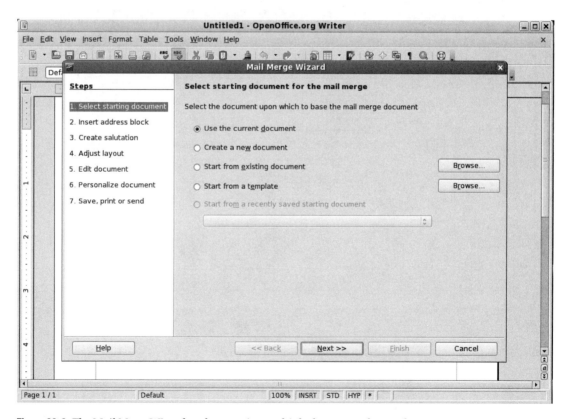

Figure 23-6. *The Mail Merge Wizard makes creating multiple documents from a data source incredibly easy.*

6. You're presented with a form for entering the data for each individual you want to receive the mail-merged letter, as shown in Figure 23-7. You don't need to fill in each field; you'll be able to choose which data fields to use in the document later on. If you wish to enter your own specific data types in addition to address details, you can click the Customize button to add your own field to the list. Using the up and down arrows in the window that appears, position the highlight where you would like the data to appear. Then click the Add button (alternatively, if there's a data field you're not using, you can highlight it and select Rename to reuse it). Obviously, you should add any new data fields you want before you begin to enter data!

7. Type in the data and press Tab at the end of each line. When you get to the last field, click the New button at the top right. When you've finished entering all the data, click OK. Then accept Writer's offer to save the data as a CSV file.

8. You're returned to the data-selection screen, and your just-saved file will be at the top of the list. Click OK.

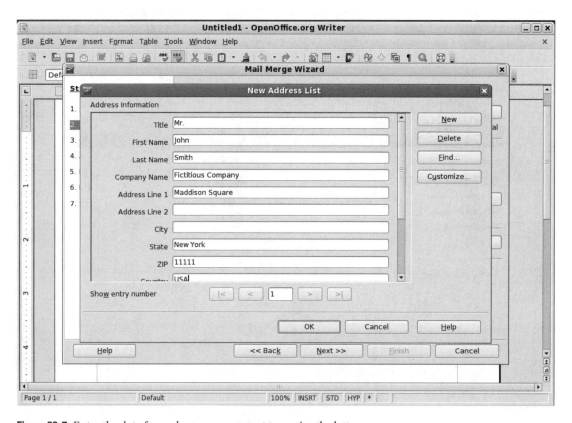

Figure 23-7. *Enter the data for each person you want to receive the letter.*

9. You're returned to the main Mail Merge Wizard window, where you can select whether to include an address block. All this means is that Writer will automatically add the merge fields to your document in what it considers the correct format (for example, title followed by first and last name, with each line of the address underneath, etc.). You can insert the merge fields manually later on if you wish; in that case, remove the check from the "This document shall contain an address block" check box. Click Next.

10. You're invited to create the salutation that will head the letter. This will contain the merge data as well, so that you can personalize the letter. Again, you can accept the default, tweak it slightly, or choose not to have an automated salutation (so that you can create your own later).

11. Depending on your previous choices, and whether you accepted the automatic address block and salutation, you are now given the choice to adjust the layout of the document in a rough way or to actually edit it (note that even if you accepted the address block and/or salutation, you'll get a chance to edit the document in the next step anyway).

12. If you opt to edit the document, you can insert your choice of merge fields by clicking Insert ➤ Fields ➤ Other. Select the Database tab in the window that appears, and then select Mail Merge Fields on the left side of the window. Click the small plus symbol next to the data file you created earlier, which should be listed on the right, and you can then select and insert the merge fields. Once you've finished, click the Return to Mail Merge Wizard button.

13. Click Next to perform the merge. You're then given a chance to edit the actual mail-merged documents (which, depending on the quantity of data entries you created earlier, could number in the tens, hundreds, or even thousands!).

14. You can save or print the *merged* document containing the data. To save the document containing the merged fields, click the Save merged document radio button and then select the Save as single document option under the Save merged document settings.

Adding Headers and Footers

You may want to add headers and footers to long documents to aid navigation. They appear at the top and bottom of each page, respectively, and can include the document title, page number, and other information. Headers and footers are created and edited independently of the main document.

As you might expect, inserting both headers and footers takes just a couple of clicks. Select Insert ➤ Header or Insert ➤ Footer, depending on which you wish to insert (documents can have both, of course). Writer will then display an editing area where you can type text to appear in the header or footer. For more options, right-click in the area, select Page, and then click the Header or Footer tab. Here, you can control the formatting and nature of the header or footer. Clicking the More button will let you apply borders or background colors.

You might wish to insert page numbers that will be updated automatically as the document progresses. OpenOffice.org refers to data that automatically updates as a *field*. You can insert a wide variety of fields by selecting Insert ➤ Fields, as shown in Figure 23-8. For example, along with the page number, you can insert the document title and author name (which is read from the details entered into the Options configuration dialog box, accessed from the Tools menu). In addition, you can enter mail merge fields by clicking Other (see the previous section for a description of how to associate mail merge data with a document).

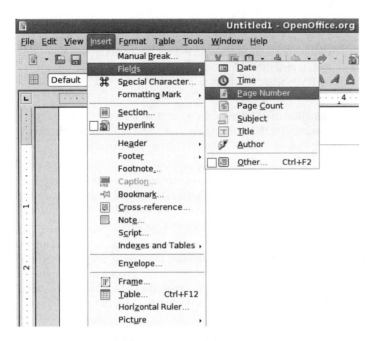

Figure 23-8. *Automatically updating data, such as page numbers, can be inserted into headers and footers.*

Summary

In this chapter, we've examined Writer, one of the core components of OpenOffice.org. We looked at the some of the key tools that enable quick and easy document creation. In particular, you've learned how to format text, use the spell-checking component, insert pictures, create and edit tables, mail merge, and add headers and footers.

In the next chapter, we move on to another vital part of OpenOffice.org: Calc, the spreadsheet component.

■■■

## CHAPTER 24

In Depth: Calc

Calc is the spreadsheet component of OpenOffice.org. Like most modern spreadsheet programs, it contains hundreds of features, many of which few average users will ever use. However, it doesn't abandon its user-friendliness in the process and remains very simple for those who want to work on modest calculations, such as home finances or mortgage interest payments. In many regards, Calc is practically a clone of Excel, and anyone who has used Microsoft's spreadsheet program will be able to get started with it immediately.

In this chapter, you'll learn about some of the best features of Calc, as well as the basics of spreadsheet creation.

Entering and Formatting Data

As with all spreadsheets, entering data into a Calc document is simply a matter of selecting a cell and starting to type. You can enter practically anything into a cell, but a handful of symbols are not allowed. For example, you cannot enter an equal sign (=) followed by a number and have it appear in a cell, because Calc will assume that this is part of a formula.

■Tip To enter any character into a cell, including an equal sign followed by a digit, precede it with an apostrophe ('). The apostrophe itself won't be visible within the spreadsheet, and whatever you type won't be interpreted in any special way; it will be seen as plain text.

Entering a sequence of data across a range of cells can be automated. Start typing the sequence of numbers, highlight them, and then click and drag the small handle to the bottom right of the last cell. This will bring up the Fill Series dialog box shown in Figure 24-1. Once you specify the details about your series, the cells are automatically filled with data.

Cells can be formatted in a variety of ways. For trivial formatting changes, such as selecting a different font or changing the number format, you can use the Formatting toolbar. For example, to turn the cell into one that displays currency, click the Currency icon (remember that hovering the mouse cursor over each icon will reveal a tooltip). You can also increase or decrease the number of visible decimal places by clicking the relevant Formatting toolbar icon.

For more formatting options, right-click the individual cell and select Format Cells from the menu. This displays the Format Cell dialog box, where you can change the style of the typeface, rotate text, place text at various angles, and so on. The Border tab of the Format Cell dialog box includes options for cell gridlines of varying thicknesses, which will appear when the document is eventually printed out.

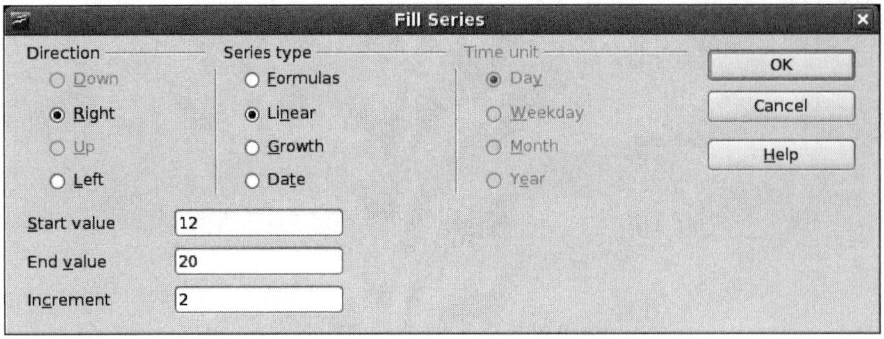

Figure 24-1. *You can automate the entering of data sequences by clicking and dragging, which brings up the Fill Series dialog box.*

Deleting and Inserting Data and Cells

Deleting data is also easy. Just highlight the cell or cells with the data you want to delete, and then press the Delete key. If you want to totally eradicate the cell along with its contents, right-click it and select Delete. This will cause the data to the sides of the cell to move in. You'll be given a choice on where you want the cells to shift from to fill the space: left, right, above, or below.

To insert a new cell, right-click where you would like to it to appear and select Insert. Again, you'll be prompted about where you want to shift the surrounding cells in order to make space for the new cell.

Working with Formulas

Calc includes a large number of formulas. In addition to simple and complex math functions, Calc offers a range of logical functions, as well as statistical and database tools. Certain formulas can also be used to manipulate text strings, such as dates.

You can reuse formulas simply by cutting and pasting them. Calc is intelligent enough to work out which cells the transplanted formula should refer to, but it's always a good idea to check to make sure the correct cells are referenced.

You can get an idea of the available functions by clicking the Function Wizard button on the Formula bar (which is just below the Formatting toolbar). This will bring up a categorized list of formulas, along with brief outlines of what function the formula performs. If you would like more details, use the help system, which contains comprehensive descriptions of most of the formulas, complete with examples of the correct syntax.

■Note The Function Wizard is actually a continuation of the wizard system you've seen in other OpenOffice.org programs, and some of the functions are also available elsewhere in the suite.

Using the Function Wizard

To use the Function Wizard to add a function, click the relevant button on the Formula bar, select the desired type of formula from the Category drop-down list, and then double-click an entry in the Function list to select it. Following this, you'll be prompted to input the relevant figures or define the appropriate data sources. Next to each text-entry box is a "shrink" button, which temporarily hides the wizard window, so you can select cells to be used within the formula.

Let's look at a quick example of using the wizard to work out an average value of a number of cells:

1. Select the cell in which you want the result of the formula to appear.

2. Start the Function Wizard by clicking the button on the Formula bar. In the left-hand list of functions, double-click AVERAGE. The wizard will then present a list of fields on the right side of the dialog box, where you can enter the values to be averaged. You could type numeric values directly into these fields, but it's more likely that you'll want to reference individual cells from the spreadsheet.

3. Click and drag the top of the dialog box to move it so that the spreadsheet underneath is at least partially visible.

4. Click the cursor in the first field of the dialog box, and then click the first cell you want to include in the calculation. This will automatically enter that cell reference into the field. You can also simply drag-select a range of cells. For example, if cells B4 and C4 have some value and you want the average in cell E4, just click B4 and drag it to the right such that C4 is also selected. The average will now appear in E4.

5. Click the next field in the dialog box, and then click the next cell you wish to include.

6. Repeat step 5 until all the fields you wish to include have been added to the fields in the dialog box (up to 30 can be selected; use the scroll bar on the right side of the wizard dialog box to reveal more fields).

7. Once you've finished, click the OK button. Calc will insert the formula into the cell you selected at the start, showing the result of the formula.

After you've added a formula with the wizard, you can edit it manually by clicking it and over-typing its contents in the Formula bar editing area. Alternatively, you can use the Function Wizard once again, by clicking the button on the Formula bar.

Summing Figures

To add the values of a number of cells, you can use the Function Wizard and select the SUM function, as shown in Figure 24-2. The procedure for choosing the cells is the same as described in the previous section.

However, Calc provides a far easier method of creating the sum formula. After positioning the cursor in an empty cell, simply click the Sum icon (the Greek sigma character) on the Formula bar, and then select the cells you wish to include in the sum. Then press Enter to see the results. If you place the cursor in a cell directly beneath a column or beside a row of numbers, Calc may be clever enough to guess what you want to add and automatically select them. If it's incorrect, simply highlight the correct range of cells.

■**Tip** You can select more than one cell by holding down the Ctrl key. You can select a range of cells in succession by clicking and dragging the mouse.

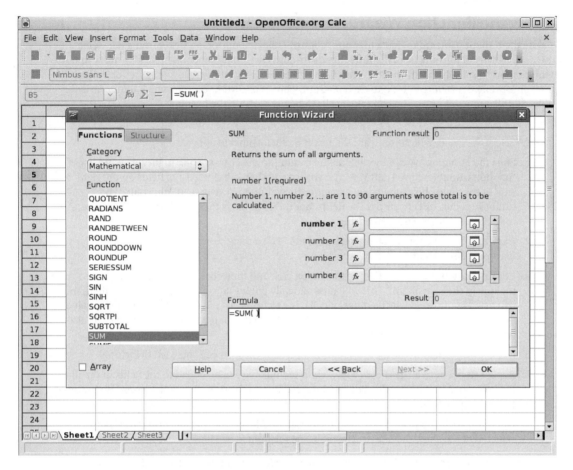

Figure 24-2. *Creating formulas is easy using the Function Wizard.*

Sorting Data

Within a spreadsheet, you may want to sort data according to any number of criteria. For example, you might want to show a list of numbers from highest to lowest, or rearrange a list of names so that they're in alphabetical order. This is easy to do within Calc.

Start by highlighting the range of data you wish to sort. Alternatively, you can simply select one cell within it, because Calc is usually able to figure out the range of cells you want to use. Then select Data ➤ Sort from the main menu. Calc will automatically select a sort key, which will appear in the Sort By drop-down list, as shown in Figure 24-3. However, you can also choose your own sort key from the drop-down menu if you wish, and you can choose to further refine your selection by choosing up to two more sort subkeys from the other drop-down menus.

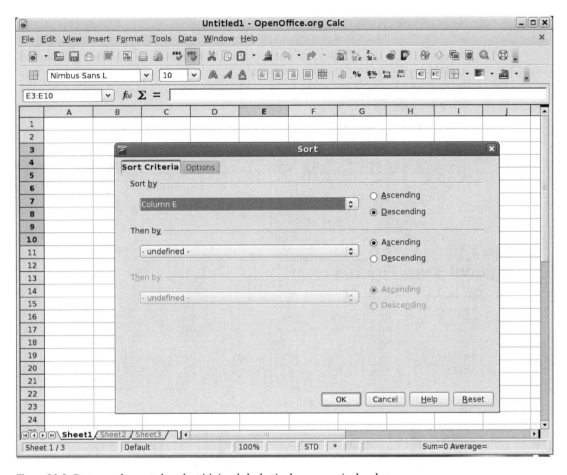

Figure 24-3. *Data can be sorted so that it's in alphabetical or numerical order.*

Creating Charts

Charts are useful because they present a quick visual summary of data. Calc produces charts through a step-by-step wizard, so it becomes very easy indeed. Here are the steps:

1. Highlight the data you want to graph. Be careful to include only the data itself and not any surrounding cells, or even the cell that contains the title for the array of data.

2. Select the Insert ➤ Chart menu option, or click the Insert Chart button on the Standard toolbar.

3. The cursor turns into a target with a small graph next to it. Click and drag on the spreadsheet itself to define the area of the graph. This can be any size. Also, you can resize it later.

4. The wizard starts. The first step is to define the range of cells to be used for the chart. By highlighting the cells before you started, you've already done this, so you can click the Next button. However, first make sure that the First Row As Label option is selected.

5. Choose the type of chart you wish to use. For simplest data selections, a bar graph is usually best. However, you might also choose a horizontal bar graph. Then click Next.

6. The wizard presents a subselection of graph types. You can also select whether gridlines are used to separate the various areas of the graph. Make your selections and click Next.

7. The last step allows you to give the chart a title and also choose whether you want a legend (a key that explains what the axes refer to) to appear next to it.

8. Click Create, and the chart will be created. Figure 24-4 shows an example.

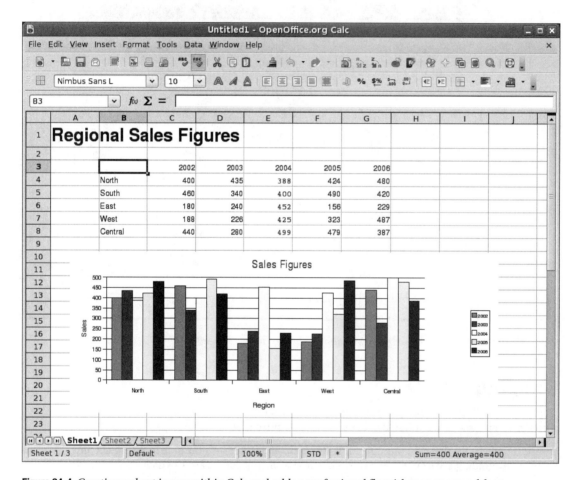

Figure 24-4. *Creating a chart is easy within Calc and adds a professional flourish to your spreadsheet.*

Once you've created a chart, you can alter its size by clicking and dragging the handles. You can also change various graphical aspects by double-clicking them. However, keep in mind that the graph is actually a picture, so the properties you edit are limited to changing the color and size of various elements.

The chart is linked to your data. Whenever your data changes, so will your chart. This is done automatically and doesn't require any user input.

Using Filters

The Filter function in Calc lets you selectively hide rows of data. The spreadsheet user then selects which of the rows of data to view from a drop-down list that appears in the cell at the top of the rows, as shown in the example in Figure 24-5.

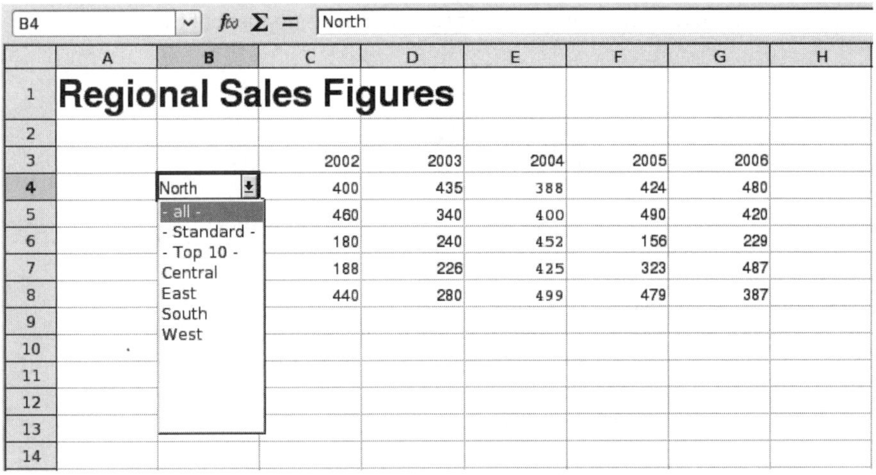

	A	B	C	D	E	F	G	H
1	**Regional Sales Figures**							
2								
3			2002	2003	2004	2005	2006	
4		North	400	435	388	424	480	
5		- all -	460	340	400	490	420	
6		- Standard -	180	240	452	156	229	
7		- Top 10 - Central	188	226	425	323	487	
8		East	440	280	499	479	387	
9		South						
10		West						
11								
12								
13								
14								

Figure 24-5. *Filters allow you to selectively hide or show rows of data in a spreadsheet.*

Note A Calc filter is a little like an Excel pivot chart, especially when it's combined with an automatically generated chart.

Using filters in this way can be useful when you're dealing with a very large table of data. It helps isolate figures so you can compare them side by side in an easy-to-follow format. For example, you could filter a table of sales figures by year.

To use the Filter function, start by highlighting the data you wish to see in the drop-down list. Make sure the column header for the data is included, too. If you're using the Filter feature on a table of data, this selection can be any column within the table, although it obviously makes sense to use a column that is pertinent to the filtering that will take place. After you've selected the data to filter, select Data ➤ Filter ➤ Autofilter. You should find that, in place of the column header, a drop-down list appears. When a user selects a various entry in the list, Calc will display only the corresponding row of the spreadsheet beneath.

To remove a filter, select Data ➤ Filter ➤ Hide Autofilter.

Summary

In this chapter, we examined OpenOffice.org Calc. We looked at the basics of how data can be entered into a cell and how it can be formatted. Then you learned how to create formulas. This is easy to do with the Function Wizard, which automates the task. Next, you saw how to sort data in a spreadsheet. We also went through the steps for creating charts using a Calc wizard. Finally, we looked at creating data filters, which work rather like pivot charts in Microsoft Excel.

In the next chapter, we move on to Impress, the presentation component of OpenOffice.org.

CHAPTER 25

███

In Depth: Impress

Impress is the presentation package within OpenOffice.org. At first glance, it appears to be the simplest of the key OpenOffice.org components, and also the one that borrows the most look and feel from Microsoft Office. However, delving into its feature set reveals more than a few surprises, including sophisticated animation effects and drawing tools. Impress can also export presentations as Adobe Flash–compatible files, which means that many Internet-enabled desktop computers around the world will be able to view the files, even if they don't have Impress or PowerPoint installed.

In this chapter, you'll learn about the main features of Impress, as well as the basics of working with presentations.

Creating a Quick Presentation

As soon as Impress starts, it will offer to guide you through the creation of a presentation using a wizard. This makes designing your document a matter of following a few steps.

You'll initially be offered three choices: Empty Presentation, From Template, or Open Existing Presentation. When Impress refers to *templates*, it means presentations that are both predesigned and also contain sample content. Only two templates are supplied with Impress, so this option is somewhat redundant. However, you might choose to look at them later, if only to get an idea of what a presentation consists of and how it's made.

Tip When you become experienced in working with Impress, you can create your own templates or download some from the Internet. To create your own template, simply choose to save your document as a template in the File Type drop-down list in the Save As dialog box. Make sure you place any templates you download or create in the `~/.openoffice.org2.0/user/template` directory. Note that this is a hidden directory in your home folder. You can change this setting by clicking Tools ➤ Options ➤ Paths.

The standard way of getting started is to create an empty presentation. This sounds more daunting than it actually is, because the Presentation Wizard will start and ask you to choose from a couple of ready-made basic designs, as shown in Figure 25-1. You'll also be given a chance to choose which format you want the presentation to take: whether it's designed primarily to be viewed onscreen or printed out.

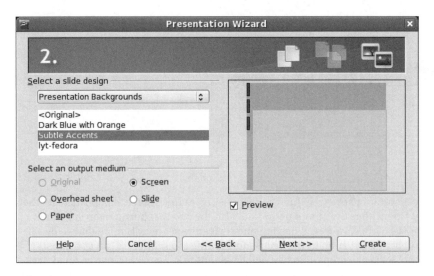

Figure 25-1. *The Impress Presentation Wizard guides you through the creation of a new presentation.*

After this, you'll be invited to choose the presentation effects, including the transition effect that will separate each slide when the presentation is viewed, and the speed of the transition. If you wish, you can set the pause between slides, too, as well as the length of time each slide stays on the screen.

After clicking the Create button in the wizard, Impress will start, and you'll be invited to choose a layout for your initial slide. These are previewed onscreen on the right side of the program window. A variety of design templates are available, ranging from those that contain mostly text to those that feature pictures and/or graphs.

Depending on which template you choose, you should end up with a handful of text boxes on your screen. Editing the text in these is simply a matter of clicking within them. The formatting of the text will be set automatically.

■**Tip** You can move and shrink each text box by clicking the handles surrounding the box. To draw a new text box, select the relevant tool on the Drawing toolbar, which runs along the bottom of the screen. Simply click and drag to draw a box of whatever size you want.

Working in Impress

When the Presentation Wizard has finished and Impress has started, you'll notice three main elements in the program window, as shown in Figure 25-2. You work in these panes as follows:

Slides pane: This pane shows the slides in your presentation in order, one beneath the other. Simply click to select whichever slide you want to work on, or click and drag to reorder the slides. To create a new slide, right-click in a blank area on the Slides pane. Right-clicking any existing slide will present a range of options, including one to delete the slide.

Main work area: This is in the middle of the program window. It lets you edit the various slides, as well as any other elements attached to the presentation, such as notes or handout documents. Simply click the relevant tab.

Tasks pane: Here, you can access the elements that will make up your presentation, such as slide templates, animations, and transition effects. Select the slide you wish to apply the elements to in the Slides pane, and then click the effect or template you wish to apply in the Tasks pane. In the case of animations or transitions, you can change various detailed settings relating to the selected element.

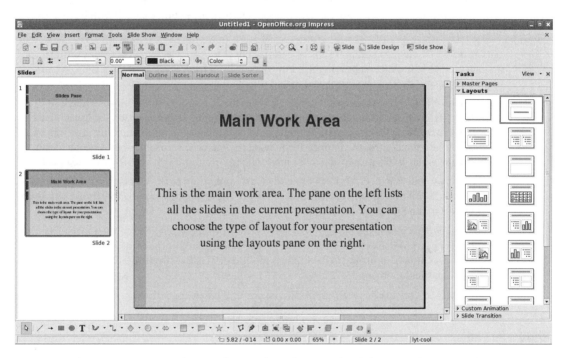

Figure 25-2. *The main Impress window is split into three elements: the Slides pane, the main work area, and the Tasks pane.*

In addition, Impress has a Drawing toolbar, which appears at the bottom of the screen. This lets you draw various items on the screen, such as lines, circles, and rectangles, and also contains a handful of special-effect tools, which we'll discuss later in this chapter, in the "Applying Fontwork" and "Using 3D Effects" sections.

You can hide each onscreen item by clicking the View menu and then removing the check next to it. Alternatively, by clicking the vertical borders between each pane, you can resize the pane and make it either more or less prominent on the screen. This is handy if you wish to temporarily gain more work space but don't want to lose sight of the previews in the Slides pane, for example.

Animating Slides

All elements within Impress can be animated in a variety of ways. For example, you might choose to have the contents of a particular text box fly in from the edge of the screen during the presentation. This can help add variety to your presentation, and perhaps even wake up your audience!

Setting an animation effect is simply a matter of clicking the border of the object you wish to animate in the main editing area so that it is selected, selecting Custom Animation in the Tasks pane, and then clicking the Add button. In the dialog box that appears, select how you want the effect to work. As shown in Figure 25-3, you have four choices, each with its own tab within the dialog box:

Entrance: This lets you animate an appearance effect for the selected object. For example, you can choose to have a text box dissolve into view or fly in from the side of the screen. When you select any effect, it will be previewed within the main editing area.

Emphasis: This gives you control over what, if anything, happens to the object while it's onscreen. As the name suggests, you can use this animation to emphasize various elements while you're giving the presentation. Some emphasis effects are more dramatic than others, and this lets you control the impact. If you want to make an important point, you can use a dramatic effect, while presenting more moderate information with a more subdued effect.

Exit: As you might expect, this lets you add an exit animation to the object. You might choose to have it fly off the side or spin away off the top of the screen. The animation choices here are identical to the Entrance choices.

Motion Paths: This makes the selected element fly around the screen according to a particular path. For example, selecting Heart will cause the element to fly around describing the shape of a heart, eventually returning to its origin. A motion path is effectively another way of emphasizing a particular object.

■**Note** You can apply only one effect at a time to an object, although several separate effects can be applied to any object.

With each animation, you can select the speed you wish it to play at, ranging from very slow to fast. Simply make the selection at the bottom of the dialog box.

Once the animation has been defined and you've clicked OK, it will appear in a list at the bottom of the Custom Animation dialog box. You can choose to add more than one animation to an object by clicking the Add button again (ensuring that the object is still selected in the main editing area). The animations will play in the order they're listed. You can click the Change Order up and down arrows to alter the order.

To fine-tune an effect, double-click it in the list to open its Effect Options dialog box (you can even add sound effects here). Under the Timing tab, you can control what cues the effect, such as a click of a mouse, or whether it will appear in sequence with other effects before or after in the list.

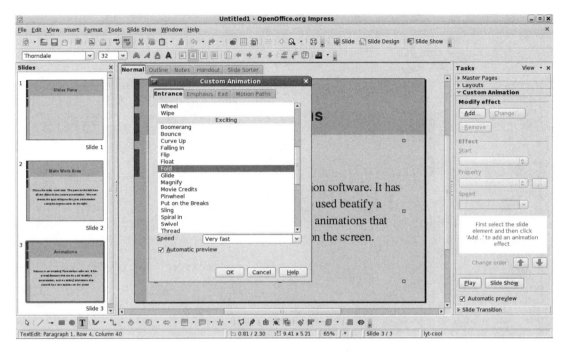

Figure 25-3. *A wide variety of animation effects is available for onscreen elements.*

Applying Fontwork

The Fontwork tool lets you manipulate text in various playful ways, such as making it follow specific curved paths. You can find this tool on the Drawing toolbar, located at the bottom of the program window.

When you click the Fontwork icon, the Fontwork Gallery dialog box appears, offering a choice of predefined font effects. Don't worry if they're not quite what you want, because after you make a choice, you'll be invited to fine-tune it.

Once you've made the selection, the dummy text "Fontwork" will appear on the screen. Editing the text is simple: just double-click the "Fontwork" text and type your own words. When you've finished, click outside the Fontwork selection.

Whenever the new Fontwork item is selected, a floating toolbar will appear, as shown in Figure 25-4. You can use this toolbar to alter various options. For example, you can select a completely different Fontwork selection from the gallery or, by clicking the second icon on the left, select your own path that you want the Fontwork item to follow.

You'll also see that the Formatting toolbar changes to allow you to alter the formatting of the Fontwork element. You can alter the thickness of the letter outlines, for example, or the color of the letters. Once again, the best way to learn how the tool works is to play around with the options and see what you can achieve.

To remove a Fontwork item, just select its border and press the Delete key on your keyboard.

Figure 25-4. *The Fontwork tool can add some special effects to your presentations.*

Using 3D Effects

In addition to Fontwork effects, Impress includes a powerful 3D tool, which can give just about any onscreen element a 3D flourish (this tool is also available in some other OpenOffice.org applications). To use it, create a text box or shape using the Drawing toolbar at the bottom of the screen. Then right-click the text box or shape and select Convert ➤ To 3D.

■**Note** The 3D Object option is designed simply to give your object depth. If you want to create a genuine 3D object that you can rotate in 3D space, select the 3D Rotation Object option.

You can gain much more control over the 3D effect by right-clicking it and selecting 3D Effects. This will open a floating palette window with five configuration panels, as shown in Figure 25-5. Click the icons at the top of the palette to adjust the type of 3D effect and its lighting, as follows:

Geometry: This defines how the 3D effect will look when it's applied to onscreen selections. For example, you can increase or decrease the rounded-edges value, and this will make any sharp objects on the screen appear softer when the 3D effect is applied.

Shading: This doesn't affect the actual texture of the 3D object, but instead alters its color gradient. This is best demonstrated in action, so select the various shading modes from the drop-down list to see the effect. In addition, you can choose whether a shadow is applied to the effect, as well as the position of the virtual camera (the position of the hypothetical viewer looking at the 3D object).

Illumination: This lets you set the lighting effect. All 3D graphics usually need a light source because this helps illustrate the 3D effect; without a light source, the object will appear flat. Various predefined light sources are available. You can click and drag the light source in the preview window.

Textures: This affects how the textures will be applied to the 3D object. A texture is effectively a picture that is "wrapped around" the 3D object. Clever use of textures can add realism to a 3D object. You could apply a map of the world to a sphere to make it look like a globe, for example, or you could add wood or brickwork textures to make objects appear as tabletops or walls.

Material: This lets you apply various color overlays on the texture. This can radically alter the texture's look and feel, so it is quite a powerful option. To change the texture itself, right-click the object and select Area. This will present a list of predefined textures. Alternatively, you can choose to use a color or pattern.

To apply any changes you make, click the check button at the top right of the palette. As with the other presentation effects, the best policy is simply to experiment until you're happy with the results.

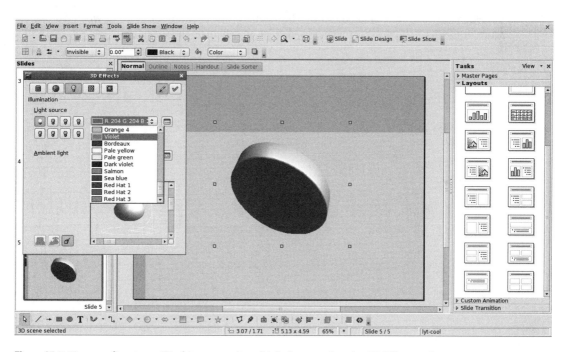

Figure 25-5. *You can fine-tune 3D objects to quite a high degree using the 3D Effects palette.*

Exporting a Presentation As a Flash File

If you plan to put your presentation online, or you want to send it to a colleague who doesn't have Impress or PowerPoint installed, outputting your presentation as a Flash animation could be a good idea. The process is simple. Just select File ➤ Export, and then select Macromedia Flash (SWF) in the File Format drop-down list (SWF is the Flash file type, which stands for Shockwave Flash). No further configuration is necessary.

In order to play the file, it needs to be opened within a web browser that has the Flash Player installed. You can do this by selecting File ➤ Open on most browsers, although you can also drag and drop the SWF file onto the browser window under Microsoft Windows. There shouldn't be much of a problem with compatibility, since the Flash Player is ubiquitous these days. If the web browser doesn't already have Flash installed, it's easy to download and install it (see www.adobe.com/shockwave/download/download.cgi?P1_Prod_Version=ShockwaveFlash).

■**Caution** When you export a presentation to Flash, some effects, such as animations and shading, might get lost.

When the Flash file is opened in a web browser, the presentation starts, as shown in Figure 25-6. You can progress through it by clicking anywhere on the screen.

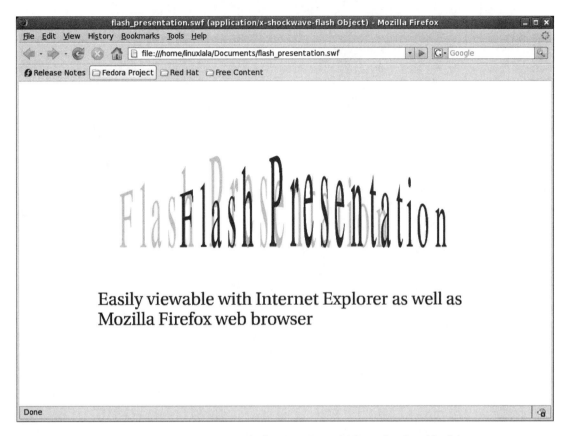

Figure 25-6. *You can save any presentation as a Flash animation, which can be played back in a suitably equipped web browser.*

Summary

In this chapter, we examined Impress, which is the presentation component within OpenOffice.org. We started by looking at how you can use the Presentation Wizard function to automate production of a basic Impress document. Then you saw how various effects can be added to the presentation, including 3D effects. Finally, we looked at how the presentation can be exported as an SWF file for playback in virtually any web browser.

In the next chapter, we will explore the database component within OpenOffice.org: Base.

CHAPTER 26

■■■

In Depth: Base

OpenOffice.org includes a number of tools to both interface with database servers and perform tasks such as entering and editing data. However, for most day-to-day users who have humble needs, creating such a setup is rather complicated. It requires some knowledge of how databases work on a technical level. For this reason, a new component was added to OpenOffice.org 2.0: Base.

Base is a relational database along the lines of Microsoft Access and is perfect for database applications of all sizes, including more modest efforts. For example, you could use it to create an inventory database to produce a report showing all products added for a certain geographical region on a certain date, or you could use it to catalog items in your personal stamp collection.

Relational databases such as those created by Base are ideal for quickly creating catalogs of information, such as inventory lists. In addition to making database creation simple and quick, relational databases let you easily query data to produce reports tailored to individual needs.

Base works on a number of levels depending on the knowledge of the user, but in its most basic form, it offers a design-based approach to the creation of tables and forms. Anyone who has previously created a database under Access will feel right at home.

In this chapter, we'll work through an example of using Base to create a simple database cataloging a collection of music. You can use the same techniques to create any kind of relational database.

Getting Started with Base

Depending on your package selection when installing Fedora, you should find Base under the Applications ➤ Office menu, listed as Database Development. In case it isn't installed, you can use the `su -c "yum install openoffice.org-base"` command to install it.

When the program first starts, the Database Wizard guides you through either creating a new database or opening an existing one, as shown in Figure 26-1.

The first step in creating a new database is to register it within OpenOffice.org. This means that it will be made available in other OpenOffice.org programs, such as Calc or Writer. Although the knowledge needed to use a database in this way is quite advanced, there's no harm in agreeing to this option. It might prove useful in the future as you learn more about OpenOffice.org.

Note Base can also connect to existing MySQL or SQL databases. You can choose the Connect to an existing database option in the Database Wizard. You can then pick up the database server you want to connect to from the drop-down list. The Database Wizard will guide you through the remaining steps. This is, however, a very convoluted procedure and is out of the scope of this book.

Following this, you can choose to open the database for editing and/or start the Table Wizard. Once you click the Finish button, you'll be invited to give the database a name and save it immediately.

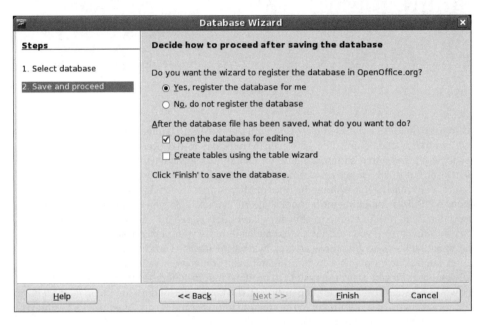

Figure 26-1. *Base starts with the Database Wizard to facilitate the quick and easy creation of new databases.*

■**Note** Databases aren't like other office files, in that they automatically save and update themselves. When using the finished database, you can simply enter data and then quit the program, without needing to deliberately opt to save the file.

Assuming that you did not opt to go directly to the Table Wizard, you'll now see the main Base program window. The right of the Base program window contains the Tasks and Data panes. The Tasks pane allows you to create new database elements, depending on what's selected in the Database pane. The Data pane shows any elements you've already created. The Database pane contains the four elements of the database that you can create and manipulate:

Tables: A table is what holds the actual data you'll eventually input. Therefore, a table is the first thing that needs to be created within a new database. Creating a table involves defining the types of data that you want to store and giving the individual data fields easy-to-understand names.

Forms: Although it's possible to enter data directly into a table, it isn't particularly intuitive or easy. Because of this, forms are used to make the data fields presentable. As the name suggests, in terms of layout these are not unlike the paper forms that you fill in to facilitate the collection of data by businesses. As with tables, forms must be created from scratch in a new database.

Forms have *controls*, which are used to facilitate data entry, or to allow users to navigate the database or otherwise manipulate it. The most common type of control is a text-entry field, which is then tied to a data field within the table, but you can also have controls that perform certain functions, such as deleting a record in the database.

Queries: A query is a way of filtering the database so that you see only a subset of it. For example, in a database detailing sales figures from across the country, you might create a query to show only the data from a particular state.

Reports: A report is a way of presenting data for human consumption, usually in a printed format. For example, you could create a report that details sales figures in the form of a letter, or you might make a report to produce address labels using addresses stored in the database.

Note The usefulness of both queries and reports are that they can be saved and used over and over again, so you could use the same query each month to examine just a small section of the data. Base offers wizards to automate the creation of both queries and reports.

Clicking an item in the Database pane displays or activates that item.

Now let's work through an example of using Base. First, you'll create a table, and then you'll create a form.

Creating a Database

As an example of using Base, you'll build a database, ready for data entry. The first step in the creation of a database is to make a table. This will hold the data that you will eventually enter using a form.

Adding a Table

As with all components within Base, you can use a wizard to create the table. The Table Wizard offers a number of predefined data fields corresponding to typical databases. It is fine for general use, but if you have a specific and unusual database in mind, you will need to create the table manually.

Here, you'll create a database to catalog CDs. This is easily accomplished with the Table Wizard, as follows:

1. Click the Tables icon in the Database pane, and then click the Use Wizard to Create Table icon. The Table Wizard will start.

2. You're given a choice between creating a business or personal database. As you would expect, business databases are likely to contain fields relating to business matters, such as accounting, and the fields in the personal section relate more to domestic matters. Choose Personal for this example.

3. Choose an entry from the Sample Tables drop-down list. For this example, select CD Collection.

4. In the Available Fields box, you now see a number of data fields that would prove handy for a CD collection. You don't need to use all of these. Instead, select only those you want in your table, and then click the single right-facing arrow button to transfer them to the Selected Fields box. For this example, select AlbumTitle, Artist, Format, Rating, and Review, as shown in Figure 26-2. Then click the Next button. (Don't worry if you find the fields lacking or if you want to add your own—you'll see how to do just that in step 6.)

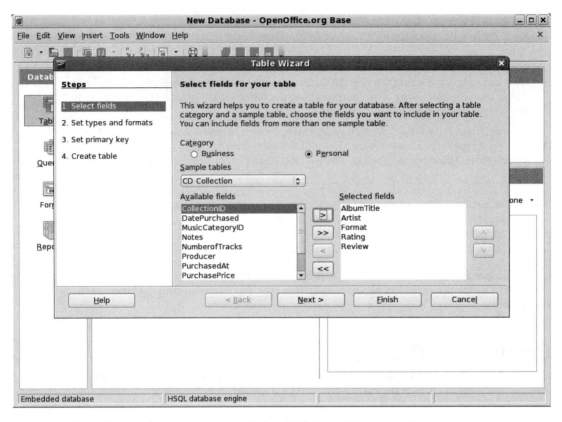

Figure 26-2. *The Table Wizard contains ready-made data fields for a wide variety of uses.*

5. Check to make sure the fields you selected are of the correct type. Click each to see the information in the right area of the dialog box. Fields can take various forms depending on what kind of data they're supposed to hold. For example, one field might be designed to contain text, while another might need to contain numbers. Yet another might need to contain dates, and some can even contain pictures. As you might expect, the wizard has automatically selected the correct data types for the predefined fields.

6. For this example, you want to add a check box that shows whether the CD is scratched. If the CD in question is scratched, the user can click the check box. If the CD isn't scratched, the box can be left blank. To create a check box, you need a special kind of data field called a Boolean. This means that the data field can be either true or false, or to put it a simpler way, it can hold either yes or no. To create a yes/no data field, click the plus button at the bottom of the Selected Fields box. This allows you to add another field. In the Field Name box, type **Scratched**. For the Field Type, click the drop-down list and locate the entry marked Yes/No [BOOLEAN]. The other options can remain as they are. Click Next to continue.

7. You're asked if you want to create a primary key. This is the unique numeric field that the database uses to keep track of each entry in the database. It's a must in a database like this one. The default choices are correct, but you must click the Auto value check box. This will automatically number each entry in the database. Now click Next again.

8. You've completed the Table Wizard. The next step is to create a form, so select Create a Form Based on This Table, and then click the Finish button.

Creating a Form

Forms are present in databases for the benefit of users to facilitate the quick-and-easy entry of data. They present data fields that you've just created within the table in an easy-to-understand form.

Base is able to walk you through the creation of forms via the Form Wizard. If you didn't select to run the Form Wizard previously, you can start it by clicking the Forms button on the Database pane, and then clicking Use Wizard to Create Form. Then follow these steps:

1. In the Form Wizard's first step, select which fields you want to appear on the form. As with the Table Wizard, this is simply a matter of selecting the fields, and then clicking the right arrow button so that they appear under the Fields on the Form heading. Alternatively, by clicking the double arrow button, you can select all of them in one fell swoop, which is what you want for this example.

2. You're asked if you want to create a subform. As its name suggests, this is effectively a form within your main form. A subform is useful with more complicated databases, where it might be necessary to view other data while filling in the form. For this simple example, leave the Add Subform box unchecked and click Next.

3. Choose a general layout for the data fields. The default is the table view, which many find ugly, so you might choose one of the first two options (in our database we chose the second option, as can be seen in Figure 26-3). These arrange the data fields in a spacious manner and make the form much more usable. If you look behind the wizard dialog box, you'll see a preview of how the form will look.

4. You're asked whether you want existing data to be displayed on the form. You can choose to treat the form as one created only for entering new data, so that you can't use it to navigate through the database and see existing data you've already entered. This might be useful in applications where you don't want users to see the other data in the database. However, for a database for your own personal use, being able to see the existing data is very handy, which is why the option The Form Is to Display All Data is selected by default. For this example, simply click the Next button to accept the default.

5. Choose a look and feel for your form from the variety of color schemes available, as shown in Figure 26-3. Again, you can see them previewed behind the wizard dialog box. Feel free to experiment with the options under the Field border heading. We suggest the 3D look option, which gives the form elements a slight interior shadow, a common feature on most modern user interfaces. The Flat option simply adds a black border to the boxes, and the No border option removes the border completely.

6. You're invited to give the form a name. Enter a suitable name, such as **CD-Collection**. You are also given the option of entering data directly into the form or modifying it manually. If you find that some field is missing from the form, you can add it yourself, by selecting to modify the form manually. You'll be doing that in the next section, so select Modify the form, and click Finish.

■Note There are no rules governing form names, and you can use virtually any symbols and also insert spaces into the name. However, it's a good idea to keep the form name simple and concise.

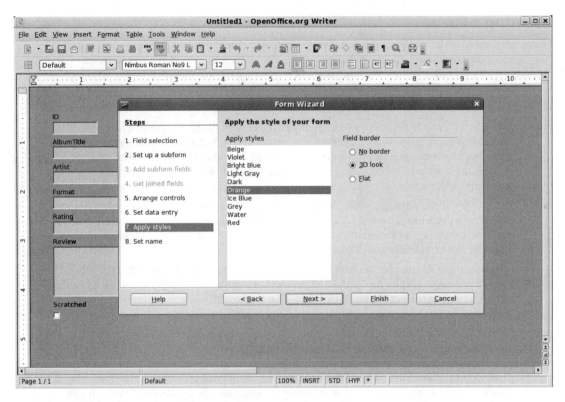

Figure 26-3. *You can choose from a variety of look-and-feel options for your form, and each will be previewed behind the wizard dialog box.*

Adding Controls to the Form Manually

When the Form Wizard finishes, you should find yourself editing the form directly. Click View ➤ Toolbars ➤ Form Controls. A floating palette—the Form Control toolbar—will appear, offering various form-specific functions.

Note The item that you wish to add to your form must already be in your table. This procedure is not for adding new items to your form.

Follow these steps to add any missing item to your form:

1. On the Form Control toolbar, click the icon that best serves the purpose of your control, be it a check box or a text box, and then click and drag to draw it on the form. You need to make it big enough so that the label can be seen. If you released the mouse button too early, simply click and drag the handles at the edges to resize the control.

2. Once the item has been drawn, double-click it. This will open the Properties dialog box. Click the Label box, delete what's there already, and type a suitable name (anything that will help you identify the item on the completed form).

3. Click the Data tab and, in the Data Field box, select the missing field from the drop-down list.

Note Creating a custom control is simply a matter of drawing it on the form, and then matching it with a data field.

---

4. Close and save the form.

You can add more custom controls following the same basic approach you used here. Simply draw them on to the form, and then match them up with an entry in the table using the Data tab.

The database is now ready for use.

Using the Database

Entering data into the finished database is easy. Click the Forms icon in the Database pane, and then double-click the form you created earlier.

The Form Control toolbar will still be visible. To hide it, click its close button at the top-right corner of the toolbar. After this, you can start to enter data into the form, as shown in the example in Figure 26-4. Note that you do not need to enter data in the ID field, because this will automatically be filled with the primary key number.

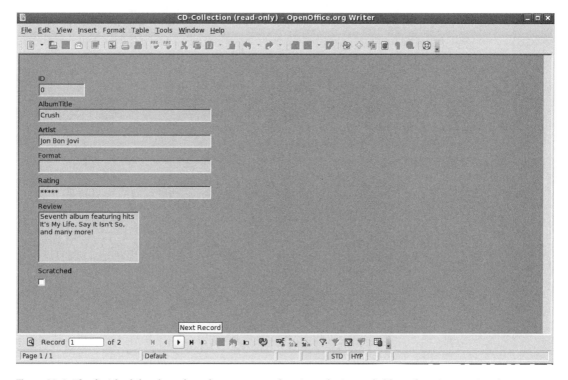

Figure 26-4. *The finished database form lets you enter data into the input fields and navigate using the toolbar at the bottom.*

Once you've filled in the form, you can click the Next Record button in the Form Navigation toolbar running along the bottom of the window (don't forget that hovering the mouse cursor over each button reveals a tooltip explaining what the button does). This will move you on to the next blank form, where you can enter more data. Repeat this as many times as necessary.

The Form Navigation toolbar contains other handy tools. For example, the first button—a magnifying glass—lets you search the database for a particular entry. It's well worth investigating the functions.

Summary

In this chapter, we looked at the Base database component of OpenOffice.org and how to use it to easily create and edit simple databases. We stepped through an example of setting up a database table and creating a database form that users can employ to enter and edit data.

In the next chapter, we will look at the Evolution e-mail client.

■ ■ ■

## CHAPTER 27

In Depth: Evolution

Evolution isn't part of the OpenOffice.org suite. It was originally created by Ximian, an organization founded by the creators of the GNOME desktop project and acquired by Novell in August 2003. Even long after the acquisition, Evolution is still developed by many of the key GNOME desktop developers.

Although it's not explicitly described as such by its developers, Evolution is considered the "official" GNOME desktop personal information manager. It provides an address book, calendar, tasks manager, and e-mail management functionality. Nearly every Linux distribution that uses the GNOME desktop system also uses Evolution. Evolution even retains the same look and feel as many elements of the Fedora desktop.

In terms of functionality, Evolution is similar to Microsoft Outlook, in that as well as being a powerful e-mail client, it incorporates contacts management, a calendar, and a to-do list. Evolution is even able to connect to Microsoft Exchange (2000 and above) groupware servers and synchronize with contact and calendar data, in addition to fetching e-mail. Of course, it can also connect to standard POP3/SMTP e-mail servers, as well as IMAP and also Novell GroupWise servers. This means it is compatible with practically every e-mail system in use today.

Although Evolution offers many of the functions of Microsoft Outlook, it differs in some key ways. Therefore, this chapter describes how to perform basic tasks, as well as more advanced everyday jobs.

Evolution Modes

Evolution consists of four components: Mail, Contacts, Calendars, and Tasks. These are interconnected but operate as separate modes within the program. Each mode can be selected from the View ➤ Window menu. The program window, toolbar, and menu system will change to accommodate whichever mode is selected. Figure 27-1 shows the program in Mail mode.

■Tip You can quicky shift between the various Evolution modes by enabling the icons. Click View ➤ Switcher Appearance ➤ Hide buttons. The bottom-left of the window will now show buttons for each Evolution mode. You can shrink the switcher component to small icons by clicking View ➤ Switcher Appearance ➤ Icons Only.

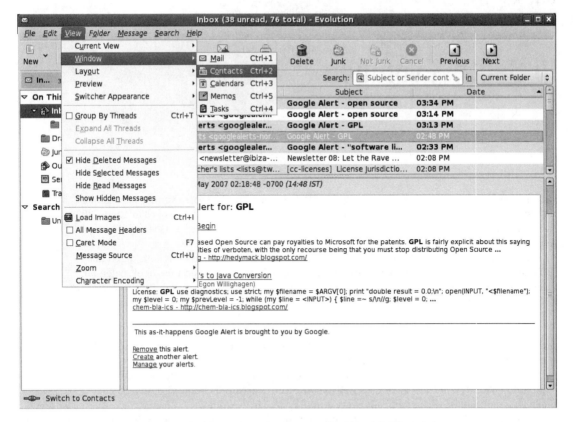

Figure 27-1. *You can switch between Evolution's modes by using the default keyboard shortcuts or through the View ➤ Window menu.*

The four Evolution modes work as follows:

Mail: At the top left of the program window are the mail folders. Here, you'll find the Inbox and Sent folders, along with any other mail folders you create. On the right is the list of e-mail messages and beneath this is the message preview pane, where the body of any message you select will be displayed. Above the message list is the search box, which works like most e-mail search routines: type the relevant word(s) and then click Find Now. Notable icons running along the top of the window include the New button, which will let you compose an e-mail message, and the Send/Receive button, which will download new messages and also send any messages in the Outbox folder.

Contacts: At the left side of the program window are listed the various contact folders. For most users, there will be just one, named Personal, but if you specified a groupware server during setup, you will also be able to connect to this by clicking its entry. At the top right is the list of contacts. Clicking any contact displays that individual's information at the bottom of the window, in the contact information area. The search bar at the top of the window beneath the toolbar lets you quickly search for contacts using their name. The New button on the toolbar lets you create a new contact.

Calendars: On the left side of the program window are the various calendars you can access. For most users, the Personal calendar will be the principal one, but you can also access shared calendars here. To the right is the monthly calendar and, in the middle of the program window, the appointment list, with half-hour entries covering the working day. By default, the current day is shown. To select a different day, simply double-click the day in the month view. You can switch between day, week, and month appointment views by clicking the Day, Work Week, and Month buttons on the toolbar.

Tasks: Your tasks are listed on the left side of the program window. Once again, most users will use just the Personal task list. The task list itself appears in the main program window.

Basic E-Mail Tasks

Evolution's e-mail functionality is arguably the heart of the program. Although it offers a lot of features, it is quite simple to use. If you've ever used any other e-mail client, such as Microsoft Outlook, you have a head start.

This section describes how to accomplish several everyday tasks within the e-mail component of Evolution. When you start Evolution, the Mail mode is selected automatically. However, if it isn't, or if you've switched to a different mode within the program, simply click the Mail button at the bottom left of the program window.

Sending and Receiving E-Mail

Once Evolution has been set up correctly to work with your e-mail servers, as outlined in Chapter 8, you can simply click the Send/Receive button on the toolbar to connect to the server(s) and both send and receive e-mail.

You may need to enter your password if you didn't enter it during setup. You can check the Remember Password box to avoid having to type it again, but this means that the password will then be stored on your hard disk, possibly posing a security risk.

■Note Although e-mail is normally sent as soon as you click the Send button when composing e-mail, if the sending has been delayed for any reason (such as because you were offline at the time), it will be sent as soon as you click the Send/Receive button. Until that point, it will be held in the Outbox folder on the left side of the program window.

Any outstanding mail is sent first, and then the receiving procedure is started. As shown in Figure 27-2, a status dialog box will tell you how many messages there are and the progress of the download. Clicking the Cancel button will stop the procedure (although some messages may already have been downloaded).

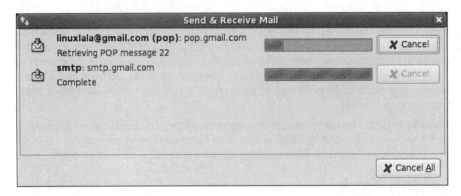

Figure 27-2. *You'll see how many messages there are to download whenever you click the Send/Receive button.*

Reading E-Mail

Simply click an e-mail message to view it in the preview pane at the bottom of the screen. Alternatively, you can double-click a message to open it in its own program window (selecting a message and pressing Enter will have the same effect).

As with most e-mail clients, any unread messages in the list appear in bold, and messages that have been read appear in ordinary type. By default, each message is marked as read after 1.5 seconds, but you can alter this value. To change it, click Edit ➤ Preferences, click the Mail Preferences icon in the Preferences dialog box, and then change the value under the Message Display heading. A value of 0 will cause the mail to switch to read status as soon as it's clicked, which can be useful if you want to quickly clear a lot of messages.

You can also mark many messages as read by highlighting them all, right-clicking an individual one, and selecting Mark As Read from the menu that appears. You can select multiple messages in the usual way: Shift-click to select a consecutive list or Ctrl-click for nonconsecutive selections.

Deleting Messages

You can delete messages by highlighting them and pressing the Delete key. Alternatively, right-click any message (or a selection of them) and select Delete.

The way Evolution handles deleted messages is rather unusual in that messages aren't deleted instantly. They simply disappear from view. You can view all deleted messages by clicking the Trash icon on the left side of the program window, but, technically speaking, the messages haven't been moved to the Trash folder. The Trash folder merely displays in one place messages marked for deletion. You can right-click each message in the Trash view and select Undelete. You can then browse each of these messages from the Unmatched folder. To empty the Trash, right-click the Trash icon and select Empty Trash.

To get rid of deleted messages permanently, you need to right-click the folder *where you deleted the message* (such as the Inbox) and click Folder ➤ Expunge. You'll be asked if you really want to delete the messages, as shown in Figure 27-3.

Note If you move any messages from folder to folder, as described later in the "Sorting and Filtering Messages" section, a copy of the mail will end up in the Trash folder. This is because Evolution doesn't literally move messages. Instead, it copies them from the old to the new location and deletes the original. This can be a little disconcerting at first, but there's nothing to worry about. The mail message will remain wherever you moved it, and it won't disappear when you expunge any folders.

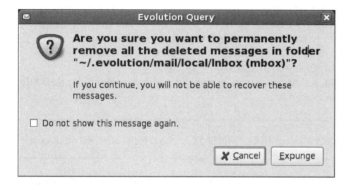

Figure 27-3. *To permanently delete messages, it's necessary to expunge them from the folder from which they were deleted.*

Flagging Messages

You can flag messages in a variety of ways to help remind you of their status or purpose. The simplest form of flagging is to mark a message as important: right-click the message and select Mark As Important, or click in the space beneath the Important column (this is located to the left of the From column).

Alternatively, you can add several different flags by right-clicking a message and selecting Mark for Follow Up. Your choices range from Do Not Forward to No Response Necessary and Review. This heading will then appear in the message preview at the bottom of the window whenever the mail is selected.

IMPORTING E-MAIL FROM THUNDERBIRD

Back in Chapter 4, we discussed a method of exporting e-mail from various Microsoft e-mail programs, which use proprietary formats, so that it can be imported under Fedora. To recap, you can install the Mozilla Thunderbird e-mail client under Windows, import your e-mail into it from Outlook or Outlook Express, and then export Thunderbird's mailbox (.mbox) files for use within Evolution.

If you followed these instructions and now have the .mbox files ready for use with Evolution, it's easy to import them. Click File ➤ Import. In the Import dialog box, click the Browse button, locate the .mbox file, and click Open. If you have more than one .mbox file, you'll need to import each one manually.

Composing a Message

Creating a new e-mail is as simple as clicking the New button at the top left of Evolution's program window. Fill in the To and Subject details as usual, and then type in the main body of the message.

To add a CC or BCC, click the To button and select addresses from your contacts list in the dialog box that appears (selecting the CC or BCC button as appropriate). Alternatively, if you would like to have the CC and BCC fields visible and available at all times, click their entries under the View menu of the Compose a Message window.

As with most Microsoft mail programs, new e-mail can be sent either as plain text or as HTML. Plain text mode is the default. To switch to HTML, click the entry on the Format menu. The advantage of HTML mail is that you can vary the style, size, and coloring of text, so you can emphasize various words or paragraphs, as illustrated in Figure 27-4. In addition, if you click Insert ➤ Image, you can insert pictures from the hard disk. Other options on the Insert menu let you insert tables, dividing lines (click the Rule menu entry), and hyperlinks.

The disadvantage of HTML e-mail is that the person receiving the message will need an HTML-compatible e-mail program to be able to read it.

■**Note** Many people in the Linux community frown on HTML-formatted e-mail and prefer plain text messages.

Words are automatically spell-checked in the new e-mail and are underlined in red if the spell checker thinks they are misspelled. To correct the word, right-click it, click Check Word Spelling, and then select the correctly spelled word from the list.

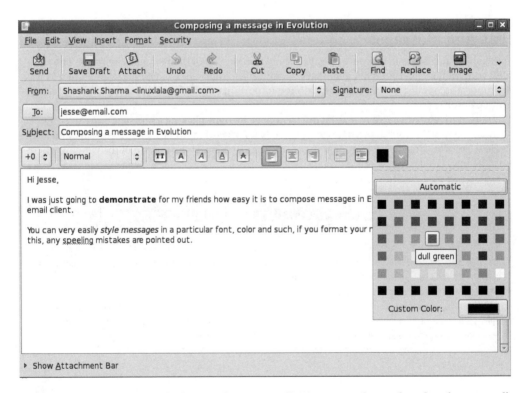

Figure 27-4. *New messages can be formatted in HTML, allowing you to change the color of text, as well as its size.*

Creating an E-Mail Signature

E-mail signatures are the blocks of text that appear automatically at the end of new e-mail messages you compose. They save you the bother of typing your name and contact details each time. To create an e-mail signature, follow these steps:

1. Click Edit ➤ Preferences. In the Composer Preferences dialog box, click the Signatures tab.

2. Click the Add button.

3. In the Edit Signature dialog box, type what you wish to appear as your signature. The signature can either be in plain text or HTML (click Format ➤ HTML). Don't forget that in HTML mode you can insert lines (Insert ➤ Rule), which can act as a natural divider at the top of your signature to separate it from the body of the e-mail, as shown in the example in Figure 27-5.

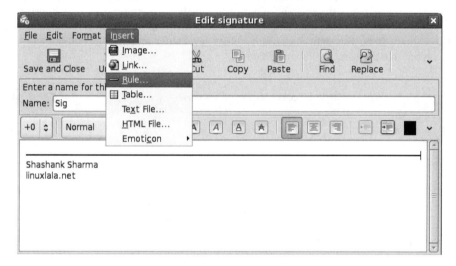

Figure 27-5. *Creating an e-mail signature saves you from having to type your contact details each time.*

4. Click the Save and Close icon at the top left.

5. Click Close to close the Preferences window.

■**Tip** Enter a few carriage returns at the top of your signature so that when you create a new e-mail, you have enough space to click and type without accidentally clicking within the signature.

Advanced E-Mail Tasks

Evolution offers several features that can help you organize your e-mail. You can create new folders, as well as filter, sort, and search through your messages.

Creating New Folders

If you want to better organize your e-mail, you can create your own folders, which will then appear in the list on the left side of the program window.

To create a new top-level folder, which will appear in the list alongside the standard folders (Inbox, Junk, Outbox, etc.), right-click On This Computer and select New Folder. Then make sure that On This Computer is selected in the folder view of the dialog box that appears. Type a name and click Create.

You can also create second-level folders, which will effectively be "inside" other folders and will appear indented below their parent folder within the list. For example, you might want to create a series of folders within the main Inbox folder to sort your mail from various individuals or organizations. To do this, right-click Inbox, select New Folder, and give the folder a name in the dialog box that appears, as shown in Figure 27-6.

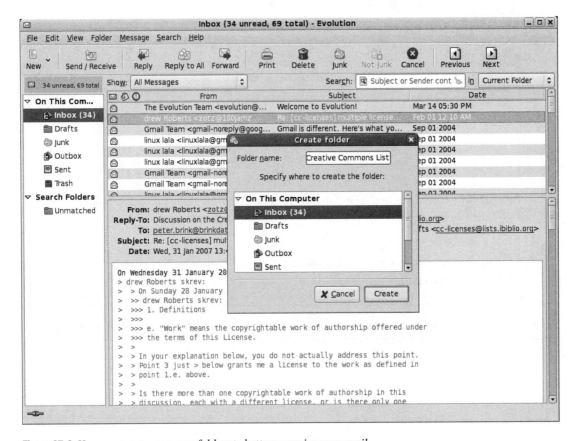

Figure 27-6. *You can create your own folders to better organize your mail.*

You can then drag and drop messages into the new folders, or simply right-click them and select Move to Folder. This can be useful if you wish to select a handful of messages by holding down the Ctrl key. All you need to do then is right-click one of them and select Move to Folder.

You can also copy messages from one location to another, thus producing two copies of the same message: simply right-click the message and select Copy to Folder. Then select the folder from the list. Alternatively, you can hold down the Ctrl key while you drag the message to the new location.

Dealing with Junk E-Mail

Evolution includes intelligent junk mail filtering. Any mail that Evolution thinks is spam or junk mail will end up in the Junk folder. When you first start using Evolution, you should check the folder regularly, because there's a chance Evolution might have made a mistake. However, this is a good thing, because by right-clicking the message and selecting Mark As Not Junk, the Evolution junk mail filter will be able to better understand what to consider as junk in your particular Inbox.

In a similar way, if you find that Evolution misses a junk e-mail and it ends up in your Inbox, you can right-click it and select Mark As Junk.

To empty the Junk folder, select all the messages (Ctrl+A), right-click, select Delete, and then click Folder ➤ Expunge. Bear in mind that, as with any folder, once the messages are deleted, they will appear in the Trash view where, if necessary, they can be restored.

Sorting and Filtering Messages

You can filter incoming messages according to practically any criteria, including who sent the message, its subject line, words within the body of the mail, its size, or even if it has attachments. Coupled with the ability to create folders, this allows you to automatically sort messages as soon as they're received.

To set up filters, click Edit ➤ Message Filters. Click the Add button and, in the Add Rule window, start by giving the new rule a descriptive name by which you'll be able to recognize it in the future. You might think that this isn't important, but you might create tens, if not hundreds, of filters, so being able to identify filters will be very helpful.

As shown in Figure 27-7, the Add Rule dialog box is split into two halves: the "Find items that meet the following criteria" section, and the Then section.

The Find items part is used to identify the mail. You can select to filter based on almost any criteria, such as who appears in the Sender field of the message, words that appear in the Subject line, the date sent, and so on. Simply select what you require from the drop-down list directly beneath the Add button. In most cases, you'll then need to specify details for the filter. For example, if you choose to filter by the address of the individual sending the e-mail, you'll need to provide that e-mail address.

■**Tip** Several Find items rules can be created. For example, you could create a rule to filter by the address of the sender, and then click the Add button to create another rule to filter by text in the Subject line. By clicking If All Criteria Are Met in the Find Items drop-down list, the mail will be filtered only if both conditions are met. By selecting If Any Criteria Are Met from the drop-down list, the mail will be filtered if either condition is met.

Figure 27-7. *Creating message filters lets you automatically organize your e-mail as soon as it's received.*

Once you've set the If conditions, you need to select from the Then section of the dialog box. This tells Evolution what to do with the filtered mail. The obvious course of action is to move the e-mail to a particular folder, which is the default choice, but you can also delete the e-mail, set a particular flag, beep, or even run a particular program! As with the Find items rules, you can set more than one condition here, so you can have Evolution beep and then delete the message, for example.

TIPS FOR USING EVOLUTION E-MAIL

In many ways, Evolution is similar to e-mail programs you might have used in the past, but also has a few of its own quirks and idiosyncratic ways of working. Here are a handful of preferences you might want to set to have Evolution behave in a more familiar way:

- *Forward e-mail inline*: If you attempt to forward a message, Evolution will attach it to a new message as a file. The person receiving the e-mail will then need to double-click the file to view the forwarded e-mail, which can be confusing. The solution is to make Evolution forward the message *inline*, which is to say that Evolution will quote it beneath the new mail message, like Microsoft e-mail programs. To do this, click Edit ➤ Preferences, click Composer Preferences on the left side of the dialog box, click the Forward Style drop-down list, and select Inline.

- *Change the plain text font*: Any messages sent to you in plain text format, rather than HTML, will appear in the message preview pane in a Courier-style font. To have messages display in a more attractive and readable typeface, click Edit ➤ Preferences, select Mail Preferences on the left side of the dialog box, and then remove the check from Use the Same Fonts As Other Applications. In the Terminal Font drop-down list, select an alternative font. The standard Fedora font is called Sans and is a good choice.

- *Always create HTML e-mail*: Evolution defaults to plain text e-mail for any new messages you create. If you want to always create HTML messages, click Edit ➤ Preferences, click Composer Preferences on the left side of the dialog box, and then put a check alongside Format Messages in HTML.

- *Empty Trash on exit*: To automatically expunge all folders of deleted messages each time you quit Evolution, click Edit ➤ Preferences, click Mail Preferences on the left side of the program window, and put a check alongside Empty Trash Folders on Exit.

Creating Search Folders

Evolution's search folder feature is a more powerful alternative to message filters. Using search folders, you can filter mail based on a similar set of criteria, but you can choose to include messages in the results that might be *associated* with the filtered messages. For example, if you choose to filter by a specific individual's e-mail address, you can select to have any replies you sent to that person included in the results, rather than simply messages received from her. In addition, you can apply search folders to specific e-mail folders on an ongoing basis, rather than all incoming e-mail.

You can create a new search folder by clicking Edit ➤ Search Folders. As with creating message filters, clicking the drop-down box beneath the Add button will let you select a criteria by which you can filter. The choices are broadly similar to those for message filters, in that you can filter by e-mail address, size of e-mail, message body, and so on.

In the Include Threads drop-down box, you can select what kind of results you would like the search filter to return:

- None simply returns e-mail messages matching the criteria.

- All Related returns every single message that is associated with the criteria.

- Replies returns results that include replies to the messages returned via the filter.

- Replies and Parents returns results that include replies and also any initial message that you or others might have sent that inspired the message included in the filter results.

- No Reply or Parent returns results that include messages that were sent to you originally and you did not reply to.

Search folder results are listed under the relevant folders on the left side of the Mail mode window.

The search folder feature is very powerful and worth spending some time investigating.

Contacts

Evolution includes a powerful contacts manager component that can catalog information about individuals. At its most basic, the contact manager stores e-mail addresses for use within the e-mail component of Evolution, but you can enter significant additional data about each individual, including addresses, phone numbers, fax numbers, and even a photograph for easy identification. This should allow Evolution to become your sole personal information manager.

To switch to Contacts mode, click the button at the bottom-left side of the program window, or click View ➤ Window ➤ Contacts. Once in Contacts mode, you can view information in several ways. Click View ➤ Current View to choose from the following views:

Address Cards: This is the default view and shows the contacts as virtual index cards arranged alongside each other at the top of the program window. Click the scroll bar beneath the cards to move through them.

Phone List: This shows the contact information as a simple list, arranged vertically, with various elements of the contact's personal information listed alongside, such as phone numbers and e-mail addresses.

By Company: This organizes the data in a similar way to Phone List view but sorted by the company the contacts work for (if such data has been entered into the contact entries).

Adding or Editing Contact Information

By far, the best way of initially building up your contacts list is to right-click e-mail addresses at the head of messages and select Add to Addressbook. This will add a simple contact record consisting of the individual's name and e-mail address.

When using Microsoft mail applications, simply replying to an e-mail from an individual is enough to add that contact to your address book. Evolution is capable of this behavior, too, but the feature isn't activated by default. To set this up, click Edit ➤ Preferences, click Mail Preferences on the left side of the dialog box, and then click the Automatic Contacts tab. Now put a check in the box marked Automatically Create Entries in the Addressbook When Responding to Mail.

You can then edit the contact details by double-clicking the entry in Contacts mode. This will let you enter a variety of information, as shown in Figure 27-8. To import a photo for this contact, click the top-left icon. You can use any picture here, and you don't need to worry about its size, because it will be resized automatically by Evolution (although its aspect ratio will be preserved). The imported photo will appear on the contact's virtual card.

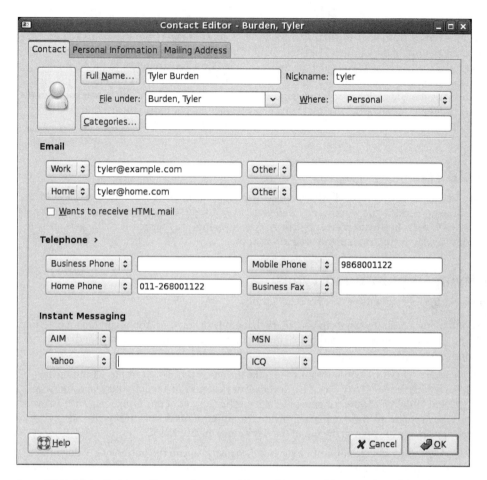

Figure 27-8. *A lot of information can be entered for each contact. You can also add a photo by clicking the button at the top left.*

Creating a Contact List

Contact lists are simply lists of e-mail addresses. Once a list is created, you can right-click its entry in the address book, and then choose to send a message to the list or forward it to someone else as a vCard. The obvious use of contact lists is for sending group e-mail messages.

Note A vCard is a virtual business card. Effectively, it's a small file that contains personal information. As well as personal data, vCards can contain pictures and audio clips. They're understood by practically all business-level e-mail programs, including Microsoft Outlook and Apple Mail.

To create a contact list, click the small down arrow next to the New button in Contacts mode, and select the option from the list. Then simply click and drag contacts from the main program pane onto the bottom of the Contact List editor pane. This will automatically add their names and e-mail addresses. Alternatively, you can type their e-mail addresses manually into the Members field, and then click the Add button, which can be useful if the individual isn't in your contact list.

By checking the Hide Addresses When Sending Mail to This List option, you can ensure that the e-mail addresses are added to the BCC field of a new message, so people on the list don't see the others on the list.

Calendars

The Calendars mode of Evolution allows you to keep an appointments diary. Entries can be added in half-hour increments to the working day, and you can easily add events to days that are weeks, months, or even years in advance. Viewing a day's appointments is as simple as clicking its entry in the monthly view at the top right of the program window.

Specifying Appointment Types

You can make the following three types of diary entries:

Appointments: These are events in your diary that apply to you only. You might have a meeting with an external supplier, for example, or might simply want to add a note to your diary to remind you of a particular fact.

All Day Events: These are appointments that take the entire day. For example, a training day could be entered as an all day event. However, all day events don't block your diary, and you can still add individual appointments (after all, just because your day is taken up with an event doesn't mean you won't need to make individual appointments during the event). All day events appear as a blue bar at the top of the day's entry in your diary.

Meetings: Meetings are like appointments, but they also give you the option of inviting others to attend. The invitations are sent as iCal attachments to e-mail, so users of Microsoft Outlook should be able to reply to them (provided Outlook is properly configured; see the program's documentation for details, and note that iCal is sometimes referred to as RFC 2446/2447). Once an individual receives a meeting invitation, he can click to accept or decline. Once Evolution receives this response, the individual's acceptance or declination will be automatically added to the diary entry.

Adding or Editing a Diary Entry

To add a new diary entry, simply select the day in the monthly view at the top right. Then right-click and choose either an appointment, an all day event, or a meeting. To edit an already existing diary entry, double-click its entry in the list.

At its most basic, all an appointment needs in order to be entered into your diary is some text in the Summary field, as shown in Figure 27-9. By default, appointments and meetings are assumed to be all day events. You can change this by clicking the All Day Event button. Now you can set the time for your appointment and meetings. You can specify the duration of your meeting in number of hours it will last or specify the time it will end. For what it's worth, appointments can go on for days—just select "until" from the "for" drop-down box and set a different date!

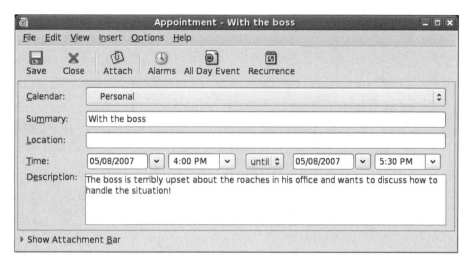

Figure 27-9. *When creating a new appointment, you can add all the details you need, but don't forget to set the end time!*

By clicking the Recurrence tab, you can set the appointment to be booked into your diary according to certain intervals. Start by putting a check in the This Appointment Recurs box, and then select a time interval. For example, selecting 1 week will mean that the appointment is booked into your diary automatically on a weekly basis. After this, select a day of the week for the recurring appointment. Following this, you must either specify the number of recurrences or simply select Forever from the drop-down list. Then click the Add button to add the details of the recurring event to the appointment.

In the case of meeting appointments, you can click the Invitations tab to invite others to the meeting, via iCal invitations that will be sent out by e-mail as soon as you've finished creating the appointment. Simply click the Add button and then, in the empty field that appears, start typing the contact name of the individual you want to invite. If the person is already in your contacts list, the name will be automatically completed, but you can also type individual e-mail addresses.

Clicking the Scheduling tab will show you who can and can't attend, according to replies to the invitations sent out (obviously, this is a feature you'll be using after you've initially created the appointment). On the left side of the dialog box, you will see the list of attendees and also their status: whether they've accepted or not, or whether they've sent a busy/tentative reply (in which case, you might choose to reschedule the meeting).

Tasks

Tasks mode is the simplest component within Evolution and allows you to create a to-do list. After you've made an entry, clicking the check box alongside it will mark it as completed. Completed items appear with a strike-through, as shown in Figure 27-10.

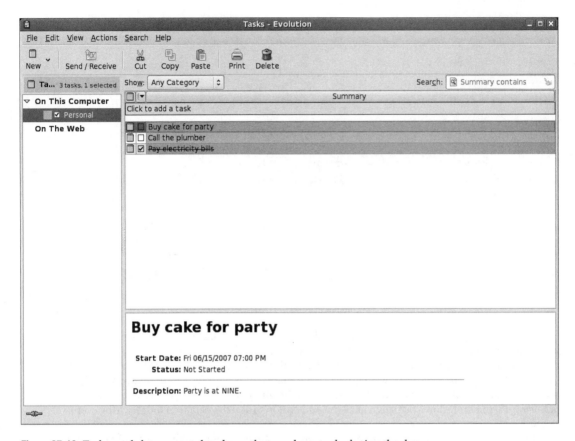

Figure 27-10. *Tasks mode lets you catalog chores that you have to do during the day.*

Switch to Tasks mode by clicking its button on the bottom-left side of the program window. To add a new task, click the bar that reads Click to Add a New Task. Type a description of the task, and then press Enter. You will then be able to enter further tasks in the same field.

Double-clicking a task allows you to fine-tune its details. For example, you can add a due date so that you'll know when the task must be completed. You can also add a description for future reference.

By clicking the Status Details button, you can also set a percentage figure for completion of the task, as well as its priority, ranging from Low to High.

Summary

This chapter has been a whistle-stop tour of Evolution's main features. We've looked at e-mail creation and organization, contacts management, working with the appointments calendar, and editing the task list.

Evolution is a powerful program. Be sure to take a look at its help documentation (Help ➤ Contents) to learn more about it.

In Part 7 of the book, starting with the next chapter, we look at the techniques you need to know to keep your Fedora system running smoothly. Chapter 28 explains how to install Linux software.

PART 7

■ ■ ■

Keeping Your System Running

CHAPTER 28

■■■

Installing and Removing Software

One of the fun things about running any operating system is the ability to expand it—for adding in new software over time to improve your workflow, or just for entertainment value.

Linux is blessed in this regard, because tens of thousands of software titles are available to meet just about every need. However, once you've tracked down the ideal software title, there's still one barrier to overcome: actually installing it on your system.

Installing software under Fedora isn't the same as with Windows. With Fedora, users are afforded a lot more power over what happens to their system, but this comes at the expense of needing to take a little time to understand the terminology and techniques.

In this chapter, you'll learn how to use the various tools available for managing software on Fedora; but first, we'll start with some basics of software installation.

Software Installation Basics

Installing programs on Windows is relatively easy. If you wish to use the Winamp media player, for example, you can browse to the appropriate web site, download the installer .exe file, and install the software.

Although you might not realize it, a lot of work goes into making this seemingly simple task possible. Once the original software has been created by the programmers, it must be made into a form that you, the end user, can run on your computer.

The first thing to happen is that the software is *compiled*. This is the process of turning the source code created by programmers into an actual file (or set of files) that can be used on a daily basis. On most systems, compiling source code involves a lot of number crunching. This takes time—whole days, in some cases—and this is why it isn't normal practice to compile the source code every time you want to run the program.

Once the program files have been compiled, there needs to be a way they can be installed on various systems and easily transported across the Internet. This is where packaging comes into the equation. Programs usually consist of many files. If each program file were made individually available, some would likely get lost or corrupted, and the program wouldn't work. Therefore, the files are usually combined into a single archive file. In addition, third-party system files are added to ensure compatibility on all computers, and an extra program, called an installer, is added so that users can quickly get the files onto their systems.

All this means that to be able to install a program like Winamp on Windows, you just need to download the installer.exe file and run it once. No more work is required.

Linux is a little more involved, largely because it never assumes that users want their environment to be simplistic and their options limited. However, most Linux distributions still embrace the paradigm of packaging software into a single, easily transported file.

Formats of Linux Installation Files

If you visit the web site of a particular Linux application, you may find that it's available to download in a number of different formats. The program will almost certainly be available as *source code*—the original listing that the developer created. But it might also be available as a binary or a package file.

■**Note** Linux isn't the only operating system for which open source programs are created and used. There are open source projects for both Windows and Apple Macintosh, many of which are hosted at the SourceForge.net web site (`http://sourceforge.net/`). Many other less widely used operating systems also rely on open source software to a greater or lesser extent.

Here are the formats by which Linux software is normally distributed:

Source code: Programmers write their software in various programming languages, such as C and C++, and the code that results is known as *source code*. To make source code usable, it must be compiled into a *binary file*. Because the cornerstone of the Linux philosophy is the sharing of source code, you'll almost always find the source code of a program available at the developer's web site. You can then download and compile this on your own system (or, if you're so inclined, study the source code to further your understanding). Although compiling source code isn't very hard to do, it's more convenient to download either a binary version of the program or a package.

Binary files: You might find binary files available at the developer's web site. This means that the programmer has taken his own source code and, as a service to users of the program, compiled it so that it's ready for use as soon as it's downloaded. For example, this is how Linux versions of Mozilla Foundation software like Thunderbird and Firefox are currently distributed if you download them directly from `www.mozilla.com`. Sometimes binary files come with scripts to help you install them. However, in most cases, you simply place the files in a convenient location on your hard disk, and then run them from there.

■**Note** In the case of both source code and binary files, the files usually come in a *tarball*, which is a single archive file containing other files. A tarball by definition isn't compressed, but usually, either the bzip2 or gzip tools are used to shrink the file to ease transportation across the Internet.

Self-installing binaries: Some larger programs are made available as self-installing binary files. This comes very close to the way Windows works in that, when the file is executed, a GUI-based installation wizard takes you through installation. If you download OpenOffice.org from the official web site (`www.openoffice.org/`), for example, you end up with a single 80-plus MB file, which you then simply run from the command line to install the program.

Package files: In many cases, you'll find that a package file of the program is available. In this case, someone has compiled the software files and put them all together in a single, easily transportable file. Package files for Fedora end with `.rpm` file extensions, but other Linux distributions use other package formats, such as `.deb` (Debian-based distributions like Ubuntu).

■**Note** As a blanket rule, an installation package created for one distribution won't be compatible with another. It's possible to use a program called alien under Fedora, which aims to convert packages between distributions and different package formats, but this should be seen as a last resort. The first resort is to simply obtain a package specifically designed for your Linux distribution.

Package Management

Of all the formats for Linux software distribution, packages are by far the most common and popular. Fedora uses packages, as do nearly all other Linux distributions. In fact, the Fedora DVD contains thousands of packages (see Figure 28-1).

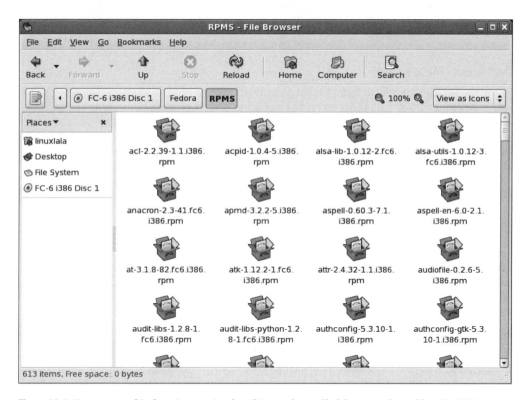

Figure 28-1. *Every part of Fedora is contained within, and installed from, package files. The DVD contains thousands of them.*

It's important to understand what a package file actually is and what it contains. With Windows, an installation.exe file is effectively a piece of software combined with an archive of files. When you run the executable, it triggers a small program contained within it that then unpacks the contents of the file and installs them to the hard disk.

In contrast, package files used by Fedora merely contain the program files, along with a handful of configuration files to ensure that the software is set up correctly. Package files are useless without the various pieces of software that are used to manipulate them and do the hard work of installing, removing, and querying them. This software is known as the *package management system*.

A well-implemented package management system is able to install programs, upgrade them, and uninstall them, all with just a few keystrokes or clicks of the mouse on the user's part. Package systems vastly reduce the amount of work required to get new software onto your system, and they make maintenance tasks easy, too.

The package management system builds its own database so that it knows exactly what programs are installed at any one time, so you can simply query the database rather than searching the application menu or the hard disk. The package management system also keeps track of version numbers. This gives you much more control over the software on your system and makes updating easy. Additionally, if a program starts to act strangely, its configuration files can simply be refreshed using the package manager. There's no need to uninstall and reinstall the software, as is so often the case with Windows programs.

Dependency Management

One of the key features offered by any package management system is *dependency management*. Put simply, the package manager must ensure that if you install a piece of software, any additional software it relies on to work properly is already present on the system. If the software isn't present, the package manager must either resolve the situation automatically or ask you what to do.

Sometimes the software you want to install might depend on other programs on your system, but more often, the dependencies take the form of system libraries. Library files contain pieces of code that are equivalent to .dll files under Windows—not software that you, as a user, will use directly. The key library on a Fedora system is the GNU C Library, without which the Linux kernel couldn't function. But practically every program has its own needs when it comes to library files, and these requirements must be handled by the package management software.

■**Note** One reason why the Windows installation files are so large is that they typically come with all the system files that they need in case those system files are not already present on the system. In other words, dependency isn't an issue under Windows because everything comes supplied. Windows isn't alone in this regard; installation files for the Apple Macintosh are similar.

Dependency management doesn't just mean adding in packages that a piece of software needs. It might also mean *removing* packages already present on your system. This might happen if certain packages are incompatible with new software you want to install—something that's referred to as *package conflict*. In addition, sometimes you might want to remove a package that other packages rely on—a situation known as *reverse dependency*. In such a case, the package manager either must stop you from removing that software to avoid breaking the software that depends on it, or remove the reverse-dependency packages as well. In most cases, it will ask you what you wish to do.

DEPENDENCY HELL

If you try to install certain software packages, you will very likely find that they depend on other packages, such as software libraries. These other packages must either be present on the system already or installed at the same time for the software to work correctly. Fedora will attempt to take care of the latter automatically. In a similar way, removing software also means that other packages that rely on that particular software must also be removed, because of reverse dependency.

Dependency hell is what happens when you have chains of dependencies. For example, let's say you install a program called Oscar. You're then told that this depends on another program called BigBird, which isn't installed. Fine, you think, I'll just add BigBird to the same installation command. But it then transpires that Big-Bird has its own dependency of Snuffleupagus. You add that, too. Alas! Snuffleupagus has its own dependency of MrHooper.

This can carry on for some time. It's less of a problem when installing software, because the sourcing of dependencies is usually automated, but it can be a problem when you're installing packages at the command line.

The concept of dependency hell is a holdover from pre-yum Red Hat Linux. Back then, you had to resolve all dependency issues manually, but nowadays, yum ensures that you never have to worry about dependency chains.

Package Management System Components

Fedora's package management system has two components: RPM and yum.

RPM is the most basic part of the system. It's used to install and uninstall software, and it can also be used to query any software that's currently installed. It's like the manager in a warehouse who is tasked with knowing exactly which boxes have been stored where. The manager doesn't know where the boxes come from, and he doesn't know anything about boxes outside his warehouse. He just manages the boxes that are delivered to him and that are stored in his warehouse.

Note RPM stands for Red Hat Package Manager, which is a technology that was created by Red Hat some time ago. It's still used on Red Hat–based versions of Linux, such as Fedora Core and CentOS, as well as a number of other distributions, such as SUSE and Mandriva. You might think it strange that software created for use in one distribution is used in rival versions of Linux, but one of the cornerstones of the world of Linux is the philosophy of sharing.

RPM is aware of dependency issues and will inform you if you don't have the necessary software for a specified package to work correctly. But it does not have the means to fix the situation automatically. Continuing with our analogy, this is like a warehouse manager who doesn't order more boxes. That's not his job. He will just tell you if boxes delivered to him are missing some of their components.

To address dependency issues, an additional layer of background software, called yum, sits on top of RPM. Yum is unique in that when you install any software using yum, any dependency issues will be worked out for you behind the scenes. In other words, the dependencies too are automatically installed.

Note Yum stands for Yellow dog Updater, Modified. It is a complete rewrite of Yellow dog Updater, used in Yellow Dog Linux, which is another Red Hat–based distribution. Yum was developed originally to update and manage the Red Hat Linux systems used at Duke University. It has been part of every Fedora Core release, and has since been adopted by several distributions, including Yellow Dog Linux!

Yum can manage dependencies because it's designed to work with *software repositories*. These are collections of software, from which the user can search and install packages. More often than not, these software repositories are online, but that's not always the case. The Fedora DVD supplied with this book is one large software repository, for example.

COMPONENTS OF AN RPM FILE

Any RPM package file consists of three basic parts: a header, a signature, and the software archive. The header contains the package's name, the package's version, a complete list of all the files the RPM file contains, a description of the package, a list of tools it requires to function properly, and a lot more details.

All this information is needed to ensure that all the packages required by the particular package to function are already installed. Also, none of the already installed packages should break, or stop working, when a new RPM package is installed. As such, the header also contains a list of packages that it conflicts with so that users can be warned before installation.

The signature section of the RPM file contains information that can be used to verify the authenticity and integrity of the package. It ensures that the package has not been changed by anyone.

The archive consists of the actual files that comprise the package. It is sometimes referred to as the payload.

Finally, every RPM package file has one more section besides these three. This is the *lead*, which identifies the package as an RPM file.

Yum relies on the RPM system to take care of the actual installation. Effectively, RPM and yum are two sides of the same coin.

■Note When we talk about RPM and yum, we are referring to behind-the-scenes system components of Fedora that are normally used by other pieces of software. Yum is used by the software management tools Pirut and Pup (discussed in the "Managing Software via the GUI" section later in this chapter). Yum is in fact a command-line utility. It's also possible to use the RPM system from the command line, as described in the "Managing Software from the Shell" section later in this chapter.

As you might have realized, the package management system means that software installation (and removal) is a fundamentally different proposition under Linux than under Windows or Mac OS X. If you want to install new software, the first place to look is the Fedora software repositories, such as the repository contained on the installation DVD. In fact, the DVD contains more than 3,000 packages, which represent most of the popular software currently available for Linux.

It's comparatively rare under Linux to visit a web site and download a package file for installation, as is often the case for Windows users. The only time this normally happens is if you can't find what you're looking for in the official repositories.

■Tip Software repositories don't have to be "official," or sanctioned by the Fedora Project, to be used under Fedora. Sometimes, you might opt to add extra repositories that contain particular software. For example, you might recall that in Chapters 18 and 19 we described how to add repositories so that you can install the multimedia codecs to play DVDs, MP3s, and so on. This is necessary because there are certain licensing issues with MP3 and DVD formats that conflict with Fedora's policies, so no official repository is available for these codecs.

SOFTWARE VERSIONS

Because most Linux software is open source, a curious thing happens when it comes to software versions. Rather than there being just one "official" version of a program, such as with most Windows software (where you must download the official version of the file), many individuals and organizations take the source code, compile it, and make their own package files available for others to use.

For example, virtually all the software installed with Fedora has been compiled by Fedora developers. This means that it can be quite different from what's "officially" available at the programmer's web site. In some cases, the source code is tweaked so that notorious bugs are fixed, or a different look and feel is applied to the software so that it integrates with the distribution. Often the configuration files are changed so that the software won't con-flict with other software packages and will work properly under Fedora.

The original programmer doesn't mind when such things happen, because this way of working is part and parcel of open source software. In fact, the programmer is likely to encourage such tweaking.

Because of this, the first place to look if you want any additional software is not the developer's web site, but the Fedora DVD. This way, you'll get an officially sanctioned Fedora Linux release that will fit in with the rest of your system and won't require much, if any, additional work to get up and running.

The tools used to manage software are detailed in this chapter. First, we'll look at graphical software that can be used to manage software, and then we'll look at the command-line tools you can use.

■**Tip** Depending on the software's release cycle, the version available on the DVD might be obsolete, and there may already be a newer version available. In such a case, it is best to install the software from the Internet using Fedora's package management tools. Refer to Chapter 9 for details on how to update your system online.

Managing Software via the GUI

To install and remove software via Fedora's GUI, you can use Pirut. Additionally, you can use Pup, a package updater, to manage the available package updates. Both these tools were released with Fedora Core 5. Of the two options, the package manager, Pirut, is the tool to use when installing or removing software. It has an easy-to-use interface and provides more details about the packages. Pup (short for Package Updater), on the other hand, is a replacement for up2date, which was the de facto software updater used in previous Fedora releases. Pup is useful when you wish to apply any new package updates.

Using Pirut to Install Software

You can start Pirut by going to Application ➤ Add/Remove Software. You'll need to enter the root password to use Pirut.

FINDING YOUR WAY AROUND PIRUT

Pirut offers a tabbed navigation window so that you can easily manage your software. You will see three horizontal tabs at the top: Browse, Search, and List (as shown in the following illustration). When you launch the package manager, you are dropped to the Browse tab. From here, you can access the seven different categories that the software is divided into. Each of the categories is listed on the left, and the right pane displays further software sections for each of the categories.

The seven categories are Desktop Environments, Applications, Development, Servers, Base System, Languages, and Uncategorized.

When you click any of the categories or their subsections, a description appears in the field immediately below the two panes. Each category has its own set of sections of software—so, for instance, when you click Applications, the right pane will display various application-specific sections like Office/Productivity, Graphics, Sound and Video, and so forth.

To get a list of software in any of these sections, you need to click the Optional packages button, at the bottom-right corner of Pirut's window. A message similar to "41 of 64 optional packages selected" will be displayed just above the Optional packages button (the actual numbers depend on how many packages you choose during installation). In this case, it means that there are 64 packages available under this section of software, out of which 41 are already installed on your system.

Clicking the Optional packages button brings up the Packages window, which has an alphabetical list of packages available under that section.

Every package in the Packages window has a check box before the name of the package. A check mark before a package's name signifies that the package is already installed. The same is true for the subsections within each category—a check mark next to a subsection of software means that some package from this section is installed on your system.

But enough about the Browse tab! Let's briefly discuss the other tabs, List and Search.

From the List tab, you can choose to view all the packages available through Fedora's repository, or just a list of packages already installed on your system. The Search tab comes in handy when you are looking for some software but can't remember its name. You can use keywords when searching for packages. For example, when looking for a screenshot tool, search for "screenshot." Pirut looks through the header files for each of the packages in the repositories to find a match.

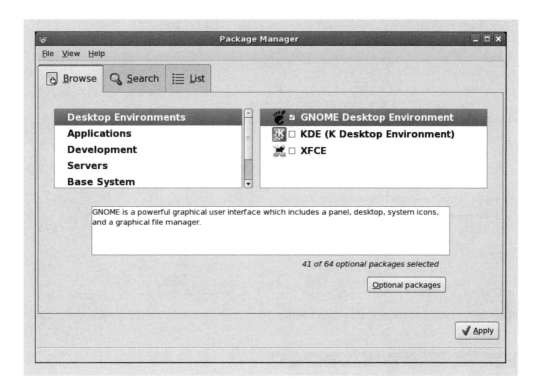

Let's say you need to install some instant messaging software to chat with your friends. From the Browse tab, click Applications. Scroll through the software sections in the right pane and click Graphical Internet. Clicking the Optional packages button now will bring up an alphabetical list of software in this section (see Figure 28-2). Select pidgin by putting a check in the box, and then click Close.

Note Pidgin is an instant messaging client that supports multiple protocols, including AIM, Yahoo, MSN, and Jabber.

Clicking Apply will install Pidgin on your system. Before installing any software, though, the package manager resolves its dependencies. To do this, the package manager reads through the header file from Pidgin's RPM, which lists all the packages that it requires to work, as described in the "Components of an RPM File" sidebar earlier in the chapter. So you need not worry about packages that Pidgin depends upon for functioning properly.

When you install any package, Pirut gives you a 20-second countdown so that you can look at the list of dependencies before continuing with the installation (see Figure 28-3). A downside of the package manager is that it never informs you about the amount of disk space the newly installed packages will take, or about the size of the dependencies. It works these things in the background, displaying only the name of each package that it's downloading and then telling you when installation is complete.

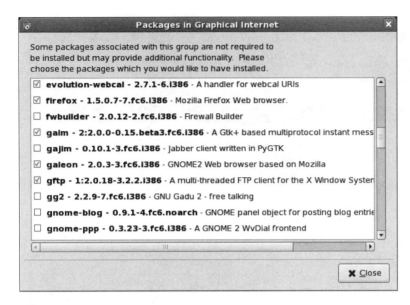

Figure 28-2. *Clicking the Optional packages button brings up an alphabetical list of packages.*

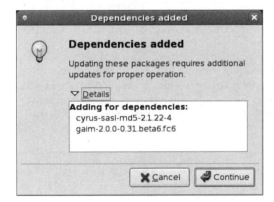

Figure 28-3. *A list of dependencies when installing Pidgin. The list comes up if you click Details within 20 seconds.*

Tip You can use the package manager to install software from different sections or categories. You don't have to install software one by one. Just select all the packages you need to install, and Pirut will resolve the dependency issues of all the selected packages and install them in turn.

Using Pirut to Remove Software

If you click Pirut's List tab, you're presented with a list of all the packages. From here, you can choose to view all the packages, only the installed packages, or only the available packages. A check mark next to the package name indicates that the package is already installed on your system. If you uncheck a box, the package manager marks the package for removal. You will be presented with a summary of actions that will be taken when you hit Apply.

The package manager is not very forthcoming in informing you about reverse dependencies. For example, if you choose to remove the Firefox web browser, Pirut asks whether you want to continue or cancel. It's only after you click Continue that Pirut looks through its database and tells you about reverse dependencies, by means of a pop-up window. At this point, you get a countdown timer that gives you 18 seconds to look at the list of dependent packages and cancel the operation. To view the dependencies, click Details.

Using Pirut to Search for Software

Sometimes, you might not be able to find some software where you expect it to be. For example, if you want to install the scrot screenshot tool, you'll probably look for it in the Graphics section. But it's not listed there. In such a scenario, you can use Search. Click Pirut's Search tab and type the name of the package. Pirut will then list all the packages associated with that software.

There may be instances when you want to install some package but can't quite remember its name. In such cases, you can use keywords that describe the purpose of the package to search. So, in the preceding example, you could simply search for "screenshot" or "screen capture," and Pirut would display all matching results.

Pirut does this by reading through header files of each of the RPM packages in the repositories and looking for a match. It will display any package that has the word you searched for in its name or description.

You can read a brief description of any package that is displayed as part of your search results by clicking that package, and then clicking the Package Details button (see Figure 28-4).

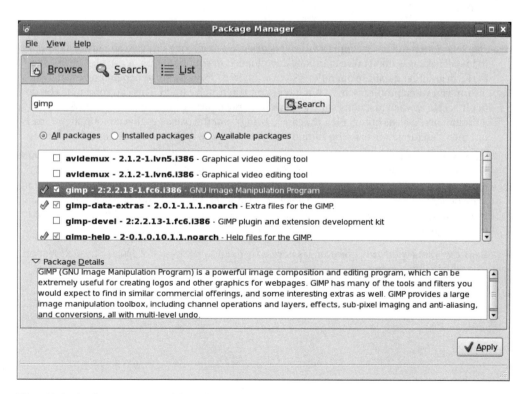

Figure 28-4. *The description is read from the RPM's header file and displayed in the Package Details section.*

Applying Package Updates with Pup

Pup is available from Application ➤ System Tools ➤ Software Updater. It lists all the package updates that are available for your system. These may be security updates, bug fixes, and so on.

■**Note**   Please refer to Chapter 9 to learn about applying security updates.

When you launch Pup, all the updates are selected by default. There is an icon in the system tray that keeps reminding you of these available updates. You can apply the updates from the system tray icon by clicking it and selecting Apply Updates, or you can apply the updates through the Pup menu by manually selecting the updates you wish to apply.

■**Note**   Both Pirut and Pup use yum to handle all the dependency issues. These tools are just graphical front-ends to yum.

Managing Software from the Shell

There may be times when command-line installation is necessary or just useful. Maybe your computer has gone wrong and you can't boot to a GUI, or maybe you're simply working at the shell and it's more convenient to type a few commands to install some software than it is to start up a GUI tool.

Two commands are available for software installation under Fedora:

rpm: This command has a simple syntax. It is designed to remove software already installed or to install packages that you've manually downloaded to your hard disk. It can also be used to perform granular database operations such as queries. rpm is aware of dependencies and will inform you when problems arise, but it relies on you to solve them. This can sometimes be difficult because, when installing software, rpm will only inform you about the actual system components, such as library files, that are missing—*not* the packages that contain them. rpm is not intended for new users, who should find yum far more appropriate for managing software.

Yum: As mentioned earlier in this chapter, yum is a command-line utility. It is designed to work with software repositories to install software. These repositories can be online, on a CD/DVD, or on your hard disk. Unlike rpm, yum is quite good at handling dependency issues. In fact, software dependencies are automatically taken care of when installing software using yum. When removing software, you'll find that solutions are automatically calculated so that all you need to do is agree or disagree. So, you should use yum whenever possible.

Before working with yum, however, it's necessary to know the basics of rpm, so the next section will start with that command.

DECODING PACKAGE FILENAMES

Fedora uses RPM package files for software installation. These are the files you'll sometimes have to deal with at the command line, and their filenames usually tell you everything you need to know about them. Here's one example:

```
firefox-1.5.0.7-7.fc6.i386.rpm
```

Dashes or periods are used to separate the four parts of each package name. At the beginning of the filename is the name of the program: the popular Firefox web browser, in this instance. Following this are the version numbers: 1.5.0.7. These aren't guaranteed to follow the version number conventions used by the developer of the software, although they're very similar in most cases. However, the numbers after the dash in a version number tend to refer to the specific version of the RPM file. Many different RPMs might be created from the same version of the original software, so it's necessary to have a way of telling the different RPMs apart. This number is sometimes referred to as the *release number*.

After the name and version number is the platform on which the RPM file will work. i386 indicates that this program will work on all Intel 80386-compatible processors—anything including a Pentium chip and above. i386 refers to the numbering system used in CPU manufacturing.

In some instances, you might find packages stipulating i686, indicating that they're designed for Pentium II processors and above. Also, many RPM files simply indicate i586, which means that they'll work on any processor from 80586 upward, including the Pentium and Pentium II, and all subsequent Intel, AMD, IBM, and other improvements. Many packages are listed as noarch, which means that they'll work on any processor and system.

The Fedora Project produces a version of Fedora Core that is optimized for the new 64-bit range of chips, such as the AMD Athlon 64. Unfortunately, RPM files compiled for use on these chips won't work on 32-bit systems, which comprise the majority of computers in use today. Such files are usually marked with an x86_64 extension.

Using rpm to Install and Remove Software

Using the rpm command, you can perform nearly all software installation and removal tasks on Fedora. All the rpm commands listed here must be run as the root user.

Installing Software Using rpm

The rpm command is never used by itself; it is controlled by various command-line options. Consider the following example:

```
rpm -i firefox-1.5.0.7-7.fc6.i386.rpm
```

The -i command option tells the rpm command to install the specified file. If you're updating software with a newer version, you can use the -U option instead. In fact, using -U all the time is a good idea because, if the program isn't installed, rpm is clever enough to realize that and will install the program instead.

Let's try this out: *fortune* is a fun command-line program that displays a pithy and/or witty saying whenever you run it. It can be found on the Fedora DVD. Insert the DVD and open a shell window. Then switch to the root user before using rpm to install the program:

```
su
[Enter root password]
rpm -U /media/FC-6_DVD/fedora/RPMS/fortune -1.0-870.i586.rpm
```

You can then run your new software by typing `fortune` at the command-line prompt. The trouble with running this command is that it will go through the process of installing the file, but give little, if any, feedback or indication of progress. Because of this, many people add the `-v` and `-h` command options. The `-v` option specifies verbose output, meaning that more information is fed back to the user. The `-h` option simply causes `rpm` to indicate its progress with a progress bar consisting of hash symbols.

Putting all this together forms what many consider the standard command that should be issued to install a package you've manually downloaded:

```
rpm -Uvh fortune-1.0-870.i586.rpm
```

You can specify more than one file for installation at the same time, simply by listing the package names one after the other, separated by a space:

```
rpm -Uvh package1.rpm package2.rpm package3.rpm
```

QUERYING WITH RPM

It's well worth reading the `rpm` man page because `rpm` is packed with features, all of which are accessed by command-line options. Perhaps the most useful, other than software installation and removal, is the query option: `-q`. The query option is unusual because it has its own set of command options. Anything that appears *after* `-q` is considered a query option.

By default, using `-q` without any query options queries installed RPM files (the main database). This is handy if you want to explore the list of installed programs. For example, typing `rpm -q nautilus` will show whether the Nautilus package is installed. The `-qa` option, used without specifying a package, will list all of the installed programs.

To query an RPM file that's not installed, you need to add the `-p` option and then specify the package filename. Used together, the `-qp` options will tell you what program is contained within the specified RPM file—nothing more. If you want a listing of the files inside the package, add `-l`. Using `-i` will return some additional information about the program. Using all these command options together will reveal all the useful data the specified package has to offer:

```
rpm -qpli packagename | less
```

Notice that this example pipes the output into `less`, because this command can sometimes return quite a lot of information, which can scroll off the screen.

Removing Software Using rpm

Uninstalling an RPM file is just as easy as installing one. Simply specify the `-e` command option, like so:

```
rpm -e firefox
```

In most cases, this is quick and simple. Note that there's no need to specify anything other than the main program name, unless you have a number of programs on your system with similar filenames. If this is the case, `rpm` will prompt you for more information.

Resolving Dependency Issues with rpm

If you try to use the rpm command to install or remove software, you'll come up against its limitations pretty quickly in the form of dependency issues. As an example, let's try to install the Dogtail test tool from the Fedora DVD:

```
rpm -Uvh dogtail-0.6.0-1.fc6.noarch.rpm
```

Here's the output we saw on our test system:

```
error: Failed dependencies:
        pyspi >= 0.6.0 is needed by dogtail-0.6.0-1.fc6.noarch
        xorg-x11-server-Xvfb is needed by dogtail-0.6.0-1.fc6.noarch
```

A quick search of the Fedora DVD should reveal that both of these package files are available. You can now install them both using a command similar to the preceding one, and then try installing Dogtail.

However, note that there can be instances in which the DVD might not have all the files needed by a package. For instance, the pyspi and xorg packages might have their own dependencies. rpm's main failing is that it creates dependency chains.

■**Caution** Resolving any kind of dependency issues when using rpm is hard work. It's possible to do so, but it's far simpler to use yum to manage software (as described in the next section). So, you should use yum whenever possible, be it for installing new packages or removing software.

RPM SECURITY

When installing programs, it's vital that some mechanism exists to prove that the RPM files used are genuine. By its very nature, open-source software is open to abuse. A nefarious individual could alter the source code of a program, implanting something such as a Trojan routine that could steal data. After inserting the code, he could then compile and package the file as if it were the genuine article provided by Fedora or the original developer.

The simplest defense is to make sure that you download only from web sites you can trust, such as that of Fedora itself. You can also use the RPM GNU Privacy Guard (GnuPG or GPG) key system.

Every officially released RPM file from Fedora is signed with a GPG hashcode. This hashcode is unique to each file and is generated based on the contents of the RPM using a so-called *secret key*, which only Fedora knows. All secret keys have public key counterparts, and the Fedora RPM public key is added by default to all Fedora installations. The public key can be used to confirm that the hashcode is correct, based on the contents of the file. This allows for a high degree of security.

RPM files also contain *checksums*, which can be used to confirm that the file isn't missing files, or that it doesn't contain altered files. Checksums are the results of mathematical formulas applied to the file. If the file changes in any way, no matter how small, then the checksum will change, too.

To check any kind of RPM file for both checksums and GPG hashcodes, type the following:

```
rpm -checksig -v filename.rpm
```

The results should read OK for each category. Of course, this depends on whether the GPG public key from the organization that created the RPM file is known to your system. If it's not, then you will see an error.

You can import public keys from third-party package sources using the following command:

```
rpm -import ftp://mysite.com/publickey
```

Ordinarily, the key is imported directly from an online source, such as an FTP server. You'll probably find the address listed somewhere on the web site, such as in the FAQ section. However, it could just as easily be imported from a text file on your own hard disk that you've downloaded, or that someone has given you. But, once again, this file must be from a trusted source. If you intend to use a new online RPM file archive, for example, you should make sure you use the key offered on its server. You certainly cannot assume that a site you stumble across using a search engine will contain an authentic public key for another download source.

Using Yum to Install and Remove Software

Yum handles all dependency issues, and should be considered the de facto software administration command-line tool. Yum should be run as root user for software installation and removal, although some tasks, such as searching through the software repositories, can be carried out as a normal user.

Installing Software Using Yum

Installing software via yum is easy. Just specify its name along with the `install` command option.

Note Not all yum commands need dashes before them. For instance, commands like `install`, `update`, and `info` do not require dashes. This is because yum requires at least one of these commands to function. You can optionally provide yum with certain configuration options, such as `-y` or `-R`, and these configuration options must be preceded by a dash. For a more detailed list of yum commands and configuration options, read the man page. To do so, open a terminal (Applications ➤ Accessories ➤ Terminal) and run the command `man yum`.

For example, to install the Dogtail test tool mentioned earlier, enter the following command:

```
yum install dogtail
```

First, yum searches through the database of packages contained in the software repositories to find out whether the software you're specifying is available. Assuming that it is, yum then attempts to work out if it needs any dependencies, and also if the dependencies themselves have dependencies (and so on).

Yum begins by downloading the RPM package for Dogtail. It then reads the header file contained in the RPM and informs you of any dependency issues. It turns out that the pyspi and xorg-x11-server-Xvfb packages are required by Dogtail. Yum also gives you some other information (most of which can be ignored), such as version number. The list of dependencies is then displayed in a nice table, and you're asked whether you wish to proceed:

```
Populating transaction set with selected packages. Please wait.
---> Downloading header for xorg-x11-server-Xvfb to pack into transaction set.
xorg-x11-server-Xvfb-1.1. 100% |=========================| 30 kB    00:01
---> Package xorg-x11-server-Xvfb.i386 0:1.1.1-47.7.fc6 set to be updated
---> Downloading header for pyspi to pack into transaction set.
pyspi-0.6.0-2.fc6.i386.rp 100% |=========================| 3.7 kB    00:00
---> Package pyspi.i386 0:0.6.0-2.fc6 set to be updated
--> Running transaction check
```

Dependencies Resolved

```
=============================================================================
 Package                  Arch      Version          Repository      Size
=============================================================================
Installing:
 dogtail                  noarch    0.6.1-1.fc6      updates         172 k
Installing for dependencies:
 pyspi                    i386      0.6.0-2.fc6      core             79 k
 xorg-x11-server-Xvfb     i386      1.1.1-47.7.fc6   updates         1.6 M

Transaction Summary
=============================================================================
Install       3 Package(s)
Update        0 Package(s)
Remove        0 Package(s)

Total download size: 1.8 M
Is this ok [y/N]: y
```

Note We have reproduced only a section of the entire output, in order to focus on the neat table that yum creates to inform you of dependencies.

Pressing the Y key installs all the packages specified. A hash bar indicates the installation's progress. Following this, you can run Dogtail by clicking its entry in the menu (Application ➤ Programming ➤ Dogtail). You can also launch Dogtail from the terminal by issuing the command `dogtail`.

USING YUM TO INSTALL RPMS

Since yum far outshines `rpm` in resolving dependencies, it is best to use yum whenever possible. But there might be times when a package that you wish to install is not available through the online repositories. In this case, your best bet is to install the RPM file.

Don't despair, yum still can serve you well. The `yum-localinstall` command can be used to install manually downloaded RPM packages. The command

```
yum localinstall dogtail-0.6.1-1.fc6.rpm
```

would install Dogtail from the RPM, using the online repositories to resolve any dependencies.

All packages available through Fedora's software repositories are signed with a GPG key. This means that Fedora can verify that the package you are about to install is not malicious. But sometimes it might be necessary for you to install unsigned RPM files. That is, you might want to install some software, but it might not be available through any of the official Fedora software repositories. In such a case, if you try to install the package with the `yum localinstall` command, yum would complain that you are trying to install an unsigned package and not proceed.

Open the `/etc/yum.conf` file in the Gedit text editor:

```
su -c "gedit /etc/yum.conf"
```

Replace the `gpgcheck=1` line with `gpgcheck=0`. Save the file and exit Gedit. You will now be able to install unsigned RPM's with the yum localinstall command. Once the package is installed, edit the `/etc/yum.conf` file and again set `gpgcheck=1`.

Removing Software Using Yum

Uninstalling software is as simple as installation. Just specify remove as the command option:

```
yum remove dogtail
```

You'll see a brief message informing you that yum is working out any dependency issues before the software is uninstalled.

When removing software, yum will work out any reverse-dependency issues, and simply mark all reverse dependencies for removal (including dependencies of dependencies, and so on).

■**Note** You need to be careful when removing software that you've previously installed with yum. This is because yum might not remove all the packages that it installed. Consider this analogy: to install software A, yum needs to install software B and C. But C needs package D to work. So yum installs B, C, and D for A to work. But when you remove A, yum might not remove B, C, or D, because they are not dependent on A to work. So effectively, you're left with three packages installed that you're not going to use.

Therefore, you should scrutinize any list of removal candidates very thoroughly. If you don't know what the packages in the list are, or what they do, then you shouldn't continue with the removal. Sometimes the best policy is simply to not remove the piece of software.

If yum suggests the removal of a particular package as a reverse dependency, but you don't know what the package does, you can use yum's info command to learn more. (This is discussed further in the upcoming "Querying Packages Using Yum" section.)

Searching Using Yum

You can use yum to search through the software repository lists for particular software packages. This will search all the repositories available to yum.

As you might expect, searching is easy—just use the search command option:

```
yum search browser
```

The search term is looked up in the description, summary, packager, and package name fields of an RPM's header. The results of the search are presented in a tabular fashion, like so:

```
# yum search clanbomber
Loading "installonlyn" plugin
Setting up repositories
Reading repository metadata in from local files

clanbomber.i386                    1.05-3.fc6              extras
Matched from:
clanbomber
ClanBomber is a free (GPL) Bomberman-like ....
```

The last line is a summary of the package. In this case, it runs into multiple lines. The search will display any exact matches that it can find. If it fails to find any exact match, it will list all packages related to the search term.

As you can see, if the package is not installed, yum will list the repository that contains it—in this case extras.

Querying Packages Using Yum

You can see a description of any package in Fedora's repositories by using the `info` command option:

```
yum info packagename
```

This will also tell you if the package is installed, and which repository it's contained in if it isn't. You'll also learn the version number of the package, and even the size (in megabytes), along with a handful of other details.

You can even get yum to list all dependencies of any package, like this:

```
yum deplist packagename
```

This will provide a list of dependency packages, along with the package that provides it. However, this is only one level deep, which is to say that dependencies of dependencies will not be calculated.

Remember the List option in Pirut? Yum can also be used to list all the installed and available packages. You need to use yum's `list` option for this:

```
yum list [options]
```

The `list` option has its own set of options. Using the `all` option will display all available and installed software. Yum will even inform you of all the obsolete packages if you use the `obsoletes` list option. Similarly, the `updates` option will display all packages with updates available in the repositories.

Updating Software Using Yum

The yum command can also update your entire system. By now, you're no doubt getting the hang of using yum and its preference for plain-English commands, so you might already have guessed the necessary command option:

```
yum update
```

This command will update every installed package. However, if you supply any package names, only those get updated. There is a special `updates` repository for this purpose. This is enabled by default and kicks into action as soon as you issue the `yum update` command. To see a list of packages for which a newer version is available, run this command:

```
yum list updates
```

You'll be presented with a very comprehensive list of packages. Just for the fun of it, run the command

```
rpm -q firefox
```

and you'll see the version of Firefox installed on your system. Compare it with the version of Firefox in the updates list, and you'll know why it's called the `updates` repository!

Adding Installation Sources

For the package management system to work correctly, it needs to have access to at least one software repository. The Fedora installation program configures yum to use its official repositories. You've already seen how to add a repository in Chapter 19. For most users, the default repositories are all that will be needed, but it's easy to add others.

Adding new software repositories is a very simple procedure. You simply need to edit the repository list in the `/etc/yum.repos.d/` directory.

This directory contains all the repositories. As you can see, all repository files need to have the `.repo` extension. To add third-party repositories, you need to create a new repository file (you need root privilege for this):

```
su -
[Enter password]
gedit /etc/yum..repos.d/new_repository.repo
```

This will open the file in the Gedit text editor. Before creating a new repository, let's read the `fedora-core.repo` file to get an idea of how the repository files are organized:

```
[core]
name=Fedora Core $releasever - $basearch
#baseurl=http://download.fedora.redhat.com/pub/fedora/\
linux/core/$releasever/$basearch/os/
mirrorlist=http://mirrors.fedoraproject.org/\
mirrorlist?repo=core-$releasever&arch=$basearch
enabled=1
gpgcheck=1
gpgkey=file:///etc/pki/rpm-gpg/RPM-GPG-KEY-\
fedora file:///etc/pki/rpm-gpg/RPM-GPG-KEY
```

As your repository file is still empty, copy this text to it, but replace the first line with the name of your repository, and also replace the `baseurl` and `mirrorlist` locations with your repository location. This may seem like a tall order, but it's actually fairly easy. Let's try to add the `livna` repository first, which can be done by simply installing an RPM. Then we'll set up our `Freshrpms` repository manually.

■**Tip** With Fedora Core 6, you can add extra repositories during initial installation. This is worth bearing in mind if you install Fedora Core on any other computer because it can save time and effort later on.

Some third-party repositories offer RPM files that you can install to enable those repositories. The RPM package has a script that will add the necessary files in order for you to use the repository. For instance, the `livna` repository can be activated by installing an RPM:

```
rpm -ivh http://rpm.livna.org/livna-release-6.rpm
```

■**Tip** You can install remote RPM packages as well as those you've downloaded to your hard disk.

This command installs the `livna` repositories. If you now browse to the `/etc/yum.repos.d/` directory, you will find a `livna.repo` file there. This file was added by the RPM you just installed. Yum uses all the files listed in this directory.

So, the next time you use yum, it will use the newly created `.repo` file.

Remember the `fedora-core.repo` file we looked at earlier? It's time to create a similar `.repo` file for the `Freshrpms` repository:

1. Open a terminal and run this command as the root user (`su -`):

   ```
   gedit /etc/yum.repos.d/freshrpms.repo
   ```

2. This will open an empty file. Copy the first line from the `fedora-core.repo` file and change it to `[freshrpms]`.

3. Now copy the second line from the `fedora-core.repo` file into the `freshrpms.repo` file. Add the word `Freshrpms` to the end of it so that the line reads as follows:

```
name=Fedora Core $releasever - $basearch - Freshrpms
```

The next line is the location of the repository:

```
#baseurl=http://ayo.freshrpms.net/fedora/linux/$releasever/$basearch/freshrpms
```

■**Note** The # at the beginning of the preceding line indicates that the repository is not used. For most configuration files under Linux, the hash symbol (#) signifies that the statement is commented out. That is, the text following a # is considered to be a comment, and is thus ignored.

---

4. You can also provide a mirror location if you wish. Just add this line to include a mirror:

```
mirrorlist= http://ayo.freshrpms.net/fedora/\
linux/$releasever/mirrors-freshrpms
```

5. Copy the next two lines from the `fedora-core.repo` file as is into the `freshrpms` file:

```
enabled=1
gpgcheck=1
```

6. Save the file and exit the Gedit text editor.

Most repository providers offer a GPG key to verify the RPM packages downloaded from that repository. You can import the GPG key from the freshrpms web site with the following command, as described earlier in the "RPM Security" sidebar:

```
rpm -import http://freshrpms.net/RPM-GPG-KEY-freshrpms
```

■**Tip** To disable a repository, you don't necessarily have to remove its `.repo` file. Each `.repo` file has an `enabled` value. When set to 1, it informs yum to use the repository. Just change `enabled` to 0, and yum will stop using that repository.

Compiling from Source

Back in the old days of UNIX, the only way to install software was from source code, through a process known as compiling. This was because most people edited the source code themselves, or at least liked to have the option of doing so. Nowadays, innovations such as package management systems make compiling all but redundant for the average user. But knowing how to compile a program from source is still a good Linux skill to have. In some cases, it's your only option for installing certain programs, because you may not be able to find a packaged binary.

It goes without saying that program compilation is usually handled at the command-line prompt. It's not the kind of thing you would do via a GUI program.

Installing the Compiler Tools

Before you can compile from source, you need to install several items of software: the make program, which oversees the process of creating a new program, and the GNU Compiler Collection (GCC), which does the hard work of turning the source code into a binary. In addition, if the software relies on certain library files, you'll need to install developer (`devel`) versions of them, as well as the libraries themselves if they're not already installed.

It's possible to install all the program compilation tools you need by installing the Development Tools component using Pirut (Figure 28-5). This will not only install gcc, but also several other packages that are required when installing programs from source.

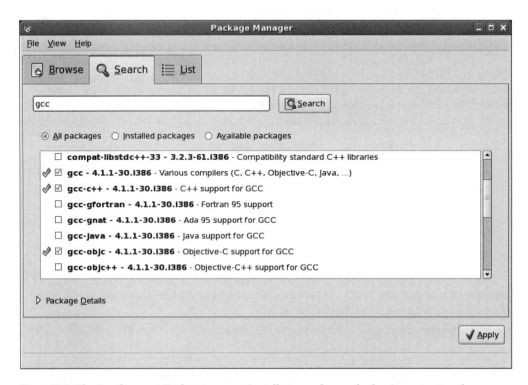

Figure 28-5. *The Development Tools component installs gcc and several other important packages*

Let's take a look at installing a program from source. This example will use Dillo, a stripped-down web browser that's designed for speed and small file size. It's a fun little program that's good to have around in the event your main browser develops a glitch that you can't fix—at least you'll then be able to get online to fix it!

First, head over to the Dillo homepage (`www.dillo.org/`) and download the latest version of the source code.

Unpacking the Tarball and Resolving Dependencies

The first thing to do is to unpack and uncompress the tarball (to learn more about the `tar` command, see Chapter 32):

```
tar jxf dillo-0.8.6.tar.bz2
```

Of course, you should replace the filename with that of the version you downloaded.

Next, you'll need to switch into the source code directory and take a look at the README file:

```
cd dillo-0.8.6
less README
```

This will tell you the dependencies Dillo has and also any caveats you may need to take into account in order to compile Dillo on a Linux system.

Note Unlike binary files, source code is rarely designed with one computer platform in mind. For example, Dillo is able to compile on all types of UNIX, including Linux, Solaris, and BSD. With a little work, it might even be possible to compile it under Windows.

Typically, the README file will be quite technical, but the trick is to let your eyes skip over anything confusing and look for the important headings. You should scout the file for important parts, such as a line that reads "Dillo needs the following packages."

Dillo needs several library files, the first of which is the glib library. This is a given on nearly all Linux systems that use the GNOME desktop, but you should check to make sure it's present. Additionally, in order to compile, Dillo will need the devel version of glib, which is unlikely to be part of the default Fedora installation.

Next, the README file tells us that Dillo also needs the GTK+ 1.2 library. You must check to make sure that this is installed, and then make sure the devel version is installed.

Beneath that in Dillo's list of requirements are support for JPEG and PNG image formats, which is definitely installed on the average Linux system, and the Wget download tool, which is also included with most versions of Linux (although it's a good idea to use yum or rpm to check whether it's installed).

After finding out about dependencies, you should scroll down the README file to look for any notes about compiling under Linux. It turns out there might be some issues with older 2.4 versions of the Linux kernel, but Fedora uses 2.6, so this isn't a problem.

In summary, before you can compile Dillo, you need to check if glib and GTK+ 1.2 are installed. Although the README file doesn't say so, you also need the devel versions of both. You can try to use yum with the info command option to check if these libraries are installed:

```
yum info gtk\* glib
```

Notice that you can specify both library names in the same command. Yum is clever enough to realize this and processes each library separately. More importantly, you can use wildcards to make your search simpler. Additionally, as with all kinds of searches, it pays to simplify the search terms, so rather than searching for GTK+ 1.2, you can simply search for gtk*, as just shown.

Tip Using wildcard characters with BASH requires that you "escape" them. Notice the \ before the * in the command above? This is called "escaping". Similarly file names with spaces in between need to be "escaped" when using BASH. For example, if you have a file called my file, then to read it with less you run the command less my\ file.

Since we searched for gtk* in the preceding command, both GTK and its devel version were displayed in the result; but the devel version for glib was not displayed. To search for that, you can use the yum search glib-devel command. It's quite easy to spot the devel versions of any package. The word *devel* is part of the package name (as shown in Figure 28-6).

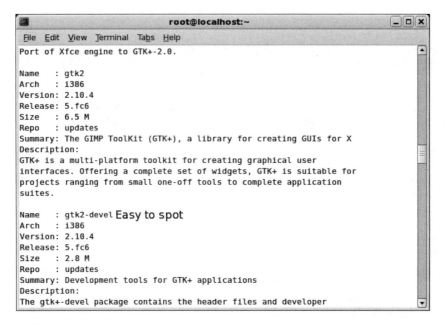

```
root@localhost:~                                    _ □ ✕

File  Edit  View  Terminal  Tabs  Help

Port of Xfce engine to GTK+-2.0.

Name    : gtk2
Arch    : i386
Version: 2.10.4
Release: 5.fc6
Size    : 6.5 M
Repo    : updates
Summary: The GIMP ToolKit (GTK+), a library for creating GUIs for X
Description:
GTK+ is a multi-platform toolkit for creating graphical user
interfaces. Offering a complete set of widgets, GTK+ is suitable for
projects ranging from small one-off tools to complete application
suites.

Name    : gtk2-devel Easy to spot
Arch    : i386
Version: 2.10.4
Release: 5.fc6
Size    : 2.8 M
Repo    : updates
Summary: Development tools for GTK+ applications
Description:
The gtk+-devel package contains the header files and developer
```

Figure 28-6. *You can spot devel packages just by looking at the package's filename.*

Notice the line that reads repo. If a package is already installed on your system, then the repository will be installed as well. If it's not installed, then the repository that offers it will be listed here. In this case, yum informs you that these packages are available from the updates respository.

If you did a typical Fedora install, chances are that none of these files are installed. Using Pirut, you can search for gtk and glib. This search will also list devel version of each (see Figure 28-7)—you should select them as well.

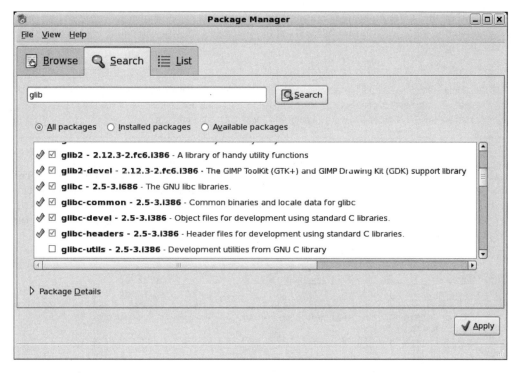

Figure 28-7. *The devel packages are also listed when you search with Pirut.*

Alternatively, you can try to manually track down the devel package files. That is, you can search for them on the Internet using your favorite search engine. The major problem with this approach, however, is that it's not always obvious which package contains which devel library file, so it can sometimes be like searching for a needle in a haystack.

Compiling the Program

Now comes the exciting process of compiling the program! This is done via three commands, issued in sequence. Before continuing, make sure that you're in the directory that you unpacked the files into.

```
./configure
make
```

You need to be root before you can issue the next command. Use su - to gain root privilege, and then run the following command (you will have to change back into the directory where the files were unpacked):

```
make install
```

The first command starts the configure script created by the Dillo programmer, which checks your system to make sure that it meets Dillo's requirements. In other words, it checks to make sure that the glib and GTK+ libraries are present. It also checks to make sure that you have the correct software required to actually compile a program, such as GCC and make.

It's when the configure script is running that something is most likely to go wrong. In that case, more often than not, the error message will tell you that you're missing a dependency, which you must then resolve.

Note   Some configure scripts are very thorough and check for components that the program you're trying to install might not even need. Because of this, you shouldn't worry, as the text scrolls past, if you see that various components are missing. Unless configure complains about it, it's not a problem.

The next command, make, takes care of the actual program compilation. When it's run, the screen will fill with what might look like gibberish (see Figure 28-8), but this is merely the output of the GNU compiler. It provides a lot of valuable information to those who know about such things, but you can largely ignore it. However, you should keep your eyes peeled for any error messages. It's possible that the configure script might not have checked your system thoroughly enough, and you might be missing an important system component—in which case, make will halt.

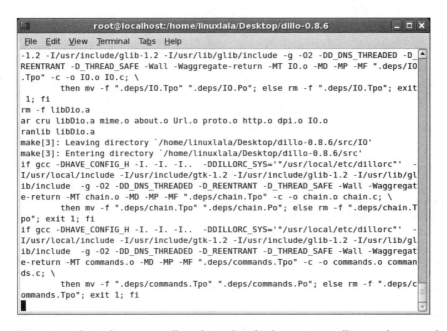

Figure 28-8. *The make process will result in a lot of information scrolling up the screen, but you can ignore most of it.*

Alternatively, the program simply might not be able to compile on your system without some tweaking to the makefile (the file that make uses). If such a situation arises, the best plan is to visit the web site of the developer of the software and see if there's a forum you can post to. Alternatively, check if the developer has an e-mail address where you can ask for help.

■**Note** Sometimes you may see an error message at the end of the make session, as we did. You should still try following up with the make install command. It too might report some error messages, as it again did on our test machine. However, we were still able to get Dillo working just fine! The moral of the story is that software compilation is something of a black art, with error messages designed for programmers—but not all error messages are fatal.

Eventually, the compilation will stop with a number of "exit" messages. Then you must run the final command: make install. This needs to be run as the root user (use the su - command) because its job is to copy the binary files you've just created to the relevant system directories, and only root can write to these directories.

Any documentation that comes with the program is also copied to the relevant location on your system.

Once the three commands have completed, you should be able to run the program by typing its name at the command prompt. If you've been playing along at home and have compiled Dillo, you can run it by typing dillo. Figure 28-9 shows an example of Dillo in action.

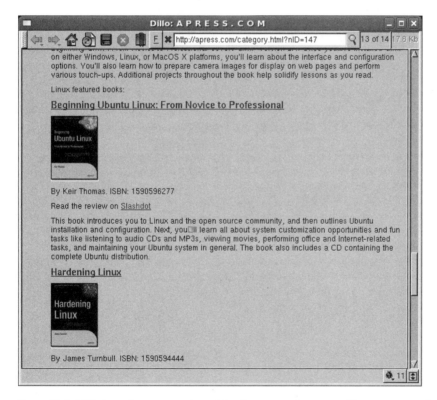

Figure 28-9. *Dillo in action—a certain satisfaction comes from compiling a program from source code.*

> ■**Tip** Perhaps it goes without saying that you'll need to add your own icon to the desktop or the Applications ➤ Internet menu. Source packages are usually designed to be installed on any version of UNIX running a variety of desktop managers. So, it's not possible for the developer to know where to create desktop shortcuts.

Summary

This chapter has described how to install software under Fedora. We looked at how this differs from Windows software installation, and how the package management system is designed to make life easier for Linux users.

You learned how to use the package management tools Pirut and Pup, and the rpm and yum command-line tools to manage software. You also learned how to add installation sources. Finally, we looked at how programs can be compiled from their source code, which is a fundamental process of all versions of Linux.

In the next chapter, we'll look at how the system of users under Fedora can be administered.

CHAPTER 29

■■■

Managing Users

Linux was designed from the ground up to be a multiuser system. When it's deployed on huge mainframe computers, it's capable of serving hundreds, if not thousands, of users at the same time, provided that there are enough terminal computers for them to log in. In a more domestic setting, such as when Fedora is installed on a desktop PC, it usually means that more than one family member can have their very own account on the PC. Any files that users create will be private, and users will also get their own desktop environment that is separate from those of the other users.

Even if you're the only person using your PC, you can still take advantage of Fedora's multiuser capabilities. Consider creating user accounts for various aspects of your life—perhaps one for work and one for time spent browsing the Web. Each user account can be tailored to a specific need.

In this chapter, you'll learn how to administer multiple user accounts.

Understanding User and Group Accounts

The concept of users and file ownership was explained in Chapter 14, but let's take a moment to recap and elaborate on some important points.

Users and Groups

Each person who wishes to use Fedora must have a user account. This will define what that user can and cannot do on the system, with specific reference to files. Because Fedora is effectively one large file system, with even hardware devices seen as individual files (see Chapter 14), this means that user permissions lie at the heart of controlling the entire system. They can limit which user has access to which hardware and software, and therefore control access to various PC functions.

Each user also belongs to a group. Groups have the same style of permissions as individual users. File access can be denied or granted to a user, depending on that person's group membership.

Note As in real life, a group can have many members and can be based around various interests. In a business environment, this might mean that a group is created for members of the accounting department, for example, or for the human resources department. By changing the permissions on files created by the group members, each group can have files that only the group members can access (although, as always, anyone with superuser powers can access all files).

On a default Fedora system with just a handful of users, the group concept might seem somewhat redundant. However, the concept of groups is fundamental to the way Fedora works and cannot be avoided. Even if you don't make use of groups, Fedora still requires your user account to be part of one.

In addition to actual human users, the Fedora system has its own set of user and group accounts. Various programs that access hardware resources or particular sets of files normally use these. Setting up system users and groups in this way makes the system more secure and easier to administer.

Root User

On most Linux systems, the root user has power over the entire system. Root can examine any file and configure any piece of hardware. Root typically belongs to its own unique group, also called root. Fedora is no different.

Because of its power, the root user can cause a lot of accidental damage, so it's rare for anyone to log in as root on bootup. Instead, you can switch to root user temporarily from an ordinary user account by typing the following:

su

This will prompt you for the root password and then log you in as root for as long as you need. The su command gives you the root user's privileges. When you've finished, type exit, and you'll be returned to your ordinary user account.

You can use the su - command to inherit the root user's environment variables. The su command retains the normal user's environment variables; so if you use su, you won't be able to execute system-level changes, despite having superuser powers.

A normal user can, however, execute system programs by specifying their full path. For example, a normal user can't run the ifconfig program because it is not in their $PATH (environment variable). They can issue the command /sbin/ifconfig to run it, but they can't use it to modify any system component.

■**Tip** You can tell when you're logged in as root user because the command prompt will end with a hash symbol (#). When logged in as an ordinary user, it ends with a dollar sign ($). The hash symbol should be seen as a warning that you now have unrestricted control over the system—when you see it, be careful what you type, and double-check everything before hitting Enter!

To quit the root user account, type exit.

UIDs and GIDs

Although we talk of user and group names, these are only used for the end user's benefit. Fedora uses a numerical system to identify users and groups. These are referred to as user IDs (UIDs) and group IDs (GIDs), respectively.

For various reasons, under Fedora, all the GID and UID numbers under 500 are reserved for the system to use. This means that the first non-root user created on a system during installation will probably be given a UID of 500. In addition, any new groups created after installation are numbered from 500. On our system, the default user had a UID of 500 and a GID of 500. The second user we added was given a UID of 501 and a GID of 501. The root user's UID is 0.

■**Note** UID and GID information isn't important during everyday use, and most commands used to administer users and file permissions understand the human-readable usernames. However, knowing UIDs and GIDs can prove useful when you're undertaking more complicated system administration.

USER SWITCHER

The User Switcher applet is located to the left of the Clock on the desktop. When creating a user account, Fedora asks you to enter your full name. It's this name that you'll find next to the clock.

The User Switcher allows you to quickly change into another user account on your machine without logging out.

When you left-click the User Switcher, you'll see a list of all the users on your machine. One user will have a check in the check-box. This signifies the user you are logged in as. Also, this user would appear to be discolored. This means that this is the current account.

When you click some other users check-box, you'll be promptly dropped to the login screen. Just enter the password for that user account to log in (you don't have to type in the username). If you now click the User Switcher, you'll find that two users have a check in the check-box but only the current user is discolored as shown in the following illustration.

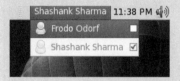

Clicking the other user now will drop you to the desktop of that user account.

Amazingly, none of your program windows are affected when you switch into a different user account. When you come back, you will find that all program windows are still open and everything is as you left it.

When you right-click the User Switcher applet, you get the option to Edit Personal Information, Edit Users and Groups or Setup the Login Screen.

Adding and Deleting Users and Groups

The easiest and quickest way to add a new user or group is to use the Users and Groups tool under the System ➤ Administration menu. Of course, you can also perform these tasks through the command line.

Adding and Deleting Users via the GUI

To add a new user, select System ➤ Administration ➤ Users and Groups. This will open the User Manager application, once you've typed in the root password. Then click Add User. You'll see the Create New User dialog box, as shown in Figure 29-1.

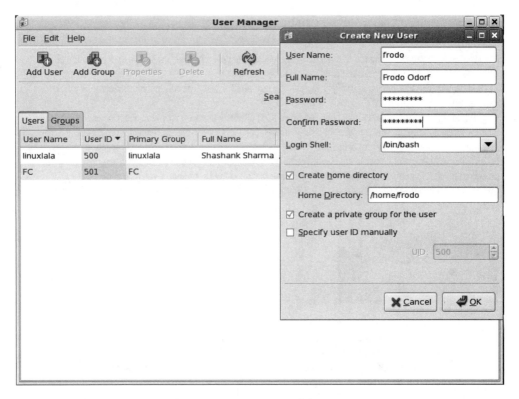

Figure 29-1. *Adding new users and groups is easy courtesy of the User Manager program.*

Fill out all the fields. When adding a new user, as during initial installation, you're invited to enter a username for the user as well as the real name. The username is how the user is identified to the system, while the real name is how the user will be identified to other users. You also need to set an initial password for the user that is at least six characters long. To ensure accuracy, enter it twice.

You can also choose to enter a custom UID, but you must keep it greater than 500.

■**Note** You can view the system users and groups that take up the first 500 UIDs by clicking Edit ➤ Preferences in the User Manager program, and then removing the check from the Hide system users and groups check box.

You'll see the User Properties dialog box when you click the Properties button, as shown in Figure 29-2. You can force a user to change his password by clicking Enable password expiration on the Password Info tab, and you can set the account expiration date from the Account Info tab.

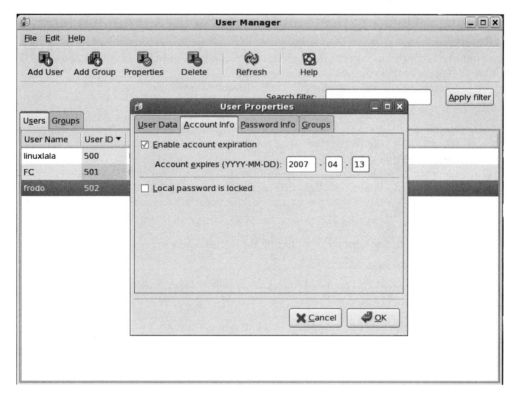

Figure 29-2. *The User Properties dialog box can be used to provide user-specific details.*

Deleting a user is simply a matter of highlighting the username in the list and clicking the Delete button. This will delete the user's /home/ directory and also any temporary files.

Creating and Deleting Groups via the GUI

Adding a group is simply a matter of clicking the Add Group button in the User Manager program window (System ➤ Administration ➤ Users and Groups). After clicking the Add Group button, you'll be prompted to give the group a name. The GID will be automatically filled in for you, but you can choose a different number if you have good reason to do so (remember to keep it over 500 to keep in line with the way Fedora operates).

It isn't essential that you add users to the group then and there. You can add users to a group from the Group Users tab in the Group Properties dialog box, but you'll see a lot of user accounts on the list that belong to the system and are vital to the way Fedora operates. You shouldn't add any of these to your new group, and you should never, ever delete any of these user accounts!

As with user accounts, deleting a group is simply a matter of highlighting it in the list and clicking the Delete button. You should ensure that the group no longer has any members before doing this because Fedora will otherwise warn you that the group can't be removed.

Adding and Deleting Users and Groups at the Command Line

You can create new users at the command-line shell by using the useradd command. This command must be run with superuser powers, which is to say that you must become the root user (use the su - command) before you can add a new user.

The command to add a user is normally used in the following way:

```
useradd <username>
```

This command will create a home directory for the user and also update system files with the new user's details. There are several other useful command options, which can be discovered by a quick browse of the command's man page.

The Fedora way of working is to give each user her own group based on her username. Therefore, you will find that the command also creates a group.

If you ever need to create a new group, it can be done with the groupadd command, as follows:

```
groupadd <groupname>
```

You can also assign a new user to a group with the -G switch when creating the new user:

```
useradd -G <username> <groupname>
```

For example, the following command creates a user called haha and adds him to the group hoho:

```
useradd -G haha hoho
```

Note that creating a new user using useradd won't automatically apply a password to the account. Fedora can't work with accounts that have no passwords, so until one is applied, the new account will be locked. You can add a password using the passwd command, as discussed in the next section.

Deleting a user is mercifully simple compared to this! Use the userdel command, as follows:

```
userdel haha
```

This won't remove haha's /home/ directory, however. You must use the -r switch to do that. Similarly, to delete a group, use the groupdel command:

```
groupdel <groupname>
```

Adding and Changing Passwords

On a default Fedora installation, ordinary users are able to change their passwords at the shell. The command for any user to change his password is simple:

```
passwd
```

The user will be asked to confirm his current password, and then enter the new password twice to confirm that it has been typed correctly.

Alternatively, by adopting superuser powers, a user can change the password of another account:

```
su -
[Enter password]
passwd <username>
```

This is necessary just after you create a new user account because it isn't given a password automatically. For obvious security reasons, Fedora won't allow blank passwords.

You can enter just about anything as a password, but you should bear in mind some common-sense rules. Ideally, passwords should be at least eight characters long and contain letters, numbers, and even punctuation symbols. You might also want to include both uppercase and lowercase letters.

A number of command options can be specified along with the passwd command when it is used with superuser powers. For example, the -l option will lock the specified account so that it can't be accessed (the -u option will unlock it).

Tip You can temporarily switch into any user account by typing su *<username>*. When you've finished, simply type exit to return to your own account. You can use the su - *<username>* command to inherit the user's environment. When no username is specified with the su - command, you inherit the root user's environment.

Summary

In this chapter, we looked at the principles behind user and group accounts under Fedora. We examined how user and group accounts can be created, edited, and deleted using the GUI, as well as the command-line prompt. We also looked at how passwords can be manipulated by the individual users themselves and by a user with superuser powers.

In the next chapter, we'll look at how the system can be optimized. You'll also learn about several interesting and important system tools.

CHAPTER 30

■■■

Optimizing Your System

One slight problem with Fedora (and all Linux distributions) is that it takes a one-size-fits-all approach—the default installation attempts to provide services for every kind of user. While this offers the widest range of compatibility, it doesn't always ensure an optimized system.

You may never attach a printer to Fedora, for example, so what's the point of keeping the printing subsystem in memory? You can remove it from your Linux setup and not only free memory, but also speed up boot times, because you no longer need to wait for the printer service to start. While this might save only a couple seconds, or just a couple of hundred kilobytes of memory, repeating the process and paring Fedora down to the bone can produce an ultra-efficient system.

In this chapter, you'll learn how to target the various subsystems of your Linux system in order to optimize and speed up your computer. We'll look at everything from bootup, to hard disks, to streamlining the kernel itself.

Speeding Up Booting

Let's take a look at what happens when a Fedora-equipped PC boots. Then we'll explore some ways to speed up the process.

Understanding Bootup

After you start your computer, and after the computer's power-on self-test (POST), the computer's BIOS searches for a boot program on the hard disk. If Fedora is installed on the computer, the boot program then runs the GRUB boot loader program. The job of the GRUB boot loader is twofold. First, it displays a menu from which you can choose which operating system to load. If you've installed Fedora alongside Windows, you'll be able to choose between the two operating systems at this stage. Second, GRUB loads the Linux kernel, if a Linux operating system is chosen from the boot menu.

Once loaded, the kernel then starts the very first program that's run on any Linux system: `init`. The principal job of `init` is to run a variety of run-level scripts, which load the hardware and software necessary for the full and correct functioning of the system. All of these are located in `/etc/init.d`.

■**Note** In this context, *scripts* can be defined as long chains of commands stored in a single file.

`init` begins its job when the `inittab` file, located at `/etc/inittab`, is read. This file describes how the init process should set up the system, with information on setting up the system in a certain run level.

■**Note** Comments within scripts are usually preceded by a hash (#) or sometimes a semicolon (;), which tells the computer not to interpret what follows on that line as an actual command. Comments are inserted to help you, as a user, understand what the script is supposed to do.

The system initialization (*sysinit*) line is read next, and the corresponding command is executed. In Fedora's case, the command is to execute the /etc/rc.d/rc.sysinit script. You can think of the rc.sysinit file as the autoexec.bat file on old MS-DOS systems. It is responsible for running all the services that are listed every time your computer boots.

■**Note** Every command in the /etc/inittab file is called an action. The most used action in this file is wait. It means that init executes the command for a specific run level and then waits for that run level to terminate.

The /etc/rc.d/rc.sysinit file is the real hero of the boot process. It is responsible for starting everything from your network devices to mounting the /proc filesystem. At this point the /etc/init.d/functions file is executed. This file contains functions that are used by almost all the scripts in the /etc/init.d directory.

Control returns to the sysinit file after the function file gets executed. Now the system clock is configured and the hardware is initialized. Apart from all this jazz, the sysinit file also verifies your root file system and mounts it. It also mounts other file systems specified in the /etc/fstab file (discussed in Chapter 14), and also turns on the swap space.

Following this, the run-level scripts are activated. These are located within the /etc/rc.d directory. Each run level has its own /etc/rc.d/rcX.d directory, where X refers to the run level in use. Figure 30-1 shows the scripts at run level 5.

Figure 30-1. *The scripts for each run level are contained in the /etc/init.d/rcX.d directories, where X is the run-level number.*

Run-level scripts do two things: they start and configure any hardware that's specific to that particular run level, and they start any necessary system software (known as *services*) that is particular to that run level.

■**Note** Because the run level defines what software and hardware are in use on the computer, the run level could accurately be referred to as the *operating mode* of the computer.

For example, if run level 5 is activated, the GNOME Display Manager (gdm) will be run to start the GUI. gdm is missing from run level 3's scripts, because run levels 1 and 3 are usually configured to boot to a command-line prompt. See Table 30-1 for a list of run levels and what they normally do.

Table 30-1. *Fedora Run Levels*

Run Level	Description
0	Halt; the computer will be shut down.
1	Single-user mode (root login); very few hardware and software services are activated.
2	Non-GUI mode; network interface deactivated. Multiple user logins are allowed.
3	Non-GUI mode; complete multiuser mode. Standard set of hardware and system services started, including network services.
4	Unused.
5	GUI mode; default run level for Fedora. Standard set of hardware and system services started.
6	Reboot; the computer will be shut down and then restarted.

On Fedora, the line id:5:initdefault in the /etc/inittab file determines which run level to run. If you change 5 to 3 in this line, init would set up run level 3.

In terms of operating system components, it's during the run-level script stage that things like the printing services are started and network file sharing subsystems are made to run in the background. If the system is configured as a web server, software like Apache will be run at this stage, too.

Run levels 2 through 5 are defined as *multiuser*. Technically speaking, this means that they allow more than one user to log on, but for most desktop users, they're better defined as the day-to-day running modes of the computer. Run level 5 is the default run level under Fedora.

■**Note** There's no reason why run levels 7, 8, and 9 can't be used under Fedora. However, only run levels 0 through 6 are normally configured.

The job of the run-level scripts is to define the user experience. When they've finished, the computer will be configured and ready for use in some fashion. However, that's not quite the end of things.

Although you'll be able to log on, the GNOME desktop will not have started yet, and it too has its own set of initialization processes. It needs to start its own set of programs, such as the system tray/notification area applets, which provide handy functions like onscreen volume control. Once all that has finished, you can use the computer!

Because so much must take place for your system to come to life, booting Fedora can take some time. On our test system, it averaged between one and two minutes. Certainly, you can shave some time from this.

> **Note** Run levels don't just contain startup scripts. They also contain "kill" scripts, designed to shut down services should you change into a particular run level from another. For example, run level 3 contains a kill script designed to terminate gdm, so that the GUI is no longer active. However, there's no need to worry about kill scripts when considering how to optimize Fedora's boot process.

Reducing the Boot Menu Delay

Getting rid of the GRUB boot menu delay can save some waiting around in the early stages of the boot process. The delay can be reduced to a few seconds, or even eradicated completely. Of course, in such a case, you won't be able to choose which operating system you want to load if you're dual-booting with Windows. Even if Fedora is the only operating system on your computer, without the boot delay, you won't have the chance to pass additional boot parameters that you normally can using the GRUB menu. So you need to consider whether this is a worthwhile time-saving measure.

The boot menu delay is stated in the /boot/grub/grub.conf file. Only the root user can edit this file. So use su - to change into the root user:

```
$ su -
Password:
# gedit /boot/grub/grub.conf
```

This loads the file in the Gedit text editor, as shown following. Look for the line that begins with timeout, and change the value to whatever you wish. The units are counted in seconds, so a value of 5 equates to five seconds. A value of 0 will mean the boot menu won't appear at all. Generally speaking, a delay of three seconds gives you just enough time to press a key at the appropriate time, and this will then cancel the countdown, meaning the boot menu will stay on your screen until you select an option.

```
# grub.conf generated by anaconda
#
# Note that you do not have to rerun grub after making changes to this file
# NOTICE:  You have a /boot partition.  This means that
#          all kernel and initrd paths are relative to /boot/, eg.
#          root (hd0,0)
#          kernel /vmlinuz-version ro root=/dev/VolGroup00/LogVol00
#          initrd /initrd-version.img
#boot=/dev/hda
default=0
timeout=3
splashimage=(hd0,0)/grub/splash.xpm.gz
#hiddenmenu
title Fedora Core (2.6.18-1.2798.fc6)
        root (hd0,0)
        kernel /vmlinuz-2.6.18-1.2798.fc6 ro root=/dev/VolGroup00/LogVol00 rhgb quiet
        initrd /initrd-2.6.18-1.2798.fc6.img
```

When you've finished, save the file and quit Gedit.

Optimizing Run-Level Services

Perhaps it goes without saying that the majority of bootup time is spent starting the boot and run-level scripts. This is when the entire system comes to life—hardware and essential software services are activated. But this isn't to say that all run-level scripts are essential.

■**Note** A *service* is a piece of background software that provides something that you, the user, need on a day-to-day basis. Some services manage hardware, such as the graphical interface, printing services, and networking. Some services provide software services, such as logging files or checking the system clock against a time server.

The one-size-fits-all approach of Fedora means that some services that are started up aren't always necessary. Approximately 60 run-level scripts start on a typical boot. By selective pruning, you can easily remove around a quarter of these, but caution is advised. You're altering a fundamental aspect of your system configuration, and one simple mistake can make the difference between a system that works and one that is no longer able to boot.

Creating a Custom Run Level

Because of the risk of seriously damaging your system by pruning run-level scripts, I recommend that you use run level 4 for your experiments. Run level 4 is officially designated as "unused" and is therefore ideal for the purpose.

For this plan to work, you need to make run level 4 into a clone of run level 5, and then configure the computer to boot to run level 4, rather than 5. Here's how to proceed:

1. Open a terminal window. Click Application ➤ Accessories ➤ Terminal.

2. Switch to the root user at the command line by typing su -.

3. Clear out the existing run level 4 scripts using the following command:

   rm /etc/rc.d/rc4.d/*

4. Copy the scripts for run level 5 to the directory of run level 4, thereby creating a clone. Because the run level 5 directory contains symbolic links to files in /etc/init.d, you need to use the -P command-line option with the cp command. That way, it copies the links, rather than the linked files. Issue the following command:

   cp -P /etc/rc.d/rc5.d/* /etc/rc.d/rc4.d/

5. The default run level that Fedora boots into is listed in /etc/inittab. You need to edit this file to switch the default to run level 4. Type the following to load /etc/inittab in the Gedit text editor:

   gedit /etc/inittab

6. In the text editor, look for the line that reads id:5:initdefault:. Change the 5 to a 4, so that the line now reads as follows: id:4:initdefault:.

7. Save the file and quit the text editor.

8. Reboot your computer.

■**Tip** While rebooting, you can verify that you're entering the newly defined run level 4 by watching for a message along the lines of "Entering run level 4." This will appear before status messages of the various run-level scripts begin to appear. When up and running, typing `runlevel` as the root user will display the current run level (two numbers will be quoted—the second indicates the current run level).

Pruning Run-Level Services

GNOME includes a tool that allows you to control which run-level services start during bootup. To access it, click System ➤ Administration ➤ Services. You should see a window similar to that shown in Figure 30-2.

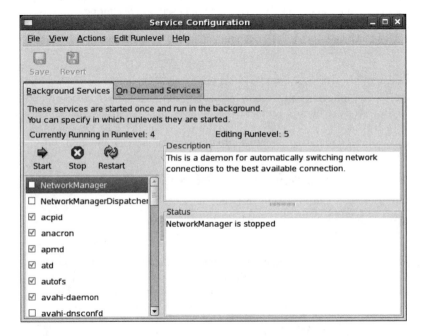

Figure 30-2. *The Service Configuration window shows each available service, whether the service is running, and a description.*

■**Caution** Before proceeding, you need to change the run level setting here as well. Click Edit Runlevel and select Run Level 4. The line above the description should now read "Editing Run Level 4." By default, the Service Configuration tool is set to edit run level 5.

Services: There are two tabs at the top of the Service Configuration window: Background Services and On Demand Services. We are concerned only with the Background Services. The various services on the system are listed on the left. This list includes all available services even if they're not active during any run level and are not used during boot (effectively, these services are contained in the /etc/rc.d/init.d/ directory).

Status: Whether the service is running or not is described here. If the service is running, you will see a message like "servicename (pid number) is running." A message like "servicename is stopped" appears in the Status pane if a service is not running.

Description: Brief descriptions of what various run level services do are displayed here.

Take a look through the list and see what the various services do. This should give you an idea of which you might consider removing. In Table 30-2, we've listed some run-level services that we consider safe to disable. By removing these services, we managed to trim about 12 seconds from the total boot time of our test PC.

You should follow some common-sense rules when removing entries:

- Don't remove a service whose purpose you don't understand. If in doubt, leave it alone! Bear in mind that several services might look innocuous but may be essential because they support other, more essential system components.

- Disable services only for run level 4. Don't disable the service for any other run level, especially run level 5, which you will want to use later if your changes prove problematic.

Table 30-2. *Services That You May Want to Disable*

Service	Description	Notes
apmd	Monitors battery status	You can disable this if you don't use a laptop.
avahi-daemon	The avahi network daemon	You can disable this if your machine is not on a network.
avahi-dnsconfd	See avahi-daemon	See avahi-daemon.
bluetooth	The Bluetooth service	Disable this if you don't have any Bluetooth hardware.
cups	The cups printing service	You can disable this if you don't have a printer attached to your computer and do not intend to print from the computer in the future.
hidd	See bluetooth	See bluetooth.
hplip	The HP Printer daemon	You can disable this if you don't use any HP hardware.
isdn	Used for ISDN modems	You can disable this if you don't have an ISDN modem.
kudzu	Probes the hardware and configures new devices	If you are sure that no new hardware will be attached, disable it.
netfs	Mounts and unmounts network file systems	You can disable this; only advanced or corporate users are likely to use it.
pcscd	The smart card daemon	Disable this if you don't use smart cards.
portmap	Portmap manager	Used by NFS and NIS protocols. You can disable it if your machine is not used as a NFS or NIS server.

Deactivating a service is easy. You can either click the Stop button to disable a service or simply click the check box and remove the check.

When you've finished, click the Save button. This will write the changes to disk. You should then reboot to test your new settings.

Restoring Run Level 5

If you are too aggressive when pruning run-level services, you may find that you've left your system in an unusable state. If this happens, you can simply switch the default run level back to 5, and then attempt to make repairs to your custom run level.

The following instructions assume a worst-case scenario, which is to say that you're unable to boot to a GUI, but they work under other circumstances as well.

1. If you see an error message effectively saying that a graphical screen cannot be started, press Alt+Ctrl+F2 (i.e., the F2 key).

2. This will drop you to a login prompt. After you've logged in, type the following, as root user (su -), to open the /etc/inittab file in the vi text editor:

   ```
   vi /etc/inittab
   ```

3. Scroll down to the line that reads id:4:initdefault:. Now press A and change the 4 to a 5 so that the line now reads id:5:initdefault:.

4. To save the file, press the Esc key and type :w. Press Enter now to save the file.

5. Next, press Esc again, type :q, and then press Enter.

6. Type reboot to restart your computer.

■**Note**   The :w and :q commands require you to type : (colon) and w or q, respectively, to save and quit the vi text editor.

STOP SEARCHING FOR AN ADDRESS

If you use an Ethernet or Wi-Fi connection to access the network, you'll find that Fedora spends a few seconds each boot acquiring an Internet address. Therefore, one way to provide an instant speed boost is to give your computer a static IP address. (See Chapter 8 for details on how to configure your network interface.)

To assign a static address, you'll need to find out what IP address range your router uses. You can discover this address by looking at the router's configuration software (sometimes this is accessed via a web browser). Look for the configuration section with a heading like DHCP Configuration.

Normally, the addresses are in the 192.168.x.x range, where x.x can be any series of numbers from 1.1 to 255.255. For instance, the router within our test setup uses the 192.168.0.1–255 range.

In our case, choosing a static IP address that will work with the router is simply a matter of selecting an IP address in this range. However, I know that the router hands out addresses sequentially from 2 upward, so it's best to choose an address that it's unlikely to reach, even if you happen to have many computers connected to the network. Starting at 50 is a good idea, so we assigned our test PC the address 192.168.1.50.

Don't forget that, when defining static IP addresses, you'll need to manually supply the gateway, subnet, and DNS addresses. In most cases, the subnet address will be 255.255.255.0. The DNS address will be the same as the gateway address.

Optimizing Hard Disk Settings

The hard disk is one of the key elements in the modern PC. Because most of your PC's data must travel to and from it, speeding up your hard disk means that your entire PC will be faster.

Fedora provides a powerful command-line tool that you can use to control every aspect of your hard disk: hdparm. This is a power-user's tool. Not only must you be the root user to run it, but you also must be careful not to mistype the commands. All changes are made instantly, so if you make a mistake, your system may crash or at least suffer from serious problems. There's even the risk of data loss, although this can be minimized by making sure that you have no other programs running at the same time you run hdparm.

■**Note** When switching to the root user to carry out the steps in this chapter, be sure to use the su - command, rather than simply su. Adding the dash will switch you to root user. You will also inherit root's path so that you can use system configuration commands like hdparm, which are normally contained in /sbin.

The good news is that changes made via hdparm will last for only the current session, so there's no risk of permanent damage. Any changes that are beneficial can be made permanent later.

In the context of optimization, hdparm lets you both benchmark the disk and change various technical settings, such as the sector multcount value. These adjustments can bring speed boosts.

Benchmarking Your Hard Disk

Because experimenting with hdparm can cause crashes, and because its benchmarking feature needs almost exclusive access to the hard disk, hdparm is best run with as few as possible additional programs up and running. Therefore, switching to run level 3 is a good idea. To do this, close all open programs, and then open a terminal window (click Applications ➤ Accessories ➤ Terminal). At the prompt, type the following to switch to run level 3:

```
su -
[Enter root password]
init 3
```

■**Note** Technically speaking, switching to run level 1 is an even better idea, because this will deactivate all unnecessary services. Run level 1 is akin to Windows Safe Mode, except without the GUI. However, you want realistic benchmark results to test the changes you make via hdparm, and it's debatable whether the restricted confines of run level 1 will provide such results.

Let's start by benchmarking your hard disk to see its performance based on the current settings. Type the following (assuming Fedora is installed on the first hard disk in your system; if it's on the second hard disk, change /dev/hda to /dev/hdb):

```
hdparm -Tt /dev/hda
```

This will benchmark your disk in two ways. The first (-T) tests the PC's memory throughput, measuring the data rate of the memory, CPU, and cache. The second (-t) actually tests the disk's data rate. The first test affects the outcome of the second, which is why the two are used together. Between them, these two methods of benchmarking present the standard way your disk is used on a day-to-day basis. Here's the result from our system:

```
[root@localhost ~]# hdparm -Tt /dev/hdg

/dev/hdg:
 Timing cached reads:   4312 MB in  2.00 seconds = 2156.45 MB/sec
 Timing buffered disk reads:  60 MB in  3.09 seconds =  19.42 MB/sec
[root@localhost ~]#
```

Make a note of the figures so that you can compare them to the results of these tests after you change hard disk settings.

■**Note**   Until not too long ago, hdparm was unable to work with SATA hard disks. But with the 2.6 kernel and newer versions of the program, SATA disks are supported too.

Changing Hard Disk Settings

You can use hdparm to view your current hard disk settings by entering the following at the command prompt:

```
hdparm /dev/hda
```

These are the results we got:

```
/dev/hda:
 multcount    = 16 (on)
 IO_support   =  1 (32-bit)
 unmaskirq    =  1 (on)
 using_dma    =  1 (on)
 keepsettings =  0 (off)
 readonly     =  0 (off)
 readahead    = 1024 (on)
 geometry     = 65535/16/63, sectors = 78125000, start = 0
```

Let's take a look at what these settings mean.

The multcount Setting

The first setting, multcount, refers to how many sectors can be read from the hard disk at any one time. On many drives, a higher setting here is best, but on other drives, a lower setting is best. You can find out what your drive's maximum multcount setting is by issuing the following command:

```
hdparm -i /dev/hda
```

Look for MaxMultSect in the results. On our machine, this read MaxMultSect=16.

You can experiment with the multcount setting on your hard disk by using the -m hdparm command option:

```
hdparm -m8 /dev/hda
```

Here, we have chosen a lower value than the original setting (16).

You can then follow this by another benchmark to see if there is an improvement:

```
hdparm -tT /dev/hda
```

The IO_support Setting

The IO_support setting refers to the input/output (I/O) mode used by the hard disk controller. This has three possible settings: 0 to disable 32-bit support, 1 to enable 32-bit support, and 3 to enable 32-bit support with a special sync signal.

You can change the IO_support setting with the -c hdparm command option; the 32-bit support with sync option (3) is generally considered the best choice:

hdparm -c3 /dev/hda

The unmaskirq Setting

The third setting, unmaskirq, allows Fedora to attend to other tasks while waiting for your hard disk to return data. This won't affect hard disk performance very much, and generally it's a good idea for the health of your system to activate it if isn't already switched on. This command activates unmaskirq:

hdparm -u1 /dev/hda

The using_dma Setting

The fourth setting refers to whether Direct Memory Access (DMA) is in use. Hard disks are sold on the basis of their DMA modes, such as UltraDMA Burst 2 and the like. DMA is considered an indicator of the speed of a hard disk, but the truth is that, like any specification, it is only a guide.

DMA is activated by default under Fedora, but you can alter the DMA mode using the -X command option. However, on most modern PCs, this isn't necessary because the computer's BIOS defaults to the fastest DMA mode.

Other Settings

The last three settings, above the summary of the geometry and sector information of the disk, are those you shouldn't change:

- keepsettings refers to the ability of the drive to remember hdparm settings over a reboot (although not if the drive loses power).
- readonly sets whether the hard disk is read-only (so that no data can be written to it). Changing this setting is not advisable!
- readahead controls how many hard disk blocks are loaded in advance. It doesn't affect the performance of modern IDE-based hard disks, because the drive electronics contain buffers that perform this task themselves.

Making Disk Optimizations Permanent

When the PC is switched off, any changes you've made with hdparm are lost. To make the command run during bootup, you can edit the /etc/rc.d/rc.local file, which exists for exactly this purpose. The rc.local file exists for you to put in all your initialization stuff. Since you want the custom settings to be used at each bootup, you need to make the hdparm run during each boot. This sounds more complicated than it actually is. Here are the steps:

1. Switch to the root user, using the `su -` command.

2. Open the `/etc/rc.d/rc.local` file in a text editor. Add the `hdparm` settings at the end of the file. Simply type the command (e.g., `hdparm -m8 /dev/hda`) in the editor window, and then save the file.

3. That's it! The `rc.local` file gets executed after all the other `init` scripts. So, during bootup, some of the last messages you'll see before the login screen are the commands you entered.

■**Note** Any hard disk performance tweaking must take place as near as possible to the end of booting, because the changes it makes can negatively affect the startup of other services. In fact, all customizations that you wish to make to Fedora's boot process should be made to the `/etc/rc.d/rc.local` file.

Prelinking

As discussed in Chapter 28, a lot of Fedora software relies on other pieces of code to work. These are sometimes referred to as *libraries*, a term that is a good indicator of their purpose: to provide functions that programs can check in and out whenever they need them, as if they were borrowing books from a library.

Whenever a program starts, it must look for these other libraries and load them into memory so they're ready for use. This can take some time, particularly on larger and more complicated programs. Because of this, the concept of *prelinking* was invented. By a series of complicated tricks, the prelink program makes each bit of software you might run aware of the libraries it needs, so that memory can be better allocated.

Prelinking claims to boost program startup times by up to 50 percent or more, but the problem is that it's a hack—a programming trick designed to make your system work in a nonstandard way. Because of this, some programs are incompatible with prelinking. In fact, some might simply refuse to work unless prelinking is deactivated. At the time of writing, such programs are in the minority. However, keep in mind that prelinking can be easily reversed if necessary.

Running Prelink

Prelink is configured by default on Fedora. It can be enabled or disabled through the `/etc/sysconfig/prelink` file. Load this file in a text editor and scroll down to the line that reads `Prelinking=yes`. Replacing `yes` with `no` will disable prelink.

To run a prelink scan of your computer whenever you want, issue this command as the root user (use `su -`):

```
prelink -a
```

The `prelink -a` command will prelink practically all the binary files on your system and may take some time to complete. You may also see some error output, but you don't need to pay attention to it.

Deactivating Prelinking

Should you find that prelinking makes a particular application malfunction or simply stop working, you can try undoing prelinking. To do this, find out where the main binary for the program resides, and then issue the prelink command with the `--undo` command option. For example, to remove prelinking from the Gedit text editor program, you could type the following, as the root user (use the `su -` command):

```
whereis gedit
prelink --undo /usr/bin/gedit
```

However, this may not work because some programs might rely on additional binaries on the system. Therefore, the solution might be to undo prelinking for the entire system, which you can do by typing the following (as the root user):

```
prelink -ua
```

You should also disable prelink at this time by editing the `/etc/sysconfig/prelink` file as described previously.

OPTIMIZING THE KERNEL

Using the Linux kernel source code, you can compile and install your own version of the program at the heart of Linux. This gives you total control over the kernel configuration, so you can leave out parts you don't want in order to free memory. You can also set certain optimization settings, such as creating a version of the kernel specifically built for your model of CPU.

Although compiling a kernel is a simple procedure, there are many complex questions that you'll need to answer, and an in-depth knowledge of the way Linux works is necessary.

In addition, compiling your own kernel brings up several issues. The first is that it may not work with any binary modules that you have installed, such as graphic cards or wireless drivers (including `ndiswrapper`, as discussed in Chapter 8). You can opt to install these yourself from scratch, but this adds to the complexity.

The second problem is that Fedora is built around precompiled kernels. Several software packages expect to work with the precompiled kernel and, in addition, Fedora may occasionally download an updated prepackaged kernel automatically as part of the system update feature and override the one you've created. In addition, you may not be able to effectively troubleshoot problems with your system, or contribute to bug reports, when using a custom kernel. If you encounter problems that involve hardware or other low-level system components, you will probably have to reboot into a precompiled kernel to see if your custom kernel is causing the problem.

If there are any security problems with the kernel version you compiled, you'll need to recompile a new kernel from scratch (or patch the one you have). This means you'll need to keep an eye on the security news sites and take action when necessary.

That said, compiling a kernel is an excellent way of learning how Linux works, and the sense of achievement if it all goes well is enormous.

Some people choose to download the kernel source code from the official Linux kernel site, at `www.kernel.org/`. However, it makes more sense to download the official Fedora release, because this will be tailored for the way your system works. Using the Software Management tool Pirut (see Chapter 29 for details), simply search for and install `kernel-source`.

You can find several guides to compiling your own kernel online. We suggest you study the Fedora-specific procedure described in the Fedora release notes, available at `http://docs.fedoraproject.org/release-notes/`. You can also read the guide at `www.digitalhermit.com/linux/Kernel-Build-HOWTO.html` for a more generic idea about compiling kernels.

Freeing Disk Space

After using Fedora for some time, you might find that the disk begins to get full. You can keep an eye on disk usage by using the following command in a terminal window (click Applications ➤ Accessories ➤ Terminal):

```
df -h
```

This will show the free space in terms of megabytes or gigabytes, and also expresses it as a percentage.

If the disk starts to get full, you can take some steps to make more space available.

Removing Unused Software

If you still need disk space, consider removing unused programs. As you learned in Chapter 29, you can manage software through Pirut (Applications ➤ Add/Remove Software).

The best way of managing software is from the Browse tab, which lets you see which groups of programs you have installed, rather than viewing individual programs (removing individual programs might not free up much space).

Note In case you created a separate /home partition and it is this partition that is filling up, this section isn't going to help you. If your /home partition is a LVM logical volume, then you should read the "Adding Space to an Existing Logical Volume" section of this chapter.

From the Browse tab, you can see the categories of software and further sections in each category, as shown in Figure 30-3. For example, you might choose to remove software under the Games section. Alternatively, if you don't use any office programs on your system, you might choose to deselect titles under the Office/Productivity section.

Caution As always, removing software can create dependency problems, in that Pirut may want to remove some packages apart from those you selected. So you might find yourself limited in what software you can actually remove. You must carefully study any warning that Pirut prints out to ensure that only unnecessary software is removed.

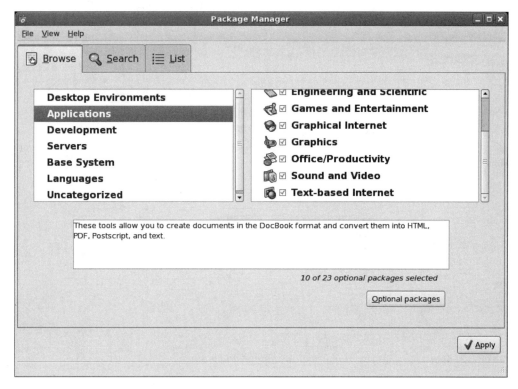

Figure 30-3. *Using the Package Group filter helps identify classes of programs that you might want to remove to free space, such as games.*

Adding Space to an Existing Logical Volume

If you followed our installation instructions in Chapter 5, or if you created a custom LVM layout during installation, you can simply add space to an existing logical volume without losing any data.

You can use the graphical Logical Volume Management (LVM) utility to do this. Click System ➤ Administration ➤ Logical Volume Management. Figure 30-4 shows the partition layout on one of our test machines.

Clicking a volume group will display all the logical volumes and the unused space on each volume. From here you can either choose to create a new logical volume using the unused space, or delete an existing logical volume.

To add space to an existing logical volume, click the logical volume's entry on the left sidebar and then click the Edit Properties button. The LVM application refers to disk space in terms of extents. You can change this to gigabytes by clicking the Extents drop-down list, as shown in Figure 30-5.

You can add all remaining space to this logical volume by clicking the Use remaining button, or you can specify the amount of space you wish to add. When you are done, press the OK button and the partition layout will be updated.

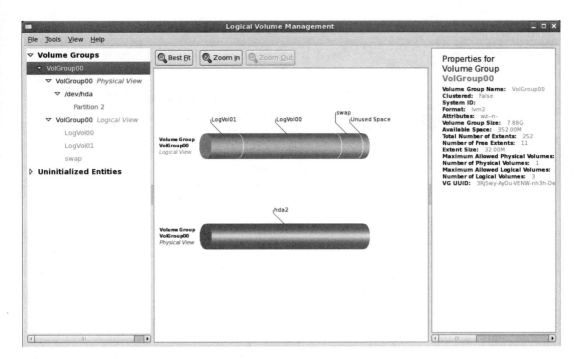

Figure 30-4. *The LVM application lets you modify logical volumes and groups.*

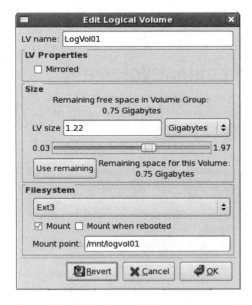

Figure 30-5. *LVM refers to disk space as extents. You can easily change this to gigabytes.*

▮**Note** You cannot modify a mounted logical volume. You can unmount a logical volume by clicking Edit Properties and removing the mark from the Mount check box.

You can similarly add a new disk drive using LVM. When you plug in a new hard disk, it will be uninitialized. To initialize it, select its name from the left sidebar and then click the Initialize button.

▮**Caution** Initializing the disk will erase all the data on the disk. Make sure you don't have any critical data on your disk in case it is not new.

A new entry, Unallocated Volumes, will appear on the left sidebar with your disk listed under it. You can now create new volume groups or add space to an existing volume group.

That's right, you can add space from one hard disk to a volume group on another hard disk. This enables you to increase the space allocated to each of the logical volumes within this volume group.

To extend a volume group, select its entry in the left sidebar and click the Extend Volume Group button. Once you have selected the disk entity to be added, the new volume will be added as unused space in the volume group.

Summary

In this chapter, we looked at streamlining your installation of Fedora. This involved speeding up the boot procedure by decreasing the boot menu delay and deactivating various unnecessary run-level scripts that get loaded at boot time. We also looked at optimizing your hard disk settings to allow for greater efficiency in loading and saving files.

Additionally, we investigated prelinking programs so that they load faster, recompiling the kernel so that it's optimized for your system, freeing disk space, adding space to LVM logical volumes, and adding a second hard disk.

In the next chapter, you'll learn how to perform backups to safeguard your data.

CHAPTER 31

■ ■ ■

Backing Up Data

Every computer user knows that backing up data is vital. This is usually because every computer user has lost data at some point, perhaps because of a corrupted file or accidental deletion.

Some of the people behind UNIX were well aware of such occurrences, and developed several advanced and useful backup tools. These have been mirrored within Linux, with the result that creating and maintaining backups is easy.

In this chapter, we'll first look at what data should be backed up, and then explore two ways to make backups: using the Pybackpack utility and from the command line.

What Data Should You Back Up?

Data on your system can be classified into three broad types: program data, configuration data, and personal data. It's traditionally reasoned that backing up all types of data is inefficient and difficult in most circumstances, largely because it would mean backing up practically the entire hard disk. Because of this, you usually want to back up the latter two types of data: configuration and personal. The theory is that if your PC is hit by a hard-disk-wrecking disaster, you can easily reinstall the operating system from the CD/DVD. Restoring your system from backup is then simply a matter of ensuring the configuration files are back in place so that your applications work as you would like them to, and making sure that your personal data is once again made accessible.

Practically all the personal configuration data for programs you use every day, as well as your personal data, is stored in your users' home folder (although the configuration files for software used system-wide are stored in the /etc folder). If you take a look in your /home directory, you might think that previous sentence is incorrect. On a freshly installed system, the directory appears largely empty. However, most, if not all, of the configuration files are hidden; their directory names and filenames are preceded with a period (.), which means that Linux doesn't display them during a standard directory listing.

To view hidden files and folders in the Nautilus file manager, select View ➤ Show Hidden Files. This can be quite an eye-opener when you see the masses of data you didn't even realize were there, as shown in the example in Figure 31-1. To view hidden files at the shell prompt, simply use the -a command option with the ls command:

```
ls -a
```

The configuration files held in your home folder relate solely to your user account. Any other users will have their own configuration files, entirely independent of yours. In this way, all users can have their own configuration settings for various applications.

Under Fedora, you can back up both configuration data and personal files using Pybackpack.

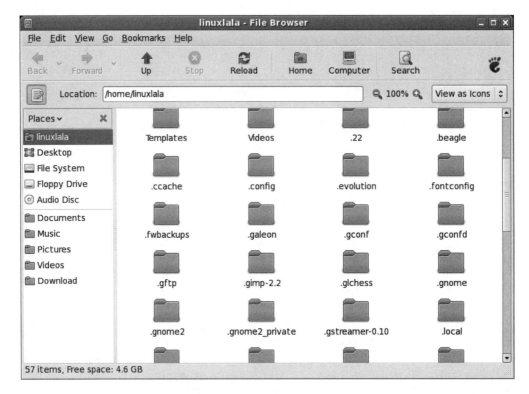

Figure 31-1. *Most of the configuration files for programs are hidden—literally—in your home folder.*

Keep in mind that there's little point in making backups if you leave the resultant archive files on your hard disk. For full backup protection, the archives should be stored elsewhere, such as on an external hard disk, a network mount, or a CD or DVD. Consider using GnomeBaker to create the CD or DVD. We'll describe the procedure for using this tool in the "Burning the Backup File to CD/DVD" section later in this chapter.

Using Pybackpack

Pybackpack is a file backup tool written in Python to facilitate the quick and easy backup and also restoration of files. Pybackpack can back up personal data as well as system configuration files and can store the resultant backup file on your hard disk, a removable drive, or a remote machine (through SSH).

Pybackpack was created courtesy of the Google Summer of Code program in 2005. To install Pybackpack, head over to the project's web site (http://andrewprice.me.uk/projects/pybackpack) and grab the latest fc7.rpm file. We downloaded it to the Downloads directory.

You need the rdiff-backup utility for Pybackpack to work, so open a Terminal (Applications ➤ System Tools ➤ Terminal) and type su -c "yum install rdiff-backup". Since Pybackpack is not available from the official Fedora repositories, it is not signed. Before you can install it, you need to disable the gpgcheck from the /etc/yum.conf file. At the terminal, type su -c "gedit /etc/yum.conf and press Enter. Look for the line that reads gpgcheck=1 and rewrite it such that it reads gpgcheck=0. You can now safely install Pybackpack. At the terminal, type the following:

```
cd /home/linuxlala/Downloads
su -c "yum localinstall pybackpack"
```

You will now find Pybackpack listed under the System ➤ Preferences ➤ System menus as File Backup Manager.

■**Note** The rdiff-backup utility is the driving force behind Pybackpack. If you wish to back up your data on a remote machine, you will need to install rdiff-backup on that machine as well. We discuss rdiff-backup later in the chapter.

Backing Up Data via Pybackpack

To configure a backup, select \System ➤ Preferences ➤ System ➤ File Backup Manager. You'll see the File Backup Manager dialog box, as shown in Figure 31-2. Using this dialog box, you can choose the files that Pybackpack backs up and where it stores the backup files.

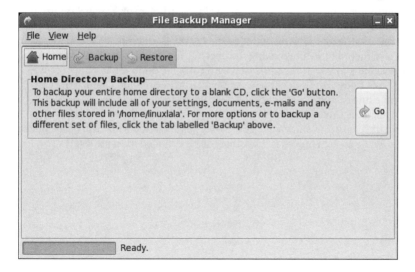

Figure 31-2. *Pybackpack can back up your entire home directory or custom paths that you specify.*

■**Note** Pybackpack doesn't create a new backup file each time it runs, because that would take too long. Instead, it creates an *incremental backup*, which means that it updates the last backup files with files that have changed or have been created since. Any files that haven't been updated since the last backup are unchanged.

Including Files and Folders in the Backup Job

You can choose to create a backup of your users' home directories by clicking the Go button under the Home tab. If you wish to back up some other files, like a collection of pictures from your past birthday or all your work files, click the Backup tab. Then click the New button on the Backup Sets sidebar, located at the bottom-left.

The Create New Backup Set dialog box will then guide you through the steps required to back up your files. You can specify a name for your backup, and you can also optionally write a brief description. Choose a destination for you backup files (the local hard disk, a CD/DVD, or a remote machine). To select files and folders to include in the backup, simply browse to the relevant location and click the "Include in set" button.

Bear in mind that directories are added recursively, which means that any directories contained within the directory you're adding are also backed up. For example, if you back up your home directory, you don't need to specifically add the Pictures and Documents directories.

Excluding Files and Folders from the Backup Job

Since directories are added recursively in the backup, it isn't hard to imagine the purpose of the "Exclude from set" button. It is best to describe it, however, by using an example. Suppose the Pictures folder in your home directory contains categorized images of your birthday, your parent's wedding anniversary, and the like. Having included the Pictures folder in a backup set, all the folders within it are also included. While making the backup, you decide you don't want to keep the birthday pictures that show your face smeared with cake. So, double-click the Pictures folder and the Birthday_Pics folder, and select the images you don't want (you can use the Ctrl or Shift keys to select multiple images), and then click the "Exclude from set" button.

The pane at the bottom of the Create New Backup Set dialog box lists the files that will be included or excluded from the backup, as shown in Figure 31-3. Files and folders that will be included are preceded with a + sign, while a – sign precedes those that will be excluded from the set.

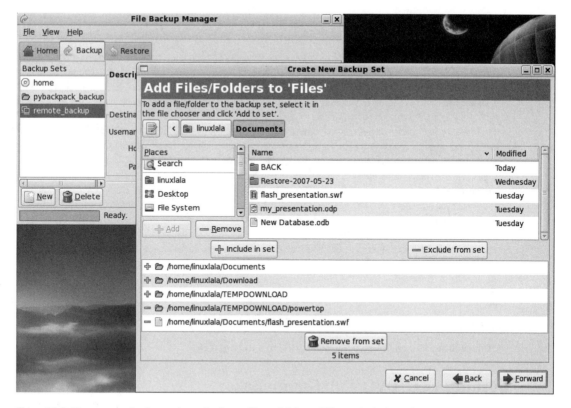

Figure 31-3. *You can easily determine whether a file or folder will be included in a backup set.*

Restoring Data via Pybackpack

If the worst happens and you need to restore any number of files from the backup, click System ➤ Preferences ➤ System ➤ File Backup Manager. The first step is to click the Restore tab. Click the "Location to restore from" drop-down list and choose a backup file from which to restore. The "Restore as of" drop-down list lists various versions of the files based on when the backups were made; it makes sense to choose the latest files (unless you want to revert to an older version of a file).

The data is restored under the restored_files/pybackpack_backup/ folder under your home directory.

WHAT ARE INCREMENTAL BACKUPS?

Rdiff-backup, the force behind Pybackpack, works on the principles of incremental backups. When you create a backup, a copy of the current file is stored somewhere. The next time you make a backup, it will overwrite the previous copy of the backup. With incremental backups, multiple copies of a backup are stored, but each original piece of information is stored only once. Successive backups will only contain files that have changed since the last backup. We'll give you an example to illustrate this.

Suppose you took ten pictures on your birthday and kept them under the `Birthday_Pics` folder. You then made a backup of the `Birthday_Pics` folder. Let's say the backup was made on the desktop and is called `backup_bday`. Later, a friend comes over, and he has some pictures from the night as well. You store these pictures in the `Birthday_Pics` folder as well and make another backup. Now, when you browse to the `bday_pics` backup folder on your desktop, you'll find that it contains all the pictures.

When you now restore the pictures, you can decide whether to restore them to the state they were in before the first backup (when the `Birthday_Pics` folder only had ten pictures), or to the state they were in just before the second backup (when you had added the pictures your friend brought to the `Birthday_Pics` folder). Also, when you made the backup for the second time, not all the pictures were copied again—only the new pictures were copied. This is the advantage of incremental backups.

Burning a Backup File to CD/DVD

For safekeeping, you can burn your backup file to a CD or DVD.

Burning a CD/DVD with GnomeBaker

To start GnomeBaker, click Applications ➤ Sound & Video ➤ GnomeBaker. Choose Data CD or Data DVD. To burn your CD/DVD, follow these steps:

1. Select the backup file you want to burn, and click Add files. The Data CD tab at the bottom of the window will list the selected file under Contents.

2. The bar at the bottom will show you how much space is left on the CD, so you can select files accordingly.

3. When you have selected the files to burn, click the Burn button, and you'll see the dialog box shown in Figure 31-4.

■**Note** Bear in mind that CD-R/RW and DVD-R/RW discs don't last forever. In fact, some estimates put the typical life span of a disc at as little as a few months! As always, quality matters. Buying more expensive, branded discs will produce far better results. Kodak estimates its Ultima CD-R discs will last 200 years, for example! Storage is also important. Store your discs in a location away from strong light and with average temperature and humidity levels.

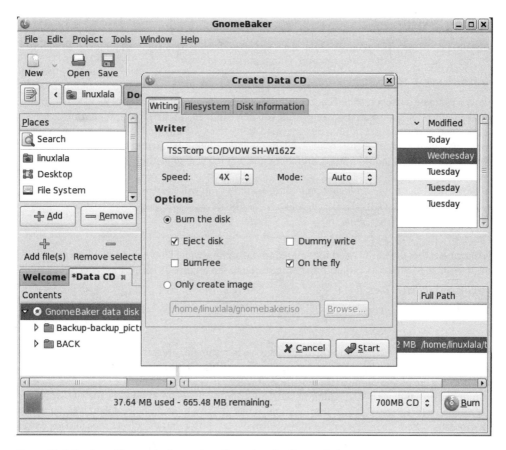

Figure 31-4. *Backup files can be burned to disc using the GnomeBaker program.*

Making Backups from the Command Line

Although Pybackpack allows the uninitiated to make quick backups, the tar program is preferred by Linux old-timers. This creates TAR files and is one of the original carryovers from UNIX. TAR stands for Tape ARchive and refers to backing up data to a magnetic tape backup device. Although TAR files are designed for backup, they've also become a standard method of transferring files across the Internet, particularly with regard to source files or other installation programs.

A TAR file is simply a collection of files bundled into one. By default, a TAR file isn't compressed, although additional software can be used to compress it. TAR files aren't very sophisticated compared to modern archive file formats. They're not encrypted, for example, but this can also be one of their advantages.

■**Note** Linux comes with a couple more backup commands, which you might choose to use. They are cpio and pax. Examine their man pages for more details.

Creating TAR Files

Perhaps unsurprisingly, TAR files are created at the console using the tar command. Usually, all you need to do is specify a source directory and a filename, like so:

```
tar -cf backup.tar /home/linuxlala/
```

This will create a backup called backup.tar based on the contents of /home/linuxlala/. tar is automatically recursive so, in this example, it will delve into all subdirectories beneath /home/linuxlala. The -c command option tells tar you're going to create an archive, and the -f option indicates that the filename for the archive will immediately follow. If you don't use the -f option, tar will send its output to standard output, which means that it will display the contents of the archive on the screen.

If you type in a command like the preceding example, you will see this message:

```
Removing leading '/' from member names.
```

This means that the folders and files added to the archive will all have the initial forward slash removed from their paths. So, rather than being stored in the archive as this:

```
/home/linuxlala/Mail/file1
```

the file will be stored as follows:

```
home/linuxlala/Mail/file1
```

The difference between the two forms concerns when the files are later extracted from the archive. If the files have the initial slash, tar will write the file to /home/linuxlala/Mail/file1. If there's already a file of that name in that location, it will be overwritten.

On the other hand, with the leading slash removed, tar will create a new directory wherever you choose to restore the archive. In this example, it will create a new directory called home, and then a directory called linuxlala within that, and so on. Of course, if these directories already exist at that location, then tar will simply write the files to them.

Because of the potential of accidentally overwriting data by specifying absolute paths in this way, a better way of backing up a directory is simply to change into its parent and specify it without a full path. The following will back up your home directory:

```
cd /home/
tar -cf backup.tar linuxlala
```

When this particular archive is restored, it will create a new folder called linuxlala wherever it's restored.

Compressing TAR Archives

You can also compress the archive from within tar, although it actually calls in outside help from either bzip2 or gzip, depending on which you specify.

To create a TAR archive compressed using bzip2, the following should do the trick:

```
tar -cjf backup.tar.bz2 linuxlala
```

This will create a compressed backup from the directory linuxlala. The -j command option passes the output from tar to the bzip2 program, although this is done in the background.

Notice that we've changed the backup filename extension to indicate that this is a bzip2 compressed archive. This is standard practice.

The following command will create an archive compressed with the older gzip compression:

```
tar -czf backup.tar.gz linuxlala
```

Note You might be wondering which you should use: bzip2 or gzip? In nearly every case, bzip2 is better. It will shrink files to a much higher degree. Gzip is used when you might have to transfer files to a computer that does not have bzip2 installed. This is very rare nowadays. However, many source code files are compressed using gzip because there's a chance they might be extracted on a UNIX system without bzip2.

This uses the -z command option to pass the output to gzip. This time, the filename shows it's a gzip compressed archive, so you can correctly identify it in the future.

Extracting Files from a TAR Archive

Extracting files using tar is as easy as creating them:

```
tar -xf backup.tar
```

The -x option tells tar to extract the files from the backup.tar archive.

Extracting compressed archives is simply a matter of adding the -j or -z option to the -x option:

```
tar -xjf backup.tar.bz2
```

Note Technically speaking, tar doesn't require the preceding hyphen before its command options. However, it's a good idea to use it anyway, so that you won't forget to use it with other commands.

Viewing TAR Archive Information

To view the contents of a TAR archive without actually restoring the files, use the -t option:

```
tar -tf backup.tar | less
```

This example adds a pipe into less at the end, because the listing of files probably will be large and scroll off the screen. Just add the -j or -z option if the tar archive is also compressed.

In addition, you can add the -v option to all stages of making, extracting, and viewing an archive to see more information (chiefly, the files that are being archived or extracted). Adding -vv provides even more information:

```
tar -cvvf backup.tar linuxlala
```

This will create an archive and also show a complete directory listing as the files and folders are added, including permissions.

Saving a TAR File to CD/DVD

Once the TAR file has been created, the problem of where to store it arises. As we mentioned earlier, storing backup data on the same hard disk as the data it was created to back up is foolish, since any problem that might affect the hard disk might also affect the archive. You could end up losing both sets of data!

If the archive is less than 700 MB, consider storing it on a CD. If it's less than 4.3 GB, you could save it to a DVD. To do this from the command line, first turn the file into an ISO image, and then burn it.

To turn the archive into an ISO image, use the `mkisofs` command:

```
mkisofs -o backup.iso backup.tar.bz2
```

You can then burn the ISO image to a CD or DVD by using Nautilus.

Burning a CD/DVD with Nautilus

To start the Nautilus CD burner, click Places ➤ CD/DVD Creator. Now you can just drag and drop the backup folder you want to burn. Once you've added the backup files, click the Write to Disc button, as shown in Figure 31-5. (We've already covered burning disks with Nautilus in Chapter 11.)

Alternatively, you can just right-click the ISO file and select Open with CD/DVD Creator.

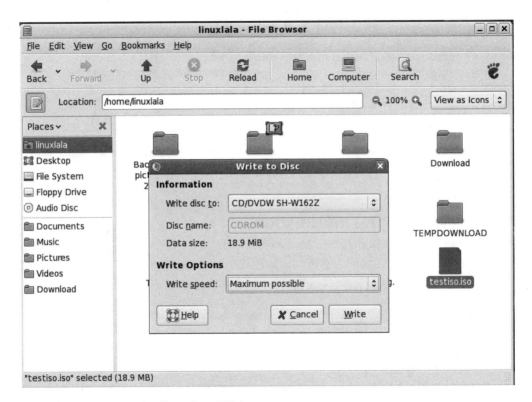

Figure 31-5. *You can use Nautilus to burn ISO images.*

Summary

In this chapter, we looked at making backups. First, you saw how to verify where your personal and other vital data is stored. Then we looked at how Pybackpack can be used to back up system configuration and personal data, and to restore data from your backup. Finally, you learned how to use `tar` at the command line to back up any kind of data.

In the next chapter, we'll look at how tasks can be scheduled to occur at various times under Fedora.

CHAPTER 32

■■■

Scheduling Tasks

In this book, you've learned about various tasks you can perform to keep Fedora running smoothly. You may decide that you want some of these tasks to occur on a regular basis. For example, perhaps you want your /home folder to be backed up every day, or perhaps you want to clean the /tmp folder to ensure that you always have enough free disk space. You could carry out each task individually, but human nature would no doubt step in, and you would forget, or you might perform the action twice, because you've forgotten that you've already done it.

As you might expect, Linux is able to automate the running of particular tasks. They can either be run periodically at scheduled times or as one-time tasks. Using Linux's scheduling features is explained in this chapter.

Scheduling with crontab

Under Fedora, the main way of scheduling tasks is via the cron daemon. This works on behalf of the user in order to schedule individual tasks, and it is also used by the system to run vital system tasks, although a different way of working is used in each case.

For cron to run user-scheduled tasks, it reads a file called crontab. Each user has her own version of this file, which is stored in the /var/spool/cron directory. This file can be edited in a text editor, but a special command should be used to do so.

Note System-wide tasks are handled by the /etc/crontab file. This runs scripts contained in /etc/cron.hourly, /etc/cron.daily, and so on, depending on when the tasks are meant to be run (every hour, day, week, or month). The average user never needs to bother with system-wide cron jobs. These are handled by the internal system, and programs create their own entries as and when necessary.

The cron daemon starts at bootup and simply sits in the background while you work, checking every minute to see if a task is due. As soon as one comes up, it commences the task, and then returns to a waiting status.

Creating a Scheduled Task

Adding a scheduled task is relatively easily and is done via the shell. Entering the following command will cause your personal crontab file to be loaded into the vi text editor, ready for editing:

```
crontab -e
```

If this is the first time you've edited your `crontab` file, it will most likely be completely empty. However, don't be put off. Adding a new entry is relatively easy. Refer to Chapter 15 to see how vi works. The `crontab` file normally takes the form of something like this:

```
01 12 15 * * tar -cjf /home/linuxlala/backup.tar.bz2 /home/linuxlala
```

Let's examine the line piece by piece. The first part—the numbers and asterisks—refers to when the task should be run. From left to right, the fields refer to the following:

- Minutes, from 0 to 59

- Hours, in 24-hour time—so from 0 to 23

- Day dates, for the day of the month, from 1 to 31 (assuming the month has that many days)

- Months, from 1 to 12

- Day, for a particular day, either from 0 to 6 (0 is Sunday), or specified as a three-letter abbreviation (`mon`, `tue`, `wed`, and so on)

In the example, the task is set to run at the 1st minute at the 12th hour (noon) on the 15th day of the month. But what do the asterisks stand for? They're effectively wildcards and tell `cron` that every possible value applies. Because an asterisk appears in the month field, this task will be run every month. Because an asterisk appears in the day field, the task will be run every day.

You might have noticed a logical contradiction here. How can you specify a day if you also specify a date in the month? Wouldn't this seriously limit the chances of the task ever running? Yes, it would. If you were to specify `sat`, for example, and put `15` in the date field, the task would run on only the 15th of the month if that happened to be a Saturday. This is why the two fields are rarely used in the same `crontab` entry, and an asterisk appears in one if the other is being used.

After the time and date fields comes the command itself: `tar`. As you learned in the previous chapter, `tar` is designed to back up your personal data.

Only standard BASH shell commands can be used in the command section. `cron` isn't clever enough to interpret symbols such as the tilde (~) as a way of referring to your `home` directory. For this reason, it's best to be very thorough when defining a `cron` job and always use absolute paths.

Let's take a look at another example, with a special day field (shown in Figure 32-1):

```
59 23 * * 0-3 tar -cjf /home/linuxlala/backup.tar.bz2 /home/linuxlala
```

The first field says that this task will run at the 59th minute of the 23rd hour (that is, one minute before midnight). The date and month fields have asterisks, so this implies that the task should run every day and every month. However, the day field contains 0-3. This says that the task should run on only days 0 through to 3, or Sunday through Wednesday.

You can have as many `cron` entries as you like; simply give each a separate line. You don't need to put them in date or time order. You can just add them as and when you see fit.

When you're finished, save the file and quit vi in the usual way (by pressing Esc and then typing `:wq`).

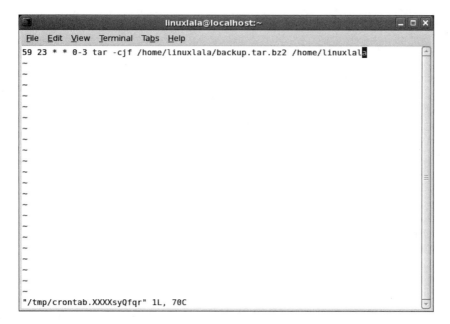

Figure 32-1. *Editing crontab lets you schedule tasks using the vi text editor.*

Scheduling with anacron

If cron has an Achilles' heel, it is that it expects your computer to be up and running all the time. If you schedule a task for around midnight, as in one of the previous examples, and your computer isn't switched on at that time, the task simply won't run.

anacron was created to fix this problem (see Figure 32-2). It also can run scheduled tasks, but unlike cron, it doesn't rely on exact times or dates. Instead, it works on the principle of time periods. For example, tasks can be set to run every day. In fact, tasks can be set to run every *x* number of days, regardless of whether that's every two days or every hundred thousand. It also doesn't matter if the computer is shut down and rebooted during that time; the task will be run only once in the specified time period. In addition, tasks can be specifically set to run at the beginning of each month, regardless of the length in days of each month.

anacron is primarily designed to be used for system maintenance, and the /etc/anacrontab file holds the details of the tasks. Unlike with crontab, each user doesn't have his own anacrontab file. However, there's no reason why you can't add your own commands to the main anacrontab file. This file can be edited in any text editor, and you don't need to use a special command to edit it (as with crontab), although you'll need to adopt superuser powers to do so.

Each line in anacrontab takes the following form:

days   delay   name of task   command

The days field holds the number of days in between the running of the task. To set the task to run every day, you would enter 1. To make the task run every nine days, you would add 9. To set it to run monthly, you would type @monthly.

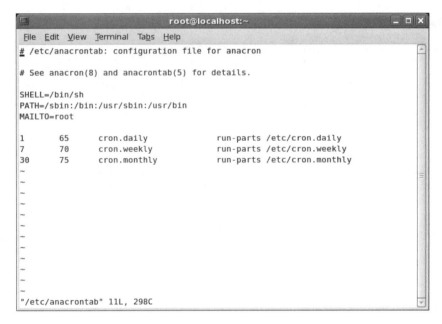

Figure 32-2. *anacron is used to run tasks periodically, such as every couple of days.*

The delay field tells anacron how long to wait after it has run before running the task, specified in minutes. It is necessary because anacron is usually run at bootup, and if it were to run the scheduled tasks instantly, the machine would grind to a halt because it is already busy. A delay of five minutes is usually adequate, although if some tasks are already scheduled to run on the same day before that task, you should allow enough time for them to finish.

The name of task field is for your personal reference and shouldn't contain either slashes or spaces. (Hint: Separate words using underscores or full stops.)

The command field is, as with crontab, the shell command that should be run.

■**Note** anacron is run as the root user, so if you do add your own entry to /etc/anacrontab, any files it creates will be owned by root, too. If you use anacron to create a backup of your /home directory, for example, the resultant backup file will be owned by root, and you'll need to use the chown command to change its ownership so you can access it. See Chapter 14 for more information about the chown command.

Let's look at an example of an /etc/anacrontab entry:

```
1 15 backup_job tar -cjf /home/linuxlala/backup.tar.bz2 /home/linuxlala
```

This will run the specified tar command every day (because 1 is in the days field), and with a delay of 15 minutes after anacron is first run.

anacron is run automatically every time you boot into Fedora.

Using at to Schedule One-Off Tasks

What if you quickly want to schedule a one-time-only task? For this, you can use the at command.

Adding a job with at is very easy, largely because the at command accepts a wide variety of time formats. For example, typing the following at the command prompt will run a job at lunchtime tomorrow:

```
at noon tomorrow
```

It really is as simple as that!

Alternatively, you can specify a time, date, and even a year:

```
at 13:00 jun 25 2008
```

This will run the job at 1 p.m. on June 25, 2008. The various time and date formats are explained in the at command's man page.

Once the at command containing the date has been entered, you'll be presented with a mock shell prompt, called the at prompt. Here, you can type the commands you want to run. Many shell commands can be entered, one after the other; just press Enter between them. Then press Ctrl+D to signal that you're finished editing. At this point, at will confirm the time and write the task into its list.

You can view the list at any time by typing atq. This will show a list of numbered jobs. You can remove any job by typing atrm, followed by its atq job number. For example, the following will remove the job numbered 9 in the atq list:

```
atrm 9
```

Summary

In this brief chapter, we looked at how you can schedule tasks under Fedora, which is essentially making programs run at certain times. We examined the crontab and anacron facilities, which can schedule tasks to run periodically, and we also examined the at service, which can schedule one-off tasks to run at certain times.

In the final chapter of this book, we will look at how you can access your Fedora computer remotely—theoretically, from any Internet-equipped location in the world.

■ ■ ■

## CHAPTER 33

Accessing Computers Remotely

One area where Linux particularly excels is in its support for networking, including the Internet. If you wish to learn about how networks operate on a fundamental level, then Linux is an ideal choice, because it puts you in virtually direct contact with the technology.

The widespread integration and support for networking extends to several useful system tools that let you access Linux across any kind of network, including the Internet. In fact, it's even possible to access a Linux machine running on a different continent just as if you were sitting in front of it!

This chapter looks at the many ways you can access your Fedora computer remotely. In addition, we look at the ways that you can use Fedora to access almost any other computer, including Windows XP Professional PCs.

Using Secure Shell

The history of UNIX has always featured computers connecting to other computers in some fashion, whether they were dumb terminals connecting to a mainframe computer or UNIX machines acting as nodes on the fledgling Internet. Because of this, a wide variety of techniques and protocols were invented to allow computers to communicate and log into each other across networks. However, while these still work fine over the modern Internet, we're now faced with new threats to the privacy of data. In theory, any data transmitted across the Internet can be picked up by individuals at certain key stages along the route. If the data isn't protected in any way, it can be easily intercepted and read.

To counter such an occurrence, the ssh suite of programs was created. Although these programs started as open source, they gradually became proprietary. Therefore, several newer open source versions have been created, including the one used on the majority of Linux distributions (including Fedora): OpenSSH.

The goal of ssh is to create a secure connection between two computers. You can then do just about any task, including initiating a shell session so that you can use the remote computer as if you were sitting in front of it, or copying files to and from ssh using various techniques at both ends of the connection to encrypt not only the data passing between the two machines, but also the username and password.

■**Note** This chapter refers to *remote* and *local* machines. The *remote* machine is the computer you're connecting to across the network or Internet. The *local* machine is the one you're actually sitting in front of. These two terms are widely used within documentation describing networking.

Logging Into a Remote Computer

The most basic type of ssh connection is a remote login. This will give you a command prompt on the remote computer, as if you had just sat down in front of it and opened a GNOME Terminal window.

But before you can log into any machine via ssh, you'll need to be sure that the remote computer is able to accept ssh connections. This means that it needs to be running the ssh server program (referred to as a *service*), and also that its firewall has an open port for incoming connections.

The two major components of OpenSSH are the client and server. Most distributions, including Fedora, install both items and run the server component all the time. This server component is automatically configured, but if you're using the Fedora firewall (see Chapter 9), you will need to configure an incoming rule to open port 22.

■**Note** If you use the Security Level and Firewall tool as described in Chapter 9, you can simply select the default incoming SSH rule. There's no need to manually specify a port number.

Initiating an ssh remote shell session with a remote machine is usually achieved by typing something similar to the following at a command prompt on the local machine:

ssh <username>@<IP address>

In other words, you specify the username you want to log in as, as well as the IP address of the machine. If there's a fully-qualified domain name (FQDN) for the system you want to access, you can specify that instead of the IP address.

■**Note** An FQDN is the hostname of a system plus its Internet address, such as mycomputer.example.com. Unless you have had this function specifically set up for you by a system administrator, you'll probably have to connect via IP addresses. However, if you rent a web server, you might be able to connect to it with ssh using the domain name of the server.

You'll be prompted for your password, which, obviously, is the password for the account you're trying to log into on the *remote* computer.

When you log in for the first time, you'll see the following message:

```
ssh linuxlala@192.168.0.102
The authenticity of host '192.168.0.102 (192.168.0.102)' can't be established.
RSA key fingerprint is b5:f4:3e:xx:xx:xx:xx:xx:xx:xx:xx:xx:c9:1a:2d.
Are you sure you want to continue connecting (yes/no)? yes
Warning: Permanently added '192.168.0.102' (RSA) to the list of known hosts.
linuxlala@192.168.0.102's password:
```

This means that the remote computer's encryption key hasn't yet been added to your PC's store file. However, once you agree to the initial login, the encryption key will be added, and it will be used in the future to confirm that the remote computer you're connecting to is authentic.

■ Note There's a fine line between security concern and paranoia. Connecting to a remote machine for the first time and accepting its ssh key is considered insecure by some people, because you cannot be 100 percent sure that the remote machine is the one you want to connect to. It might have been swapped for a different machine by hackers (or some such theory). In addition, the key might be intercepted on its journey to you. Because of this, those who are highly security conscious can use the ssh-keygen program to create a key on the remote machine first, and then import it to the local machine via floppy disk before logging in.

VERIFYING KEY FINGERPRINTS

Now that you have established an ssh connection, wouldn't you want to verify whether you are indeed connected to the right machine? The trick lies in verifying the RSA key fingerprint. Fedora automatically creates these keys. To create your own RSA key, open a Terminal window and type ssh-keygen -t rsa.

In the example just discussed, look at the line that begins with RSA key fingerprint. This is then followed by a 16-digit string of colon-separated text. You can verify whether you are connected to the right machine by checking its RSA key against this key fingerprint.

You can store this RSA key fingerprint in a file and compare this with the fingerprint on the remote machine. Once connected to the remote machine, run the command ssh-keygen -l -f /etc/ssh/ssh_host_rsa_key.pub. You will see something like the following:

```
b5:f4:3e:xx:xx:xx:xx:xx:xx:xx:xx:xx:xx:c9:1a:2d. ssh_host_rsa_key.pub
```

Note that the colon-separated value is the same as what you saw when making the connection with the remote machine. If you own the remote machine, you should copy this 16-digit key (write it down on paper or store it on another machine) and use it to confirm that you're connected to the right machine.

If you don't own the remote machine, you can still verify the key fingerprint by contacting the owner of the remote machine. Depending on whether you know this person, the conversation can occur in person or over the phone. If you don't know the person, you can use GPG-signed e-mail, such that you can verify the signature of his GPG public key to confirm his identity. (This is important because you have no means of otherwise knowing if you are talking to the genuine owner.)

GNU Privacy Guard (GPG) allows you to encrypt your personal data. Using public and private keys, you can verify the authenticity of data, e-mails, and so on (www.gnupg.org/ has excellent documentation on how you can set up and use GPG).

After confirming that you want to make the connection, you'll be invited to enter the password for the user account under which you initiated the ssh connection. Once this is done, you should find yourself with a shell login on the remote computer. You can run the same commands as usual and perform identical tasks.

The machine you're logged into will show no symptoms of being used remotely. This isn't like the movies, where what you type on your local machine is somehow mirrored on the remote machine for all to see. However, obviously, if a user of the remote machine were to view her network connections using something similar to the netstat command, then she would see another computer attached via ssh.

To end an ssh session, simply type exit. This will then return you to the command prompt on your own machine.

Tip There's a version of the `ssh` client that runs on a variety of non-Linux operating systems, making it possible to log into your Fedora machine from a Windows computer. The program is called PuTTY, and can be downloaded from `www.chiark.greenend.org.uk/~sgtatham/putty/`.

MANAGING REMOTE SESSIONS

Whenever you open any kind of shell to enter commands and run programs, you'll notice that any commands you start running last only as long as the shell window is open. When the shell window is closed, any task running within it ends, too. This is because the shell is seen as the "owner" of the process, and when the owner dies, any processes it started also die.

When using `ssh` to start a remote shell session, this also applies. Whenever you log out, any tasks you were running are ended. This can be annoying if, for example, you've started a lengthy download on the remote machine. Effectively, you must remain logged in via `ssh` until the download has finished.

To get around this, you can use the handy `screen` program. This isn't specifically designed to be an aid to remote logins, but there's no reason why it cannot be used in such a situation.

The `screen` program effectively starts shell sessions that stick around, even if the shell window is closed or the `ssh` connection is ended or lost. After logging into the remote computer via `ssh`, you can start a `screen` session by simply typing the program name at the prompt: `screen`.

This will start the program, but there won't be any indication that you're running a `screen` session. There's no taskbar at the bottom of the Terminal window, for example; `screen` works completely in the background.

Let's consider what happens when you detach and then reattach to a `screen` session. To detach from the `screen` session, press Ctrl+A and then Ctrl+D. You'll then be returned to the standard shell and, in fact, you can now disconnect from your `ssh` session as usual. However, the `screen` session will still be running in the background on the remote computer. To prove this, you could log back in, and then type this:

```
screen -r
```

This will resume your `screen` session, and you should be able to pick up quite literally where you left off; any output from previous commands will be displayed.

To quit a `screen` session, type `exit` from within it. If you start multiple windows within a `screen` session, you must individually close each of those windows before you can exit `screen`.

The `screen` program is very powerful. To learn more about it, read its man page. To see a list of its keyboard commands, press Ctrl+A, and then type a question mark (?) while `screen` is running.

Transferring Files Between Remote Computers

The `ssh` utility brings with it two basic ways of transferring files between machines: `scp` and `sftp`. `scp` is fine for smaller file transfers, but if you want to copy a lot of files, `sftp` is probably a better choice.

Using scp

Strictly speaking, `scp` is merely a program that copies files from one computer to another in a secure fashion using the underlying `ssh` protocol. You don't have to be logged into another computer via `ssh` to use it. For example, if we wanted to transfer a file from one of our test computers to a remote computer, we could type the following:

```
scp somefile linuxlala@<IP address>:/home/linuxlala/Desktop
```

Replace <IP address> with the IP address of the computer to which you want to send the file. In other words, you must first specify the local file you want to copy across, and then provide the login details for the remote computer in the same format as with an ssh login. Then, after the colon, you specify the path on the *remote* computer where you would like the file to be copied.

■**Note** If it helps, consider the latter part of the scp command after the filename as one large address—first you provide your username, then the computer address, and then the path.

Using the command when you *are* logged into another computer via ssh works in exactly the same way. Let's consider a simple analogy.

Assume there are two computers: A and B. You have a user account on each one. Sitting at the keyboard of A, you establish a ssh connection with B by typing the following:

```
ssh linuxlala@computer_B
```

This lets you log into B as if you were sitting in front of it. You can now copy files from the remote machine to the local machine.

On our test machines, B has a file called formula1.xls that we want to copy to our local machine (A). We do this with the following command:

```
scp formula1.xls linuxlala@computer_A:/home/linuxlala/
```

This will copy the file from computer B to computer A and place it in the /home/linuxlala/ directory.

■**Note** With scp, you can copy entire directories, too. Simply add the -r command option, like so: scp -r mydirectory <username>@<IP address>:/path/.

Using sftp

To copy a lot of files to or from a remote computer, the sftp program is the best solution. If you've ever used a shell-based ftp program, you'll feel right at home, because sftp isn't very different.

The difference compared to scp is that you use sftp to establish a connection with the remote computer in a similar way to ssh, except you can use only certain commands. You can initiate a sftp session by using this command format:

```
sftp <username>@<IP address>
```

The same rules as when you're logging in with ssh apply, both in terms of formatting the login command and also confirming the encryption key if this is the first time you've logged in.

The sftp commands are fairly basic. For example, to copy a file from the remote machine, simply type this:

```
get <filename>
```

This will copy the file into the directory you were in on the local machine before you started the sftp session.

By specifying a path after the filename, the file will be copied to the specified local directory:

```
get formula1.xls /home/linuxlala/racing_stuff/
```

Sending files from the local machine to the remote machine is just as easy:

```
put <filename>
```

By specifying a path after the filename, you can ensure that the file is saved to a particular remote path.

One useful thing to remember is that any command preceded by an exclamation mark (!, called a bang in Linux-speak) is executed on the local machine as a shell command. So, if you wanted to remove a file on the local machine, you could type this:

```
!rm -rf <filename>
```

Simply typing a bang symbol on its own starts a shell session on the local machine so that you can perform even more tasks. When you're finished, type exit to return to the sftp program.

For a list of popular sftp commands, see Table 33-1.

Table 33-1. *Common sftp Commands*

Command	Function
cd	Change the remote directory.
lcd	Change the local directory.
get	Download the specified file.
ls	List the remote directory.
lls	List the local directory.
mkdir	Create a directory on the remote machine.
lmkdir	Create a directory on the local machine.
put	Upload the specified file to the remote machine.
pwd	Print the current remote directory.
rmdir	Delete the remote directory.
rm	Delete the remote file.
exit	Quit sftp.
!command	Execute the specified command on the local machine.
!	Start a temporary local shell session (type exit to return to sftp).
help	Show a list of commands.

Accessing GUI Applications Remotely

So far, we've looked at connecting to a remote machine using command-line tools. But Fedora is based around the graphical desktop, so is there any way of running, say, a Nautilus file browser window to manipulate files on the remote machine? Yes!

The graphical subsystem of Linux, X, is designed to work across a network. In fact, if you run Linux on your desktop PC, X *still* works via a loopback network within your machine (meaning that network commands are sent out but addressed to the very same machine on which they originated). Because of this, it's possible to make programs on a remote machine run on a local machine's X server. The actual work of running the application is handled by the *remote* machine, but the work of displaying the graphics is handled by the *local* machine.

■**Caution** X connections across a network can be a little slow and certainly not as snappy as running the same application on the local machine. This lag can become irritating after a while.

Running X Applications on a Remote Computer

Unfortunately, X server communications aren't normally encrypted, so if one machine were to simply connect to an X server over a network (or even the Internet), the data transfer would be unencrypted and open to eavesdroppers.

But ssh once again comes to the rescue. You can configure ssh so that X applications on the remote computer can be run on the local machine, with the data sent through the ssh connection. Log into the remote machine using ssh, but also specify the -X flag:

```
ssh -X <username>@<IP address>
```

When you're logged in, you can simply start any application by typing its name as usual. The only difference is that the program will appear on the screen of the local machine, rather than on the remote machine, as shown in Figure 33-1.

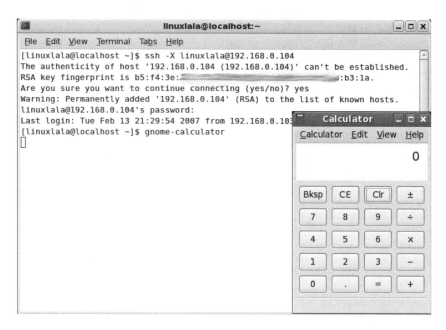

Figure 33-1. *Although the calculator application appears on the local computer's display, it's actually running on the remote machine.*

Using X across the Internet or even a local network isn't very fast, and you can expect delays when you open menus or if the screen must frequently redraw. However, you will notice some slight improvement if you use the -C command option along with -X when attempting to run X applications using ssh.

Running the GNOME Desktop Across a Remote Connection

It's even possible to run the entire GNOME desktop across an ssh connection. In other words, you can access the desktop of a remote computer as if you were sitting in front of it.

You can do this by starting a stripped-down X server shell on the local computer, and then initiating the GNOME desktop on the remote computer via an ssh connection.

On the local machine from which you would like to initiate the connection, close all open programs and then kill the X server by pressing Ctrl+Alt+Backspace. Then switch to any one of the virtual terminals by pressing Ctrl+Alt+F1–6. Log in and run this command as root: `init 3`. This command will kill the X server. Now run the command `xinit`. This will start a rudimentary X session, complete with an `xterm` shell window. You can then use the `ssh` command to log into your remote machine, specifying that X communications should be allowed over the connection:

```
ssh -X <username>@<IP address>
```

Then type the following:

```
gnome-session
```

After a few seconds, the remote computer's GNOME desktop will appear. Make sure you don't close the original `xterm` window, because this owns the `gnome-session` process, so closing it will kill the desktop.

Once again, the remote desktop will be somewhat slow to respond to mouse clicks and keyboard strokes, but it should be usable.

If you intend to do this often, you may wish to configure a command line–only run level on the local machine. This means that you can boot to a non-GUI login prompt and then initiate your own X session manually (either running GNOME on your local machine or on a remote machine). Most Linux distributions (including Fedora and SUSE) define run level 3 as command line–only, so you can do the same.

Note Under Fedora, run level 5 runs the GUI, and is the default. Run level 3 is command line–only and run level 4 is unused.

To stop the GUI from starting automatically under run level 3, you need to modify the `/etc/inittab` file so that you'll boot to the modified run level 3. You need to be root to modify the file, so use the `su -` command. The following will load it into the Gedit text editor:

```
gedit /etc/inittab
```

Look for the line that begins `id:5:initdefault:` and change it so that it reads `id:3:initdefault:`. Then save the file and reboot.

Once you've logged in, you'll have the choice of either starting the X server shell for a remote connection, as described earlier, or starting the usual GNOME desktop on the local machine by typing `startx`.

Accessing Fedora via Remote Desktop

A less secure but more convenient way to access your PC's desktop across a network is to use Fedora's Remote Desktop feature. The advantage of this method is that the desktop of the remote computer appears in a window on the local computer's desktop, so there's no need to kill the existing X server and start a new one.

Remote Desktop uses the Virtual Network Computing (VNC) software to share the desktop. *Sharing* is the key word because, effectively, anyone who connects will take control of the main desktop, including the mouse and keyboard input.

However, there are a couple of important differences compared to accessing X across an `ssh` connection:

- Although the password is sent encrypted, the rest of the VNC data transfers aren't. Complete encryption is possible using special versions of VNC, or via an OpenSSH tunnel.

- The remote desktop isn't blanked, so anyone standing in front of the computer will be able to see what you're doing. This could present a security/privacy risk.

If you're prepared to put up with these caveats, then allowing remote desktop access on a computer is easy. You will need to install the Terminal Server Client program before you proceed. Start Pirut Package Manager (Application ➤ Add/Remove Software) and click the Search tab. Look for tsclient and click the check box to mark it for installation.

Here's the procedure:

1. Click System ➤ Preferences ➤ Internet and Network, and then click Remote Desktop. Put a check alongside "Allow other users to view your desktop" and ensure there's a check in the box alongside "Allow other users to control your desktop," as shown in Figure 33-2. Beneath this option, you can choose whether the user should confirm each connection and whether you want to set a password. Both options add to the security of your system, although the confirmation option means that someone will have to be at the computer to authorize an incoming connection.

Figure 33-2. *Fedora's Remote Desktop feature lets you share your desktop, but isn't as secure as making an X server connection with ssh.*

2. On the computer from which you want to connect to the remote desktop, click Applications ➤ Internet ➤ Terminal Server Client. In the Computer field, enter the IP address of the computer you wish to connect to. In the Protocol drop-down list, select VNC. Then click Connect.

3. You'll be prompted to enter the password, if one is applicable, and you should then see the remote computer's desktop in a window. Once you've finished, simply close the window to terminate the connection.

Controlling the Fedora Desktop from Windows

You can easily control the Fedora remote machine from Windows by installing a couple of programs. You will need to allow other users to control the Fedora desktop, as shown in Figure 33-2. To begin, download PuTTY and RealVNC for Windows.

The PuTTY program is actually an EXE file that doesn't need to be installed. Just double-click it to start PuTTY. You will, however, need to install RealVNC.

When you have installed RealVNC, double-click the PuTTY EXE file to bring up the PuTTY Configuration dialog box. Click SSH on the left sidebar, and under Preferred SSH Protocol Version, click the 2 radio button.

Next, click Tunnels (under SSH on the left sidebar), and type the IP address of the Fedora machine as well as the port number. The port number for a VNC connection is 5900. For the destination, type **192.168.0.105:5900**, as shown in Figure 33-3, and click Add.

Now open RealVNC and fill in the server address (192.168.0.105:5900), and click OK (see Figure 33-3). You will now be able to control the Fedora desktop.

Figure 33-3. *You can use PuTTY and RealVNC on the Windows machine to control the remote Fedora machine.*

VNC AND PORTS

You will frequently encounter a four-letter acronym in many Linux documents/guides on the Internet: YMMV (your mileage may vary). This means that depending on your system configuration, you might not get the same results. In our VNC example, we use port 5900, but depending on your firewall and your network settings, you might have to use different ports.

The VNC protocol by default uses the 59xx ports. For Windows, the port is 5900. You can run multiple VNC sessions under Linux, so the first instance of VNC would use port 5901, the second instance would use port 5902, and so on. To determine the IP address of your Linux machine, open a Terminal window (Applications ➤ System Tools ➤ Terminal) and type `/sbin/ifconfig`. To determine the IP address of a Windows machine, click Start ➤ Run and type `cmd`. Then type `ipconfig` at the command prompt, and note the IP address.

Connecting to Remote Windows Computers

The Terminal Server Client program allows you to connect to a variety of remote desktop server programs and, in particular, Windows XP or Windows 2000 computers via the Remote Desktop Protocol (RDP). Unfortunately, Windows XP Home, Me, 98, and 95 don't support RDP connections, which means that they aren't able to run an RDP server and allow other computers to access their desktops. However, there is a way to access the desktop of these computers remotely using some add-in software.

Connecting to Windows XP Professional, 2000, and NT

Using Terminal Server Client to access a Windows XP Professional, 2000, or NT computer is easy. Here, we use an XP Professional machine as an example, but the instructions are valid for 2000 and NT, too.

You'll find the Terminal Server Client program on the Applications ➤ Internet menu. Once it's running, in the Computer field, type either the IP address of the machine or its FQDN (if applicable). You don't need to type the username, password, or any other details. Click Connect, and a new window should appear in which you should see an XP login prompt. You should then log into Windows using your username and password.

■**Caution** If you haven't set a password for your user account on the Windows machine, you won't be able to log in. This is a quirk of the Windows XP RDP system. The solution is simple: use the User Accounts applet within the Windows Control Panel to assign yourself a password.

Of course, the XP computer will need be configured to allow incoming RDP connections. To configure it, right-click My Computer, select Properties, click the Remote tab, and make sure "Allow users to connect remotely to this computer" is checked. Figure 33-4 shows the XP desktop under Fedora. The Windows computer to which you want to connect may also need to be updated with the latest service packs, particularly in the case of a Windows 2000 computer.

Figure 33-4. *You can access remote Windows XP Professional machines using RDP and the Terminal Server Client program.*

If this is the first time you've accessed the Windows computer over an RDP connection, you might be wondering why the graphics look so bad. This is because of the default display settings of the Terminal Server Client program. You can, however, use custom settings to get better graphics (as shown in Figure 33-5).

Note As with Fedora's Remote Desktop feature, when logging in via RDP, you will be literally sharing the same desktop as anyone who might be standing in front of the computer. Because of this, for privacy and security, the desktop on the remote computer will be blanked when you log in.

Figure 33-5. *You can provide custom graphics settings from the Display tab of the Terminal Server Client program.*

Connecting to Other Windows Computers

You can download a VNC server for just about any operating system. Windows and Linux are supported, as is Macintosh OS X. In fact, a VNC server will run on any Windows computer, from 95 onward. Once it's installed, you can then use the Terminal Server Client program within Fedora to connect to that computer's remote desktop.

■**Note** In fact, any computer that's running the VNC Viewer program can access a computer running a VNC server (including the one set up by Fedora's Remote Desktop feature). Various VNC Viewer programs are available for Linux, Windows, Macintosh OS X, and other operating systems, including PocketPC. Just search the Web for "VNC Viewer" to find viewer programs.

Of course, you'll have the same insecurities and lack of desktop blanking that plague VNC connections to a Fedora desktop, as described previously. But if you're prepared to accept this, you'll be pleased to hear that setting up the VNC server on the Windows machine is easy. TightVNC, available from www.tightvnc.com/, is one of the best variations of VNC around. You should download the self-installing package for Windows. During installation, you'll be asked if you want to register TightVNC as a system service. Click the check box alongside this option. This will activate the VNC server every time the computer starts.

Once the program is installed, the server configuration program will appear. You should change the password by overtyping the default in the Password field. Connecting to the remote Windows machine is also a piece of cake. On the Fedora system, open Terminal Server Client (Applications ➤ Internet) and type the remote computer's IP address into the Computer field. In the Protocol drop-down list, select VNC. Then click Connect. You'll be prompted for the remote computer's VNC server password and, once you enter this, the remote desktop will appear in a window. Figure 33-6 shows an example of connecting to a Windows 98 computer.

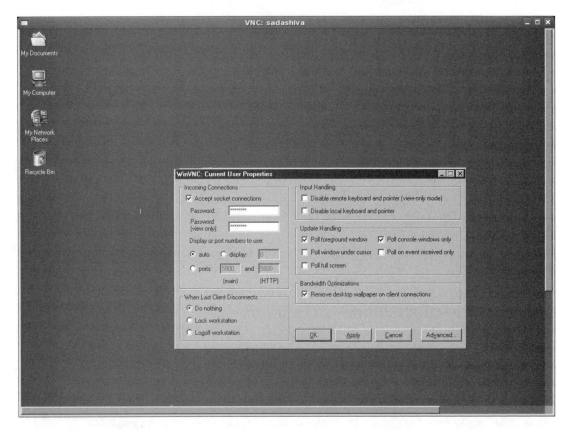

Figure 33-6. *By installing a VNC server, you can connect to just about any remote operating system, including Windows 98.*

Summary

In this chapter, we looked at how you can access your Fedora computer remotely across the Internet. We examined how you can access the computer as if you were sitting in front of it, using the ssh program. This allows you to start a command-line prompt and even run GUI programs on the remote computer.

In addition, we discussed how the screen program can be used to keep sessions alive across various logins, and how you can transfer files using the sftp and scp programs. Then we looked at how to use the Terminal Server Client tool to access the desktop of remote Windows computers.

APPENDIX A

■ ■ ■

Glossary of Linux Terms

This appendix provides brief explanations of common terms used in the Linux and UNIX environments. These include technical terms, as well as conventions used within the Linux community. Due to space limitations, this glossary is somewhat selective, but still should prove a lasting reference as well as a helpful guide for those new to Linux.

Cross-referenced terms are set in italics.

.

Symbol that, in the context of file management, refers to the current directory.

..

Symbol that, in the context of file management, refers to the parent directory of that currently being browsed.

/

Symbol that, in the context of file management, refers to the *root* of the file system; also separates directories in a path listing.

~

Symbol that, in the context of file management, refers to a user's home directory.

|

Pipe symbol; used at the *command prompt* to *pipe* output from one *command* to another.

>

Symbol that, when used at the *command prompt*, indicates output should *redirect* into a file.

<

Symbol that, when used at the *command prompt*, indicates a *command* should accept input from a file (see *redirect).*

#

Symbol that, when it appears on the *command prompt*, usually indicates the user is currently logged in as *root*; also, when used in configuration files, like those in the /etc directory, signals the start of a comment.

$

Symbol that, when it appears on the *command prompt*, usually indicates the user is currently logged in as an ordinary user. (Note that some versions of *Linux/UNIX* use % or > instead of $.)

?

Wildcard character indicating that any character can be substituted in its place.

*

Wildcard character indicating that zero or more characters can appear in its place.

*nix

Popular but unofficial way of describing the family tree that comprises *UNIX* and its various clones, such as *Linux* and *MINIX*.

administrator

Another word for either the *root* user or one who has adopted that user's powers temporarily.

AIX

IBM's *proprietary* form of *UNIX* that runs on the company's proprietary hardware, as well as *commodity* hardware based around AMD and Intel processors. Nowadays, IBM is slowly deprecating AIX in favor of *Linux*.

alias

Method of creating a user-defined *command* that, when typed, causes another command to be run or a *string* to be expanded.

Apache

Popular *open source* web server software that runs on *UNIX*, *Linux*, and other operating system platforms. Considered responsible in part for the rise in popularity of Linux in the late 1990s.

applet

Small program that, in the context of the *Fedora* desktop, runs as part of a larger program and offers functions that complement the main program. The *GNOME* desktop incorporates several applets in its notification area.

archive

Any file containing a collection of smaller files, compressed or otherwise (see also *tar*).

BASH

Bourne Again SHell. The most common *shell* interpreter used under *Linux* and offered as default on many Linux systems.

binary executable

Another way of referring to a program that has been compiled so that it can be used day-to-day. See also *compile*.

block device

How the *Linux kernel* communicates with a *device* that sends and receives blocks of data; usually a hard disk or removable storage device. See also *character device.*

BSD UNIX

Berkeley Software Distribution UNIX; form of *UNIX* partially based on the original UNIX *source code* but also incorporating recent developments. BSD is *open source* and free for all to use and share with practically no restrictions. There are various forms of BSD UNIX, such as FreeBSD, NetBSD, and OpenBSD. BSD doesn't use the *Linux kernel*, but it runs many of the same programs. Some of the programs offered within the Linux operating system come from BSD.

bzip2

Form of file compression. Together with the older and less efficient *gzip*, it is a popular form of file compression under *Linux* and the equivalent to ZIP compression under Windows. Files employing bzip compression are usually given a `.bz2` file extension. See also *tar.*

C

Programming language in which much of the *Linux kernel* is written, as were later versions of *UNIX* before it. C was created by some of the same people who created UNIX, and its development mirrors that of UNIX.

C++

Object-oriented programming language; originally designed to be an enhancement to *C*, but now seen as a popular alternative.

C#

Modern programming language that uses syntax similar to *C*, created by Microsoft and implemented on *Linux* via the Mono project.

character device

How Linux refers to a *device* that sends/receives data asynchronously. For various technical reasons, this typically refers to the *terminal* display. Character devices are called this because data is transferred one character at a time. Apart from terminal display, serial modems and teletype machines too are character devices. See also *block device.*

checksum

Mathematical process that can be applied to a file or other data to create a unique number relative to the contents of that file. If the file is modified, the checksum will change, usually indicating that the file in question has failed to download correctly or has been modified in some way. The most common type of checksum program used under *Linux* is md5sum.

client

Shorthand referring to a computer that connects to a *server.*

closed source

The opposite of *open source*, in which the *source code* is not available for others to see, share, or modify. See also *proprietary.*

code

See *source code.*

command

Input typed at the *shell* that performs a specific task, usually related to administration of the system and/or the manipulation of files.

command prompt

See *shell.*

commodity

In the context of hardware, describes PC hardware usually based around Intel or AMD processors that can be bought off the shelf and used to create sophisticated computer systems (as opposed to buying specially designed hardware). One reason for *Linux*'s success is its ability to use commodity hardware.

community

The general term for the millions of *Linux* users worldwide, regardless of what they use Linux for or their individual backgrounds. By using Linux, you automatically become part of the community.

compile

The practice of creating a binary file from *source code*, usually achieved using the ./configure, make, make install series of commands and scripts.

config file

Configuration file; any file that contains the list of settings for a program. Sometimes it's necessary to edit config files by hand using programs like *vi* or *Emacs,* but often the program itself will write its config file according to the settings you choose.

copyleft

The legal principle of protecting the right to share a creative work, such as a computer program, using a legally binding license. Copyleft also ensures future iterations of the work are covered in the same way.

cracker

Someone who breaks into computer systems to steal data or cause damage. The term is not necessarily linked to *Linux* or *UNIX* but was created by the *community* to combat the widespread use of hacker in this sense. The word *hacker* has traditionally defined someone who merely administers, programs, and generally enjoys computers.

cron

Background *service* that schedules tasks to occur at certain times. It relies on the crontab file.

CUPS

Common UNIX Printing System; set of programs that work in the background to handle printing under *UNIX* and *Linux.*

curses

Library that lets software present a semi-graphical interface at the *shell*, complete with menu systems and simple mouse control (if configured). The version of curses used under *Linux* and *UNIX* is called ncurses.

CVS

Concurrent versioning system; application that allows the latest version of software packages to be distributed over the Internet to developers and other interested parties.

daemon

See *service*.

Debian

Voluntary organization that produces *distributions* of *free software* operating systems, including *Linux*. It is a nonprofit organization run by passionate free software advocates. Many distributions use Debian as the basis for their software because of its claimed reliability.

dependency

A way of referring to system files that a program requires in order to function as intended. If the dependencies are not present during program installation, a program might refuse to install.

device

Linux shorthand describing something on your system that provides a function for the user or that the system requires in order to run. This usually refers to hardware, but it can also describe a virtual device that is created to provide access to a particular Linux function.

directory

What Windows refers to as a folder; areas on a hard disk in which files can be stored and organized.

distribution

A collection of software making up the *Linux* operating system; also known as a *distro*. The software is usually compiled by either a company or organization. A distribution is designed to be easy to install, administer, and use by virtue of it being an integrated whole. Examples include *Fedora*, Ubuntu, SUSE Linux, and *Debian*.

distro

Shorthand for *distribution*.

documentation

Another way of describing written guides or instructions; can refer to online sources of help as well as actual printed documentation.

Emacs

Seminal text editor and pseudo-*shell* beloved by *UNIX* aficionados; can be used for programming tasks, simple word processing, and much more. This editor has cultural significance as one of the core pieces of software offered by the *GNU Project*. Emacs was originally developed principally by *Richard Stallman*. See also *vi*.

environment

Shorthand referring to a user's unique *Linux* configuration, such as variables that tell the *shell* where programs are located.

FAT32

File Allocation Table 32-bits; file system offered by Windows 98, Me, 2000, and XP. *Linux* can both read and write to FAT32 file systems. See also *NTFS* and *VFAT*.

Fedora

A community-driven and *Red Hat*–sponsored set of projects. The most popular of these products is the Fedora distribution of *Linux*, which combines the best software offered by *FOSS*, to provide a stable and easy-to-use Linux distribution. Fedora is run by passionate advocates of *free software*. This is why non-free components (for playing MP3s, DVDs, etc.) are not included in the Fedora distribution. The Fedora distribution is offered in various formats such as installable DVD's and LiveCD variants.

Firefox

Web browser program used under *Fedora* and produced by the *Mozilla Foundation*.

FLOSS

Free, Libre, or Open Source Software; used within the *community* to describe all software or technology that, broadly speaking, adheres to the ethical approach of *open source* software and/or *free software*, as well as its legal guidelines.

FOSS

Free or Open Source Software; alternative term for *FLOSS*.

free

When used to describe software or associated areas of technology, "free" indicates that the project abides by the ethical (if not legal) guidelines laid down by the *GNU Project*. It doesn't indicate that the software is free in a monetary sense; its meaning is quite different from "freeware."

free software

Software in which the *source code*—the original listing created by the programmer—is available for all to see, share, study, and adapt to their own needs. This differs from the concept of *open source* because the right of others to further modify the code is guaranteed via the *GNU Public License* (GPL) or a compatible license.

gcc

GNU Compiler Collection; programs used when creating *binary executable* files from *source code*.

GID

Group ID; numbering system used by the operating system to refer to a *group*.

GIMP

GNU Image Manipulation Program; high-powered image-editing program that runs under *Linux*, *UNIX*, Windows and other operating systems. Often preceded by the definite article (i.e., "The GIMP"). See also *Tux*.

GNOME

Initially an acronym for GNU Network Object Model Environment; this expansion is now considered obsolete. It is the *GUI*-based desktop environment used by *Fedora*, as well as several other *distributions*. It uses the GTK+ *libraries*. See also *KDE*.

GNU

GNU's Not UNIX; see the *GNU Project*.

GNU/Linux

Another name for the operating system referred to as *Linux*. The name GNU/Linux gives credit to the vast quantity of *GNU Project* software that is added to the *Linux kernel* within a *distribution* to make a complete operating system. As such, GNU/Linux is the preferred term of many *free software* advocates.

GNU Project

Organization created by *Richard Stallman* in order to further the aims of *free software* and create the body of software that makes up the *GNU* operating system.

GNU Public License

Software license principally created by *Richard Stallman* in order to protect software *source code* against *proprietary* interests and ensure that it will always be shared. It does this by insisting that any source code covered by the GNU Public License (GPL) must remain licensed under the GPL, even after it has been modified or added to by others. The *Linux kernel*, as well as much of the software that runs on it, uses the GPL.

GPL

See *GNU Public License*.

grep

Global Regular Expression Print; powerful *shell command* that lets you search a file or other form of input using *regular expressions*. Because of the ubiquity of the grep program, many *Linux* and *UNIX* users refer to searching as "grepping." To "grep a file" is to search through it for a *string*.

group

Collection of users under one heading (group name) to facilitate system administration.

GRUB

GRand Unified Bootloader; boot manager program that offers a menu from which you can choose which operating system you wish to boot. It's needed to load the *kernel* program and thereby initiate the *Linux* boot procedure.

GUI

Graphical user interface; describes the software that provides a graphical system to display data and let you control your PC (usually via a mouse).

guru

One who is experienced and knowledgeable about *Linux*/*UNIX* and is willing to share his or her knowledge with others.

gzip

One of the two preferred forms of file compression used under *Linux*. Files employing gzip compression usually have a `.gz` file extension. See also *bzip2*.

hack

Ingenious and/or extremely efficient solution to a problem, particularly within the programming world.

hacker

Term used within the *community* to describe anyone who enjoys computers and possesses some skill therein, either in a professional capacity or as a hobby. This term is distinct from connotations of maliciously breaking into computers propagated by the media. See also *cracker*.

host

Shorthand referring to any computer that acts as a *server* to another computer. See also *client*.

HP-UX

Hewlett-Packard's *proprietary* form of *UNIX* designed to work on its own hardware platform.

Hurd

Kernel being developed by the *GNU Project*. It's not associated with the *Linux* kernel in any way.

info

Source of *documentation* accessible from the *shell*; an alternative to the more established *man page* system. Also known as Texinfo.

init

The program that is automatically run after the *kernel* has finished loading, and therefore early in the boot procedure. It's responsible for effectively starting the operating system.

init.d

Collection of startup *scripts* that make up the components of a *run level*. Under *Fedora*, these are found at `/etc/init.d/`. *Symbolic links* to selected `init.d` scripts are contained in folders within `/etc` that are named after *run level* numbers, such as `rc0.d`, `rc1.d`, `rc2.d`, and so on.

initrd

Initial RAM disk; system used by the *Linux kernel* to load *modules* that are essential for the kernel to be able to boot, such as disk controllers.

inode

Part of the usually invisible file system structure that describes a file, such as its ownership permissions or file size.

ipchains

Now deprecated component of version 2.2 of the *Linux kernel* that allows the creation of network security setups, such as firewalls or port-forwarding arrangements. Note that some *distros* still prefer to use ipchains. See also *iptables*.

iptables

Component of versions 2.4 and 2.6 of the *Linux* kernel that allows powerful network security setups. Iptables is chiefly used in the creation of firewalls, but can be used for more elementary arrangements such as network address translation (NAT) routers.

job

How the *BASH shell* refers to a running program in order to facilitate administration by the user.

journaling

File system technology in which integrity is maintained via the logging of disk writes.

KDE

K Desktop Environment; *GUI* and set of additional programs used on various *distros*, such as Mandriva and SUSE.

kernel

Essential but ordinarily invisible set of programs that run the computer's hardware and provide a platform on which to run software. In the *Linux* operating system, the kernel is also called Linux, after its creator, *Linus Torvalds*.

kernel panic

Error message that appears when the *kernel* program in *Linux* cannot continue to work. In other words, it's a polite way of indicating a crash or, more often, a problem arising from user misconfiguration. This is most often seen when booting up after making incorrect changes to the system.

kludge

Community slang describing an inelegant way of making something work, usually not in a way that is generally accepted as being correct. Pronounced *kloodge*.

LAMP

Acronym describing a series of programs that work together to provide a complete *Linux*-based web-hosting environment. Stands for "Linux, Apache, MySQL, and Perl, PHP, or Python" (the last three in the list are scripting languages; see *script*).

LGPL

Lesser GPL; version of the *GNU Public License* (GPL) in which some use restrictions are slackened at the expense of various freedoms laid down by the main GPL. The LGPL is mostly used for *library* files.

library

General term referring to code that programs need to run and that, once in memory, is frequently accessed by many programs (leading to the phrase "shared library"). The most common and vital library is glibc (GNU C Library), created by the *GNU Project* and the fundamental building block without which *Linux* could not operate. *GNOME* relies on the GTK+ libraries, among others.

link

File system method of assigning additional filenames to a file; also known as a "hard link." See also *symbolic link*.

Linux

You mean you don't know by now? Linux is what this book is all about. It is a *kernel* program created by *Linus Torvalds* in 1991 to provide an inexpensive operating system for his computer, along with other components. These days, Linux is used to describe the entire operating system discussed in this book, although many argue that this is inaccurate, and use the term *GNU/Linux* instead.

local

Shorthand referring to the user's PC or a device directly attached to it (as opposed to *remote*).

localhost

(1) Network name used internally by *Linux* and software to refer to the *local* computer, distinct from the network.

(2) Default name given to a Linux-based PC when no other name is defined during installation.

man page

Documentation accessible from the *shell* that describes a *command* and how it should be used.

MINIX

Operating system that is a rough clone of *UNIX*, created by Professor Andrew Tanenbaum. It was the inspiration for *Linux*.

module

Program code that can be inserted or removed from the *kernel* in order to support particular pieces of hardware or provide certain kernel functions. Drivers under Windows perform the same function.

mount

To add a file system so that it is integrated (and therefore accessible) within the main file system; applies to external file systems, such as those available across networks, as well as those on the *local* PC, such as the hard disk or CD/DVD-ROMs.

Mozilla Foundation

Organization founded by Netscape to create *open source* Internet software, such as web browsers and e-mail clients; originally based on the Netscape *source code*. At the time of writing, it produces the *Firefox* and Camino web browsers, the Thunderbird e-mail and Usenet client, the Bugzilla bug-tracking software, and other programs.

MySQL

Popular and powerful *open source* database application. See also *LAMP*.

newbie

Term used to describe anyone who is new to *Linux* and therefore still learning the basics. It's not a derogatory term! See also *guru*.

NFS

Network File System; reliable and established method of sharing files, printers, and other resources across a network of *UNIX*-based operating systems. See also *Samba*.

NTFS

NT File System; file system offered by Windows NT, 2000, and XP. It can be read by *Linux*, but usually writing to it is considered unsafe. See also *FAT32*.

OpenOffice.org

Open source office suite project created with the continuing input of Sun Microsystems and based on code Sun contributed to the open source *community*. Its commercial release is in the form of StarOffice (although StarOffice has several *proprietary* components added).

open source

(1) Method and philosophy of developing software whereby the *source code*—the original listing created by the programmer—is available for all to see. Note that open source software is not the same as *free software*; describing software as open source doesn't imply that the code can be shared or used by others (although this is often the case).

(2) A community of users or any project that adheres to open source values and/or practices.

partition

Subdivision of a hard disk into which a file system can be installed.

PID

Process ID; the numbering system used to refer to a *process*.

pipe

Method of passing the output from one *command* to another for further processing. Piping is achieved within the *shell* by typing the | symbol.

POSIX

Portable Operating System Interface; various technical standards that define how *UNIX*-like operating systems should operate and to which the *Linux* operating system attempts to adhere.

PPP

Point-to-Point Protocol; networking technology that allows data transfer across serial connections like telephone lines. In other words, it's the technology that lets you connect to your Internet service provider using a modem.

process

The way the system refers to the individual programs (or components of programs) running in memory.

proprietary

Effectively, software for which a software license must be acquired, usually for a fee. This usually means the *source code* is kept secret, but it can also indicate that the source code is available to view but not to incorporate into your own projects or share with others.

Red Hat

A well-known company, founded in 1993, committed to open source software. See also *Red Hat Enterprise Linux* and *Fedora*.

Red Hat Enterprise Linux

The *Linux* distribution produced by *Red Hat*; intended for commercial users, each Red Hat Enterprise Linux release is supported by Red Hat for seven years. Often abbreviated to *RHEL*, all of Red Hat's training and certification courses are based on it.

redirect

To send the output of a *command* into a particular file. This also works the other way around: the contents of a particular file can be directed into a command. Redirection is achieved within the *shell* using the left and right angle brackets (< and >).

regex

See *regular expression*.

regular expression

Powerful and complex method of describing a search *string*, usually when searching with tools such as grep (although regular expressions are also used when programming). Regular expressions use various symbols as substitutes for characters or to indicate patterns.

remote

Indicates a computer or *service* that is available across a network, including but not limited to computers on the Internet (as opposed to *local*).

RHEL

See *Red Hat Enterprise Linux*.

root

(1) The bottom of the *Linux* file system directory structure, usually indicated by a forward slash (/).

(2) The user on some versions of *UNIX* or *Linux* who has control over all aspects of hardware, software, and the file system.

RPM

(1) Acronym for RPM Package Manager, earlier known as Red Hat Package Manager; system used to install and administer programs under *Red Hat Enterprise Linux*, *Fedora*, SUSE *Linux* and some other *distributions*.

(2) Refers to a software package file format.

RTFM

Read the fine manual/*man page*; exclamation frequently used online when a *newbie* asks for help without having undertaken basic research.

run level

Describes the current operational mode of *Linux* (typically, the *services* that are running). The arrangement under *Fedora* is as follows: run level 1 is single-user mode (a stripped-down system with minimal running services); run level 2 is the same as 3, but without *NFS*; run level 3 provides a text interface; run level 4 is unused; run level 5 provides a *GUI*; run level 6 is reboot mode (switching to it will cause the computer to terminate its processes and then reboot); and run level 0 is shutdown (switching to it will cause the PC to shut down).

Samba

Program that re-creates under *UNIX* or *Linux* the Microsoft *SMB*-based system of sharing files, printers, and other computer resources across a network. It allows Linux to become a file or printer *server* for Linux and Windows computers, and also allows a Linux client to access a Windows-based server.

scalable

Term describing the ability of a single computer program to meet diverse needs, regardless of the scale of the potential uses. The *Linux kernel* is described as being scalable because it can run supercomputers, as well as handheld computers and home entertainment devices.

script

Form of computer program consisting of a series of *commands* in a text file. Most *shells* allow some form of scripting, and entire programming languages such as Perl are based around scripts. In the context of the *Linux* operating system, shell scripts are usually created to perform trivial tasks or ones that frequently interact with the user. Shell scripts have the advantage that they can be frequently and easily modified. The Linux boot process relies on several complex scripts to configure essential system functions such as networking and the *GUI*. See also *init*.

server

(1) Type of computer designed to share data with other computers over a network.

(2) Software that runs on a computer and is designed to share data with other programs on the same PC or with other PCs across a network.

service

Background program that provides vital functions for the day-to-day running of *Linux*; also known as a *daemon*. Services are usually started when the computer boots up and as such are constituent parts of a *run level*.

shell

Broadly speaking, any program that creates an operating environment in which you can control your computer. The *GNOME* desktop can be seen as a shell, for example. However, it's more commonly understood within *UNIX* and *Linux* circles as a program that lets you control the system using *commands* entered at the keyboard. In this context, the most common type of shell in use on Linux is *BASH*.

SMB

Server Message Block; network technology for sharing files, printers, and other resources. See also *Samba*.

Solaris

Form of *UNIX* sold by Sun Microsystems; runs on *proprietary* hardware systems as well as on *commodity* systems based on Intel and AMD processors.

source code

The original program listing created by a programmer. Most programs that you download are precompiled—already turned into *binary executables* ready for general use—unless you specifically choose to download and *compile* the source code of a program yourself.

SSH

Secure SHell; program that lets you access a *Linux*/*UNIX* computer across the Internet. SSH encrypts data sent and received across the *link*.

SSL

Secure Sockets Layer; form of network data transfer designed to encrypt information for security purposes. It's used online for certain web sites and also within *Linux* for certain types of secure data exchange.

Stallman, Richard M.

Legendary *hacker* who founded the *GNU Project* and created the concept of *copyleft*, as well as the software license that incorporates it: the *GNU Public License* (GPL). See also *Torvalds, Linus*.

standard error

Linux and *UNIX* shorthand for the error output provided by a *command*.

standard input

Linux and *UNIX* shorthand for the *device* usually used to provide input to the *shell*. For the majority of desktop PC users, this refers to the keyboard.

standard output

Linux and *UNIX* shorthand for the *device* usually used to display output from a *command*. For the majority of desktop PC users, this refers to the screen.

string

A word, phrase, or sentence consisting of letters, numbers, or other characters that is used within a program and is often supplied by the user.

SVG

Scalable Vector Graphics; vector graphics technology. SVG is actually an XML markup language designed to create 2D graphics, increasingly used for *Linux* desktop icons and web graphics.

swap

Area of the hard disk that the *Linux kernel* uses as a temporary memory storage area. Desktop or *server* Linux differs from Windows in that it usually requires a separate hard disk *partition* in which to store the swap file.

symbolic link

Type of file akin to a Windows shortcut. Accessing a symbolic link file routes the user to an actual file. See also *link*.

sysadmin

Systems administrator; a way of describing the person employed within a company to oversee the computer systems. In such an environment, the sysadmin usually is the *root* user of the various computers.

System V

Variant of *UNIX* used as a foundation for modern forms of *proprietary* UNIX.

tainted

Describes a *kernel* that is using *proprietary modules* in addition to *open source* modules. Can also refer to insecure software.

tar

Tape Archive; software able to combine several files into one larger file in order to back them up to a tape drive or simply transfer them across the Internet. Such files are usually indicated by a `.tar` file extension. Note that a tar file isn't necessarily compressed; the *bzip2* and *gzip* utilities must be used if this is desired.

TCP/IP

Transmission Control Protocol/Internet Protocol; standard protocol stack used by most modern operating systems to control and communicate across networks and also across the Internet (as opposed to NetBEUI, commonly available on older versions of Windows, and IPX/SPX, used on Novell's NetWare operating system).

terminal

Another word for *shell*.

TeX

Method and set of programs for typesetting complex documents. Invented prior to word processors and desktop publishing software, and now considered a specialized tool for laying out scientific texts. An updated version of the program called LaTeX is also available.

Torvalds, Linus

Finnish programmer who, in 1991, created the initial versions of the *Linux kernel*. Since then, he has taken advantage of an international network of volunteers and staff employed by various companies who help produce the kernel. Torvalds himself contributes and oversees the efforts.

tty

TeleTYpewriter; shorthand referring to underlying *Linux* virtual *devices* that allow programs and users to access the *kernel* and thereby run programs.

Tux

The name of the penguin character that is the *Linux* mascot. The original Tux graphic was drawn by Larry Ewing using GIMP.

UID

User ID; numbering system used by the operating system to refer to a *user.*

UNIX

Seminal operating system created as a research project in 1969 by Kenneth Thompson and Dennis Ritchie at Bell Labs (later AT&T). Because it was initially possible to purchase the *source code* for a fee, subsequent revisions were enhanced by a variety of organizations and went on to run many mainframe and minicomputer systems throughout the 1980s, 1990s, and up to the present. Nowadays, UNIX is fragmented and exists in a variety of different versions. Perhaps most popular is its *open source* rendition, *BSD UNIX,* which has seen many developments since the source code was first released. This means that BSD UNIX no longer exists but has instead diversified into a number of separate projects. *Proprietary* versions are also available, including *Solaris, HP-UX,* and *AIX.*

user

The way the operating system refers to anyone who accesses its resources. A user must first have a user account set up, effectively giving that user his or her own private space on the system. In addition to actual human users, an average *Linux* system has many other user accounts created to let programs and *services* go about their business. These are usually not seen by human users.

variable

A changeable value that stores a certain data type (such as a number, date, or *string*), remembering it for future reference by the system or *script* it is defined by. Variables defined by and for the *Linux kernel* are vital to it.

verbose

Command option that will cause it to return more detailed output (or, in some cases, to return actual output if the command is otherwise "quiet"); usually specified by adding the -v command option.

VFAT

Virtual File Allocation Table; technical name of Microsoft's FAT file system offered under Windows and also on removable storage devices such as flash memory cards.

vi

Arcane text editor and pseudo-*shell* beloved by *UNIX* aficionados that can be used for creation of text files or programs. Traditionally, UNIX users either love or hate vi; some prefer *Emacs.*

Wine

Short for Wine Is Not an Emulator; software that re-creates the Windows Application Programming Interface (API) layer within *Linux* and lets users run Windows programs.

workspace

X terminology referring to a *GUI* desktop.

X

Short for X Window System; software that controls the display and input devices, thereby providing a software foundation on top of which desktop managers like *GNOME* are able to run.

X11

Version 11 of the *X* software, currently in use on most desktop *Linux* systems.

XFree86 Project

Organization that creates *X* software. At one time, every *distribution* of *Linux* used XFree86 software, but most now use similar software from the *X.org* organization.

xinetd

The *service* responsible for starting various network *servers* on the computer.

XMMS

Audio player program.

X.org

Organization that produces the X Window software and, in particular, a set of programs called *X11*. X11 is used on most modern distributions of *Linux*. It is backed by a number of *UNIX* and Linux industry leaders.

xterm

Simple program that allows you to run a *shell* under *X*. This program has the advantage of being available on most *Linux* systems that offer a *GUI*.

Yum

Yellow dog Updater, Modified; command-line package management utility that is the underlying system by which software is installed and managed under *Fedora* and other *RPM*-based Linux distributions. Yum still requires *RPM* at the back-end to administer the software. Under *Fedora*, Pirut Package Manager and Pup provide a *GUI* method of using yum.

APPENDIX B

■ ■ ■

BASH Command Index

This appendix provides a whistle-stop tour of commands that can be used at the BASH shell. This is a highly selective listing, intended to provide a guide to commands that see day-to-day use on average desktop systems. In a similar fashion, although some command options are listed, they're strictly limited to those that receive regular deployment.

The descriptions of each command are deliberately simple. Note that the quantity of space a command is given is not an indication of its importance or usefulness. To this end, commands in the list with an asterisk after their name offer far more than hinted at by their brief descriptions. In such cases, we strongly advise that you refer to the command's man page for more information.

Various conventions are used in the list:

- Substitute your own details wherever italicized words appear.

- Commands that can be run by ordinary users are preceded with a dollar sign ($).

- Commands that require root privileges, or are not in an ordinary user's $PATH, are preceded with a hash symbol (#).

Commands that present dangers to the system through misuse are clearly marked. Such commands should not be used without research into their usage and function.

Command	Description	Typical Command Options	Examples of Use
$ alias	Create or display command aliases		alias *list*=ls
$ alsamixer	Alter audio volume levels		alsamixer
$ apropos	Search man pages for specified words/phrases		apropos "*word or phrase*"
$ bzip2	Compress specified file (replaces original file with compressed file and gives it .bz2 file extension)	-d: Decompress specified file -k: Don't delete original file -t: Test (use only with -d); do a dry run without writing any data	bzip2 *myfile*
$ bzip2recover	Attempt recovery of specified damaged .bz2 file		bzip2recover *myfile.tar.bz2*
$ cal	Display calendar for the current month (or specified month/year)		cal 8 2006

Continued

Command	Description	Typical Command Options	Examples of Use
$ cat	Display a file on the screen or combine and display two files together		cat *somefile*
$ cd	Change to specified directory		cd */usr/bin*
$ cdparanoia *	Convert CD audio tracks to hard disk files	-B: Batch mode; convert all tracks to individual files -S: Set CD read speed (2, 4, 8, 12, etc.; values relate to CD drive spin speed; used to avoid read errors)	cdparanoia -S 8 -B
# cdrecord *	Burn audio or CD-R/RW data discs (the latter usually based on an ISO image; see mkisofs)	dev=: Specify the drive's device number (can be discovered by running cdrecord with the scanbus option) -scanbus: Scan to see which CD-R/RW drives are present and return device numbers speed=: Specify the write speed (2, 4, 6, 8, etc.) -v: Verbose output; obligatory for feedback on cdrecord's progress	cdrecord *dev=0,0,0* *-speed=16 -v* *myfile.isos*
# chgrp	Change group ownership of a file/directory	-R: Recursive; apply changes to subdirectories	chgroup *groupname* *filename*
$ chmod	Change permissions of a file/directory (where a=all, u=user, g=group; and r=read, w=write, x=executable)	-R: Recursive; apply to subdirectories --reference=: Copy permissions from specified file	chmod a+rw *filename*
$ chown	Change file ownership to specified username	-R: Recursive; apply to subdirectories	chown *username file1*
# chroot	Change the root of the file system to the specified path		chroot */home/* *mydirectory*
# chvt	Switch to the specified virtual terminal (equivalent of holding down Ctrl+Alt and pressing F1–F6)		chvt *3*
$ clear	Clear terminal screen and place cursor at top		clear
$ cp	Copy files	-r: Recursive; copy subdirectories and the files therein -s: Create symbolic link instead of copying	cp *file1 directory/*
$ crontab	Edit or display the user's crontab file (scheduled tasks)	-e: Edit the crontab file (create/amend) -l: List crontab entries -r: Delete the crontab file -u: Specify a user and edit their crontab file	crontab -e
$ date	Display the date and time		date

Command	Description	Typical Command Options	Examples of Use
$ df	Display free disk space within file system	-h: Human readable; display sizes in kilobytes, megabytes, gigabytes, and terabytes, as appropriate -l: Restrict to local file systems, as opposed to network mounts	df -h
$ diff	Display differences between specified files	-a: Consider all files text files (don't halt when asked to compare binary files) -i: Ignore lowercase and uppercase differences	diff *file1 file2*
$ diff3	Display differences between three specified files		diff3 *file1 file2 file3*
$ dig	Look up IP address of specified domain	-x: Do a reverse lookup; map the specified IP address to a domain name	dig *somesite.com*
$ dmesg	Display kernel message log		Dmesg
$ du	Show sizes of files and folders in kilobytes	-h: Human readable; produce output in megabytes, gigabytes, and terabytes -s: Summary; display totals only for directories rather than for individual files	du -h *home/username*
$ eject	Eject a removable storage disk	-t: Close an already open tray	eject */media/dvd-rom*
$ ex *	Start a simple text editor program used principally within shell scripts		ex *myfile.txt*
$ exit	Log out of shell (end session)		exit
# fdisk *	*Dangerous!* Hard-disk partitioning program	-l: List partition table	fdisk */dev/hda*
$ fg	Bring job running in background to foreground		fg 1
$ file	Display information about specified file, such as its type		file *myfile*
$ find *	Find files by searching directories (starting in current directory)	-maxdepth: Specify the number of subdirectory levels to delve into, starting from 1 (current directory) -name: Specify name of file to search for -type: Specify file types to be returned; -type d returns directories and -type f returns only files	find -name "*missingfile*"

Continued

Command	Description	Typical Command Options	Examples of Use
$ free	Display information about memory usage	-m: Show figures in megabytes -t: Total the columns at bottom of table	free -m
# fsck *	Check file system for errors (usually run from rescue disc)		fsck /dev/hda1
$ ftp *	FTP program for uploading/ downloading to remote sites		ftp ftp.mysite.com
# fuser	Show which processes are using a particular file or file system	-v: Verbose; detailed output	fuser -v myfile
$ grep *	Search specified file for specified text string (or word)	-i: Ignore uppercase and lowercase differences -r: Recursive; delve into subdirectories (if applicable) -s: Suppress error messages about inaccessible files and other problems	grep "find this text" somefile.txt
# groupadd	Create new group		groupadd groupname
# groupdel	Delete specified group		groupdel groupname
$ groups	Display groups the specified user belongs to		groups username
$ gzip	Compress files and replace original file with compressed version	-d: Decompress specified file -v: Verbose; display degree of compression	gzip myfile
$ halt	Initiate shutdown procedure, ending all processes and unmounting all disks	-p: Power off system at end of shutdown procedure	halt -p
# hdparm *	*Dangerous!* Tweak or view hard disk settings		hdparm /dev/hda
$ head	Print topmost lines of text files (default is first 10 lines)	-n: Specify number of lines (such as -n 5)	head myfile.txt
$ help	Display list of common BASH commands		help
$ history	Display history file (list of recently used commands)		history
$ host	Query DNS server based on specified domain name or IP address	-d: Verbose; return more information -r: Force name server to return its cached information rather than query other authoritative servers	host 82.211.81.166
$ hostname	Display localhost-style name of computer		hostname
$ id	Display username and group info of specified user (or current user if none specified)		id username

Command	Description	Typical Command Options	Examples of Use
# ifconfig *	Display or configure settings of a network interface (assign an IP address, subnet mask, and activate/deactivate it)	down: Disable interface (used at end of command chain) netmask: Specify a subnet mask up: Enable interface (used at end of command chain)	ifconfig *eth0 192.168.0.10* netmask *255.255.0.0* up
$ info *	Display info page for specified command		info *command*
# init	Change current run level		init *1*
$ jobs	Display list of jobs running in background		Jobs
$ kill	Kill specified process		kill *1433*
$ killall	Kill processes that have specified names	-i: Confirm before killing process -v: Verbose; report if and when successful	killall *programname*
$ last	Display details of recent logins, reboots, and shutdowns		last
$ ldd	Display system files (libraries) required by specified program		ldd */usr/bin/program*
$ less	Interactively scroll through a text file	-q: Quiet; disable beeps when end of file is reached or other error is encountered -i: Ignore case; make all searches case-insensitive unless uppercase letters are used	less *myfile.txt*
$ ln	Create links to specified files, such as symbolic links	-s: Create symbolic link (default is hard link)	ln -s *myfile1 myfile2*
$ lpr	Print file (send it to the printer spool/queue)	-V: Verbose; print information about progress of print job	lpr *myfile.txt*
$ lpstat	Display print queue		lpstat
$ ls	List directory	-a: List all files, including hidden files -d: List only directory names, rather than their contents -h: Human readable; print figures in kilobytes, megabytes, gigabytes, and terabytes -l: Long list; include all details, such as file permissions -m: Show as comma-separated list	ls -h *mydirectory*
# lsmod	Display currently loaded kernel modules		lsmod
$ man	Display specified command's manual		man *command*

Continued

Command	Description	Typical Command Options	Examples of Use
$ md5sum	Display MD5 checksum (normally used to confirm a file's integrity after download)		md5sum *myfile*
# mkfs *	*Dangerous!* Create specified file system on specified device (such as a floppy disk)	-t: Specify type of file system	mkfs -t *vfat /dev/hdb1*
$ mkisofs *	Create ISO image file from specified directory (usually for burning to disc with cdrecord)	-o: Options; this must appear after command to indicate that command options follow -apple: Use Mac OS extensions to make disc readable on Apple computers -f: Follow symbolic links and source actual files -J: Use Joliet extensions (make ISO compatible with Windows) -R: Use Rock Ridge extensions (preferred Linux CD-ROM file system) -v: Verbose; display more information (-vv for even more info)	mkisofs -o *isoimage.iso* -R -J -v *mydirectory*
# modinfo	Display information about kernel module		modinfo *modulename*
# modprobe	Insert specified module into the kernel, as well as any others it relies on	-k: Set module's auto-clean flag so it will be removed from memory after inactivity -r: Remove specified module as well as any it relies on to operate	modprobe *modulename*
$ more	Interactively scroll through text file (similar to less)		more *myfile.txt*
# mount *	Mount specified file system at specified location	-o: Specify command options, such as rw to allow read/write access; various types of file systems have unique commands	mount */dev/hda4 /media/win_c*
$ mv	Move (or rename) specified files and/or directories	-b: Back up files before moving	mv *myfile mydirectory/*
$ netstat *	Show current network connections		netstat -a
$ nice	Run specified command with specified priority	-n: Specify priority, ranging from the highest priority of -20, to 19, which is the lowest priority	nice -n *19*
$ nohup	Run specified command and continue to run it, even if user logs out		nohup *command*
$ passwd	Change user's password		passwd *username*
$ ping	Check network connectivity between local machine and specified address	-w: Exit after specified number of seconds (such as -w 5)	ping *mydomain.com*

Command	Description	Typical Command Options	Examples of Use
$ printenv	Display all environment variables for current user		printenv
$ ps *	Display currently running processes	a: List all processes (note that command options don't require preceding dash) f: Display ownership of processes using tree-style graphics u: Limit results to processes running for and started by current user x: Include processes in results not started by user but running with the user ID	ps aux
$ pwd	Display current directory		pwd
$ reboot	Reboot computer		reboot
$ renice	Change a process's priority while it's running (see nice)		renice 19 3953
$ rm	Delete single or multiple files and/or directories	-r: Recursive; delete specified directories and any sub-directories -f: Force; don't prompt for confirmation before deleting (use with care!)	rm -rf directory
$ rmdir	Delete empty directories		rmdir directoryname
# rmmod	Delete module from kernel		rmmod modulename
$ rpm *	Complex package management tool that can be used to manage software; can install, query, and verify software packages. Note that direct interaction with rpm is not recommended. You should instead use yum as often as possible	--version: Prints the version number of the package -i: Install; install a new package -v: Verbose; display detailed output -qa: List all installed packages -U: Upgrade; upgrade the currently installed package to new version -q: Query; display information about packages -e: Erase; uninstall or remove packages	rpm -ivh package.rpm
# route *	Add and create (or view) entries in routing table (see ifconfig)		route add default gw 192.168.1.1
# runlevel	Display current run level		runlevel
$ screen *	Program that runs pseudo-shell that is kept alive regardless of current user login	-ls: Display list of currently running screen sessions -R: Reattach to already running screen session or start new one if none available	screen

Continued

Command	Description	Typical Command Options	Examples of Use
$ sftp *	Secure Shell FTP; like FTP but running over an ssh connection (see ssh)		sftp *username@192.168.0.104*
$ shred	Overwrite data in a file with gibberish, thereby making it irrecoverable	-u: Delete file in addition to overwriting -v: Verbose; show details of procedure -f: Force permissions to allow writing if necessary	shred -fv *myfile*
$ sleep	Pause input for the specified period of time (where s=seconds, m=minutes, h=hours, d=days)		sleep *10m*
$ smbclient *	FTP-style program with which you can log into an SMB (Windows)-based file share		smbclient *//192.168.0.101/*
$ sort	Sort entries in the specified text file (default is ASCII sort)		sort *myfile.txt* -o *sorted.txt*
$ ssh *	Log into remote computer using secure shell		ssh *username@192.168.0.100*
$ startx	Start GUI session (if GUI isn't already running)		startx
$ su	Temporarily log in as specified user; log in as root if no user specified	-: Adopt user's environment variables, such as $PATH	su -
$ tac	Display specified text file, but in reverse (from last to first line)		tac *myfile.txt*
$ tail	Display final lines of specified text file	-n: Specify number of lines to display (such as -n4)	tail *myfile.txt*
$ tar *	Combine specified files and/or directories into one larger file, or extract from such a file	-c: Create new archive -j: Use bzip2 in order to compress (or decompress) files -f: Specify filename (must be last in chain of command options) -r: Add files to existing archive -x: Extract files from existing archive -z: Use gzip to compress (or decompress) files	tar -zcf *file.tar.gz directory*
$ tee	Display piped output and also save it to specified file		ls -lh | tee *listing.txt*
$ top *	Program that both displays and lets the user manipulate processes		top
$ touch	Give specified file current time and date stamp; if it doesn't exist, create a 0-byte file with that name		touch *myfile*

Command	Description	Typical Command Options	Examples of Use
`$ tracepath`	Discover and display network path to another host		`tracepath 192.168.1.20`
`$ umask`	Set default permissions assigned to newly created files		`umask u=rwx,g=r,o=`
`# umount`	Unmount a file system		`umount /media/cdrom`
`# useradd`	Add new user	-m: Create home directory for user	`useradd -m username`
`# userdel`	Delete all mention of user in system configuration files (effectively deletes the user, although files owned by the user might remain)	-r: Remove user's home directory	`userdel -r username`
`$ unalias`	Remove specified alias	-a: Remove all aliases (use with care!)	`unalias command`
`$ uname`	Display technical information about current system	-a: Display all basic information	`uname -a`
`$ unzip`	Unzip a Windows compatible ZIP file	-l: Display archive content but don't actually unzip	`unzip myfile.zip`
`$ uptime`	Display uptime for system, as well as CPU load average and logged-in users		`uptime`
`$ vi *`	Text editor program		`vi`
`$ wc`	Count the number of words in a file		`wc myfile.txt`
`$ whatis`	Display one-line summary of specified command		`whatis command`
`$ whereis`	Display information on where a binary command is located, along with its source code and man page (if applicable)	-b: Return information only about binary programs	`whereis -b command`
`$ xhost`	Configure which users/systems can run programs on the X server	+: When followed by a username and/or system name, gives the user/system permission to run programs on the X server; when used on its own, lets *any* user/system use the X server -: Opposite of +	`xhost +`
`$ xinit`	Start elementary GUI session (when not already running GUI)		`xinit`

Continued

Command	Description	Typical Command Options	Examples of Use
`$ yum *`	Package management utility; uses software repositories to manage RPM-based Linux distributions	`install`: Install the package and all dependencies `update`: Update the specified packages to latest version. Update all installed packages if no package is specified `remove`: Remove the specified package as well as other packages that depend on the specified package `localinstall`: Install RPM packages that you have downloaded manually	`yum install` *packagename*
`$ zip`	Create Windows-compatible compressed ZIP files	`-r`: Recursive; include all subdirectories and files therein `-u`: Update ZIP file with specified file `-P`: Encrypt ZIP file with specified password `-v`: Verbose; display more information `-#`: Set compression level (from 0, which is no compression, to 9, which is highest)	`zip -r` *myfile*`.zip` *mydirectory*
`$ zipgrep`	Search inside ZIP files for specified text string		`zipgrep "search phrase"` *myfile*`.zip`

■ ■ ■

Getting Further Help

So you've read through this book and have a good working knowledge of Linux. Fedora is running exactly as you want it to, and things are going OK. But then you hit a brick wall. Perhaps you want to perform a task but simply don't know how. Or maybe you know roughly what you need to do but don't know the specifics. Although this book tries to be as comprehensive as possible, it can't cover every eventuality.

You need to find some help, but where do you turn? Fortunately, many sources of information are available to those who are willing to help themselves. Linux contains its own series of help files in the form of man and info pages, and these are good places to start. In addition, some programs come with their own documentation. If neither of these sources provides the help you need, you can head online and take advantage of the massive Linux community around the world.

Read the Manual!

Before asking for help online, it's important that you first attempt to solve your problems by using Linux's built-in documentation. If you go online and ask a question so simple that it can be answered with a little elementary research, you might find people reply with "RTFM." This stands for "read the fine manual." In other words, do some basic research, and then come back if you're still stuck.

It's not that people online don't want to help. It's that they don't like people who are too lazy to help themselves and expect others to do the hard work for them. Although not all the people you encounter will take such a hard line, doing a little homework first can provide answers to a lot of questions, removing the need to ask others. This is particularly true when it comes to the fundamentals.

Documentation typically comes in three formats: man pages, info pages, and README files.

Man Pages

Man pages are the oldest form of UNIX documentation. In the old days, once an individual had created a piece of software, he would write a brief but concise man page in order to give others a clue as to how to operate it. The programmer would come up with a few screens of documentation that could be called up from the command prompt. This documentation would outline what the software did and list all the ways in which it could be used.

Nowadays, depending on the software package, man pages are usually created by technical writers, but the concept of providing essential information still applies. Man pages under Linux provide all the information you need about how to use a particular command or piece of software.

Sounds great, doesn't it? Alas, there's a problem: man pages are written by software engineers *for* software engineers. They expect you to already understand the technology being discussed. This is illustrated very well by the man page for `cdrecord`, software that can be used to burn CD images to disc. You can view this man page by typing `man cdrecord` at the command prompt.

The first line of the Description section of the man page states, "Cdrecord is used to record data or audio Compact Discs on an Orange Book CD-Recorder or to write DVD media on a DVD-Recorder." Most of that is clear, but what do they mean by "Orange Book"? They don't explain. (If you're curious, head over to http://searchstorage.techtarget.com/sDefinition/0,,sid5_gci503648,00.html.)

Further down in the man page, it reads, "Cdrecord is completely based on SCSI commands . . . Even ATAPI drives are just SCSI drives that inherently use the ATA packet interface as [a] SCSI command transport layer."

What's SCSI, or ATAPI for that matter? Again, the man page doesn't explain. (They're methods of interfacing with storage devices attached to your computer.) But why should man pages explain as they go along? Their function is to describe how to use a piece of software, not to provide a beginner's introduction to technology. If they did that, a single man page could run to hundreds of pages.

In other words, man pages are not for complete beginners. This isn't always the case, and because Linux sees widespread usage nowadays, man pages are sometimes created with less knowledgeable users in mind. But even so, the format is inherently limited: man pages provide concise guides to using software. Luckily, there are some tips you can bear in mind to get the most from a man page. But before you can use those tips, you need to know how to read a man page.

How to Read a Man Page

To read a man page, you simply precede the command name with man. For example, to read the man page of cdrecord, type the following command:

```
man cdrecord
```

This opens a simple text viewer with the man page displayed. You can move up and down line by line with the cursor keys, or move page by page using the Page Up and Page Down keys (these are sometimes labeled Pg Up and Pg Down). You can search by pressing the forward slash key (/). This will highlight all instances of the word you type. You can search for other examples of the word in the document by pressing the N key.

The average man page will include many headings, but the following are the most common:

Name: This is the name of the command. There will also be a one-sentence summary of the command.

Synopsis: This lists the command along with its various command options (sometimes known as *arguments* or *flags*). Effectively, it shows how the command can be used. It looks complicated, but the rules are simple. First is the command itself. This is in bold, which indicates it is mandatory. This rule applies to anything else in bold: it must be included when the command is used. Anything contained within square brackets ([ ]) is optional, and this is usually where you will find the command options listed. A pipe symbol (|) separates any command options that are exclusive, which means that only one of them can be used. For example, if you see [apple|orange|pear], only one of apple, orange, or pear can be specified. Usually at the end of the Synopsis listing will be the main argument, typically the file(s) that the command is to work on and/or generate.

Description: This is a concise overview of the command's purpose.

Options: This explains what the various command options do, as first listed in the Synopsis section. Bearing in mind that command options tell the software how to work, this is often the most useful part of the man page.

Files: This lists any additional files that the command might require or use, such as configuration files.

Notes: If this section is present (and often it isn't), it sometimes attempts to further illuminate aspects of the command or the technology the command is designed to control. Unfortunately, Notes sections can be just as arcane as the rest of the man page.

See Also: This refers to the man pages of other commands that are linked to the command in question. If a number appears in brackets, this means the reference is to a specific section within the man page. To access this section, type man `<section number>` command.

Although there are guidelines for the headings that should appear in man pages, as well as their formatting, the fact is that you may encounter other headings, or you may find nearly all of them omitted. Some man pages are the result of hours if not days of effort; others are written in 10 minutes. Their quality can vary tremendously.

Tips for Working with Man Pages

The trick to quickly understanding a man page is decoding the Synopsis section. If you find it helps, split the nonobligatory command options from the mandatory parts. For example, cdrecord's man page says that you *must* specify the dev= option (it's in bold), so at the very least, the command is going to require this:

```
cdrecord dev=X filename
```

■Tip The preceding paragraph points out a very serious issue; namely, the preceding step is actually no longer required in Fedora. So, you should take note that man pages aren't always up to date! So you shouldn't rely solely on man pages as a source of information. You must always look up the project page on the Internet for the latest news, updates, and details.

Next you should skip to the Options section and work out which options are relevant to your requirements. While you're there, you'll also need to figure out what the dev= command option requires.

Although the command options contained in square brackets in the Synopsis section are, in theory, nonobligatory, the command might not work satisfactorily without some of them. For example, with cdrecord, you can use the -speed command option, which sets the burn speed, and also the -v option, which provides verbose output (otherwise, the command runs silently and won't display any information, including error messages!).

Another handy tip in decoding man pages is understanding what standard input and standard output are. In very simple terms, standard input (stdin) is the method by which a command gets input—the keyboard on most Linux setups. Standard output (stdout) is where the output of a command is sent, which is the screen on most Linux setups. (See Chapter 15 for more details about standard input and standard output.)

Often, a man page will state that the output of a command will be sent to standard output. In other words, unless you specify otherwise, its output will appear on screen. Therefore, it's necessary to specify a file to which the data will be sent, either by redirecting the output (see Chapter 17) or by specifying a file using a command option. For example, the mkisofs command can be used to create ISO images from a collection of files for subsequent burning to CD. But unless the -o option is used to specify a filename, mkisofs's output will simply be sent to standard output—it will appear on the screen.

Finally, here's the best tip of all for using man pages: don't forget that man has its own man page. Simply type man man.

Info Pages

Man pages date from the days of relatively primitive computers. Back then, most computers could only display page after page of text, and allow the user to scroll through it. In addition, memory and disk space were scarce, which is why some man pages are incredibly concise—fewer words take up less memory!

The *Texinfo* system is a valiant attempt by the GNU Project to overcome the shortfalls of man pages. Often, this is referred to as *info*, because that's the command used to summon Texinfo pages (normally, you type info command).

For starters, info pages are more verbose than the equivalent man pages, and that gives the author more space to explain the command or software. This doesn't necessarily mean that info pages are easier to understand, but there's a better chance of that being the case.

Secondly, info pages contain hyperlinks, just like web pages. If you move the cursor over a hyperlinked word, which is usually indicated by an asterisk (*), you can proceed to a related page (by pressing the spacebar or the Tab key). In a similar sense, pages are linked together so that you can move back and forth from topic to topic.

The bad news is that the man page system is far more popular and established than Texinfo. If a programmer creates a new application, for example, it's unlikely she'll bother with an info page, but she will almost certainly produce a man page.

In fact, in many cases, typing info command will simply bring up the man page, except in the software used to browse info pages.

However, nearly all the GNU tools are documented using info pages, either in their own pages or as part of the coreutils pages. For example, to read about the cp command and how to use it, you can type this:

```
info coreutils cp
```

To browse through all sections of the coreutils pages, type this:

```
info coreutils
```

Because man pages are so established, everyone expects to find one for every utility. So most utilities that have info pages will also have man pages. But in such a case, the man page will state near the end that the main documentation for the utility is contained in an info page and you may find it more fruitful to use that instead.

Navigating through info pages is achieved via the keyboard and is something of an art. But, as you might expect, there's a user-friendly guide to using info: just type info info. Remember that words preceded with an asterisk are hyperlinks, and you can jump from link to link using the Tab key.

README Files and Other Documentation

Some programs come with their own documentation. This is designed to give users the information they need to get started with the program (as opposed to the man page, which is a concise and complete guide to the software). Alternatively, program documentation sometimes gives a brief outline of the program's features.

The files are usually simple text, so they can be read in any text editor or word processor, and are normally called README. Under Fedora, these documents are usually stored in a program-specific directory within /usr/share/doc.

Every program directory has the version and build number as part of its name. For example, there is no directory called gedit for the text editor. It is named gedit-2.18.0.

Not all programs are friendly enough to provide such documentation, but even so, you'll still find a directory for the software in /usr/share/doc. This is because the software might also come with a getting started guide written by the Fedora package maintainer. Such guides detail specifics of using the software under Fedora, such as where configuration files are located or how the program interoperates with other software on the system.

In addition, the directory will probably contain copyright information, explaining the software license used by the software, as well as a CHANGELOG, which is a text file listing features that have been added to each release of the software. The directory might contain some other files, too, detailing where to send information about bugs, for example.

Viewing the README documentation is easy. For example, for the Gedit text editor, you could type this:

```
cd /usr/share/doc/gedit[tab]
less README
```

Sometimes, the README documentation is in a compressed tarball, in which case it will have either a .tar.gz or a .tar.bz2 file extension. However, less is clever enough to realize this and extract the document for reading.

Getting Help Online

If you can't figure out the answer by referring to the documentation, then there's little choice other than to look online. Linux benefits from a massive community of users, all of whom are usually willing to help each other.

Usually, the best way of getting help is to visit a forum. Here, you can post messages for others to reply to. Alternatively, you might choose to sign up for a mailing list. This is a way of sending e-mail to several hundreds, if not thousands, of people at once. Any individual can then reply. Mailing lists often have the benefit of allowing personal attention and interaction, but this comes at the expense of each subscriber receiving a whole lot of mail.

Forums

The official Fedora project forums are located at www.fedoraforum.org/. You'll find forums for just about every need, from security to beginner's issues. Because there are dedicated forums for installation help, networking issues, and so on, you can easily find what you're looking for. This also means that you must take care before asking questions; post your question in the forum that best suits your purpose.

Before you can post, you need to register by providing an e-mail address. This is designed to keep down the quantity of unwanted junk postings to the forum.

You might think it fine to post a new question immediately after registering, but don't forget the simple rules mentioned at the beginning of this appendix: if you don't do elementary research first and try to solve your own problem, you may elicit a hostile response from the other posters, especially if your question is one that comes up time and time again, and has been answered several times.

So, first make use of the comprehensive search facility provided with the forums. For example, if you're looking for advice on getting a Foomatic D1000 scanner working, use this as a search term and see what comes up. The chances are that you won't be the first person who has run into problems with that piece of hardware, and someone else may have already posted a solution.

Often, you'll need to read the full thread to find an answer. Someone may start by asking the same question as you but, with the help and guidance of the forum members, they might find a solution, which they then post several messages later.

In addition, some individuals write their own HOWTO guides when they figure out how to do something. These are normally contained in the How-To Articles forum (`http://forums.fedoraforum.org/forumdisplay.php?f=12`).

If you're unable to find a solution by searching, then consider posting your own question. Keep your question simple, clear, and concise, because no one likes reading through acres of text. If possible, provide as many details about your system as you can. You will almost certainly want to provide the version number of the Linux kernel you're using, for example. You can find this version number by typing the following in a GNOME Terminal window:

```
uname -sr
```

In addition, any other details you can provide may prove handy. If you're asking about hardware, give its entire model name and/or number. Don't just ask for help with a Foomatic scanner. Ask for help with a Foomatic D1000 scanner, model number ADK1033, Revision 2. If you're asking about a piece of software, provide its version number (click Help ➤ About).

Sometimes in their replies, other forum members may ask you to post further details or to provide log files. If you don't understand the question, simply ask the poster to give you more details and, if necessary, instructions on what to do. Just be polite. Explain that you're a newbie. If you think the question is extremely obvious, then say so—apologize for asking what may be a stupid question, but explain that you've tried hard to answer it yourself but have failed. This is not so that others can embarrass or ridicule you, but so that others can provide detailed and easy-to-understand answers.

Mailing Lists

Mailing lists have a number of advantages and disadvantages. The advantages are that they provide an excellent way to learn about Fedora. All you have to do is read through the e-mail messages you receive in order to partake in the constant information drip-feed. In addition, some mailing lists are designed to make public announcements, so you'll find it easy to learn about the latest happenings in the Fedora community.

Mailing lists also have a terrific sense of community. They offer a neat way of getting to know other Fedora users and talking to them. E-mails often drift off topic into humor and general discussion.

■**Note** Interestingly, the most-complained-about thing regarding mailing lists is that discussions often drift off topic. Since a message to a mailing list gets delivered to potentially thousands of subscribers, it is advised that discussion be kept strictly on topic.

A disadvantage of mailing lists is that you can easily receive in excess of 200 messages a day, depending on which mailing list you join. Even if you have a moderately fast Internet connection, that quantity of messages can take a long time to download. In addition, you'll need to sort out any personal or business e-mail from the enormous quantity of mailing list traffic (although the mailing list messages usually have the list title in square brackets in the subject field; you can therefore create a mail rule that sorts the mail according to this).

You can sign up to the Fedora mailing lists at `www.redhat.com/mailman/listinfo`. There are far too many listed here, look for those that have Fedora in their name.

Other Official Sites

One of the sites that you must devote time to browse is `http://fedoraproject.org/`. You will find links to Fedora mailing lists, frequently asked questions, documentation, and other useful resources for Fedora.

To get started with the official documentation, visit `http://fedoraproject.org/wiki/Docs`.

IRC

Internet Relay Chat, or IRC, is one of the most popular ways of communicating with the community. It is a means of having real-time text conversation with multiple people. You will have to register yourself at `http://freenode.net/` before you can chat with other Fedora users.

You will find more details about Fedora and its IRC channels at `http://fedoraproject.org/wiki/Communicate`.

Third-Party Sites

Of course, the Fedora project doesn't have a monopoly on sites that discuss Fedora. Several third-party web sites are worth at least an occasional visit, and there are other forum web sites devoted to Linux.

Perhaps the king of third-party Fedora sites is the Unofficial Fedora FAQ, at `www.fedorafaq.org/`. This contains brief instructions on how to do a variety of common tasks under Fedora, such as installing certain types of software or administering particular hardware. It covers a lot of the same ground as this book, but is still worth investigating if you wish to browse through some excellent tips and advice.

Finally, one of the best Linux forums and general advice sites can be found at `www.linuxquestions.org/`. This has a forum dedicated specifically to Fedora, but also contains many more devoted to just about every aspect of Linux, including forums for beginners.

Index

Find it faster at http://superindex.apress.com/

Find it faster at http://superindex.apress.com/

Find it faster at http://superindex.apress.com/

Find it faster at http://superindex.apress.com/

You Need the Companion eBook

Your purchase of this book entitles you to buy the companion PDF-version eBook for only $10. Take the weightless companion with you anywhere.

We believe this Apress title will prove so indispensable that you'll want to carry it with you everywhere, which is why we are offering the companion eBook (in PDF format) for $10 to customers who purchase this book now. Convenient and fully searchable, the PDF version of any content-rich, page-heavy Apress book makes a valuable addition to your programming library. You can easily find and copy code—or perform examples by quickly toggling between instructions and the application. Even simultaneously tackling a donut, diet soda, and complex code becomes simplified with hands-free eBooks!

Once you purchase your book, getting the $10 companion eBook is simple:

❶ Visit **www.apress.com/promo/tendollars/**.

❷ Complete a basic registration form to receive a randomly generated question about this title.

❸ Answer the question correctly in 60 seconds, and you will receive a promotional code to redeem for the $10.00 eBook.

2855 Telegraph Avenue • Suite 600 • Berkeley, CA 94705

eBookshop

THE EXPERT'S VOICE™

Offer valid through 1/30/08.

Apress®

Apress License Agreement (Single-User Products)

THIS IS A LEGAL AGREEMENT BETWEEN YOU, THE END USER, AND APRESS. BY
OPENING THE SEALED CD PACKAGE, YOU ARE AGREEING TO BE BOUND BY THE
TERMS OF THIS AGREEMENT. IF YOU DO NOT AGREE TO THE TERMS OF THIS
AGREEMENT, PROMPTLY RETURN THE UNOPENED DISK PACKAGE AND THE
ACCOMPANYING ITEMS (INCLUDING WRITTEN MATERIALS AND BINDERS AND
OTHER CONTAINERS) TO THE PLACE YOU OBTAINED THEM FOR A FULL REFUND.

DISCLAIMER OF WARRANTY

NO WARRANTIES. Apress disclaims all warranties, either express or implied, including,
but not limited to, implied warranties of merchantability and fitness for a particular purpose, with respect to the software and the accompanying written materials. The software
and any related documentation is provided "as is." You may have other rights, which vary
from state to state.

NO LIABILITIES FOR CONSEQUENTIAL DAMAGES. In no event shall Apress be
liable for any damages whatsoever (including, without limitation, damages from loss
of business profits, business interruption, loss of business information, or other pecu-
niary loss) arising out of the use or inability to use this product, even if Apress has
been advised of the possibility of such damages. Because some states do not allow the
exclusion or limitation of liability for consequential or incidental damages, the above
limitation may not apply to you.